Earnestly Contending for the Faith

A Study of Jude

Dr. Frank W. Parsons

PUBLISHED BY FIDELI PUBLISHING, INC.

Earnestly Contending for the Faith: A Study of Jude

Unless otherwise noted, all Scripture is quoted from the
New American Standard Bible, 1995 updated edition.

ISBN: 978-1-962402-28-6

Published by

Fideli Publishing, Inc.
119 W. Morgan St.
Martinsville, IN 46151

www.FideliPublishing.com

This volume is dedicated Pastor Sam Infante of the Philippines
and to all faithful servants in Christ the Lord

Preface

The Epistle of Jude, though brief is fully packed and with some controversial issues. Addition, Jude's uses some controversial texts from non-canonical sources in his letter.[1] His use of non-canonical writings raises difficult issues and questions since the origin of some his material used is not from the period of writing prophets. Moses is indeed the chief paradigm or pattern for all genuine writing and speaking prophets for the OT and NT Bible.[Deut. 18:15ff] The period for writing prophets is approximately from 1450 unto 400 BC. There are no writing or speaking prophets after above period until John the Baptist. John the Baptist prophesied as forerunner preparing the way for the Messiah, Christ the Lord.[Mal. 4:4-6; Matt. 11:14; Luke 1:17] Moreover, there are no biblical prophets or apostles today as established according to Moses.

Initially, Jude appears as though he intends to write a letter of encouragement or an exhortation to his readers. For some reason, Jude seems to be troubled with the gross corruption and wicked of men, professing believers, coming into the church. Jude warns that the same thing happened to Israel as they were coming out of Egypt. These were also corrupt men in whom Jude says,

> For certain persons have crept in unnoticed, those who were long beforehand marked out for this condemnation, ungodly persons who turn the grace of our God into licentiousness and deny our only Master [GK *depostes*, *Supreme Sovereign*] and Lord, Jesus Christ. (Jude 1:4)

Therefore, Jude felt *compelled* to exhort the saints to contend or fight and stand firmly in declaring the Word of God as faithful men called by the Lord Jesus.

> Beloved, while eagerly preparing to write to you about the salvation we share, I find it necessary to write and appeal to you to contend for the faith that was once for all entrusted to the saints. (Jude 1:3 NRS)

v

So, Jude lays out the urgent and critical theme of "**Earnestly contending for the faith**" that has already been deposited and entrusted to the saints, which is the complete Word of God and the sound doctrine of the Gospel.

While the word "contend" suggests that the meaning that might imply *to fight* and *to hold on to the faith*, Jude's intention is far greater. His appeal is a *good old fashion house cleaning in the church if necessary* and *getting busy doing the work of the ministry* (work of the Lord) to which we have been called to do. Hence, Jude implies removing the ungodly unbelievers that only profess faith in Christ but are totally void of regeneration. The church needs to get busy proclaiming the Gospel. That is, going out to *reach the lost* and *establishing* and *equipping the saints* that they may properly *do the full work of the ministry*.^{Eph. 4:11f}

Jude is quick to point out the corruption and wickedness among leaders that must be rebuked. (Some may only need a sharp rebuke, but some unfortunately may have to be dismissed.) NIV does a good job of pointing this out.

> Dear friends, although I was very eager to write to you about the salvation we share, I felt compelled to write and urge you to contend for the faith that was once for all entrusted to God's holy people. For certain individuals whose condemnation was written about long ago have secretly slipped in among you. They are ungodly people, who pervert the grace of our God into a license for immorality and deny Jesus Christ our only Sovereign and Lord.   (Jude 1:3, 4 NIV)

Jude seems to allude to spiritual leaders and their wickedness in the church. Jude insinuates that the problem centers or lies with some of the spiritual leaders. NIV helps to clarify the context dealing with Elders in the church and the corruption existing within the leadership. Paul, however, warns the church at Ephesus that they must be careful in bringing any alleged charges, especially against an Elder. There must be at least two or three **eyewitnesses**; otherwise, you do not accept any such accusations.

> [17]The <u>elders</u> who direct the affairs of the church well are worthy of double honor, especially those whose work is preaching and teaching. [18] For Scripture says, "Do not muzzle an ox while it is treading out the grain," and "The worker deserves his wages." [19] **Do not entertain an accusation against an <u>elder</u>** unless it is brought by two or three [*eye*[a]]-**witnesses**.[20] But those *<u>elders</u>*[a] **who are sinning** you are to reprove before everyone, so that the others may take [*heed of the*] warning. [21] I charge you, in the sight of God and Christ Jesus and the elect angels, to keep these instructions without partiality, and to do nothing out of favoritism

[partiality]. [22] Do not be hasty in the laying on of hands, and do not share in the sins of others. Keep yourself pure. (1 Tim. 5:14-22 NIV)

[a]Note: the meaning of a biblical witness is that they are eyewitness to the event. Hearsay is not a witness and is inadmissible. The word _elder_ (GK _presbuteros_) refers to leaders in the church including particularly Pastor. The **elder** is not in v 20, but NIV rightly includes the word elder according to subdivisional contexts.[1 Tim. 5:17-25]

Rebuking others in the church is indeed in order.[2 Tim. 4:2; Titus 1:3] Still, caution on rebuking others publicly. Exhorting other will go farther in the long run. Rebuking, correcting, or disciplining others, especially elders, is used only as a last resort. Let us learn and practice "godly grace and mercy" towards everyone. For this is how the Lord deals with all humanity.[Rom. 2:4] Therefore, we likewise need to exercise *godly grace and mercy* to others whether to saints or unbelievers.

Many churches are too carnal, worldly, and immature to properly excise *godly correction*. Many are too worldly to be corrected. Some churches have few godly men and notably men called of God and walking in Christ. The church has moved away from the actual significant mandates established and dictated by our risen Lord Jesus Christ and confirmed by the apostles.

In some respects, Jude seeks to points out how the people of God drift off-center from the Word of God. Part of the drifting off course is just simply the fickleness of human nature. As humans, we often <u>do</u> <u>not</u> stay the course. As the world becomes more and more *mechanized* and *integrated cultures* and *cognitive mindsets* and *ideologies*, the Gospel may become even more burred.

However, human nature is such that it gives into whims of the flesh, the world, and most certainly the influence of the devil. Jesus is the plumbline, and we need to keep our eyes focused on Him,

> Wherefore seeing we also are compassed about with so great a cloud of witnesses,[a reference to Heb. 11] let us lay aside every weight, and the sin which doth so easily beset *us*, and let us run with patience the race that is set before us, Looking unto Jesus the author and finisher [perfecter] of *our* faith; who for the joy that was set before him endured the cross, despising the shame, and is set down at the right hand of the throne of God.
>
> (Heb. 12:1, 2 KJV)

Listen to me now and pay close attention: many churches believe or not are telling and instructing the risen Lord of glory what to do. This is shame upon shame! We have it backwards! We do not tell the Lord what to do; He tells and instructs the churches what to do. Friend, we are supposed to get order from Heaven and not give orders to Heaven. Our Lord doesn't take orders; He gives orders! Jesus is the King of kings, Lord or lords, and the only Sovereign. Praise the Lord!

Still others are assuming that it is up to them to build the Kingdom of God, the church, its programs, and layout the ministries just any way they want to do it. Well, I hate to break anyone's bubble of pride, but no! We are not given the right *to do as we want*. The Lord has not handed the church over to the whims of carnal, rebellious, and natural man. Israel did things their way during the Judges: "— every man did *that which* [*he imagined*] *was* right in his own eyes.Judges 17:6 KJV As a result, Israel had evil practices at every turn. I tell you the church is fully ripe for judgment of God unless the people of God repent and start walking godly as a witness for Christ.

If anyone thinks he can do whatever he wants in the ministry without following Jesus' plan and void of fervent prayer, I warn you that our Lord will come and put your church lights out! Friend, I am not joking. You might have your mechanical lights on in church, but your spiritual lights will be off, dead. The risen Lord said to the thriving church of Ephesus,

> "To the angel [e.g., *messenger* or *Pastor*] of the church in Ephesus write: These are the words of him who holds the seven stars [e.g., *Pastors*] in his right hand, who walks among the seven golden lampstands [*seven churches*]: 2"I know your works, your toil and your patient endurance. I know that you cannot tolerate evildoers; you have tested those who claim to be apostles but are not, and have found them to be false. 3I also know that you are enduring patiently and bearing up for the sake of my name, and that you have not grown weary. 4But I have this against you, that you have abandoned the love you had at first. 5Remember then from what you have fallen; **REPENT**, and do the works you did at first. If not, I will come to you and remove your lampstand [e.g. *I'll punch your lights out*] from its place, unless you **REPENT**. 6Yet this is to your credit: you hate the works of the Nicolaitans, which I also hate. 7**Let anyone who has an ear listen to what the Spirit is saying to the churches**. To everyone who conquers, I will give permission to eat from the tree of life that is in the paradise of God.   (Rev. 2:1-7 NRS)

The churches are **not** going out to win souls for Christ. For shame; this the heart of the Gospel of God. The churches are not going out and evangelizing, and friend, this is Jesus' chief command,

> — **REPENTANCE for the FORGIVENESS of sins will be preached
> in his name TO ALL NATIONS**, beginning at Jerusalem. You are
> witnesses of these things. (Luke 24:47, 48 NIV)

Listen, the above command must begin with the surrounding area of the church. What good is the church's light if it remains locked up in a building? The community cannot change unless the Light is brought to them, and as they receive God's Word are built up in the faith. Then missions will truly thrive and there will be money to get the job done.

Jesus gave a parable, which exemplifies the *necessity* of evangelism by the saints, and this applies to any dispensation and not just our Lord's ministry to Israel.

> And the lord said unto the servant, Go out into the highways and hedges,
> and **COMPEL** *them* to come in, that my house may be filled.
>
> (Luke 14:23 KJV)

Many church leaders are **deficient in the exercising of their faith**. Some leaders are **not matured** or **grounded in the faith**. We will not properly build a NT church without Jesus' standards, instructions, and leading with *godly men*. The church needs men who are totally committed, and these must be men that have been properly well-equipped and trained and grounded in the Word. There are too many in churches where men that are void of total surrender and firm commitment to the risen Lord Jesus and His commands or mandates. They are too much in love with the world and others are simply too immature or too lazy.

The problem is that there is little or no proper equipping or training of the saints. Friend, I mean all the saints ought to be laboring in the ministry and not just a few people.[Eph. 4:12] Additionally, the fervent need of *training* and *recruiting* must be **ongoing** and **continual**. You cannot have too many trained teachers and workers. We do not wait until we need teacher and workers; we must have them ready and willing to serve before the need of the increase. If you think the increase will not come, shame on you for your lack of faith and dependance on the power of the Holy Spirit.

Regrettably, some come in one door and leave through another door and never to return. Some families are too mobile. Yes, praise the Lord, some families do not stay very long in one place. If churches do not provide ongoing training, this is what the Bible declares will happen, and it will happen just as the apostle Paul declares it would,

> And he gave some, apostles; and some, prophets; and some, evangelists; and some, pastors and teachers; ¹²For the perfecting [the building up] of the saints, for the work of the ministry, for the edifying of the body of Christ: ¹³Till we all come in the unity of the faith, and of the knowledge of the Son of God, unto a perfect [fully mature] man, unto the measure of the stature of the fullness of Christ: ¹⁴That we *henceforth* be no more children, tossed to and fro, and carried about with every wind of doctrine, by the sleight of men, *and* cunning craftiness, whereby they lie in wait to deceive; ¹⁵But speaking the truth in love, may grow up into him in all things, which is the head, *even* Christ: (Eph. 4:11-15 KJV)

The churches **are not** even calling upon people to repent. People in the community around the church are not being evangelized with the Gospel. People are not being given the opportunity to confess their sins and receive Christ as Lord in many churches. Churches are playing "Churchianity" not practicing "Christianity." Churches have become more like a social gatherings rather that in-depth study of the Word of God. Preaching is reduced to a lecture and not preaching through "rebuke, exhort with all longsuffering and doctrine."² Tim. 4:2 KJV Yes, there is a passionate need to call people for commitments and earnestly challenge them to faithfully serve Christ the Lord.

Shame upon many leaders in the churches! Listen, the churches are in shambles. The churches need urgent godly renewal and *spiritual reformation.* There is no confession of their sin anymore.¹ John1:7ff No one sins anymore? So, there is no need for *repentance, renewal, or spiritual revival*? This is a major point with Jude. Let us be gracious to one another, amen, but let us also rebuke the ungodly. Let us continue to reach out to those who are caught or ensnared by the world, flesh, and devil, "snatching them out of the fire."Jude 1:23

Well, as it relates to our individual walk in Christ, let me ask you point blank: *When was the last time you asked the Lord to forgive you of your sins*? The trouble is we do not even remember when we sin let alone confess our sins and biblically repent. (Come on and be honest with yourself.) We have become too cozy with the world, too carnal, and even too callused to hear the Holy Spirit. We are spiritually lazy now days: *we have been spoon fed like an infant*. The churches are tuned-in to the world, and they have tuned-out to the Word of God.

Hebrews writer says,

> Therefore, as the Holy Spirit says: "Today, if you will hear His voice, **Do not harden your hearts** as in the rebellion, In the day of trial in the wilderness." (Heb. 3:7, 8 NKJ)

> Again He designates a certain day, saying in David, "Today," after such a long time, as it has been said: "Today, if you will hear His voice, **Do not harden your hearts**." (Heb. 4:7 NKJ)

My friend, let us not harden our hearts and refuse to hear the blessed wooing of the Holy Spirit. Let us listen and obey the beckoning of the Holy Spirit as we hear God's Word. Let us hear the Word of God as it given to from the pulpit. Let us not allow our traditions to override the plain teaching of Scripture. What use is it, my brother, if we say, 'I believe in the Scriptures, but we do not do what the Bible teacher?'"

We are being ensnared by our natural man, the old nature, the carnal flesh. And yes, some of us are ensnared by the world, and some of us are even ensnared by devil as the apostle declares.

> And the Lord's servant must not be quarrelsome but kindly to everyone, an apt teacher, patient, [25]correcting opponents with gentleness. God may perhaps grant that they will repent and come to know the truth, [26]and that they may escape from the snare of the devil, having been held captive by him to do his will. (2 Tim. 2:24-26 NRS)

Jude's message to the churches is right on target for our generation today. If we say that we believe God's Word, then, let us put the Word of God into practice. But **we need godly and committed men**. Sorry, but the Lord uses men to fight wars; He does not need women, children, or youth. The Lord is seeking godly men.[Ezek. 22:30] Will you make a commitment right now to yourself and to the Lord and follow the risen Lord Jesus and His mandates? Will you make the commitment to not just say that you believe His Word, but will you stand and be counted that you shall indeed also obey His Word? We have only one life to live for Christ; let us make our life count for Christ the Lord for His glory and praise!

Footnote:

1. Non-canonical, meaning "not relating to, part of, or sanctioned by a canon. It can also mean **not** belonging to the canon of Scripture." From Google Search

TABLE OF CONTENTS

Part Three: Rebellious and Head-strong, 1:8-13

Part Four: The Judgment of God is coming, 1:14-16

Part Five: Pressing forward in your high calling in Christ, 1:17-23

Introduction

The style and study of this volume by the author is slightly modified from his previous writings. There is some formatting that has been changed. There are aspects that remains the same. For example, memory verse(s) in the beginning of the chapter. There is also a brief introduction and a short conclusion at the end. At the top of each page, there will be the *chapter title* on one side of page and *on the opposite page there is the chapter subtitle*. I am encouraged that this particular format is helpful for the reader working through *"Earnestly Contending for the Faith*, the study of Jude" more effectively. There are occasional footnotes, which you will read, which have been placed at the end of each chapter. In addition, at the end of the book, you find a list of acronyms, an index, and other books, tracts, and songs by Dr. Parsons.

Scripture quotations are from various translations. The various translations have been used for variety of purposes. When Scripture is quoted in a separate paragraph, the texts will be indented and in smaller fonts. When Scripture quotations are within the paragraph, the font size remains the same size within the paragraph. The Scripture quotations will be from the New American Standard, 2020, and from the 1995 *updated* edition unless noted in the text. Some of the other major Scripture quotations are from the Textus Receptus ENG version; Geneva Bible (GNV) 1599; King James Version (KJV) 1611; American Standard Version (ASV) 1901; New Revised Standard (NRS) 1989; New English Translation (NET) 2005; the New International Version (NIV) 2011; English Standard Version (ESV) 2011; the Berean Study Bible (BSB) 2016; the Majority Standard Bible (which uses the BYZ text, 2022). There are other quotes from the Aramaic Bible in Plain English (ABPE) 2010; and the Common English Bible (CEB) 2011. There are quotes from the Literal Standard Version 2020. The Latin Vulgate ENG version is noted particularly, Jude 1:5, 25.

If a Hebrew (HEB) or a Greek (GK) word is given, the word is spelled out phonetically in English (ENG). Small and large brackets ([], []) are used to indicate a word or phrase is added to clarify the Scripture text, but the insertion is not part of the original translation. The GK OT is quoted in the ENG from Septuagint [LXX] by Brenton (1851). When the author uses personal paraphrases, the word(s) are placed in *italics and indented.*

There are occasional footnotes at the end of the chapter as noted above. The footnotes are placed at end of each chapter for quick reference but to avoid disruption of the reading. The footnotes are for those who are inclined to probe more into the subject. Similarly, for the clarity of a word, there are inserted *like footnote fashion* in the Scripture texts quoted and placed at the bottom of the text. For example, instead of a footnote at end of the chapter, the author has also added notes in brackets within the main text but in a reference format. In addition, occasional footnotes are marked by footnote letter, e.g. [], but the brackets "[a]" are sometimes not used. Please keep in mind that annotations are placed in the text similarly to footnotes but remains in the text for immediate clarity. For instance,

> For if there come into your synagogue [GK, *sunagoge*] a man with a gold ring, in fine clothing, and there come in also a poor man in vile [*poor*] clothing; ³and ye have regard to him that *wears* the fine clothing, and say, Sit thou here in a good place; and ye say to the poor man, Stand thou there, or sit under my footstool. ⁴Do ye not make distinctions among yourselves, and become judges with evil thoughts?　　　　(James 2:2-4 ASV)

Here is another example,

> ¹⁴I have given them thy word; and the world hath hated them, because they are not of the world, [*they were sanctified by Jesus*] even as I am not of the world. ¹⁵I pray not that thou shouldest take them out of the world, but that thou shouldest keep them from the evil [*one*]ᵈ. ¹⁶They are not of the world, even as I am not of the world. ¹⁷**Sanctify them through thy truth** [*certainty of inspiration*]: thy word is truth. ¹⁸As thou hast sent me into the world, even so have I also sent them into the world. ¹⁹And for their sakes **I sanctify myself**, that **they** also **might be sanctified through the truth.**　　　　(John 17:14-18 KJV)

> ᵈNote: evil, GK *poneros*, is genitive masculine, and it refers to Satan; the word is not neuter as to a thing.

The insertions are to keep the flow going for reader but provide an immediate clarity without disrupting the flow and reading.

Many books have been written with a general outline. However, the study the Epistle of Jude is not written from a strict structured outline. The author's study of Jude has chosen to use a *thematic* and *verse by verse* approach. Jude is only one chapter and with 25 verses. The Epistle of Jude is subdivided into six themes and marked off with a general theme to each part. Encompassing each theme are the latent topics or subject within those verse(s).

For those a little more meticulous, the GK NT with various readings and difference by variance in translations are usualized. This includes consulting various GK lexicons. The Holy Spirit is precise in what He reveals. Nevertheless, there things as the apostle Peter says concern Paul, which can certainly apply to you and me as well today. Peter says,

> [*As Paul is*] speaking of this as he does in all his letters. There are some things in them hard to understand, which the ignorant and unstable twist to their own destruction, as they do the other scriptures.

(2 Peter 3:16 NRS)

So, let us give careful attention to the Scripture text and especially the more difficult texts and issues. Thus, challenging each of us to pay close attention to the verse at hand.

Here is how the book is laid out:

Occasion and Purpose, Jude 1:1-4: some today preach cheap grace. Their teaching is indeed scandalous, obscene, and wicked. Jude is transparent leaving no doubt what are the issues. When a person is genuinely saved by grace of Christ our Lord, that person's spiritual life change ought to be evident and show a transformed life. This is the true Bible doctrine of the grace of God. As the apostle Peter says, "- this is the true grace of God. Stand firm in it!"[1 Peter 5:2b]

Jude calls the churches to *clean house* when necessary. Jude warns us to watch out for the wicked. There are some that have turned the grace of God into living in sin and even boasting of doing it. Therefore, the Elder Jude is exhorting the saints to "earnestly contend for the faith which was once delivered unto the saints."[Jude 1:3 KJV]

Vengeance is mine, I will repay, says the Lord, Jude 1:5-7. Jude warns the people of God that they cannot rebel against the Lord or His Word without receiving serious consequences. Warning: rebellion and wickedness shall be dealt with by the Lord. Again, there will be serious consequences for Christians living in wickedness. There may be consequences for their action or lack of actions. Jude illustrates the consequences of disobedience through history of the OT. The Lord brought judgment on the people of God that openly rebelled and sinned against Him.

For example, Jude says that the Lord destroyed some of the people coming out of Egypt due to their rebellious acts. Even angels were not exempted. When angels sinned, God's judgment was swift and with no recourse or appeal. Consider God's judgment upon Sodom, Gomorrah, and surrounding cities. Such severe judgment by God stands as witness even to this day. So, immorality and wickedness should not be tolerated by God in the churches. Know for certain that God will judge His people.

Rebellious and Head-strong, Jude 1:8-13. Jude refers to book of Enoch which is a non-canonical book, and its writing is no earlier than 3rd century BC. Some who desire to probe deeper into Jude's Epistle may find some things very challenging. Others less meticulous may be less prone to probe into Jude any deeper. While Jude uses non-canonical writing like Enoch, he is not giving credence or endorsing any of its doctrines. So, watch out that you are not snared by it.

It is easy apparently for some people to overlook or ignore certain issues or obvert actions in the church. However, to things that we do or omit to do, we may awake and realize that the Lord will not overlook our actions or attitudes. Balaam and Korah certainly discovered that "your sin will indeed find you out."[Num. 32:23]

Shockingly, Jude warns about what he calls, "spots in your feasts of charity."[Jude 1:12 KJV] The meaning is literally "**hidden reefs** in your love feast." Jude is referring to the church observing Communion (the Lord's Supper). Jude alludes to other problems and issues in the church to which he is writing. The leadership had better properly handle it.

The Judgment of God is coming, Jude 1:14-16. Once against, Jude raises controversy by using the book of Enoch. The use of the book of Enoch raises serious issues for those of us that desire to probe deeper into text. The use of non-canonical books like Enoch was a common practice among some Jews. Some Jews in writing might allude or actually refer to outside non-biblical sources in their writings. However, Jude nor his readers consider the writing of Enoch as inspired by God or authentic.

In addition, Jude warns about fault-finders coming into the assembly and disturbing the peace in the church. These are *accusers of the brethren*.[Rev. 12:10] The leadership is expected to deal with such troubles in godly way. There are people driven by the old nature. There are others, to be sure, that shall attempt to exploit the people. Let us be alert and watch out and deal with them in a godly manner.

Pressing forward in your high calling in Christ, Jude 1:17-23. Jude gives his final exhortation just before he unveils his mighty doxology and blessings. He moves rapidly through this section, verses 17-23. Jude deals with five issues in such short of space. He alerts people to God's Words through apostles concerning the last days before our Lord returns. Then, he alerts us to people we all need to watch out for in the church. Unfortunately, we need to watch out for and anticipate trouble makers in the church; Satan will be working to disrupt the Lord's work. These are people that may be unregenerate and without the Holy Spirit.

Then, Jude quickly reminds everyone that they need to build ourselves up in our most holy faith in Christ the Lord. That is, being faithful in doctrine, and being faithful in putting the doctrine into practice.

Jude is exhorting and reminding us as saints to eagerly look for and anticipate with eagerness our Lord's coming. Therefore, let us get busy doing the work of our Lord. We may even need to *snatch some right out of fire*. Others may be so *polluted by the flesh* that we need to extend mercy to them reminding ourselves that the Lord gives mercy also to us.

Presented Faultless in God's Presence, Jude 1:24, 25. If Jude's awesome doxology does not cause you to want to jump up and down and shout with amazing joy, you had better reexamine the genuineness of your faith in Christ. The Living God, the Lord, is going to greet us with excitement and bubbling joy. This alone should exhibits the greatness of our redemption in Christ.

Then, in the mist of this tremendous doxology, Jude is extremely careful to point out that all glory, majesty, dominion and authority belong to Jesus Christ the Lord who is the Designer, Creator, the Sustainer, and only Redeemer. Friend, this is indeed one of the most wonderful doxologies in Scripture. We need to read it again and again and share with other saints the blessings of the momentous doxology.

The Epistle of Jude is certainly short, but his letter is very pungent and fully packed. His epistle is also packed with controversy. Here the controversy will only be more noticeable to those who desire to probe deeper into God's Word. Listen, when you are reading through Jude and this study, please give serious thought to his overall theme. Ah, but with Jude's theme, there is coupled with it an urgent underlining challenge and passionate plea for all genuine saints in Christ: **Earnestly Contending for the Faith**.

Part One

Occasion and Purpose

[1] Jude, a bond-servant of Jesus Christ and brother of James, to those who are the called, beloved in God the Father, and kept for [*by*] Jesus Christ: [2] May mercy, peace, and love be multiplied to you. [3] Beloved, while I was making every effort to write you about our common salvation, I felt the necessity to write to you appealing that you contend earnestly for the faith that was once for all *time* handed down to the saints. [4] For certain people have crept in unnoticed, those who were long beforehand marked out for this condemnation, ungodly persons who turn the grace of our God into indecent behavior and deny our only Master and Lord, Jesus Christ. (Jude 1:1-4 NAS)

CHAPTER 1

Sustaining grace of Christ

Memory verse

And He has said to me, "My grace is sufficient for you, for power is perfected in weakness." Most gladly, therefore, I will rather boast about my weaknesses, so that the power of Christ may dwell in me.

(2 Cor. 12:9)

Introduction

The author of the Epistle of Jude is questionable by some scholars today. Equally and unfortunately, tradition has only helped to muddle *the water* and made it more obscuring. For instance, one issue that is among adamant traditionalists is that Mary remained a virgin after the birth of Jesus. This is more than just misguided; this is a barefaced lie. The Scriptures are abundantly clear that Mary remained a virgin only until the birth of Jesus, the Messiah our Lord.

But he [*Joseph*] kept her [*Mary*] a virgin[a] until she had given birth to a Son [her firstborn child]; and he named Him Jesus (The LORD is salvation).

(Matt. 1:25 AMP)

[a]Note: more connotatively, "but did not have marital relations with her until she gave birth to a son."[NET]

So Mary, the mother Jesus, after she gave birth to Jesus, she indeed had other children by her husband Joseph.

Is this not the carpenter, the son of Mary and brother [b] of James, Joses, Judas, and Simon? And are His sisters[b] not here with us?" And they took offense at Him. (Mark 6:3)

[b]The GK words are *adelphos* [lit. *male sibling*] and *adelphe* [lit. *female sibling*]. This means biological siblings of Jesus.

Mary was chosen to carry the Lord in the womb, and she was empowered by the Holy Spirit to conceive the Christ.

Therefore, Mary, the mother of Jesus, indeed had other children, which were biological siblings of Jesus. Ecclesiastical traditionalists tends to circumscribe the Scriptures, thus making the Word of God none effect. For example, our Lord said concerning the Pharisees and their overemphasis of tradition, '- [*you Pharisees make*] the Word of God none effect through your tradition ___.' Mark 7:12.

Jude (author of this letter), is the brother of Jesus, our Lord. Jude actual name is Judas in NT GK. In HEB, the root name would be *Judah*. As to the name Jude, some have alleged that Jude did not want to be connected to Judas Iscariot, the one that betrayed Jesus. So, some traditions say that he shortened his name to Jude, but the GK text reads, Judas.

Jude (Judas) today would be address as Judah, *Yehuda* in the HEB community. (The Yiddish form is spelled and pronounced differently.) Yehuda means "praise" or "thanksgiving.'" Leah (the mother of Judah) said when she gave birth to *Yehuda*,

> And she conceived again, and bore a son: and she said, Now will I
> **praise the LORD**: therefore she called his name *Judah*; and left [*ceased*]
> bearing.   (Gen. 29:35 KJV)

Jude addresses himself a **slave** of Jesus. When Jude and his other siblings fully realize who Jesus was, their life was radically transformed as they trusted in Jesus as Lord and Savior. Jude's siblings (brothers and sisters) came to the realization through saving faith that they were now "**slaves** of Christ the Lord." Unfortunately, many in the churches today do not realize who Jesus is nor do they comprehend their utter sinfulness before our Lord.

I think it significant that Jude refers to himself in GK as a slave.

> GK: "Joudos *doulos Iesous* Christos –"

> Lit: "Judas a *slave* of Jesus Christ –"

Today, the idea of being one's **slave** is too demeaning, repulsive, and revolting in the minds of many in world today. Even in the time of the NT, slaves were considered the lower in rank in the Roman world.

What do you suppose will be the reaction of the skeptics' and mockers when many stand before Jesus as Supreme Sovereign and Lord of all? Friend, then they shall understand what petrifying fear really means. It is like that of Nabal who initially belittled David but later he found out that David was the

King of Israel.[1 Sam. 25:36-38] Nabal became like a stone. This my friend is *petrifying fear*.

However, Jude and the other family clan of Joseph and Mary were not given sufficient illumination by Spirit of God until after Jesus' resurrection. Christ's true identity was hidden from the family in order not to interfere with the plan of God and redemption of humankind. As Jude was to discover, our Lord provides all sufficiency of grace to all that genuinely placed their trust in Him as the Christ and Redeemer of all mankind.

A. Some preach cheap grace

Nowadays, many are preaching *cheap grace*. "Human works salvation," or "free to live in sin, we are saved by grace!" When Jesus calls His redeemed, He calls us by infinite and mighty grace. Friend, there is nothing cheap about the grace from Heaven. Christ's grace come with a total commitment to each of His redeemed, He "saves us to the uttermost."[Heb. 7:25] Ah, but my friend, the true grace of the Lord will transform and change our lives for the better. Jesus delivers us from the bondage of sin, and His grace gives new view on life through the power with the risen Christ within us.

Moreover, to all that are genuinely saved in Christ, our Lord excepts from each of His redeemed total commitment to Him. Jesus said, "- whoever does not bear his cross and come after Me cannot be My disciple."[Luke 14:25-27 NKJ]

Paul implores the Corinthians, "As we work together with *Him* [Christ], we urge you also not to accept the grace of God in vain."[2 Cor. 6:1 NRS] This is why the apostle could also say of himself,

> But by the grace of God I am what I am, and His grace to me was not in vain. No, I worked harder than all of them—yet not I, but the grace of God that was with me. (1Cor 15:10 MSB)

Many people today would <u>not</u> prostrate at the name of Jesus by choice; but believe me, at the Judgment, every person shall be petrified in fear and bow their knee before Him as Sovereign Lord. Even the apostle John when he is carried into the presence of the risen Lord Jesus in Heaven. "When I saw Him, **I fell at His feet like a dead man**."[Rev. 1:17]

Later, after Jesus' resurrection, Jude begins to awaken to the truth as our Lord appears to him and his siblings. Jude no doubt immediately prostrated himself at the feet of the Lord Jesus in His presence. Jude saw himself as utterly undone and wretched in Christ presence. Jude was now Jesus' love-

3

slave forever.[see Exo. 21:5, 6] Friend, being Jesus' **love-slave**, is that too repulsive for you? Or are you one who espouses "cheap grace?"

I think it is very noteworthy that like his brother James who also said in the beginning of his letter, "From James, a **slave** [*doulos*] of God and the Lord Jesus Christ —."[James 1:1] Equally important, there is nowhere in Scripture that teaches nor implies that Jude or James were ever declared apostles. Jude or James were Jesus' servants for all eternity. Jude says, "From Jude, a **slave** [*doulos*] of Jesus Christ --."[Jude 1:1 NET] The brothers may have been *Elders* in the church at Jerusalem, but there is no Scripture declaring Jude or James were even *Elders*. Still, there is no Scripture revealing they were apostles. This is the fabrication ecclesiastical tradition overriding the plain teaching of Scripture.

Friend, I say again, "Do you consider yourself a *doulos* (*slave*) of Jesus Christ?" Well, are you Jesus' slave? Similarly, "Is Jesus **Lord of all** your life?" "Is Jesus the Ruler of your life, or do you rule your life?"[Col. 3:15] "If Jesus is not Lord of our life, how can He be your Savior of your life?" You better watch out.

Friend, you had better know this for certain if you claim Jesus as your *savior*: Jesus' Lordship shall be very apparent when you stand before Him, and stand you shall. So, it is not surprising to read Jude says near the close of his letter,

> Maintain [*keeping*] yourselves in the love of God, **while anticipating the mercy of our Lord Jesus Christ** that brings eternal life.

> (Jude 1:21 NET)

It is popular today to speak to people on first name bases. People no longer address others as "Mr. Smith" or "Mrs. Jones." Even the titles are rarely used any more. For many nowadays, even the omission of degrees or designations of positions does not fit the profile and imagine some desire to portray of themselves to others. Even in business places, people have their first name appear on their nametag. People even encourage others by saying, "Oh, please call me by my first name, Bob".

For some, there appearance of humility is only a pretense, mockery, and sham. True! There are people that put on a false-front (a mask) sheepishly.[2] Sheep are easily intimidated and quiet, but there are people that enjoy putting on a front that appears like a sheep, humble. These are people who are not humble or timid in any means like sheep. These are people wearing a mask. They give a persona[3] as one easily approachable. Interestingly, their pretenses are indeed obvious or known by others. Their pretenses or facades are easily detected in the *inflection* of their voice. The *pitch* in their voice is slightly different from their regular tone, or it is even evident in their *roles* of mannerism as they masquerade themselves with others.

I think we are better off by addressing people with special names or titles if they have one. We ought to give respect or honor to whom it is due them. Unfortunately, sometimes *familiarity can breed contempt!* True brotherly love and genuine cordiality will create a proper atmosphere instead of addressing people with their first name.

However, if Jesus is only recognized as Savior, maybe Christ has never been made the Lord of their life? Let me say again, be assured of this fact: Jesus Christ is indeed truly the Lord of our lives right now whether anyone knows it or believe it. Friend, surrendering to the Lordship of Jesus ought to be the first step in a godly walk of faith in Christ. I warn you, if Jesus is not the Lord of you like, how can be truly the Redeemer of your life?

Do you know that when anyone walks humbly as a slave of Christ, *boldness* and *confidence* shall be at their side. The world, the flesh, and demonic forces seek only to muzzle the praises of some of the redeemed today. In some churches, Jesus is not the central attraction-getter. Instead, the churches are using *gimmicks*, *lures*, *games* and *trinkets* as the central drawing card. But those who love the Lord Jesus, let this thought be chiseled in your mind for all eternity: *the Lord Jesus is forever the center of all that God is*. Jesus came to free us that we might be His love-slave forever.

> The thief cometh not, but for to <u>steal,</u> and to <u>kill,</u> and to <u>destroy</u>: I am come that they **might have life**, and that they **might have *it* more abundantly**. I am the good^c shepherd: the good shepherd giveth his life for the sheep. (John 10:10, 11 KJV)

> ^cThe word <u>*good*</u> is the GK word <u>*kalos*</u>. The meaning of <u>*kalos*</u> is that Jesus has come to **do good things for you**. 'I am come that they might have life, and that they might have *it* more abundantly'. While it is true Jesus is intrinsically good as Lord and Savior, kalos implies one doing good things for others. He will do good things for you when you know Him and walk in His will.

The abundant life or life to the full only comes as we seek to *<u>walk with Jesus</u>* and we seek to *<u>follow Him</u>* and as *<u>He leads and guides</u>* us in His will. Does Jesus lead and guide your life, or *are you egocentrically guided*? I sometimes wonder, *are we follow the Lord or are we attempting to have Him follow us*. That is to say, *is Jesus just to tag alone with us as we go through life?* If we are **not** walking and loving the Lord as we should, then the godly and abundant life, a full life in Christ, cannot be yours or mine. Our Lord is not referring to the false and evil doctrine "Prosperity Doctrine". He is discussing (in John 10:1ff) Shepherding and Watch-care over His sheep. And as we shall see, this is the emphasis of Jude.

Too many of us are just "fair-weather Christians." A *fair-weather* Christian is someone that gages the climate of the weather for church <u>attendance</u> and faithfully <u>service</u> for Christ the Lord. If the weather is too bad, the "fair-weather Christians" may go to church or do service for Him. If the weather is too nice, the "fair-weather Christians" don't go to church or do any service for King. If it is a holiday, the "fair-weather Christians" don't go to church or do any service for Master. *Church attendance* and *service* for our Lord tends to be based upon a whim or impulse of the natural man not the new man in Christ. Church attendance and service for Christ should be based on a **total commitment** rather than gaging our action on the *whims* in life.

Sadly, some may discover as *the two doors to eternity opens* that it is too late now. The person may only have had an intellectual confession of faith in Jesus. Meaning that a person has only a confession of an intellectual or historical faith of fact. Hence, they are without a genuine possession and confession of true saving faith in Christ's redeeming grace. The shocker is that they were void of genuine faith in Jesus Christ as a personal commitment of their life. Jesus is indeed first Lord and then He is our Savior. Is Jesus only recognized as Savior to you? Then, He may have never been made the Lord of your life. Friend, as I have repeatedly said, surrendering to the Lordship of Christ is **the first step** in a genuine walk of saving faith in Christ. Let us remind ourselves that if Jesus is not Lord of our life, He may not be the Redeemer of our life.

Regeneration by the Holy Spirit ought to change our *thinking* and our *way of life* forever. Jude and James initially failed to realize Jesus is more than some itinerate Rabbi or Teacher. Jude and James came to the realization that Jesus is the King of kings, LORD or lords, and the only Sovereign. As the apostle Paul says and Jude and James definitely came to know and agreed,

> For <u>Christ's</u> <u>love</u> **compels** [GK *sunecho, engulfs, overwhelms*] us, because we are convinced that one died for all [*redeemed*], and therefore all [*redeemed*] died. And he [*Christ*] died for all [*redeemed*], that those who live should no longer live for themselves but for him [*Christ*] who died for them and was raised again. So from now on we regard no one from a worldly point of view. Though we once regarded Christ in this way, we do so no longer. Therefore, if anyone is in Christ, the new creation has come: The old has gone, the new is here! (2 Cor. 5:14-17 NIV)

ᵈNote: while Christ's sacrifice is indeed available for all, but the GK "*huper*"[v 15] is very explicit: Christ died in our place on the cross. Jesus took our place as a substitute. Jesus is no substitutionary death for the unbeliever.

Jesus is indeed King of kings, LORD of lords, and the only Supreme Sovereign. What is Jesus to you? My friend, Jesus does not give cheap grace: "Now because we are fellow workers [*with Christ*], we also **urge you not to receive the grace of God in vain**."2 Cor. 6:1 NET

B. Tradition or all sufficiency of grace

Roman Catholic Church, Eastern Orthodox Church, Coptic Orthodox Church, and other similar churches continues to cling to these *super-imposed manufactured ecclesiastical traditions* overriding the plain teaching of Scripture. The Roman Church and those who endorse Rome's tradition maintain that James and his brother Jude (author of their Epistles) were part of the original twelve apostles and not siblings of Jesus. Thus, perpetuating the error that Mary, though she was married to Joseph and a sinner like her husband, had no more children but that she remained a virgin throughout her life. There are many sincere and devoted Roman Catholic believers and other church traditionalists that strongly endorse the ecclesiastical traditions. Nevertheless, the Church of Rome and other likeminded ecclesiastical groups have overridden the authority of Scripture with their super-imposed *ecclesiastical traditions*. In so doing, they have *distorted* God's Word and continue to *perpetuate a blatant lie*.

To the contrary, Scripture is explicit and obliterates the above sincere ecclesiastical traditions. Jude and his brother James and the rest of the siblings' children were born to Joseph and Mary.Mark 6:3 Joseph was indeed the husband and father of all the siblings, in whom Mary was sole mother of all the children. Jesus was born by Mary and conceived by the Holy Spirit. Still, Scripture declares Mary remained a virgin only **until after** the birth of Jesus,Mat. 1:25 which by such a time later she had other children by Joseph, her husband.

So, let the blind continue to lead the blind. As our Lord said,

'Let them alone, they be the *blind* leaders of the *blind*: and if the *blind leaders* ye *blind*, both shall fall into the *ditch* [*pit*].'   (Matt. 15:14 GNV)

ᵉWords in *italics* and their spelling are updated, but no words have been changed.

Jude identifies himself as *the servant* [GK *doulos*] of Jesus Christ, as well as his brother James. Hence, James identifies himself also as a slave of Jesus Christ.

[James 1:1] Jude and James were the siblings of Mary, the mother of Jesus, and Joseph was indeed Mary's husband and father of all the children born after Jesus.

So, how is Rome able to come up with such concoction? Like the Pharisees, ecclesiastical tradition is not only equal with Scripture, but Rome espouses that ecclesiastical tradition also supersedes it. Rome and other church bodies adhere to such ecclesiastical traditions. Not only that but Rome uses ecclesiastical tradition as the bases of interpretation. Thus, such groups actually succeed the Scripture with their traditions. If you do not get it yet: ecclesiastical tradition superimposes its dogma as the final authority over Scripture. As a result, tradition has the final authority over Scripture according to Rome and all those who follow her.

Jude's brother James was said to be a fervent man of prayer. Eusebius (a church historian and Pastor) says that James had *callus on his knees like camel*. Eusebius gives this alleged account of James' prayer life:

Below is Eusebius' letter to Pastors in the 4th century:

> *"These days many of us, especially those within evangelical traditions, rarely get on our knees in prayer. In fact, it is so out of the ordinary that when I recently invited our church community to kneel, I had to take extra time to set it up ahead of time. Those in what would [be] described as traditional churches likely find it more common to descend to a kneeler each week for the confessional prayer. Regardless of our worship tradition, I would like to suggest that all of us could learn quite a lot from the Apostle' James in his example of dedicated, humble prayer through appropriate kneeling.*
>
> *"However, let me take it a step further, and say that pastors and ministers of all sorts should take a cue on prayer from "Old Camel Knees."[a reference to James] It would be an invaluable breakthrough in ministry practice if all of us serving in ministry left a legacy like James of dedication in prayerful worship of God and intercession before God on behalf of our people. May God give us grace that our bodies would be marked by our dedication in prayer."[4]*

> [f] Note: however, *James* (brother of our Lord) *was **never** an apostle*. He may have been an Elder (though there no Scripture even declaring him as an Elder), but he certainly was never one twelve apostles.

Still, I wonder if Jude was as zealous for the Law like his brother James?[Acts 21:20].

It may be that our Lord saw the Gentiles perhaps being influence by zealous Jewish Christians as "a sect of Nazarenes"[Acts 24:5] and living under the

Mosaic Law. So, our Lord raised up Paul as an apostle to the Gentile. '–the Gentiles, to whom I now send you."Acts 26:17; Rom. 11:13

Some people today are so deficient in the Scripture, but they are also burdened down with very many ecclesiastical *traditions, customs,* and *practices* that are unscriptural. True! Today, some assume or even erroneously teach that there are two supposed programs of salvation co-existing today with the Gospel. How ignorant is that? It is alleged by such groups that there is the *Gospel of the Circumcision* for *Jewish Christians living under the Mosaic Law.* Then, there is the *Gospel of the Uncircumcision* for *Gentiles [non-Jewish] Christians* not living under the Law for righteousness before God.

Friend, Paul declares there are **NOT** two Gospels. That is, there is no Gospel which is allegedly for the Jewish Christians following the tradition under the Law. There is no so-called Gospel to the *Gentiles* where others live without obligation to the Law for righteousness.(See Gal. 5:1-5.) The fact that the Temple in Jerusalem was destroyed in 70 AD by Titus ought to awaken us to the Scriptures. The Law is indeed holy and righteous, but the Law is not the Lord's basis for being made righteousness before God.

Friend, the Law itself is indeed **holy** and **righteous**, but righteousness can never be attained by attempting to be righteous (justified) through the obedience under the Mosaic Law or by human works. Listen to me, the Mosaic Law is only a mirror. True my friend! The Mosaic Law reveals the sinfulness of mankind. Ah, but the Mosaic Law also reveals the infinite holiness and righteousness of God. The Bible is clear that by works of the Law, no one shall be justified (that is, made righteous before God). First, no one except the Lord Jesus is able to completely obey the Mosaic Law. Second, no sinful man is able to obey the Mosaic Law. Humankind is under sin,Rom. 3:11, 12 alienated from God due his sin, already condemnation,John 3:18 and abides under the wrath of God.John 3:36 Jesus Christ offered Himself upon the cross in order to propitiate our sins satisfying the righteous demand of a holy God. Hallelujah! The Bible is clear that no one will be considered righteous through works of the Law.Gal. 2:16 Thirdly, if righteousness were attainable by the Law, then Christ's death on the cross was in vain.Gal. 2:21

Personal commitment of faith and trust in Christ's sacrifice on the cross is the sole means for righteousness before God. When a person truly trusts in Jesus as Lord and Savior, Christ imputes His righteousness to us.2 Cor. 5:21 So, we are saved by faith in Christ through grace alone.Eph. 2:8-10 Unfortunately, ecclesiastical traditions and the annals of church history and church dogma has superimposed themselves over the authority of Scripture. Hence, such ecclesiastical traditions have change and distort the Scriptures.

9

Some scholars suggest Jude's and James' writings were written later to counteract misunderstanding of Paul's meaning of grace. There is no basis to the alleged claim that Jude or James was written to counteract any misunderstanding of Paul's writing.

The church was well on its way by conversation of Paul and his commission as an apostle.[Acts 13:1, 2; Acts 26:17, 18] James gives an emphasizes of living under the Law as means of righteousness. Jude and James though now saved and slaves of Christ, the brothers had not yet fully realized that God's dispensation or administration changed from Mosaic Law to the administration of Grace. Israel and the life under the administration of the Mosaic Law is ended. There is now the change to the administration of the Church.

The book of Acts reveals the distinctive transitioning from the Mosaic Law unto the church under the New Covenant of Grace. (Though the New Covenant was inaugurated at the cross,[Eph. 2:14-22] the New Covenant cannot be fully be realized until Israel is back into a covenant relationship).

Jesus said of the day coming for Israel,

> For I say unto you, Ye shall not see me henceforth, till ye shall say,
> Blessed *is* he that cometh in the name of the Lord. (Matt. 23:39 KJV)

Now in Christ, the sufficiency of *the saving grace* of the Lord Jesus. Friend, it is not the Law plus Jesus. It is all by the grace and mercy of Christ the Lord that saves. Have you my brother experienced the *all sufficiency of the grace* of the Lord Jesus in your life? If you say, "Yes, I have experienced the all sufficiency of the grace of the Lord Jesus", does it show in your life? Well, is that grace evident in your life for others to see?

Reasons for Jude and James early writing:

Here are some examples that might suggest that Jude's and James' writings might have actually occurred during the infancy of the church:

- ✓ The twelve apostles (Judas Iscariot was replaced by Mathias [Acts 1:26]) continued worshipping in the temple in Jerusalem, [Acts 3:1ff].
- ✓ Jewish Christians may have withdrawn to avoid offending Old Covenant Jews living under the Law.[Gal. 2:1-15]
- ✓ A Jewish delegation came from James to the Antioch Church perhaps to influence its direction and doctrine.[Gal. 2:12]
- ✓ James reports how many Jewish Christians were now zealous to living under the Law.[Acts 21:20]

✓ The fact that in James' Epistle he refers to the worship center as a <u>syn-agogue</u> (GK <u>*sunagoge*</u>, [James 2:2]) and not as a church, which is a red flag.

✓ Let us also recall that at Stephen's arrest, Stephen was charged that Jesus declared that He was going to *change <u>the</u> <u>tradition</u> and <u>customs</u>* of <u>the</u> <u>elders</u>. Some Jews said of Stephen.[Acts 6:14]

The above seems to solidify and confirm an early writing of Jude and James for me. The above suggests definite reasons why James even directs Paul to take vow and present an animal sacrifice of purification. It further reveals how some people incorrectly assume there are two different Gospels today: Gospel of the Circumcision and the Gospel of the Uncircumcision. Hence, this is like attempting to mix of Law and Grace for righteousness, which is like mixing oil and water, it **does** **not** mix.

Paul said,

> And if it is by grace, then it is no longer by works. Otherwise, grace would no longer be grace. But if it is by works, then it is no longer grace. Otherwise work is no longer work.   (Rom. 11:6 MSB)

Other MSS simply reads,

> But if it is by grace, it is no longer on the basis of works; otherwise grace would no longer be grace.   (Rom. 11:6 ESV)

Do you lean on your traditions for "righteousness by works," or do you rely on "all sufficiency of grace of the Lord Jesus?"

C. Set apart by the grace

Note parallel texts:

Jude, the servant of Jesus Christ, and brother of James, to them that are **sancti-fied** by God the Father, and preserved in Jesus Christ, *and* **called**:	Jude, a servant of Jesus Christ, and brother of James To those who are **called sanctified** by God the Father, and preserved in Jesus Christ.	Jude, a servant of Jesus Christ, and brother of James, to them that are **called**, **beloved** in God the Father, and kept for Jesus Christ:	Jude, the servant of Jesus Christ, and brother of James: to them that are **be-loved** in God the Father, and preserved in Jesus Christ, and **called**.
KJV	Coptic	ASV	LT/ENG

The words "<u>*sanctified*</u>" and "<u>called</u>" does appear in some GK text, but the word *sanctified* is not found some GK MSS. Whether the word "<u>*sanctified*</u>"

is part of original letter of Jude or not is too complicated to answer in this study. Still, the NT teaching concerning *sanctification* is an extremely important doctrine to know and understand. So, "*sanctified*" must be included in the study here. Also, the word "*called*" is another important word. However, the word "*called*" ("the *called*") will be discussed in the last section under, [D. Empowered of grace].

Other manuscripts have the "-<u>beloved</u> in God the Father —."[v 1 ASV] The KJV reads, "<u>sanctified</u> by God the Father." The order once again:

to them that are **sanctified by God the Father**, and preserved in Jesus Christ, *and* **called**: KJV	To those who are **called, sanctified by God the Father** NKJ	to them that are **called, beloved in God the Father** ASV	To those who are the **called, beloved in God the Father** NAS

The GK spelling of *sanctified* and *beloved* are similar. Whether the similarity in spelling is sufficient for error by the copying scribe or some other reason is unknown.

BYZ text reads: *sanctified* is [ἡγιασμένοις]-

Earlier GK text: *beloved* is [ἠγαπημένοις]-

For the moment, let us focus the words *sanctified* and the word <u>beloved</u>. Both of these concepts are greatly misunderstood. Both *sanctified* and *beloved* are taught in Scripture. The issue is too complicated as to which belongs to the original GK text. Besides, both the biblical doctrines are not only true but extremely important Scriptural teaching. The confusion of on the words *sanctified* and <u>beloved</u> is the result of the influence of the natural man reasoning. Another reason for the confusion is the dominance of ecclesiastical dogma overriding the Scripture declaration. Let us examine *sanctification* and *beloved*.

Sanctification:

"–to them that are *sanctified* by God the Father," [Jude 1:1 KJV]

The more contemporary GK scholars favors "*beloved*" (GK *agapao*), but the word "*sanctified*" (GK *hagiazo*) is omitted by some GK texts. I am persuaded by evidence that the word intended is probably *beloved* instead of *sanctified*. The word "*sanctified*" is not in earlier GK texts. Due the importance of the word *sanctified*, we need to carefully examine it as well here.

First, *sanctification* is the same words used in the Bible as *holy, set apart, dedicated,* and *consecrated* to name a few. For example, we have been *set apart* or *sanctified* <u>by</u> and <u>for</u> God in Christ Jesus our Lord. In Scripture, things were dedicated or sanctified for God when the temple of Solomon was being built. Hence, these items were given to the temple and were dedicated or holy unto the Lord.

So, in the same way, when a person is genuinely saved in Christ, he/she is then *sanctified* or *set apart* by the Holy Spirit. All genuine believers in Christ belong to the Lord. So, we have been *set apart* or *sanctified* or made *holy* unto God.

The Father, the Son, and Holy Spirit sanctifies every genuine believer. We were sanctified by the blessed Trinity's work. The Trinity works in absolute harmony and as One. For instance, Jesus said,

> Do you say of Him, whom the Father <u>sanctified</u> and sent into the world, 'You are blaspheming,' because I said, 'I am the Son of God '? If I do not do the works of My Father, do not believe Me; but if I do them, though you do not believe Me, believe the works, so that you may know and understand that the Father is in Me, and I in the Father."
>
> (John 10:36-38)

Again, in Jesus' prayer for the apostles that He had chosen, He said:

> [14]I have given them thy word; and the world hath hated them, because they are not of the world,[they were sanctified by Jesus] even as I am not of the world. [15]I pray not that thou shouldest take them out of the world, but that thou shouldest keep them from the evil [*one*][g]. [16]They are not of the world, even as I am not of the world. [17] **Sanctify them through thy truth** [certainty of inspiration]: thy word is truth. [18]As thou hast sent me into the world, even so have I also sent them into the world. [19]And for their sakes **I sanctify myself**, that **they** also **might be sanctified through the truth.** (John 17:14-18 KJV)

> [g]Note: evil, GK *poneros*, is genitive masculine, and it refers to Satan; the word is not neuter as to a thing.

At calling and commissioning of the apostle Paul, the risen Lord Jesus said,

> To open their eyes, *and* to turn *them* from darkness to light, and *from* the power of Satan unto God, that they may receive forgiveness of sins, and inheritance among **them which are sanctified by faith that is in me** [Christ]. (Acts 26:18 KJV)

Paul's ministry or service to the Gentiles was sanctified, [Rom. 15:16]. Through prayer, our food is sanctified as we are given the freedom eat whatever we want, [1 Tim. 4:5]. The genuine believer is also sanctified by the Holy Spirit.[1 Cor. 6:11]

Three-fold aspect of sanctification upon all believers:
Sanctification upon the believer is a three-fold-process from the human perspective. Yet, from God's perspective, sanctification is a single action. God's feats and actions or deeds are not bound by time. (God is eternally present and not bound by time within creation.) So, sanctification is one single action for God. Here is the three-fold aspect of sanctification: 1. We are sanctified when saved. 2. We are *presently* being sanctified in our life today by the Spirit. 3. Finally, we will be completely sanctified by rapture.

1.   We are sanctified when we are saved.
The moment a person is genuinely saved (they have personally confessed and received Jesus[John 1:12; Rom. 10:9, 13]). As the redeemed in Christ, he/she is set apart or sanctified by the Holy Spirit.

> [9]Or do you not know that the unrighteous shall not inherit the kingdom of God? Do not be deceived; neither fornicators, nor idolaters, nor adulterers, nor effeminate, nor homosexuals, [10]nor thieves, nor *the* covetous, nor drunkards, nor revilers, nor swindlers, shall inherit the kingdom of God. [11]And [*But*] such were some of you; but you **were washed**, but you **were sanctified**, but you **were justified** [*declared righteous*] **in the name** of the Lord Jesus Christ, and **in the Spirit of our God**.
>
> (1 Cor. 6:9-11)

The Holy Spirit **washes**, **sanctifies**, and **justifies** [GK dikaioo, made us *righteous* in Christ]. We are now made citizens of Heaven.[Phi. 3:20] We are *washed, sanctified*, and made *righteous* by redemption of Christ. This sanctification is a once for all action completed by God. Thus, this sanctification by God is not repeated since it is completed. It is a once for all action by God.

2.   We are *presently* being sanctified.
There is another element in sanctification once we are genuinely saved. We are also *presently being set apart* for God from the world, the flesh, and the devil. For example, Hebrews says,

> And have you forgotten the exhortation addressed to you as sons?[h] "My son, do not scorn the Lord's discipline or give up when he corrects you. [6]"For the Lord disciplines the one he loves and chastises every son he accepts." [7]Endure your suffering as discipline; God is treating you as

sons. For what son is there that a father does not discipline? [8]But if you do not experience discipline, something all sons have shared in, then you are illegitimate and are not sons.   (Heb. 12:5 NET)

[h]The word GK *huos* in v 5 is "sons" (not *children*). Son refers to all the redeemed, male and female.[Gal. 3:26-29]

A person may allegedly profess faith in Christ without a genuine commitment of genuine regeneration in which case they only intellectually believe the historical facts. However they remain unsaved without Christ. It may be evidence they are void of genuine faith in Christ since he/she is without discipline.[Heb. 12:5-8] God only disciplines His children in the faith. We are children of God in Christ. Yet, as His children, we unfortunately sin.[1 John 1:8-10] In 1 John 3:6, the apostle John's intended meaning is that as saints in Christ, we no longer live *habitually a wicked life of sin*. The saved's life has been change by the grace of God.

The reason for the change in life of genuine believer is because of present *sanctifying* work of the Holy Spirit in the life. The believer is empowered by the Spirit of God. If a Christian habitually and rebelliously sins and continually lives a wicked life, there is one of three things that shall surely take place.

a.   God will *chasten* or *discipline* the person. However, the saint unfortunately may not recognize the discipline is from the Lord since he/she is walking in rebellious sin.[Rev. 3:19]

b.   God may either take you home to Heaven (He will kill you), or friend, you may wish He had taken your life,[1 Cor. 11:27-32.]

c.   We must keep this in mind at all times: if anyone is *without discipline* from the Lord, then friend, this may be a definite evidence that the person is still unregenerate, unsaved and lost in sin and on the road to Hell![Heb. 12:8]

3.   Finally, we will be completely sanctified.

In the final state of sanctification, we are present in our gloried bodies. We shall then be completely sanctified in Christ and set apart from sin forever. Death is swallowed up in victory.

[53]For the perishable must clothe itself with the imperishable, and the mortal with immortality. [54]When the perishable has been clothed with the imperishable, and the mortal with immortality, then the saying that is written will come true: "Death has been swallowed up in victory."

15

[55]"Where, O death, is your victory? Where, O death, [GK *hades*, lit. *hades* or implying *grave*] is your sting?"
(1 Cor. 15:53-55 NIV)

In this last aspect of sanctification, this is total removal from the presence of sin. Then, we shall have a glorified body in Heaven. Hallelujah!

I shall discuss the words "the **called**" in the last section of this study [D. Empowered of grace]. For the present, let us look at the word "**beloved**;" a very important element redemption.

Beloved:

"to them that are called, *beloved* in God the Father." [Jude 1:1 ASV]

The GK texts various here. The oldest GK text reads, "**beloved**;" while the much less older GK text reads, "**sanctified**." Still, both words are important doctrines. Now, let turn our attention on the word "*beloved*."

I suppose some will sneer at the possibility that the GK text reads as "-*beloved* in God the Father."[Jude 1:1 ASV] Listen friend, I advise you to wipe that smear off your face. Anyone depositing all of their marbles, eggs, or apples, so to speak, into one bag is very foolish. Leave room for the illumination and insight by the Holy Spirit, least your be found as blind and following the blind.

In the same way, let me also say to those who lean to a more contemporary scholarship in textual criticism. Friend, do not turn your nose up at those that lean toward the textual reading as "*sanctified*," which is in other GK manuscripts. The shoe fits you as well: you do not know with certainty whether the word is "*beloved*" or if the word is "*sanctified*." You had better leave room for the illumination and insight by the Holy Spirit least you find yourself following the blind leading the blind!

Other GK manuscripts read in contrast to the word above, "sanctified:" *To those who are the called, **beloved in God the Father*** –.[Jude 1:1 NAS] Both are true in that we are *sanctified* or *beloved* in God the Father. So then, let us be careful in making a conclusive decision

For example, we are *beloved by God the Father*. So, we possess the *love* of God within us by the Holy Spirit. We are now recipients of the love of God since we are saved and in Christ. As to the unsaved without Christ, God is offering or extending His love to the unregenerate. Watch out and be careful here. The unregenerate **do not possess** the love God. Let me be very clear: "the unregenerate **DO NOT POSSESS** the love God." The unregenerate only become *recipients* of the love of God when they are genuinely saved and sanctified by faith Christ's redemption. God's love is already ours in Christ when we are in the Lord Jesus' redemption.[Rom. 5:5] As receipt of this infinite love by God, the apostle says:

> Yet in all these things we are more than conquerors[i] through Him who loved us. For I am persuaded that neither death nor life, nor angels nor principalities nor powers, nor things present nor things to come, nor height nor depth, nor any other created thing, shall be able to separate us from the love of God which is in Christ Jesus our Lord.
>
> (Rom. 8:37-39 NKJ)

> [i]"Conquers," NAS e.g. says: "in all these things we overwhelmingly conquer through Him who loved us." The NAS uses *conquer* in the singular (the NAS does read, "**we** overwhelmingly conquer." The GK is "conquer<u>s</u>," plural.

As to the love of God: the world **is being offered** *the love of God*. The **love of God** is a legitimate offer to each one in the world and without prejudice. This is the error of *electionists*. Therefore, the love of God is indeed a legitimate offer to the world through Christ the Lord.

Know this however for absolutely certain that the unregenerate world is **not** yet a recipient of the love of God. The unregenerated are presently under the pending wrath of God.[John 3:18, 36] Therefore, there is light-years difference between being a *recipient* or *benefactor* of the love of God. The unsaved are presently facing the infinite wrath of God since the lost are outside Christ's redemption. The unsaved are being offered the love of God. God is willing to rescue unsaved from His wrath but only through saving faith in Christ. No one can be a recipient of the love of God without being saved and in Christ. This is why the apostle John says,

> By this the children of God and the children of the devil are revealed [*clearly made known*]: Everyone who does not practice righteousness [*even though a profess the faith*] — the one who does not love his fellow Christian— is not of God. (1 John 3:10 NET)

John is saying that the evidence of regeneration is the love generated by the Holy Spirit in the life of the genuine believer. We do not love our brother to be saved. We truly love our brother in Christ because we are now saved!

However, there is one exception. The exception is those who are mentally incompetent to believe and be saved. The mentally incompetent includes: the Unborn, infants, children, and the mentally deficient. For example, when David's son died which was born in adultery situation with Bathsheba, he said,

> Therefore, because he [e.g., *the son*] is dead, why would I fast? Is he [*the son*] able to return again? I shall go to him and [*but*] he cannot come to me"
>
> (2 Sam. 12:23 ABPE)

Listen carefully, all humanity is alienated and cut off from God because of our sin.[Rom. 3:10f, 5:12; 1 Cor.15:22] We are **not** children of God at birth. We were all children of wrath without Christ as our Redeemer.[Eph. 2:1-3] Mankind stands condemned not because he is an unbeliever, but all humanity is condemned because all are sinners before a holy and righteous God. Get right: all humanity is condemned due our sin in Adam.[Rom. 5:12; 1 Cor.15:22] (It is an ecclesiastical liar to allege one's original sin is removed by water baptism. Jesus' meaning is the wash regeneration of the Spirit: compare John 3:3-7 to Titus 3:3-7).

If one hears the Gospel but rejects it, he has condemned himself twice. He is condemned due his sin, but second condemnation is rejection of the love of God to him. So, his judgment is more severe because he heard the Gospel and refused it. Everyone shall surely perish forever in their sin without Christ Jesus' redemption.[John 3:18, 36; 1 John 5:13]

In 1 John 4:9, the apostle John is **not** saying that if anyone love others, then we are children of God. The apostle is saying that if we are *born from above* by the Spirit of God and genuinely in Christ, our new nature will be evident by loving our brother because we have new nature within us.

So, it is incorrect to say the *world already possesses the love of God.* Listen, God is indeed **extending** or **offering** His love to the world through Christ. The Lord has His arms wide open to receive anyone in the world that is willing to come through Jesus Christ as Lord and Savior. God has His arms open wide to receive anyone willing to come to the Lord through saving faith in Jesus Christ. *Electionists* espouse that only the <u>selected</u> <u>chosen</u> <u>ones</u> shall come and be saved. According to many *electionists*, no one is willing to come to be saved. So, the Lord *elects* some to be saved.

Upon the above proposed *theological premise*, the *electionists* are categorically in error. While I deeply respect those holding the doctrine election, the offer of salvation in Christ to the world is indeed **legitimate** and **truly offered to the world**. The problem is the churches are **not** going out "door to door" and <u>compelling</u> <u>people</u> <u>to come</u> <u>to</u> <u>Christ</u>. *Electionists'* are disobedient to the risen Christ mandates.

The Gospel offered by God is: "**Come as you are right now.**" There are *no strings attached.*[5] The Lord will not allow anyone to be lost and condemned due to Satan blinding and leading people astray[2 Cor. 4:3, 4] or due to luring world's

18

attractions which the devil influences.[Act 26:18] Nevertheless, mankind is a sinner, and all will perish without faith in Christ.[John 8:24] The Bible is clear,

> "He who believes in the Son has everlasting life; and he who does not believe the Son shall not see life, but the wrath of God abides on him."
>
> (John 3:36 NKJ)

When Christ died for sinners, God proved His love towards the world when Christ Jesus died on the cross.

> But God *commended* [GK sunistemi, *sustained, proved, demonstrated*] his love toward us, in that, while we were yet sinners, Christ died for us. (Rom. 5:8 KJV)

In our above text in Jude 1:1, the believer is the **BELOVED IN GOD** the Father." Those that did not believe in Jesus, our Lord said:

> You are of *your* father the devil, and you want to do the desires of your father. He was a murderer from the beginning, and does not stand in the truth because there is no truth in him. Whenever he speaks a lie, he speaks from his own *nature*, for he is a liar and the father of lies.
>
> (John 8:44)

Jesus means that the unsaved "are of *your* father the devil" since they are unsaved and have not trusted in Christ. So, the unregenerate are children of the devil because they are without Christ and remain unregenerate. Therefore, the unregenerate are **not** children of God. However, the unregenerate can become children of God through faith in the risen Lord Jesus Christ.

Those beloved in God the Father are everyone born again through saving faith in Christ. What is so ironic here is that both *electionists* and *free-will* miss the point. Everyone that comes to Christ Jesus as Lord and Savior God is *the beloved*. Before all eternity the **beloved in God** the Father became reality through personal faith in Christ. God is willing to save all coming through Jesus Christ.

Let us keep in mind that God's actions are always in the present tense. The Lord is always in the eternal present tense. Yet, by human time frame, God is calling and He is extending the love of the Father to everyone. [John 3:16]

The above statement is paradoxical. We are "called, **beloved in God** the Father," [Jude 1:1 ASV]. Ah, but *"God is calling and God is extending the love of the Father to everyone."* The *electionists* maintain God's is only available to the *elect*. To human mind, it is paradoxical because humankind can only think in time (past, present, and future.) As I have said, God Himself is not bound by time. This is similar to:[Rom. 8:22, 23] we are "eagerly waiting the redemption which is glorification of our bodies," which is the resurrection, the raptured of saints.

Yet, in the mind of God, it is already completed: "whom He **called**, He also **justified**; and these whom He justified, He also **glorified**."[Rom. 8:30] Glorification is referring to the union of body, soul, and spirit. The final and complete state of the redeemed. While our glorification from a human point of view is future, God sees our redemption as already completed since He is eternally present.

The apostle John in his second letter refers to the church as, 'the elect lady.' The *elect lady* because God is in the present tense and not bound by human time frame.

> "The elder [which is the apostle John] unto the elect [*chosen*] lady [which is the Pastor] and her children [which is the believers], whom I love in the truth; and not I only, but also all they that have known the truth."   (2 John 1:1 KJV)

Some interpret that John is writing to an unknown Christian woman, which I think is a possible meaning. Yet, I prefer rather to think that John is referring to a *Pastor* and the *assembly of believers* where he is pastoring. (Church is the GK word *ekklesia*, which is feminine.) So, the apostle John may be using "the elect lady" a cryptic name for church. John uses *"to the elect lady"* as cryptic name due to the intense persecution of Christians in the late first century. So, "elect lady" is referring to believers: the Pastor and church as the *elect* or *chosen*. Yet, the people had to believe in Christ to be "unto the elect [*chosen*] lady and her children." Listen: it is not the elect and then believe. It is believe first and then you will be saved and be *the elect of God*. If you do not truly believe, then you cannot be among the elect!

If anyone is persuaded John is writing a Christian woman and family, this is fine. Still, the rule for genuine faith in Christ stands. You cannot be chosen until you believe. If one does not personally commit their life to Christ and trust in Him as Lord and Savior, they cannot be of the elect. Personal commitment is required to be in Christ. Again, this is paradox, and the statement is a contradiction to the human mind. God's actions are not based upon finite time (past, present, and future.) God is always in the eternally present.

Some hyper-*electionists* seem to suggest humans have no action in *"being saved."* So, a person remains passively waiting to be chosen in strong *electionist's* churches. This, friend, is such travesty. Believe and genuinely trust and receive Christ and you will be saved.[John 1:12f; Acts 16:31; Rom. 10:9-13]

On the other hand, there are other people that may be a little insecure and hoping that they will make it to Heaven, hang on and be saved. The promise of God is "believe or trust on [or *"in"*] the Lord Jesus, and you shall be saved," [Acts

[16:31]. The Lord began the work in us, and He shall complete it.[Phi.1:6; 2:12,13] Listen to me: you take action and trust in Jesus, and then, God shall take action and you shall be saved. Our action of faith in Christ occurred in time, but God is eternal and knowing all things; He is not bound by time. He called us in eternity. Nevertheless, you must personally believe in Christ as Lord and Savior to be saved.

Here again, God sees from all eternity. The Lord is not bound by time: God is eternal with no beginning or end, eternally present. I am a creature of creation (being set in time), I am bound by time. So, chose and receive the Lord Jesus and you shall be saved. We must each personally believe and receive Christ to be saved since I am a creature bound by time to be saved.

D. Empowered of grace

Now let us look at the last phrase in verse one of Jude. The expression [Jude 1:1] in the KJV and NAS:

"-to them that are <u>sanctified</u> by God the Father, and preserved in Jesus Christ, *and* <u>called</u>	"-To those who are the <u>called</u>, beloved in God the Father, and kept for [lit. *by*] Jesus Christ
KJV	NAS

Now, let us note the <u>called</u>. The order the word "<u>called</u>" is a slight variance. KJV place "<u>called</u>" at end of verse, but other translations place the phrase first. The NAS order in ENG is preferred though the word "<u>called</u>" is the last word in GK, *kletos*.

Let us note variances in the text again,

Jude, a servant of Jesus Christ, and brother of James, to those who are **sanctified** by God the Father, and preserved in Jesus Christ: *and* **called**.	Jude, a servant of Jesus Christ, and brother of James To those who are **called** **sanctified** by God the Father, and preserved in Jesus Christ.	Jude, a servant of Jesus Christ, and brother of James, to them that are **called,** **beloved** in God the Father, and kept for Jesus Christ:	Jude, the servant of Jesus Christ, and brother of James, to them that are **sanctified** by God the Father, and preserved in Jesus Christ, *and* **called:**	Jude, the servant of Jesus Christ, and brother of James: to them that are **beloved** in God the Father, and preserved in Jesus Christ, and **called.**
TRE[6]	Coptic	ASV	KJV	LT/ENG

The order in ENG by the Coptic and ASV are similar except the *sanctified* or *beloved*. (The KJV and LT/ENG places *called* at the end of the verse as it appears in the GK.) The order is editorial translation preference, to which we can agree or disagree. The *called* is from God who is eternally present and not bound by time. We are creatures set in time.

No one can be "the called" unless the person truly trusts in Christ and he is saved. As I have already explained, this is a biblical paradox. The saved are "the called" of God, but cannot be *the called* unless we personally <u>believe</u> and <u>receive</u> Jesus Christ as Lord. Then, we are <u>spiritually engrafted</u> or *baptized* and <u>sealed</u> by the Holy Spirit into Christ.[1 Cor. 12:13]

God is not bound by time. So, God knows from all eternity who are "the called." However, from human perspective, each person is responsible to personally believe and receive Jesus Christ, or else, they cannot be part of those called of God. As humans or angels, we cannot understand or unravel the mystery of the seemingly paradox of the sovereignty of God and the human will to believe. Like the mystery of Trinity: we believe it, but we cannot understand or unravel the mystery of the blessed Trinity of God.

Now, let us look at next phrase by Jude.

GK BYZ, Jude 1:1:

> GK transliteration: *tois en theoi patri egapemenois kai Iesou Christoo tetepemenois kletios*

> ENG GK order: to them in God the Father and Jesus Christ preserved by called

> ENG translation: to them called in God the Father and preserved [watch over, guarded] by Jesus Christ

> Please see the end of this chapter and the Gingrich lexicon notes on the word "*preserved*" or "*kept*," the GK word *tetepemenois*.[7]

Jude's emphasis seems to be more on the risen Lord's role as the Chief Shepherd, which is given by the apostle Peter as title for our Lord. (In essence, Peter is saying that Christ is the **number One Shepherd** or perhaps the **Supreme** or **Ruling Shepherd**) over His entire redeemed, His church. As Peter says,

> And when **the Chief Shepherd appears**, you will receive the crown of glory that does not fade away.　　　　　　(1 Peter 5:4 NKJ)

Let us note Jude expression might sound like in a strict Orthodox Jewish setting but using ENG phonic.

> *Yehuda, a slave of Yehoshua the Messiah, and an akh[i] of Yaaqob, to those called, beloved [sanctified] by Elohim the Abba, and preserved* [guarded] *by Yehoshua the Messiah.*　　　　　　(Jude 1:1)

[j]Note: "akh" means "*brother*" in HEB.

"–kept [*preserved* KJV] for Jesus Christ –"

Many contemporary translations reads "kept **for** Jesus Christ." I must disagree that this is the less likely the intended meaning by Jude. The saints are already *saved*, and *paid for in full* by the death and shed blood of Christ the Lord on Calvary, and now *citizens of Heaven*. Therefore, we are already Christ's possession.[1 Cor. 6:19, 20] The redeemed are the Lord Jesus' possession right now. Jesus said,

> "**My sheep hear My voice**, and **I know them**, and they follow Me."
>
> (John 10:27 NKJ)

In John 10, Jesus' emphasis is His on-going shepherding over His sheep. 'I know them, and **they follow Me**. ' There is a continual and permit role of the Lord Jesus' shepherding over His sheep, which He paid for and already owns. I prefer the meaning "**kept by** Christ as the Chief Shepherd over the sheep." We are not kept for Christ; He already owns and keeps us.[John 6:39; 10:28-30] The redeemed are under the "protection" or "guarded" by Jesus Christ.

So, the expression "kept *for* Jesus Christ" is less favorable meaning. The GK word "*tereo* is dative, (*tetērēmenois*, verb participle perfect passive dative masculine)." The KJV is closest to the meaning here, though I prefer the NKJ:

> To those who are called, sanctified [or *beloved*] by God the Father, and preserved in [*by*][k] Jesus Christ: (Jude 1:1 NKJ)

> [k]Note: the dative can be translated as *in*, *by*, or even *with*. So, the meaning is "preserved by Jesus Christ."

The meaning is implying that the Chief Shepherd, Jesus Christ, is vigilantly "**watching over** or **guarding**" His redeemed. Christ the Lord is actively *watching over* His sheep. The sheep are not being guarded *for* Christ. Rather the sheep are **being guarded by** Christ Himself as the Chief Shepherd. As our Lord said of His redeemed and His shepherding over his sheep,

> [37]Everyone the Father gives Me will come to Me, and the one who comes to Me I will never drive away. [38]For I have come down from heaven, not to do My own will, but to do the will of Him who sent Me. [39]And this is the will of the Father who sent Me, that **I shall lose none** of those He has given Me, but raise them up at the last day. [40]And it is the will of Him who sent Me that everyone who looks to the Son and believes in Him shall have eternal life, and I will raise him up at the last day."   (John 6:37-40 MSB)

This is the doctrine of ***the perseverance of the saint***. This is eternal security of every true believer. Listen, eternal security of saints is a very important doctrine. We continue in the faith in Christ because God began the work in us, and He shall indeed complete our salvation unto His eternal glory and praise. As the apostle says,

> Wherefore, my beloved, as ye have always obeyed, not as in my presence only, but now much more in my absence, work out your own salvation with fear and trembling. **For it is God which worketh in you both to will and to do of *his* good pleasure.** (Phil. 2:12, 13 KJV)

Again,

> Now the God of peace, that brought again from the dead our Lord Jesus, that **GREAT SHEPHERD** of the sheep, through the blood of the everlasting covenant, **Make you perfect in every good work to do his will, <u>WORKING IN YOU</u> that which is well-pleasing in his sight**, through Jesus Christ; to whom *be* glory for ever and ever. Amen.
>
> (Heb. 13:20, 21 KJV)

And I am sure of this, that **he** who **began a good work** in you will bring it to **completion at the day of Jesus Christ.** (Phil. 1:6 ESV)

> So do not be ashamed of the testimony about our Lord or of me, a prisoner for his sake, but **by God's power accept** your share of suffering for the gospel. [9]He is the one who saved us and called us with a holy calling, not based on our works but [*based*] on **his own purpose** and **grace**, granted to us in Christ Jesus before time began, [10]but now made visible through the appearing of our Savior Christ Jesus. He has broken the power of death and brought life and immortality to light through the gospel! (2 Tim. 1:8-10 NET)

In addition to all that has been said, Paul is using a perfect passive participle which, implies that Christ in us is continuing His work in us. Hallelujah! Christ is continuing the Shepherding over each of His redeemed. The meaning here is: that the saints expected to *stay alert* and *walk circumspectly* since our Lord watches over us *for good* and *for loving discipline*.

> [14]Therefore he says, "Awake, you who sleep, and arise from the dead, and Christ will shine on you." [15]Therefore watch carefully how you walk, not as unwise, but as wise, [16]redeeming the time, [e.g., *use* your time wisely] because the days are evil. [17]Therefore, don't be foolish, but understand what the will of the Lord is. [18]Don't be drunken with wine, in which

is dissipation [*reckless indiscretion*], but be filled with the Spirit, [19]speaking to one another in psalms, hymns, and spiritual songs; singing and making melody in your heart to the Lord; [20]giving thanks always concerning all things in the name of our Lord Jesus Christ to God, even the Father; [21]subjecting yourselves to one another in the fear of Christ.

(Eph. 5:14-21 WEB)

As Christians, we should not live any longer under the carnal and worldly mindset. Paul warns the childish and carnal church at Corinth, "Or are we trying to provoke the Lord to jealousy? Are we really stronger than he is?" [1 Cor. 10:22 NET.] We shall be corrected or disciplined by the Lord when we sin. Ah, but if we are without discipline, then we are unsaved and still lost in sin. The Scriptures do not warn us for nothing. Paul exhorts us to examine ourselves and be sure that we are in the faith and have trusted Christ.[2 Cor. 13:5]

Listen my friend, profession of faith does not guarantee that a person is in the faith. There is the necessity we must possess truly genuine commitment and trust in Christ.

Not *everyone* that saith unto me, Lord, Lord, shall enter into the kingdom of heaven; but he that *does* the will of my Father which is in heaven. [22]Many will say to me in that day, Lord, Lord, have we not prophesied in thy name? and in thy name have cast out devils?[lit. *demons*]? And in thy name done many wonderful works? [23]And then will I profess unto them, I **NEVER** KNEW YOU: depart from me, **ye that work iniquity**. (Matt. 7:21-23 KJV)

Paul says,

Nevertheless, God's solid foundation stands firm, sealed with this inscription: "**The Lord knows those who are his**," and, "[*Let*] **everyone who confesses the name of the Lord must turn away from wickedness**." (2 Tim. 2:19 NIV)

Check the genuineness of your faith in Christ to see if you are truly saved. If you are genuinely redeemed in Christ, "*Let us then be a vessel of honor and not vessel of dishonor*" for the glory and praise of Jesus Christ out Lord.

The wording is preferred in the KJV, but I would slightly modify the expression by saying instead of "preserved in Jesus Christ," I would stress Jude's intent is "**preserved BY Jesus Christ**."[Jude 1:1]

In closing this section, let me say once again,

Therefore, my beloved, just as you have always obeyed me, not only in my presence, but much more now in my absence, work out your own

25

salvation with fear and trembling; [13]for it is **God who is at work in you, enabling you both to will and to work for his good pleasure**.

(Phil. 2:12, 13 NRS)

Conclusion

Jude's and James' Epistles may have been written particularly to the Jewish Christian community. James leaves an impression that he is addressing Orthodox Jewish Christians believers in a synagogue setting. He even addresses the place of worship as a synagogue; James does not address the worship center a church..

> For if there come into your **synagogue** [GK, *sunagoge*] a man with a gold ring, in fine clothing, and there come in also a poor man in vile [*poor*] clothing; [3]and ye have regard to him that *wears* the fine clothing, and say, Sit thou here in a good place; and ye say to the poor man, Stand thou there, or sit under my footstool. [4]Do ye not make distinctions among yourselves, and become judges with evil thoughts? (James 2:2-4 ASV)

Like Jude's letter, James' letter also may be among the earliest epistles written. Jude, therefore, is writing particularly addressing Orthodox Jewish Christians in the infancy of church that were zealous for obedience under the Mosaic Law. Like James, Jude is addressing his audience probably in Jerusalem or Judea. The Christian Jews in Jerusalem were indeed "very zealous for the Mosaic Law, 'You see, brother, how many thousands there are among the Jews of those who have believed, and they are all zealous for the Law.' [Acts 21:20] Such observations suggest to me that the church was troubled early on in Jerusalem and Judah. Jude says,

> For **certain men have crept in unnoticed**, who long ago were marked out for this condemnation, ungodly men, who turn the grace of our God into lewdness [*license for evil* NET] and deny the only Lord God and our Lord Jesus Christ. (Jude 1:4 NKJ)

"Certain men have crept in unnoticed:" Jude may be referring to Jewish Christians. (Jude might also be referring to Jews that only had a profession of faith but **void** of having the possession of genuine faith in Christ.) There was no need for Gentiles "creeping in." Jude even traces the history as an Orthodox Jews as we shall observe throughout his epistle.

Jude addresses himself as "a slave Jesus Christ," and he identifies him as a true believer in Christ. He identifies himself as the brother of James. He does not address himself an apostle or even as an Elder. Jude identifies himself as

26

just simply "a slave of Jesus Christ." Some may have given him the title of "Elder" or even "Apostle," but there is no evidence in Scripture where Christ called Jude or James the brothers of Jesus as apostle. Jude and James refer to themselves as "slave of Jesus Christ." I wonder: "Friend, do you consider yourself '*a slave* of Jesus Christ?'"

Footnotes:

1. Judah (or Yehuda) *Gen.* 29:35:https://en.wikipedia.org/wiki/Judah (son of Jacob)

2. "*Sheepishly*:" but sheepish is an adjective (though I used as adverb *sheepishly*). Sheepish means feeling embarrassed or bashful, especially for having done something wrong or foolish. For example, you might say, "She gave me a sheepish smile and apologized.' Google

   Sheepish can also mean like a sheep, as in meekness or docility. For example, you might say, 'Mary gave her a sheepish grin.' Google

   The word "sheepish" comes from the words 'sheep.' It [*sheepish*] was originally used of describe qualities of good Christians, such as meek, modest, docile, and simple. Google

3. "*Persona*:" the aspect of someone's character that is presented to or perceived by others.

    'Her public persona has been sold to millions of women as the ideal.'

    A role or character adopted by an author, actor, etc. or in a game. Definition is from Oxford Languages

4. Calluses on James like that of a camel:

    Camel knees, EPISTLE OF JAMES, EUSEBIUS, INTERCESSORY PRAYER, James, James the just, PASTOR AT PRAYER, PRAYER, WORSHIP.

    https://mwerickson.com/2019/08/29/old-camel-knees-a-brief-reflection-on-the-remarkable-prayer-life-of-james-the just/

5. *No strings attached*, meaning it is free. "If there are no strings attached to an offer or arrangement, there is nothing that is unpleasant that you have to accept:"

    Cambridge Dictionary on-line. https://dictionary.cambridge.org/dictionary/learner-english/no-strings-attached

6. "TRE:" this is an acronym or abbreviation for Textus Receptus in modern ENG. It is a quote from Jude 1:1, http://textus-receptus.com/wiki/Jude_1:1

7. *tetepemenois*: Gingrich Lex 1. *keep **WATCH OVER, GUARD*** Mt 27:36, 54; 28:4; Ac 12:5; 24:23.—2. *keep, hold, reserve, **PRESERVE*** J 2:10; 17:11f, 15; Ac 25:21; 1 Cor 7:37; 1 Ti 6:14; 2 Ti 4:7; 1 Pt 1:4; Jd 1, 13; Rv 3:10; 16:15.—3. *keep, **OBSERVE**, pay attention to* Mt 23:3; 28:20; Mk 7:9 v. l.; J 9:16; 14:15, 21; 1 J 3:22, 24; Rv 3:8, 10; 12:17; 22:7. From Bible Works 10

tetepemenois: Friberg, *Analytical Greek Lexicon* concurs similarly. From Bible Works 10

CHAPTER 2

Blessed greetings by grace in Christ

Memory verse

But if it is by grace, it is no longer on the basis of works, otherwise grace is no longer grace. (Rom. 11:6)

Introduction

The faithful saints, and I do mean faithful saints in Christ, will be giving ten percent of his/her income to the Lord's ministry. If anyone giving ten percent, they are faithful and commendable by all means. However, I have a question, if I may be so bold to ask you: *"Is the ten percent before taxes? Is the ten percent after taxes?"* Ha, ha! What about the rest of things we have, "Our *home* that you sold, *car*, the return on your *investments*, or any other unexpected *income*, like income tax returns if you receive any return?"

The Bible says of Abraham, "And he [Abraham] gave him [Melchizedek] tithes of all." Another question. Did Abraham *give to Melchizedek only ten percent of the spoil* of the battle with the kings? Did Abraham *give the servant of God ten percent of all that he had*?

Many of us might only give a very quick glance at Jude's greeting but not much thought. What a pity. I suppose that some of us might give little thought to this small epistle and much less to his greeting! "What does Jude's Epistle contribute to me?" you might imagine to yourself. Nevertheless, what do you think? is Jude just giving a general greeting to his readers which was indeed a very common greeting during NT times? Jude says,

Jude, the servant [a slave] of Jesus Christ, and brother of James, to them
that are sanctified [or beloved] by God the Father, and preserved in [by] Jesus
Christ, *and* called: Mercy unto you, and peace, and love, be multiplied.

(Jude 1:1, 2 KJV)

Some scholars think, "Verse 2 is just a standard greeting during NT times."
Yes, Jude's greeting is no doubt a *common greeting* during the NT period. For
example,

"Grace to you and peace from God our Father and the Lord Jesus
Christ."   (Rom. 1:7)

Grace to you and peace from God our Father and the Lord Jesus Christ.

(Phil. 1:2)

Grace, mercy *and* peace from God the Father and Christ Jesus our Lord.

(1 Tim. 1:2)

Grace and peace be multiplied to you in the knowledge of God and of
Jesus our Lord   (2 Peter 1:2)

Yes, Jude's greeting is a standard or common greeting in NT in the Roman
world. Still, Jude's Epistle is given to us by the Spirit of the living God. Since
the letter is given to us by the Spirit of God, then the greeting of Jude is certainly a little bit more than a standard greeting. (Hopefully, this is the attitude
as one's begins reading the letter.) So then, if I may add, this is a personal
greeting but with it the Spirit of the living God breathing through the letter
with a definite message! Agreed? The fact that Jude has the breath of God
energizing through him, this ought to change everything.

There are three words used by Jude describing what ought to abound in the
lives of all the people of God. These three things are:

A. Continue abound all the more in *mercy*.

B. Continue abound all the more in *peace*.

C. Continue abound all the more in *love*.

These thoughts are qualities that ought to be vibrantly taking place in the
church. Jude says that the church was *abounding in grace, mercy, and love.*
Similarly, as Paul says to the Thessalonian church,

Now concerning brotherly love you have no need for anyone to write to
you, for you yourselves have been taught by God to love one another,

30

for that indeed is what you are doing to all the brothers throughout Macedonia. But we urge you, brothers, to do this more and more.

(1 Thess. 4:9, 10 ESV)

Jude is then exhorting his people *all the more* to **increase** in their *mercy, peace*, and *love* for one another. *Keep on, keep on* **increasing** in mercy, peace, and love towards one another all the more. In simply language, you cannot overdo it when continually increasing *in grace, mercy, and love*. My friend, do you think the church needs to increase all the more *in grace, mercy, and love?*

A. Continue to abound all the more in His mercy

When studying the Bible, we should not be using secular or general dictionary of the ENG or any other language except a Bible dictionary of the original language. This is because that may not be the precise meaning. When studying the Bible, a person ought to have a Bible dictionary if possible, or a person can access a Bible dictionary online over the internet. (However, be certain it is an **Evangelical** or **Fundamental** Bible dictionary.)

So, what is the biblical meaning of "*mercy*?" The GK word is *eleos*. Friberg's lexicon says, "(*Eleos*) mercy, compassion, used of attitudes of both God and man; (1) as an attitude and emotion roused by the affliction of another *pity, compassion, sympathy* (Luke 1.78); (2) especially of gracious action demonstrating God's compassion *mercy, lovingkindness, faithfulness* (Rom. 11.31)."[1]

Mercy is reaching out to others even if they are undeserving. (Reaching out to even the undeserving is the hallmark of mercy.) Biblical mercy also implies being compassionate to someone that cannot help themselves, or perhaps there is no one to help them. There is even implied being merciful to someone that may not merit help, such as the profane or wicked person. So, mercy reaches out even to the profane.

Jesus illustrates mercy as He listens to a father pleading for help for his demon possessed son. (Please read Mark 9:17-27.) The parallel text is in Matt. 17. Mark uses a different word rather than *mercy* [GK *splagchnizomai, pity, compassion, or sympathy*, Mark 9:22]. Still, the same thought in Matthew's Gospel is being applied in Mark's Gospel. In Matthew's Gospel (Matt. 17:14 some translation it is verse 15), it is fro the verb root word for *mercy*. Likely, the father felt totally helpless. Apparently, the disciplines seemingly unable to heal the young boy, even though our Lord had given them all authority to heal, Matt. 10:1ff. Had His apostles taken the authority to heal too much for granted? Did the apostles assume an innate authority that didn't belong to them? If the apostles took things for granted with Jesus, did the apostles bother to pray about the situation in healing the father's son?(See Mark 9:28, 29.)

Also troubling, how often do any of us bother to really pray? (Sadly, some only pray once but rarely pray more frequently for same issue). I wonder, "Do we taking Jesus for granted?" This is one serious weakness in the ministry. We can get too busy in doing the same thing over and over again that we fail to pray fervently and sufficiently pray. We just *assume* "the ministry, 'Oh, it is the same old thing.'" Wow! What contempt we sometimes do without giving any thought of the living God's presence. Oh yes, the Lord is indeed present with us.Heb. 13:5 How gross is that we simply take Jesus for granted? Listen friend, let us be very careful with our attitude that says, "Oh, I do not need any help in this situation; **I CAN HANDLE IT**; **I HAVE IT UNDER CONTROL**."

The father pleads to Jesus for *mercy* for his demon possessed son since he was at his wit's end. The Lord in His mercy healed the boy. Yet, the disciples are wondering, *"Hey, why couldn't we heal the boy?"*[Mark 9:28] The disciplines may have assumed they could do anything with all the power Jesus gave them: "We have the power". But like many of us today, let us carefully note that the apostles may have forgotten for a moment where their power actually resides.

The power did not reside within the apostles; oh, no! The authority and power continue to reside solely in Christ and Him alone. Like so many of us, the apostles may have *assumed* they had complete intrinsic power within themselves. No! The authority and power resides in Christ. (Some MSS include the words, "prayer and fasting."v 29) Like the apostles, maybe we today tend forget that our dependence resides solely on Christ and not our wit and authority.

The power resides with Christ the Lord. The authority resides with Him. We are in a supernatural battle. This is a war which we cannot even see. So, it is extremely important that we completely relying on Christ the Lord in our walk and service for Him. Are you taking Christ for granted too often in your life? Friend, our communion and prayer life is our only vital link in Him.

Jesus told the apostles, which equally applies to us in our perspective ministries,

> **"Abide in Me**, and I in you. As the branch cannot bear fruit of itself, unless it abides in the vine, neither can you, unless you **abide in Me**. I am the vine, you *are* the branches. **He who abides in Me**, and **I in him, bears much fruit; for without Me you can do nothing**."
>
> (John 15:4, 5 NKJ)

So, we are totally dependent on Him.[John 15:5] Unfortunately, we might pray when we may feel helpless or we are up against a wall. The Bible says, "Pray without ceasing."[1 Thess. 5:17 KJV] In simple language, stay tuned-in!

Mercy, an awesome word, but mercy is not always seemingly present among us as saints. (Mercy is rarer than you might think). The mercy that we generate ourselves is more *plastic* or *manufactured*. Mercy is comes through carnal mind. So, mercy is generated by natural man. If this is true of the Christian, how much more then that the mercy of the unregenerated derived its source from carnal world and its standard?

So, mercy is overshadowed through influence and standards of the world. This kind of mercy is synthetic (plastic) or of carnal origin, and such mercy soon runs out of gas. This is because mercy is generated by the natural man. This kind of mercy is not from the Spirit of God. Listen my friend, mercy must come from the Spirit of God if it is to be effective and lasting. As Paul said to the Galatians,

> If we live by the Spirit, let us also be guided by the Spirit. Let us not become conceited, competing against one another, envying one another.
>
> (Gal. 5:25, 26 NRS)

This is why fervent prayer is so vital in our lives. We as humans tend to be a *day late and a dollar short* when it comes to prayer. As Christians, we are too much like the world: *we tend to be more reactive rather than being proactive*. For example, just before getting married, we might pray if it is God's will, which is only reactive. However, if we are proactive, we would be praying that Lord find us the right husband or wife long before we start dating someone. Also, pray for the right college and/or career while in elementary school. Again, pray for children long before expecting a child and continue praying after the child is born.

Well, it is for certain prayer is often nothing more than *form but with little substance*. Unfortunately, prayer is only an *appendage* or "a tack-on." Prayer must be an urgent need and a deliberate and conscious effort in seeking God's will. Yet, we know that prayer is exceedingly important and powerful when praying in accordance to the Spirit of God.[Rom. 8:26-29; 1 John 5:14] Prayer is too often a last-minute action with little forethought. Listen, prayer is a live communication with Eternal God who hears our every word, whether the prayer is audible or from the heart or mind. Scripture exhorts us to:

> Let your hope make you glad. Be patient in time of trouble and never stop praying. (Rom. 12:12 CEV)

33

(Check these verses as an example: Luke 21:36; Eph. 6:18; Phi. 4:4-6; Col. 4:2; 1thess. 5:17; 1 Tim. 2:8). Stay **tuned-in**!

Ah, but Jude's audience was already exercising mercy or so it seems to me. Jude is encouraging his hearers as to imply, *Come on, put more effort into in your mercy towards one another*. Jude might have said it this way: *continue to overflow in the abundance of mercy towards others*. Life can be at times stressful. So, let us then be tuned-in to the Lord, and let us be prayed up! For the Lord is always tuned-in to the saints who see to do His will.

Jude's brother James says, "Is anyone among you suffering? Let him pray."James 5:13a James reveals that are prayers sometimes may be wrongly directed. Take James' words as one thought at a time.

> Ye lust, and have not: ye kill,ª
>
> and desire to have, and [*but*] cannot obtain:
>
> ye fight and war [*among one* another],
>
> yet ye have not, because ye ask not [*we didn't bother to pray*].
>
> [*Then*] Ye ask [*prayed*],
>
> and receive not, because ye ask amiss [*prayed for wrong reason*],
>
> that ye may consume *it* upon your lusts.
>
> (James 4:2, 3 KJV)
>
> ªNote: obviously James is saying we "kill *spiritually with anger at* a person in our hearts, but we fail to realize it."

Mercy is short-lived in many us because mercy is being generated by the natural man. We come up short. Mercy is in short supply in the church today because we are not longsuffering or patient with the Spirit of God. We are not walking in the Spirit of God. The Bible says,

> For you, brethren, have been called to liberty; only do not *use* liberty as an opportunity for the flesh, but through love serve one another. [14]For all the law is fulfilled in one word, *even* in this: "You shall love your neighbor as yourself." [15]But if you bite and devour one another, beware [*careful now*] lest you be consumed by one another! [16]I say then: **WALK IN THE SPIRIT**, and you shall not fulfill the lust of the flesh. [17]For the flesh lusts against the Spirit, and the Spirit against the flesh; and these are contrary to one another, so that you do not do the things that you wish. [18]But if you are led by the Spirit, you are not under the law.
>
> (Gal. 5:13-18 NKJ)

As we noted above, the apostle challenges the Galatians by exhorting them to:

> If we live in the Spirit, **LET US ALSO WALK IN THE SPIRIT**. Let us not become conceited, provoking one another, envying one another.
>
> (Gal. 5:25, 26 NKJ)

Mercy is needed more than ever in the churches today, but if we continue walk or live in carnal ways of the world, we had better be careful least as the apostle says, "- watch out that you are not consumed by one another."[Gal. 5:15 ESV]

B. Continue to abound all the more in His peace

Shalom, a common word in HEB, which means *peace*. The inference however when given with the phrase, "shalom aleichem," implies *"Peace be upon you."* In return, the other who is aware of the meaning will reply, "shalom aleichem," which again is implied, "Peace be upon you."

There are few people pondering or thinking about peace in *hustle and bustle* of life for those reaching out for the gold or just striving to make it in this life. Still, peace is something even the most powerful men and richest person cannot possess by his own might even with the endless things at his fingertips. Even the most astute and brilliant minds are unable achieve the ultimate peace within. Even those who practice Eastern Meditation cannot achieve peace; they can only achieve a cheap brief moment of cosmic-fantasy of peace.

Truly peace is available now and continuing throughout eternity. Even the most wealthy and strongest nations cannot establish peace in the world or even on its own turf. The world is like a very dangerous powder-keg ready to *blow everything to smithereens*[2] *at any moment.*

Unless you have just crawled from underneath a rock or just awakened from sleep like Rip Van Winkle, peace is something no mortal possesses in their own will and strength. This is even more so today. The fool is senseless, and he/she cares less about himself, others, or anything else in life. The fool lives only for today; tomorrow he is sadly gone. So, peace is meaningless to a fool. "The fool has said in his heart, "There is no God.""[Psa. 53:1]

Peace is not reachable or attainable by *one pulling themselves up by their own bootstraps.* The peace I am talking about is not *plastic* or peace through some pill. Neither is peace achieved through an altered state of self-induced mind. This is real, genuine, and lasting peace from the Lord our God. This is a peace that can only come from the Eternal and Everlasting God, the Lord Almighty and only Supreme Sovereign. Isaiah the prophet said,

35

> Thou wilt keep *him* in perfect peace, *whose* mind *is* stayed *on thee*: because he *trusts* in thee. (Isa. 26:3 KJV)

Mock what I am saying about peace if you want, but this is a peace that only comes from the Prince of Peace, Yehoshua (Jesus), our blessed Lord and Savior.

> For unto us a Child is born, Unto us a Son is given; And the government will be upon His shoulders. And His name will be called Wonderful,[3] Counselor, Mighty God, Everlasting Father, **Prince of Peace**. Of the increase of *His* government and peace *There will be* no end, Upon the throne of David and over His kingdom, To order it and establish it with judgment and justice From that time forward, even forever. The zeal of the LORD of hosts will perform this. (Isa. 9:6, 7 NKJ)

Jesus gave us this assurance of a lasting and forever peace. This is a peace that comes from the Prince of Peace which only He is able to give. This is a peace from Jesus for all those that genuinely love Him and walk in His will. This is a peace that Jesus promises, and He gives and keeps. There is peace for all that genuinely trusted and have received Him and seek to walk in His will. This is a peace to those genuinely and totally committed to Him as we seek to be obedient to His Word.

> "Peace I leave with you, My peace I give to you; not as the world gives do I give to you. Let not your heart be troubled, neither let it be afraid." (John 14:27 NKJ)

Conversely, the Bible declares,

> "*There is* no peace," says the LORD, "for the wicked."(Isa. 48:22 KJV)

There is little peace for the wicked outside the redemption of Christ Jesus the Lord. Neither is there any peace for the Christian living in sin. Hello! There is no peace for those that follow the world. Neither is there peace for Christians remaining infantile in the faith. Most of all, there is no peace for any Christian that continues to be stagnant in their worship and service for Christ. I do not mean to just be a worshiper and be available to serve. I mean a person aggressively and passionately active worshipping and serving Christ the Lord. The Bible says,

> And whatsoever ye do, do *it* **HEARTILY** [e.g., *do it enthusiastically with your heart and soul in it*], as to the Lord, and not unto men. (Col. 3:23 KJV)

> Do not love the world or the things in the world. If anyone loves the world, the love of the Father is not in him. For all that is in the world—the desires of the flesh and the desires of the eyes and pride of life— is not from the Father but is from the world. And the world is passing away along with its desires, but whoever does the will of God abides forever. (1 John 2:15-17 ESV)

There is no genuine peace without the Lord and that our all is on the alter for His glory as one hymn writer asked. Let us note the second and third stanzas with the chorus:

Is Your All on the Altar[4]

2. Would you walk with the Lord,
In the light of His Word,
And have peace and contentment always?
You must do His sweet will
To be free from all ill-
On the altar your all you must lay.

Chorus

Is your all on the altar of sacrifice laid?
Your heart does the Spirit control?
You can only be blest,
And have peace and sweet rest,
As you yield Him your body and soul.

3. Oh, we never can know
What the Lord will bestow
Of the blessings for which we have prayed,
Till our body and soul
He doth fully control,
And our all on the altar is laid.

Some are too much in love with the world. So, why would any such person that is walking with the world even begin to think about peace? Those walking with the world have no concern for peace. They are too wrapped up in their own little world to even care. There is indeed a genuine and real lasting peace offered through the Prince of Peace, our blessed Lord and Savior Jesus Christ. If you will seek Jesus with all your heart and mind, He will come to you and be your greatest Friend now and forever. Those following the world, they may mock such words "peace of mind" or "peace of heart." Know this for certain that the Day of Reckoning is coming.

What I say here some people will think the idea of such peace is a little *hokie.*[or *hoky*] (By hokie, it is meant: *something silly, sentimental, fake, or artificial.*) There is nothing silly or fake in God's Word. So, pay attention!

Jesus said the night before going to Calvary,

> "These things I have spoken to you, that **in Me you may have peace**. In the world you will have tribulation; but **be of good cheer, I have overcome the world**." (John 16:33 NKJ)

Jesus and His Word must rule in our hearts if we want peace that can only come from the Lord our God.

> And **let the peace of Christ <u>rule</u> <u>in</u> <u>your</u> hearts**, to which indeed you were called in one body. And be thankful. **Let the word of Christ dwell in you richly**, teaching and admonishing one another in all wisdom, singing psalms and hymns and spiritual songs, with <u>**thankfulness in your hearts**</u> to God. And whatever you do, in word or deed, **do everything in the name of the Lord Jesus, giving thanks to God the Father through him**. (Col. 3:15-17 ESV)

Again, the Word of God instructs us with this promise,

> Rejoice in the Lord always. Again I say, rejoice! Let everyone see your gentleness. The Lord is near! Do not be anxious about anything. Instead, in every situation, through prayer and petition with thanksgiving, tell your requests to God. And the peace of God that surpasses all understanding will guard your hearts and minds in Christ Jesus.
>
> (Phil. 4:4-7 NET)

C. Continue to abound all the more in His love

Anger, bitterness, and internal conflicts seem to rage everywhere. The only love the world can generate is eros, which is nothing more than *erotic* or *sensual* driven from an *animalistic* and *unregenerate nature and carnal impulse.* Did you know that the Bible never uses the GK word eros?

After Jesus' resurrection, Peter persuaded six apostles to left Jerusalem and go fishing with him. (Only four apostles remain in Jerusalem.) Yet, Jesus had sternly instructed all the apostles to remain in Jerusalem until they receive power from on High. Shortly after our Lord was risen, He appears to the apostles. In one incident after resurrection, He ask Peter pricking question,

> "Simon, *son* of John, do you love [GK *agapao*] Me more than **these**[b]?"
>
> (John 21:15)

38

[*Peter said,*] "Yes, Lord; You know that I love [GK *phileo*] You."

(John 21:15)

[b]Note: "**these**" is in reference to going fishing. The meaning implied is 'Do you Peter love me *more than these things*?' That is, '*Peter do you love fishing more than Me?*' Jesus is not comparing the apostles' love against one another. Jesus is asking which is more important: Me or the fishing? Keep in mind, our risen Lord had given the apostles definite orders, "He commanded them not to depart from Jerusalem, but to wait for the Promise of the Father -."[Acts 1:4 NKJ] Peter disobeyed a command and influenced six other apostles to go fishing 80 miles away. Wow!

I wonder, if the Lord was to ask you or me if we loved Him, "(concerning our private or most intimate things we do), how would we respond?" Let us not forget that the Lord is able to read our hearts or minds today, 'I am he who searches hearts and minds, and I will repay each of you according to your deeds.'[Rev. 2:23 NIV]

Wasn't there fishing around Jerusalem? Besides, Jesus gave explicit instructions to the apostles that they were to remain in Jerusalem *until they were empowered from on high*! Hello! Do you see Peter's influence? Peter persuaded six other apostles to leave Jerusalem and go fishing with him deliberately disobeying the direct command from the risen Lord Jesus. This left only four apostles that remained obedient to Jesus' command. (Do you see now?) This is a direct disobedience to Jesus' command! Do you realize this was a deliberate and direct act of disobedience to Jesus' charge: '- tarry in the city of Jerusalem until you are endued with power from on high.'[Luke 24:49 NKJ] In addition, Peter persuaded six other apostles to go fishing and disobey Christ instruction.

What about our Lord's command to us today? What commands are you disobeying? The churches are failing to knock on doors; just a few hours a week is at best only a dribble. Most churches are **not** knocking on any doors. Who are you influencing to disobey Jesus' command? However, I must say that many Pastors and church leaders **do** **not** even know what are the commands are? Even if they happen know the commands of the risen Lord, they are likely disobeying His commands. How sad is that?

I wonder, do you just have an *affectionate/friendship love* as an *acquaintance of Jesus*, or is your love for Jesus really deep and abiding love and sold out completely for His Lordship? Peter and the other apostles were strictly told,

39

Listen carefully: I am sending the Promise of My Father [the Holy Spirit] upon you; but you are to remain in the city [of Jerusalem] until you are clothed (fully equipped) with power from on high."

(Luke 24:49 AMP)

Was Peter *bored at the monotony* of sitting around in Jerusalem? But friend, there was plenty of work to be done even in Jerusalem in sharing the Gospel without just sitting around and doing little or nothing and getting bored. Is Jesus: *"Out of sight, out of mind* like a child, to you?" Our Lord didn't mean *to twiddle our thumbs* in Jerusalem and do nothing. At any rate, Peter **did not** stay in Jerusalem. Peter went fishing and convinced six others apostles to travel 80 miles to Galilee to go fishing.[John 21:2] (Traveling 80 miles was no easy task in that day.) Wow!

Jesus gave a command to the disciples, and He gives a similar commands to us today:

GO therefore and **MAKE DISCIPLES** of all the nations, **BAPTIZING THEM** in the name of the Father and the Son and the Holy Spirit, **TEACHING THEM** to observe all that I commanded you; and lo, **I AM WITH YOU ALWAYS**, even to the end of the age."

(Matt. 28:19, 20)

And He opened their [*minds in*] understanding, that they might comprehend the Scriptures. Then He said to them, "Thus it is written, and thus it was necessary for the Christ to suffer and to rise from the dead the third day, "and that **REPENTANCE AND REMISSION OF SINS should be PREACHED in HIS NAME to ALL NATIONS**, beginning at Jerusalem. [48]"And you are witnesses of these things.

(Luke 24:45-48 NKJ)

Jesus gave the command, where is our commitment today? Listen, there is no commitment unless we are actively doing His commands. Perhaps like Peter, we only have an affectionate friendship-love for Jesus. (Maybe our love for the world is a little stronger.) Perhaps our love for the Lord Jesus is not one of an abiding and lasting love like an *agape* love? Maybe we need to remind ourselves once again?

He said to them, "Thus it is written, that the Christ would suffer and rise again from the dead the third day, and that **repentance** for **forgiveness** of sins would **be proclaimed in His name** to all the nations, beginning from Jerusalem. (Luke 24:46, 47)

40

Friend, I am not beating up on Peter or making him the scapegoat or the fall guy. As Christians, we are doing little to be going out reaching the lost enthusiastically and zealously for the lost.

So, when we look at Jude's salutation, maybe he is implying more than just brotherly affection for one another. Perhaps Jude is expressing a lasting love that only the Holy Spirit is able to instill and perpetuate in and through us if we have surrendered to the Lordship of Christ over our lives. This is why we need to strive as the apostle Paul says to the Galatians by the NRS,

> **If we live by the Spirit, let us also be guided by the Spirit.** Let us not become conceited, competing against one another, envying one another.
>
> (Gal. 5:25, 26 NRS)

Even our priority of love for one another is a command. He said,

> A new commandment I give unto you, That ye **love one another; as I have loved you,** that ye also love one another. **By this shall all *men* know that ye are my disciples, if ye have love one to another.**
>
> (John 13:34, 35 KJV)

When we truly love one another, the Bible declares as given by the New Living Translation,

> Most important of all, continue to show deep love for each other, for love covers a multitude of sins. (1 Peter 4:8 NLT)

When we genuinely love one another with an *agapao* love generate by the Holy Spirit, there will be forgiveness, restoration, sweet-communion and fellowship will occur. The sinner will see what you have and he will want to have such love as well.

The Bible continually exhorts believers to love one another. However, when we walk in the carnal ways the world, God gives us this warning,

> For all the *Law* is fulfilled in one *word*, which is this, Thou shalt *love* thy *neighbor* as thy *self.* If ye bite and *devour* one another, take *heed* least ye be consumed one of another. (Gal. 5:14, 15 GNV)

> Note: there are no changes in wording, only the spelling is corrected in the GNV.

When the flesh reigns, there is *division, discord, rifts, fractions, separation, ego-centralism,* and *alienation.* There are fellowship or cluster churches and individual churches that seem to separate over nearly anything. The Lord is not pleased with such wickedness. Yes, I said "wickedness." We may pacify

41

our conscious and attempt to justify our actions, but we will not be pleasing to God who knows our hearts. We are to love our brother. Division implies discord and disunity. Such actions do not come from the Spirit of God. The Gospel is to bring peace and reconciliation.

The flesh can never be at peace. There is only internal conflict, upheaval, and destruction. The Holy Spirit alone is able bring healing, provide forgiveness, restoration, peace and harmony. It is only as the churches starts living and walking in the Holy Spirit that there will be mighty victory and sinners will come to the Lord. Carefully read Psalm 51, and hopefully, you will see what I mean.

The repentance of King David is illustration to what God will do when we genuinely confess out sin and seek to walk in His will and way by the Holy Spirit,

> Grant me the ultimate joy of being forgiven! May the bones you crushed rejoice! [9] Hide your face from my sins! Wipe away all my guilt! [10] Create for me a pure heart, O God! Renew a resolute spirit within me! [11] Do not reject me! Do not take your Holy Spirit away from me!
>
> (Psa. 51:8-11 NET)

Conclusion

The next time you read a Scripture of a salutation (a greeting), take a few moments to ponder over the words. *Mercy, peace,* and *love* is greatly needed in and through the churches today, but this must be the love from God living and radiating in and through by the Holy Spirit. There is a serious need for a genuine revival by the Holy Spirit. However, the revival must begin with you and me.

God's Word gives us this wonderful promise, and this promise is just a call away. This is a horizonal or universal promise that runs throughout the Scripture for all the people of God and not just a promise limited to Israel.

> If my people, which are called by my name, shall humble themselves, and pray, and seek my face, and turn from their wicked ways; then will I hear from heaven, and will forgive their sin, and will heal their land.
>
> (2 Chro. 7:14 KJV)

Footnotes:

1. "Mercy (*Eleos*)," Jude 1:2: Friberg's Analytical Lexicon, from Bible Works 10.

2. *Blow everything to smithereens*: "If something is blown or smashed to smithereens, it breaks into very small pieces. She dropped the vase and smashed it to smithereens." https://www.collinsdictionary.com/us/dictionary/english/smithereens

3. Isa. 9:6, 7: Some scholars think the word "Wonderful" is modifying Counselor; hence, implying "Wonderful Counselor." Whether Judges 13:17, 18 establishes as separate and distinct word, I shall leave to the HEB scholars to discuss.

    Christ the Lord is addressed as "Everlasting Father." The meaning is the Messiah is the Creator and Sustainer of all life. Christ (the Messiah or the Anointed One) is **not** God the Father. Jesus said (as literally given in the GK), 'I and the Father **We are** one. John 10:30. There is but one God but He is three persons: The Father, the Son, and Holy Spirit.

4. "Is Your all on the altar?"
    https://hymnary.org/text/you_have_longed_for_sweet_peace
    (From Google search)

CHAPTER 3

Purpose and reason of writing

Memory verse

I charge *you* therefore before God and the Lord Jesus Christ, who will judge the living and the dead at His appearing and His kingdom: Preach the word! Be ready in season *and* out of season. Convince ^[convict, reprove, expose], rebuke, exhort, with all longsuffering and teaching.

(2 Tim. 4:1, 2 NKJ)

Introduction

Jude says to his audience as given by NET,

Dear friends, although I have been eager to write to you about our common salvation, I now feel compelled instead to write to encourage you to contend earnestly for the faith that was once for all entrusted to the saints. (Jude 1:3 NET)

I suppose many of us prefer the word "beloved" rather than "Dear friends." Well, yes, I like the word "beloved," but nevertheless, the translation by the NET is closer to Jude's intention than some other translations. This is because the NET captures Jude's immediate shift in his present thought to his readers.

Jude says, "although I have been eager to write to you about our common salvation." That is, Jude wanted to write to the people of God concerning their *shared* or *common faith* in the risen Lord and Savior Yehoshua the Messiah.

There are not many ways to Heaven as the natural man thinks. Yes, even the ill-informed Christians are deficient in the Bible's teachings concerning going to Heaven. There is only one way into Heaven. As Paul says in his *seven-fold unity* of the Gospel:

There is **one body** and **one Spirit**, just as also you were called in **one hope** of your calling; **one Lord, one faith, one baptism, one God** and Father of all who is over all and through all and in all. (Eph. 4:4, 5)

Seven-fold unity of Gospel

One body— this is **not** the local church (though the text applies to the local church); this is body of Christ, all the redeemed in the church.

One Spirit— there is but one blessed Holy Spirit that unifies everyone in Christ.

One hope— this is the blessed hope, the resurrection and glorification of the body, Acts 26:6-8; Phi. 3:20, 21

One Lord— "the appearing of the glory of our great God and Savior Jesus Christ" Titus 2:13 ESV

One faith— this refers to one body of doctrine (OT and NT), the doctrine has been deposited with us, complete and lacking nothing.

One baptism— water baptism does not unify us; this is the one Spirit, in which we are all baptized into Christ, 1 Cor. 12:13.

One God— Triune God, the Father, the Son, and the Holy Spirit.

Then, Jude shifts quickly into his main thoughts, which the NET captures,

"I now feel COMPELLED INSTEAD to write to encourage you to contend earnestly for the faith that was once for all entrusted to the saints."   (Jude 1:3b NET)

"It was needful," v 3 KJV, which is a good translation, but the meaning is a little stronger. Jude *felt compelled*! "Needful," the GK word is *anagke*. Friberg Analytical Lexicon says, of the word *anagke*: "*necessity, compulsion, force*; (a) from a feeling of inward necessity *constraint, compelling obligation*."

Danker's lexicon says, "- the primary idea in Hellenic thought: inevitability as an inherent component of human experience and indicating that over which one has no control. – 1. 'constraining/compelling force', **necessity, constraint**: w. — *under pressure*."[1]

My friend, are you *compelled* to preach the Gospel everywhere you go? I am sorry to say, but many behind the *pulpit* **do not exhibit the urgency to share the Gospel**. The urgency and passion to share the Gospel has been abandoned!

45

We need to have the sense of **urgency** to get the Gospel out. We need to feel **compelled** to preach the Word! Preaching God's Word is more than being sincere in declaring the truth of God's Word. Preaching God's Word ought to be *__compelling__* and with a sense of *__urgency__* because people need to be given the Gospel lest they perish in Hell.

As Christians, we shall give a full account of our words and actions.[Mat. 12:36f, 2 Cor. 5:10] The unregenerate stand condemned already in sin whether they hear the Gospel or not.[John 3:18, 36] I say again, *the unsaved stand condemned whether hear the Gospel* or not.[John 3:18] All of humanity is lost because of their sin.[Rom. 3:23] Those who reject the Gospel even stand in greater condemnation. Our Lord gave us this parable in the urgency for saints to get the Gospel out to the lost,

> "'Go out at once into the streets and lanes of the city and bring in here the poor and crippled and blind and lame.' And the slave said, 'Master, what you commanded has been done, and still there is room.' And the master said to the slave, 'Go out into the highways and along the hedges, and __compel__ [GK *anagkazo*] *them* to come in, so that my house may be filled.'" (Luke 14:21-23)

Paul did not tell young Timothy to teach or lecture the Word of God. Paul said as given by LSB,

> I solemnly **charge**[a] *you* in the **presence of God** and of Christ Jesus, who is to judge the living and the dead, and by His appearing and His kingdom: **PREACH THE WORD**; be ready **IN SEASON** *and* **OUT OF SEASON**; **REPROVE, REBUKE, EXHORT**, with great patience and teaching. (2 Tim. 4:1, 2 LSB)

> [a]Note: the word *charge* is GK *diamarturomai* very strong. The root word is *witness* or to *testify*: *marturreo* with the prefix, *dia*; as Danker's lexicon says, 'solemnly invite attestation' esp. through indication of witness by higher powers; an emphatic aspect is dominant in the use of this term] 'solemnly affirm.'[2]

If anyone cares to know, the word "**compel**" in Jude 1:3 comes from the same root word in Luke 14:23. Friend, do you see it? We ought to sense a compelling urgency in warning people to come into the Kingdom of God. Maybe you are more a middle-of-roader, "Come if you want"?

Many people do not want to respond to Jesus' call, to the water of life and live, but once they enter the Kingdom of God, they are very glad they did. Let us then **compel** them with **urgency** to come, the King wants His banquet hall filled.

A. Intention to write concerning our common salvation

The Gospel of salvation is for everyone. The Gospel needs to be shared *one on one* to be more effective. The Gospel needs to be given with a sense of urgency and passionately. This is the saving mercy, peace, and loving of the Savior, Christ the Lord. Here is the simple Gospel message (nothing more and nothing less) we are commanded to bring to the world:

> For I delivered to you as of first importance what I also received, that **Christ died for**[b] **our sins** according to the Scriptures, and that **He was buried**, and that **He was raised on the third day** according to the Scriptures. (1 Cor. 15:3, 4)

> [b]Note: GK is *huper* "*for*-" Again, the meaning is very strong, meaning Christ died as a **vicarious substitute**: He took the place of every believer, and He took the wrath of God "for" the believer. There is no idea "blank check" sacrifice. Christ died in particular for every believer.

Peter says,

> **He himself BORE OUR SINS** in his body on the tree [the cross], that we may cease from sinning and **live for righteousness**. By his wounds you were healed[c].[e.g. healed of all sins] (1 Peter 2:24 NET)

> [c]Note: Peter is referring to healing of our sin debt which separated us from God. This healing is eternal or everlasting and forever. When God does heal someone of their illness, it is temporal healing since the death rate is the same for all.

The Lord is indeed the Healer of all infirmities and sickness. There is no one else able to genuinely heal like the Lord from all sickness. However, this is **not** the point being driven by the apostle Peter. Some of our Pentecostal and Charismatic friends give great emphasis on Peter's words here for temporal healing illnesses. Listen, all healing of sicknesses are temporary or short-term: healings of sickness or disease. The apostle Peter's emphasis is upon the eternal and lasting healing. This is healing from sin which will separate us from the love, mercy, and grace of God. The Lord will forgives you of all your sin but only in Christ. God in Christ will make you completely holy and righteous, fit for Heaven forever and ever.

People shall continue to chase and run after *fake healers* who claim healing through them. (Claiming to heal you if <u>have</u> <u>enough</u> <u>faith</u> or <u>sufficient</u> <u>faith,</u> but friend this is a "*cop out and lie.*" Jesus said that doing the will of the King is more important than having our faith increased.

⁵And the apostles said to the Lord, "Increase our faith!" ⁶And the Lord said, "If you have faith like a mustard seed, you would say to this mulberry tree, 'Be uprooted and be planted in the sea'; and it would obey you. ⁷But which of you, having a slave plowing or tending sheep, will say to him when he has come in from the field, 'Come immediately and sit down to eat'? ⁸But will he not say to him, 'Prepare something for me to eat, and, clothe yourself *properly*, serve me while I eat and drink; and afterward you may eat and drink'? ⁹Is he grateful to the slave because he did the things which were commanded? ¹⁰In this way, you also, when you do all the things which are commanded of you, say, '**We are unworthy**ᵈ **slaves; we have done *only* that which we ought to have done.**'"

(Luke 17:5-10 LSB)

ᵈ"Unworthy, or unprofitable" KJV is preferred. The meaning **is not** *worthless* or *without any value*. Christ did not die for worthless people.

Now, as to faith, faith is the key to pleasing God.^Heb.11:6 Yet, faith without action is dead faith. The NIV is on target that says, "In the same way, faith by itself, if it is not accompanied by action, is dead." ^James 2:17 NIV James sums up his point this way about faith,

For as the body without the spirit is dead, so faith without works [action] is dead also. (James 2:26 KJV)

Do you really desire to please God? Then, study to know God's will through all of God's Word, OT and NT.^2 Tim. 2:15 Then, friend get busy doing His will with all your strength. However, our worship must come first.^Deut. 6:4, 5 Let us be **compelling** and **urging** people to come to the Savior while there is still time.

The common salvation is for everyone that will come to the Savior, and the Lord's salvation is forever for the ones that will come, even the very worse of sinner. Friend, there is room at the cross for you. Yes, there's still room at the cross for you. As one hymn write wrote, Ira F. Stanphill:

There is room at the cross³

2. Tho' millions have found Him a friend
And have turned from the sins they have sinned
The Savior still waits to open the gates
And welcome a sinner before it's too late

Chorus
There's room at the cross for you
There's room at the cross for you
Tho' millions have come
There's still room for one

As I have often said, Paul is indeed a great example of saving sinners. He said himself,

> This *is* a faithful saying and worthy of all acceptance, that Christ Jesus came into the world to save sinners, of whom I am chief. However, for this reason I obtained mercy, that in me first Jesus Christ might show all longsuffering, as a pattern to those who are going to believe on Him for everlasting life. Now to the King eternal, immortal, invisible, to God who alone is wise, *be* honor and glory forever and ever. Amen.
>
> (1 Tim. 1:15-17 NKJ)

B. Yet, there's necessity to contend for the faith

Now, Jude does an uncommonly thing. He immediately sifts into very urgent announcement:

> Dear friends, although I have been eager to write to you about our common salvation, I **now feel compelled** instead to write to encourage you to contend earnestly for the faith that was once for all entrusted to the saints. (Jude 1:3 NET)

If Jude indeed makes a sudden change in his purpose for writing, why did he do it so quickly? His sudden change may seems odd. Right in his very beginning of his letter, he changes from encouragement to an urgent plea *"to earnestly contend for the faith."* Did some person come into Jude's home while he was preparing to write and deliver the urgent plea? I doubt this was some technique or a writer's ploy that Jude uses to draw his reader into his letter. He says that *"to earnestly contend for the faith."* As I have already said that the churches have *indeed lost the urgency* in preaching the Word of God today. Yes, I think the urgency is definitely obvious in preaching, but the churches and saints have dropped the urgency of sharing the Gospel. What is this urgency no longer presence with the saints or in churches? Today, preaching is a lecture or *simple talk*. Shame, shame!

Jerusalem, where Jude writes, was a place where the unexpected can flair up and out of control at any moment. (Even more so today.) The Romans

49

learned that the Jews could be a *hotbed* of people that could explode at any moment for seemingly the least little thing. Whereas, in other places in the world, "People would not even give a yawn for such issue." So, the inference or thought by Jude is that something came to his mind that sparked the shift and urgency.

Well, the immediate shift and seemingly change in the topic by Jude indicates a serious or grave concern while writing. Then, it seems he abruptly changes the topic. (Jude may have been at his residence or friend's home in or near Jerusalem.) Jude seems to sense a <u>divine</u> <u>urgency</u> that he was *under compulsion* and *felt compelled* to start writing his small but fully packed letter. This urgency was going to affect the saints not only in and around Jerusalem and Judah to Galilee, but this was an urgency threatening the Gospel message everywhere in the world. Do you sense the significance or urgency today? Many do not sense such urgency, and friend, this how sick the church is.

Today, we pick up the little Epistle of Jude, but without saying anything, we are not prone to feel such urgency. "What's the big deal? What is so urgent?" we might think to ourselves. Listen, the enemies are attacking the churches world-wide from all sides and even internally and externally. Well, in your little assembly, maybe you are asleep. Yet, Satan's bombs exploding everywhere. The world around us is raging against the saints. The carnal flesh seeks to short-circuit the ministry. There is war right at our doorstep. Still, "We see nothing," and "we hear nothing." Shocking! Is that being *callused* and *insensitive* or what? We are *so out of tune* to the beckoning and wooing of the blessed Holy Spirit and the marching orders of our Lord and His mandates that it is beyond unbelief.

As saints, we urgently need a **spiritual renewal**; we need **to be revived**. We urgently need to be recharged. We need to renew our commitment to Christ. We ought to cry unto the Lord, "**I surrender all Lord**." Instead, Christian are "ducking their heads" or "hiding" to avoid being called. Others callously say to themselves, "*Hey, I don't feel called.*" Sadly, some do not even know what the word "*commitment*" means in the walk of faith in Christ. What, Jesus doesn't thrill our soul anymore? Friend, the Christian walk is not a walk among the tulips or a walk in the park. **This is <u>WAR</u>**! Every genuine saint (every true Christian) has been drafted! Look, the enemies are real. Listen, we are acting like little children, "Let's play church!" "Oh, I don't want to go to church; it's too boring."

We don't even hear ourselves when we are thinking that way. Church is a little bit of Heaven. Only an unregenerate would dare say or think the church is boring. Heaven is being with Jesus. If you even have a brief moment of nonsense thinking like "the church is boring," you had better do as the apostle say, "Reexamine the genuineness of your saving faith in Christ."[2 Cor. 13:5] Friend, I am not joking! If you have no change within; then you have never met the risen Christ.

Be honest with yourself. Do you feel there is a deep and very urgent need **to share the Gospel** and not just to believe it or just to defend it? "Well, do you?" Jude felt *compelled*. You read me right: not just defend the Gospel. Is there a burning desire inside you to get out and faithfully and fully passionately preach the Gospel around you? I dare say that the pulpit is void of any urgency, especially an urgency upon high. I mean urgency to see people come into the Kingdom of God. The churches are not only void of any urgency, but there is also **no urgency to go door to door to share the Gospel**. Triple shame! Even worse, there is no urgency from the pulpit urging people to come to know Jesus as Lord and Savior, now, today even in church services. There is not even an invitation given in the worship service in church to come and receive Jesus as Savior before it is too late.

No battles are won holding the ground. We must press forward to **compel** the sin to come right now. In addition, there is the *urgency to equip* the saints for work of the ministry.[Eph. 4:12] Listen, contending for the faith does not just mean to "*hang on and be faithful.*" Yes, we do need to stand fast in the faith.[1 Cor. 15:57, 58] But, we even more so need to push the enemies back. There is a need to urgently push the darkness back and let the Light shine in. We need to seize new ground. We must win the lost for Christ. *The world is going to Hell in a handbasket.* Do you have any urgency to win the lost for Christ, or do you just image the "the elect" will come whether you get out and preach the Gospel or not?

Jude is urging his reader to get out and give the Gospel so that more people will be saved. Reach the lost for whom Christ did. **<u>Compel</u> them to come** into Kingdom now before they are swallowed up by the world, the flesh, and the devil. Or do you even believe the unsaved without Christ are on the collision course for Hell? If they do not come to Jesus, they shall indeed be swallowed by the world, the flesh, and the devil. They shall surely perish in their sins.[John 8:24] The sad truth is that Christians families have no urgency to compel their love to come to Christ. It is rather: "Well, you've heard the Gospel; it's your choice?" The urgency and the necessity of the Gospel has been forsaken by many churches today.

As Peter says, we need to watch out,

51

> Be sober, be vigilant; because your adversary the devil walks about like
> a roaring lion, seeking whom he may devour.   (1 Peter 5:8 NKJ)

Yes, we must be aggressively sharing the Gospel and continually reaching out to the lost. Let us bring them into the Kingdom. One of the biggest areas overlooked in reaching the lost is **night time and the places of businesses for evangelism**. Thousands are overlooked in these places because the saints are too much desiring the comfort of resting in the morning or in the evening. Well, the saints have all their *entertaining* and *lounging* to do: radio, TV, internet, videos, sports, etc. The saints are too busy at home in the morning and too tired at night. Some are too tired or exhausted to do anything at night or go to the businesses in the community during the day time. Yet, I tell you that early **morning** in the business places and **night time** in homes **are goldmines** ready for harvest. "Friend, get off your duff." Meaning, stop being lazy.

Also watch out for the enemies right under your nose

There are many who are distorting or corrupting the Gospel message of the cross. As Paul says,

> Brethren, be followers together of me, and mark them which walk so as
> ye have us for an *example*. (For many walk, of whom I have told you
> often, and now tell you even weeping, *that they are* the **enemies of the
> cross of Christ**:   (Phil. 3:17 KJV)

As Paul was leaving the elders at Ephesus, he says with certainly of the battle,

> "For I have not shunned to declare to you the whole counsel of God
> [*the whole counsel in 3 years, wow*]. Therefore take heed to yourselves and to all the
> flock, among which the Holy Spirit has made you overseers, to shepherd
> the church of God which He purchased with His own blood. For I know
> this, that after my departure **savage wolves will come in** among you,
> **not sparing the flock**. Also from **among yourselves men will rise up**,
> **speaking perverse things**, to draw away the disciples after themselves
> [*sheep stealers*]. Therefore watch, and remember that for **three years I did
> not cease to warn everyone NIGHT AND DAY** with tears. So now,
> brethren, I commend you to God and to the word of His grace, which is
> able to build you up and give you an inheritance among all those who
> are sanctified [*by faith in Christ*]."   (Acts 20:27-32 NKJ)

The apostle Peter equally warns,

But false prophets also arose among the people, just as there will be false teachers among you, who will secretly bring in **destructive heresies**, even denying the Master who bought them, **bringing upon themselves swift destruction**. And many will follow their sensuality, and because of them **the way of truth will be blasphemed**.   (2 Peter 2:1, 2 ESV)

Paul warns Titus of the waring problems facing the church,

For many are rebellious and full of empty talk and deception [*deceivers*ᵉ], especially those of (the) circumcision, who must be silenced. For the sake of dishonorable gain, they undermine entire households and teach things they should not. As one of their own prophets has said, "Cretans are always liars, evil beasts, lazy gluttons." This testimony is true. Therefore rebuke them sternly, so that they will be sound in the faith and will pay no attention to Jewish myths or to the commands of men who have rejected the truth.   (Titus 1:10-14 MSB)

ᵉNote: Friberg lex. deceiver, "one who causes people to no longer believe what is true *deceiver*." Bible works 10.

You may recall that in Paul's last letter to Timothy, he gives us a very stern warning,

I charge *thee* therefore before God, and the Lord Jesus Christ, who shall judge the quick [*living*] and the dead at his appearing and his kingdom; Preach the word; be instant in season, out of season; reprove, rebuke, exhort with all longsuffering and doctrine. For the time will come when they will not endure sound doctrine; but after their own lusts shall they heap to themselves teachers, having itching ears; And they shall turn away *their* ears from the truth, and shall be turned unto fables. But watch thou in all things, endure afflictions, do the work of an evangelist, make full proof of thy ministry.   (2 Tim. 4:1-5 KJV)

The deposit of God's Word has now been entrusted to each of us today. The Bible exhorts us to be continuous (*continually ongoing*) in our recruiting and training for more and more workers for the Kingdom of God. (If you do not train the workers, there will be no work done.)

So you, my child, be strong in the grace that is in Christ Jesus. And entrust what you heard me say in the presence of many others as witnesses to faithful people who will be competent to teach others as well. Take your share of suffering as a good soldier of Christ Jesus. No one in military service gets entangled in matters of everyday life;

otherwise he will not please the one who recruited him. Also, if anyone competes as an athlete, he will not be crowned as the winner unless he competes according to the rules. The farmer who works hard ought to have the first share of the crops.   (2 Tim. 2:1-6 NET)

Paul alludes to five generations:

(1) Jesus, "Follow me as I follow Christ-" [1 Cor. 11:1 KJV]

(2) Paul, "-- you have heard from me-" [2 Tim. 2:2]

(3) Timothy, following Paul.

(4) Disciples of Timothy reaches, "the same commit thou to faithful men-" [2 Tim. 2:2 KJV]

(5) The disciples of Timothy reaches, "who shall be able to teach others also." [2 Tim. 2:2 KJV]

Do you see the generations connected? Friend, this is five generations, at least 200 years. (A biblical generation is at least forty years.) Do you see it? The impact is very, very great. Finding faithful men that shall follow and pattern their ministry after you is indeed very important. So, did Jude purpose to build a building or people? He is building people.

Also, the apostle illustrates his point with three different people and their way in life: the soldier, athlete (masters, KJV), and farmer (husbandman, KJV). There is a reward for all those striving honestly and faithfully preaching and **compelling** people to come now into the Kingdom of God while there is still time. There are no shortcuts in our service and life with Jesus.

Conclusion

I guess many miss Jude's point of *earnestly contend for the faith*. There is a sense I suppose we really need to fight for the faith. The really and big issue is **contending for the faith** as Jesus said, *go out the highways and byways and **compel** people to come* to Savior while there is time. This will not happen through just talking and lecturing. We need to **preach** and **preach the Word** with the **urgency** and **zealous** passion by the **Holy Spirit**.[2 Tim. 4:1, 2]

Yet, there is more: there is a sense of urgency: there is a need to be a *burning desire*. Have we dropped the ball in urgency of sharing the Gospel today? If it was urgent in Jude's day, then, how much more is there urgency in our day? The prophetic clock is ticking away, and time is shorter than we may thing. Jesus said,

> "Therefore you also be ready, for the Son of Man is coming at an hour you do not expect." (Luke 12:40 NKJ)

Jude's was feeling compelled with a passionate urgency to get the message out and to earnestly contend for the faith in his epistle. Again I ask, "Has your church drop the ball? Have we lost the urgency? Where is the fire?" Jeremiah said that he was going to stop giving the Word out due to the continual warring and persecution he experienced. Jeremiah said,

> Then I said, "I will not make mention of Him [*the Lord's name*], Nor speak anymore in His name [*of the Lord*]." But *His word* was in my heart like a burning fire Shut up in my bones; I was weary of holding *it* back, And I could not. (Jer. 20:9 NKJ)

Do you honestly feel the urgency or your church where you worship feel compelled to reach out to the lost and compel them to come? Our Master is giving a great banquet and He wants the banquet hall filled. Let us compel them to come! People are glad once they enter the Kingdom of God. You will be glad they enter the Kingdom of God. Best of all, the angels of Heaven and our Lord will be glad they enter the Kingdom of God.

Footnotes:

1. "Needful," GK *anagke*, Jude 1:3: Bible Works 10. See 1 Cor. 9:7, 16; Heb. 7:12.

2. GK *diamarturomai* [2 Tim. 4:1]: Bible Works 10, Danker's lexicon. Paul's appeal to Timothy is more than faithful teaching. Paul is calling the Eternal Christ the Lord in Heaven as witness. Sharing the Gospel my friend is serious and urgent. The apostle even includes in the charge the compelling and urgency to preach as witness before Christ and the holy angels of God! [1 Tim. 5:21] The reason: people will not endure sound doctrine, note [2 Tim. 4:3-5].

3. " There is room at the cross," from Digital Songs and Hymns, https://digitalsongsandhymns.com/songs/theres-room-at-the-cross

CHAPTER 4

Ungodly and wicked perverting the grace of God

Memory verse

They profess that they know God; but in works they deny *him*, being abominable, and disobedient, and unto every good work reprobate.

(Titus 1:16 KJV)

Introduction

Now Jude wraps up his introduction by declaring that there were wicked men who were turning the grace of God into an evil lifestyle. (This sounds like today.) These are people that Jude says have slipped in unnoticed by anyone in the church. These are men perverting the grace of God by turning the grace of God into a means of living depraved lives. Believe it or not they even deny Christ the Lord the only Redeemer. The NIV reads this way in verse four:

> For certain individuals whose condemnation was written about long ago have secretly slipped in among you. They are ungodly people, who pervert the grace of our God into a license for immorality and deny Jesus Christ our only Sovereign and Lord. (Jude 1:4 NIV)

Peter even says,

> But there were false prophets also among the people, even as there shall be false teachers among you, who privily [secretly] shall bring in damnable [GK *apoleia*, perdition] heresies, **EVEN DENYING THE LORD**

56

THAT BOUGHT THEM, and bring upon themselves swift destruction.[GK *apoleia*, perdition]   (2 Peter 2:1 KJV)

As you read Jude, you can't but help be shocked and stunned by such attitude and behavior in the church. "How can anyone enter the church unnoticed?" The church does not have its guard up. The church is not carefully receiving new members. So, people enter the easy and unnoticed. Additionally, the church has few with the *spirit of discernment*. As result of the lack discernment, wickedness is coming into the church undetected.

Are people that naïve, or are some just compromisers with no spiritual backbone? Even if the leader(s) have their guard up, so speak, once the person is in the church, the saints drop their guard. Friend, this is exactly why membership is important. Membership helps safeguard the church and sound doctrine for the next generation. Amazingly, still other leaders fail to realize that maybe some people's confession is not genuine. The person is a chameleon and void being born from above. "Hey, they couldn't be an implant, could they?" The person may change his theology once in the church.

I went to join the church near our home. Then, that coming Sunday AM I attended the church, and I arrived early for Sunday school. (The Pastor was apparently gone that Sunday.) There was no Sunday school, but two men did invited men into a room to talk. One man appallingly said, "*I do not believe in Hell*." Then, even more astonishingly, other man I think said that he *did not believe in the Trinity*. I acknowledged very clearly I did believe there is a Hell and I strongly believe in the Trinity.

A few days later, I met with the Pastor for coffee, and I informed him of my encounter with the two men and who they were. The Pastor said, "Well, they signed the membership claiming to believe in these things." Nothing more was done or said by the Pastor. Needlessly to say, I never joined the church. It was a Baptist church claiming that they believe and preach the Bible.

In war time, there is a tactic that is known as *infiltration*. Infiltration is a very deadly encounter. Someone who you may look up to has infiltrated the church and now he is a leader. The person turns out to be the deadly enemy of the Gospel.[Phi. 3;18f] (This happens more often than many Pastors realizes; their guard is not up.) Friend, there are deadly enemies that are out to destroy you and the troops.

Infiltration is much more than getting in among the troops undetected. This is infiltration for the purpose of *destruction* and to *cause mayhem*: causing havoc, confusion, disorder, chaos to bring total devastation and ruin. So, infiltration by the enemy is very serious and deadly. (Oh, *you smile*; you do not think Satan will infiltrate your church? Shame on you!) Too many Pastors (young and old) have their guard down, and they are too naïve and lack spiritual discernment.

Satan enters the church in a way that is nearly impossible to detect. Satan will have the appearance as an angel of light.[2 Cor. 11:13-15] Oh, but yes he certainly will! This is because Satan sneaks upon you to destroy you from a blindside. You cannot see him. You are unable recognize the demons accompanying him to do their evil plots. This is because he attacks the ***mind*** and certainly affects our ***emotions***. (Oh, but he will certainly attack the mind and emotions.) Satan penetrates the ***mind*** and ***emotions*** as though he is an angel sent by God. (Keep in mind that our emotions are part of our unregenerate nature. Hello! Our emotions are not part of our new nature.) Satan is **no** holy angel from God. These are the wickedest angels masquerading themselves as a holy angel from God.

Paul warned the Church at Corinth of the particular tactics by the devil, but his tactics are sometimes overlooked or undetected by many in the church leaders today. That is, as I have said, many overlook the devil who can insert things into our ***minds*** and yes even in our ***emotions***!

> But I'm afraid that **YOUR MINDS** might be **SEDUCED** in the same way as the snake [*the devil*] deceived Eve with his devious tricks [*tactics*]. You might be unable to focus completely on a genuine and innocent [*sincere*] commitment to Christ. (2 Cor. 11:3 CEB)

While the Pastor is teaching in church, Satan is filling people's minds with things that are not from God. Hear me! Satan is a master illusionist. He is more than lying and deceiving. The apostle Paul says,

> For such people are **false apostles, deceitful workers, disguising themselves** as apostles of Christ. And no wonder, for even **Satan disguises himself as an angel of light**. Therefore it is not surprising his servants [*demons*] also **disguise themselves** as **servants of righteousness** [*having an appearance of godliness*], whose end will correspond to their actions. (2 Cor. 11:13-15 NET)

The issue is similar to Ananias and his wife Sapphira. Notice as Young Literal Translation captures Peter's words:

> Peter said, 'Ananias, wherefore did the Adversary [Satan] fill thy heart —' (Acts 5:3a YLT)

Apparently, Satan put the idea into the ***minds*** and ***emotions*** of Ananias and Sapphira. It is easy to lie when Satan is feeding the mind and emotions. When

Satan put an evil thought in your mind, recognize it immediate and cry to God, "Help the Lord!"[2 Cor. 10:4, 5]

Even Peter was not immune from Satan's onslaught of deception. That's right, even Peter was tricked in his mind and emotions by the devil. Remember, Jesus told His disciplines that He must die and rise again. Then, at that time, Satan took the opportunity to introduce and reject the idea and affect Peter's thoughts and emotions.

> From that time Jesus began to show His disciples that He must go to Jerusalem, and suffer many things from the elders and chief priests and scribes, and be killed, and be raised up on the third day.
>
> Peter took Him aside and began to rebuke Him, saying, "God forbid *it*, Lord! This shall never happen to You."
>
> But He [*Jesus*] turned and said to Peter, "Get behind Me, Satan! You are a stumbling block to Me; for you are not setting your mind on God's interests, but man's." (Matt. 16:21-23)

There is nowhere we might conclude that Satan filled Peter's mind and emotions without the Lord revealing it to us. If Satan can put thoughts into Peter's mind and even affect his emotions, Satan is able to fill our minds and affect our emotions today. Watch out! It may be very difficult to know with certainty when Satan planted the thoughts in our minds and affect our emotions but he certainly will.

A. God knows who are the distorters of the Gospel

Therefore, it should be clear that the church will indeed face the enemy within its doors. Unfortunately, we do not know who is in *sheep's clothing* but inside *vicious wolves*. Sometimes even those who enter doors of the church do not know themselves that they will be either aiding or abetting the enemy. (Satan sees a person as a potential easy target). Yes, there are some that will unknowingly take up the cause of the adversary, Satan, but they are unaware being used as a pawn by the evil one. This means the devil's presence in church might be undetected and remain out of sight to nearly everyone. Hello! We just cannot imagine an enemy coming through doors of the church undetected or unnoticed, but the enemy of our souls surely shall.

Once in the church, the adversary begins to plot and implant the seeds into our minds and *emotions*. As these seeds grow, other seeds that the enemy has implanted will also begin to grow as well. The seeds bloomed and destruction is with those that the devil has seduced. So, we are caught off guard. We

59

fail to recognize or remain alert, spiritually vigilant, and realize that this is an *invisible* and *supernatural war* we are facing. We cannot fight this war without continual fervent prayer and be ardently tuned into God's Word.

The plan of the wicked are all plainly known to the Lord. He has known their heinous plans from all eternity.

> But God's firm foundation stands, bearing this seal: "The Lord knows those who are his," and, "Let everyone who names the name of the Lord depart from iniquity." (2 Tim. 2:19 ESV)

Thus, God surely knows those who are His truly redeemed, and the Lord certainly knows all those who are not His redeemed but turnout to be destructive enemies. This is why **continuous prayer** and **being tuned-in** to the will of God and His blessed Holy Spirit is an absolute necessity. Let us be fully armed with the Sword of the Spirit, the Word of God: study and memorizing the Scripture for war.

Satan has many ways to *trip us up* (trick us) as saints today, but Paul said to the Church at Corinth,

> I have done this to keep Satan from getting the better of us. We all know what goes on in his mind.[a] [GK *noema*, mind, thinks] (2 Cor. 2:11 CEV)

> [a]Note: the GK is literally the *mind* or *thoughts*, *noema*. KJV uses *devices*, NAS *schemes*, or NRS *designs*. We are easy prey since we remain ignorant of his attack in our minds.

We must strive to remain on our guard and become sensitive and attentive to **the leading of the Lord** and ever **fervent in prayer**. Without the guidance from the Lord and His leading, we are as I have said, *easy prey*.

> Above all, taking the shield of faith, wherewith ye shall be able to quench all the fiery darts of the wicked-[*one*[b]]. And take the helmet of salvation, and the sword of the Spirit, which is the word of God: Praying always with all prayer and supplication in the Spirit, and watching thereunto with all perseverance and supplication for all saints.
>
> (Eph. 6:16-18 KJV)

> [b]Note: GK noun, *poneros*, a reference to Satan.

Paul is not talking about some unusual method in prayer when he says, "-pray at all times in the Spirit."[Eph. 6:18 NET] This is just fervent and earnest prayer but being continually **tuned-in** to the Lord. As Paul says in Romans,

Likewise the Spirit also *helps* our infirmities [*impotence*]: for we *know* not what to pray as we ought [*to*]: but the Spirit *itself* [*Himself*] makes [*our*] *requests* for [GK *huper-entugchano*, *pleads or intercedes with us an on our behalf*] us with sighs, which cannot be expressed. [27] But *He* that *searches* the *hearts, knows* what is the meaning [GK *phronema, thoughts*] of the *Spirit*: for *He makes* request [GK *entugchano*, pleads or intercedes] for ye *saints*, according to the *will* of God. [28] Also we *know* that all *things work* together for the best *unto* them that *love* God, *even* to them that are called of his purpose.

(Rom. 8:26-28 GNV)

ᶜNote: *italics* indicates the old ENG spelling was updated but no changes have been made in words. Words brackets are only for clarity.

Paul **does not mean** that we are somehow ignorant or unable to know how to pray. The meaning here is that we don't always know **what the will of God is** in some situations. God's will is always better than our will, and He has our best interest at heart. God's will shall surely be done. So then, we ought to be praying in accordance with the will of God. Please hear me again, the Lord always has our best interest and welfare more than we do ourselves. This is why we ought to be praying in accordance to God's will in all matters. In addition, the Spirit is a filter in our prayers to the throne of God.

If we walk in an attitude of prayer (*staying tuned-in to the Lord*) and *seeking His will*, we are less likely to be caught off guard. The problem is we do not walk in a continual attitude of prayer. We are quick to change stations or channels like changing the dial on a radio or TV. We seem to easily lose our focus and are quickly distracted and lose our spiritual focus. We fail to stay tuned-in to the will of God. If Satan attacks our minds and emotions (which he does), we do not bother to pray. We do not bother to even ask for help from the Lord. We can handle it and may tend to shrug it off as nothing; it is no big deal.

We are more tuned-in to the world due to our carnal walk in Christ. Have we forgotten as the apostle says,

> But I say, **walk by the Spirit**, and you will not carry out the desire of the flesh. For the flesh sets its desire against the Spirit, and the Spirit against the flesh; for these are in opposition to one another, so that you may not do the things that you please. (Gal. 5:16, 17)

> Put on therefore, as God's chosen ones, holy and beloved, a heart of compassion, kindness, lowliness, humility, and perseverance; bearing with one another, and forgiving each other, if any man has a complaint against any[one]; even as Christ forgave you, so you also do [*forgive*

them]. Above all these things, walk in love, which is the bond of perfection. And **LET THE PEACE OF GOD RULE IN YOUR HEARTS**, to which also you were called in one body, and be thankful. **LET THE WORD OF CHRIST DWELL IN YOU RICHLY**; in all wisdom teaching and admonishing one another with psalms, hymns, and spiritual songs, singing with grace in your heart to the Lord. Whatever you do, in word or in deed, **DO ALL IN THE NAME OF THE LORD JESUS, GIVING THANKS TO GOD THE FATHER THROUGH HIM**.   (Col. 3:12-17 WEB)

If we are walking godly in Christ, we are well ahead and going in the right directions. Let us keep our attitude and action in check. In this way, we are less likely to get tripped up and fall. For example, the Bible tells us,

Don't have anything to do with foolish and stupid arguments, because you know they produce quarrels. And the Lord's servant must **not** be quarrelsome but must be <u>kind</u> to everyone, able to teach, not resentful. Opponents must be gently instructed, in the hope that God will grant them repentance leading them to a knowledge of the truth, and that they will come to their senses and escape from the trap of the devil, who has taken them captive to do his will.   (2 Tim. 2:23-26 NIV)

Let us continually *to be bathed in prayer* and *saturated in the Word* of God and *attentive to the Holy Spirit's leading* as we *walk humbly* before the Lord which is the best antidote against the bite of the serpent.

Solomon reminds us that-

The horse is prepared for the day of battle, But the victory belongs to the LORD.   (Proverbs 21:31)

B. They turned the grace of God into a license for evil

This is unbelievable, but unfortunately very true, my brother. These are people that while they like to sing the praise of the Lord in choir, they are also *sensual* and indulging in the things of the carnal flesh. (I am not singling out the choir since there are many godly saints singing in the choir; this could be any position in church.) Such people tend to give much attention to the things of the world. Their minds are on earth things. Remember, what the apostle said of some workers at Philippi?

Brothers, join in imitating me, and keep your eyes on those who walk according to the example you have in us. For many, of whom I have often told you and now tell you even with tears, walk as enemies of the cross of Christ. Their end is destruction [GK *apoleia, perdition or perish*], their god is their belly [*sensual appetite*], and they glory in their shame, with minds set on earthly things. (Phi. 3:17-19 ESV)

These are the people that "- turned the grace of our God into a license for evil [*wickedness*]." Jude 1:4 NET When the wicked sing in the choir, the leader(s) may overlook or give a blind-eye if their lifestyle is known. Leaders may overlook or ignore their lifestyle because, "But they sing so good, and the people love it." Certain singers or performers in church "are a drawing card for the church." **This brings in money**. Apparently, Jesus is not sufficient as a drawing card today for many churches. Besides, with such entertainment, church attendance is higher, and as I have said, the revenue for the church is increased. "We can do more for the Lord with the money." Oh, really now!

All the while, the leader(s) are ignoring the warning:

Do not be deceived: "Bad company ruins good morals."

(1 Cor. 15:33 ESV)

Again, the apostle Paul tell us,

Now the one who receives instruction in the *Word* [*by spiritual leaders*] must share all good things with the one who teaches it. Do not be deceived. God will not be made a fool [*mocked*]. For a person will reap what he sows, because the person who sows to his own flesh will reap corruption from the flesh, but the one who sows to the Spirit will reap eternal life from the Spirit. So we must not grow weary in doing good, for in due time we will reap, if we do not give up. So then, whenever we have an opportunity, let us do good to all people, and especially to those who belong to the family of faith. (Gal. 6:6-10 NET)

Those who ignore God's warning and associate or fellowship with the sensual or worldly people shall wear down their own godly walk in Christ. In time, we may become callused or insensitive to their wicked influence of such friends on our lives when we continually associate with them. Behind scenes of our lives, Satan is luring the naïve and immature to imitate and follow the ungodly and their example of the carnal minded. Hence, there begins a *spiritual erosion*. Then, we may find ourselves **ensnared** but we cannot get out. It is *too late to put the fires out with its passion*. The fire has already been lit.

Listen, sin will have a luring attraction to draw us away from the Lord. For example, when Lot and Abraham separate, the Bible says,

And Lot lifted his eyes and saw all the plain of Jordan, that it *was* well watered everywhere (*[this was]* before the LORD destroyed Sodom and Gomorrah) *[these cities were]* like the garden of the LORD, *[even]* like the land of Egypt as you go toward Zoar. Then Lot chose for himself all the plain of Jordan, and Lot journeyed east. And they separated from each other. Abram dwelt in the land of Canaan, and Lot dwelt in the cities of the plain and **pitched *his* tent even as far as Sodom**. But the men of Sodom *were* exceedingly wicked and sinful against the LORD.

(Gen. 13:10-13 NKJ)

Perhaps Lot was viewing the plain of the Jordan with its lush grass, plenty of water, and cities to sell his livestock and make plenty of money. But the Bible says,

But the men of Sodom *were* **exceedingly wicked** and **sinful against the LORD**.   (Gen. 13:13 NKJ)

I doubt Lot prayed about the decision. He could only imagine the money he might make. Well, friend, Lot lost everything. He lost all his wealth; his wealth was gone. He lost his sons-in-law in the judgment. His wife perished in the destruction though they were warned, "Do not look back." His daughter committed incest with their drunken father, which no doubt Lot's daughters learned while living in Sodom. The Bible gives us this account in Lot's life after he move towards Sodom. The apostle Peter says,

And [*the Lord*] turning the cities of Sodom and Gomorrah into ashes, condemned *them* to destruction, making *them* an example to those who afterward would live ungodly and delivered righteous Lot, *who was* **oppressed** by the **filthy conduct** of the wicked (for that righteous man, dwelling among them, **tormented** *his* righteous soul from **day to day by seeing and hearing *their* lawless deeds**)—   (2 Peter 2:6-8 NKJ)

Again, the Bible says of Lot,

For that righteous man, dwelling among them, **tormented *his* righteous soul** from day to day by **SEEING** and **HEARING** *their* **lawless deeds**. (2 Peter 2:8 NKJ)

His two daughters commit incest, but his two daughters no doubt were influenced by the wicked cities lifestyle. Five thousand years later, nothing can grow in those cities. The area of those cities the Bible says,

> — turning the cities of Sodom and Gomorrah into ashes, condemned *them* to destruction, making *them* an example to those who afterward would live ungodly —   (2 Peter 2:6 NKJ)

Nowadays, many people have either forgotten the dreadful destruction of those cities or they do not believe God destroyed the cities.

The price of sin is very high:

Sin will cost you more than you want to pay;
Sin will take further than you want to go;
Sin will bring you to ruin from which you may never recover!

This is why James says,

> Come now, you who say, "Today or tomorrow we will go to such and such a city, and spend a year there and engage in business and make a profit." Yet you do not know what your life will be like tomorrow. For you are *just* a vapor that appears for a little while, and then vanishes away. Instead, *you ought* to say, "If the Lord wills, we will live and also do this or that." But as it is, you boast in your arrogance; all such boasting is evil. So for one who knows *the* right thing to do and does not do it, for him it is sin.   (James 4:13-17)

So, there may be some Christians that are easily lured and enticed into certain wickedness since they may tend to be always in *limelight*. Why are the easily lured? These are people that may only profess to be Christians and live ungodly lives. (They may seem to be unscathed even though they live in sin.) There are others like Lot who are genuine believers, but they have given into the enticement of the world around them. Yet, as I have said that there may be some people who seem to be getting away with their immoral walk. Friend, they shall not escape the Lord. We may not see any consequences initially in their life of wickedness, but no one escapes unscathed by sin.[Num. 32:23]

Also, keep in mind that forgiveness does not remove the consequences of sin. "You have made your bed, you shall lie in it!"

No one escapes the hand of the Lord. The apostle Paul reminds us as he writes to young Pastor Timothy,

> The sins of some are obvious, reaching the place of judgment ahead of them; the sins of others trail behind them.   (1 Tim. 5:24 NIV)

C. They turn from Jesus Christ, denying Him as LORD

Here again is Jude's final concluding remarks in his introduction. He sternly warns us by saying,

> For certain intruders have stolen in among you, people who long ago were designated for this condemnation as ungodly, who pervert the grace of our God into licentiousness and **deny our only Master and Lord, Jesus Christ**.   (Jude 1:4 NRS)

First, let me say how some profess to believe in Christ, but on the other hand, they actuality deny Christ in the same breath. These teachers or preachers of the Gospel are even very well-known all over the world. In one breathe, they espouse that they believe in Jesus as the Christ and Lord. (So far so good? No!)

These same people turn around in the very next breathe declare, but Jesus is not the only way to Heaven. This is a lie right out of Hell. Their words are a farce! Jesus said that He is the only way.^{John 14:6} He that has the Christ the Lord, the Son, has life, but those without Christ the wrath of God abides on them.^{John 3:36} Those without the Son are already condemned.^{John 3:18; 1 John 5:10-13}

So, this how some declare Jesus. Oh, yes, they do not use the name Lord. The word "Lord" is too offensive. Friend, regardless of how they say it, people are offended at the Gospel. Nevertheless, there is no other name whereby we must be saved.^{Acts 4:12}

No one that genuinely comes to Jesus Christ and has been truly born from above by the Holy Spirit walks away. I am talking about what Jude concludes in the introduction: "deny our only Master and Lord, Jesus Christ." Jesus is the **Pearl of Great Price**! Only as we genuinely and truly know Jesus Christ and actually know who He really is will never walk away. For only a fool would walk away.

> "Again, the kingdom of heaven is like a merchant seeking beautiful pearls, who, when he had found one **PEARL OF GREAT PRICE**, went and sold all that he had and bought it." (Matt. 13:45, 46 NKJ)

Jesus said to His apostles when people begin to get offended at His Words and walk away,

> ⁶⁶As a result of this many of His disciples abandoned Him, and no longer walked with Him. ⁶⁷So Jesus said to the twelve [disciples], "You do not want to leave too, do you?" ⁶⁸Simon Peter answered, "Lord, to whom shall we go? **You [alone] have the words of eternal life** [you are our only hope]. ⁶⁹We have believed *and* confidently trusted, and [even more] **we have come to know** [by personal observation and experience] that **You are the Holy One of God** [the Christ, the Son of the living God]." ⁷⁰Jesus answered them, "Did I not choose you, the twelve [disciples]?

> And yet one of you is a devil (ally of Satan)." [71]Now He was speaking of Judas, *the son* of Simon Iscariot; for he, one of the twelve [disciples], was about to betray Him. (John 6:66-71 AMP)

Judas Iscariot though He saw all the miracles, signs, and wonders and he was even given the power to heal, he did not actually know who Jesus really is. Judas Iscariot was lured and blinded by Satan. In his spiritual blindness, he threw away the greatest gift from God, Jesus the **Pearl of Great Price**. Judas Iscariot sold himself out for thirty pieces of silver!

Two weeks from graduation, a Bible College student ready to graduate openly denied the faith in class. The professor, faint in his Bible doctrine and theology, said, "Well, we shall see him in Heaven." I said loudly, "**NO!** We shall not see him in Heaven."

Anyone who continuously and adamantly openly denies and rejects Jesus as Lord God and only Savior has condemned himself. He only had an intellectual profession of faith. He did not have genuine possession of saving faith in Christ. There is no way that a person can recover once they continuously and adamantly reject Jesus Christ after professing to have known him. Peter out of fear for his life initially denied knowing Jesus, but openly recanted and continued to be a mighty bullwork for God. This is because Peter possessed genuine saving faith witness by the Spirit of God.

If anyone is without witness of the Spirit, he/she is not saved,

> However, you are not in the flesh but in the Spirit, if indeed the Spirit of God dwells in you. But if anyone does not have the Spirit of Christ, he does not belong to Him. [10]If Christ is in you, though the body is dead because of sin, yet the spirit is alive because of righteousness [*imputed righteousness of Christ*]. [11]But if the Spirit of Him who raised Jesus from the dead dwells in you, He who raised Christ Jesus from the dead will also give life to your mortal bodies through His Spirit who dwells in you.
>
> [14]For all who are being led by the Spirit of God, these are sons of God. [15]For you have not received a spirit of slavery leading to fear again, but you have received a spirit of adoption [*placing as sons*: referring men and women] as sons by which we cry out, "Abba! Father!" [16]The **Spirit Himself testifies** [GK *summartureo, bears* witness] **with our spirit that we are children of God.**
>
> (Rom. 8:9-11; 14-16)

My brother, it matters not how many times we may fall. Jesus is always there to pick us up. Regardless of the depth of sin we may fall into, Jesus is present to pick you up cleanse you from all your sin.[1 John 1:7-10] However, if there is **no repentance** like the Bible college student that denied the faith in Christ, then, that person may actually provide he was never regenerated, without salvation, and void of the indwelling of the Holy Spirit.

The doctrine of eternal security does not mean that a person can open reject Jesus Christ and still remain in the faith. Neither can anyone continue to live in a sinful life and also claim genuine faith. This is a lie! You had better erase that kind of thinking from your carnal mind right now.

> Therefore I endure all things for the elect's sakes, that they may also obtain the salvation which is in Christ Jesus with eternal glory. *It is* a faithful saying: For if we be dead with *him*, we shall also live with *him*: If we suffer, we shall also reign with *him*: if we deny *him*, he also will deny us: If we believe not, *yet* he *abides* [remains] faithful: he cannot deny himself. (2 Tim. 2:10-13 KJV)

The genuinely saved will continue or persevere in the faith. The saints will continue in the faith because the Lord began the good work in us. Praise the Lord, He shall indeed keep that which I have commit unto Him.[2 Tim. 1:12-17; Phi. 1:6; 2:12f, 13; 1 Peter1:3-9]

Still, turning away from the Author of life, Jesus the Lord, is committing *eternal spiritual suicide*. Friend, there is no one that can help you if you turn away from our Lord Jesus. Christ the Lord is the **only source** of eternal life. Without Him, there is nothing, and there is nothing anyone can do for you.

Let me also say to anyone who imagines that they pulled themselves up by their own bootstraps or their ministry by their own strength and will, you have forgotten the exhortation of our Lord that said,

> "Abide [remain] in Me, and I in you. As the branch cannot bear fruit of itself, unless it abides [remains] in the vine, neither can you, unless you abide [remain] in Me. I am the vine, you *are* the branches. He who abides [remains] in Me, and I in him, bears much fruit; for **WITHOUT ME YOU CAN DO NOTHING.**" (John 15:4, 5 NKJ)

Oh, yes, you may have a performance or show in the flesh. However, let us all remember what the Holy Spirit said through the apostle Paul.

> **We are coworkers belonging to God.** You are God's field, God's building. [10]According to the grace of God given to me, like a skilled master-builder I laid a foundation, but someone else builds on it. And each one must be careful how he builds. [11]For no one can lay any foundation other than what is being laid, which is Jesus Christ. [12]If anyone builds on the foundation with gold, silver, precious stones,

wood, hay, or straw, [13]each builder's work will be plainly seen, **for the Day** will make it clear, because it will be revealed by fire. And the fire will test what kind of work each has done. [14]If what someone has built survives, he will receive a reward. [15]If someone's work is burned up, he will suffer loss. He himself will be saved, but only as through fire. [16]Do you not know that you are God's temple and that God's Spirit lives in you? (1 Cor. 3:9-16 NET)

No one is in competition with his brother even if you live in the same city. Yet, I see sheep stealing from other churches. (Hear me: you shall have no reward from the Lord; you thief!) Immorality, selfishness, and false doctrines overtaking churches. Do you know what? The leaders are boasting of it all in the name of grace. As I have already warned you, we cannot escape the hand of God. We bear His name in us, and woe unto the fool who spurns the grace of God as a license to sin.

Once again, hear the Hebrews writer as he gives a very severe warn:

Of how much worse punishment, do you suppose, will he be thought worthy who has trampled the Son of God underfoot, counted the blood of the covenant by which he was sanctified a common thing, and insulted the Spirit of grace? For we know Him who said, **"Vengeance is Mine, I will repay,"** says the Lord. And again, **"The LORD will judge His people." It is a fearful thing to fall into the hands of the living God**. (Heb. 10:29-31 NKJ)

Some are seemingly throwing their rewards away. As the Hebrews writer continues,

Therefore do not throw away your confidence, which has a great reward. [36]For you have need of endurance [**to persevere**], so that when you have done the will of God you may receive what is promised. [37]For, "Yet a little while, and the coming one will come and will not delay; [38]but my righteous one shall live by faith, and if he shrinks back, [I *the LORD*] my soul has no pleasure in him." [39]But we are not of those who shrink back and are destroyed, but of those who have faith and preserve their souls.

(Heb. 10:35-39 ESV)

Some see the ministry as nothing more than a carnal vocation or personal career. If it does not work out, they just change the vocation. What a fool! Woe unto the fool who walks away from the King's service. Jesus gives us this parable,

As they were going on the road, someone said to Him, "I will follow You wherever You go." And Jesus said to him, "The foxes have holes and the birds of the sky *have* nests, but the Son of Man has nowhere to lay His head." And He said to another, "Follow Me." But he said, "Lord, permit me first to go and bury my father." But He said to him, "Allow the dead to bury their own dead; but as for you, go and proclaim everywhere the kingdom of God." Another also said, "I will follow You, Lord; but first permit me to say goodbye to those at my home." But Jesus said to him, "**No one, after putting his hand to the plow and looking back, is fit for the kingdom of God.**"　　(Luke 9:57-62)

Woe unto anyone that forsakes the ministry like leaving secular career. This is especially true if they have been called to serve as a Pastor. The abandonment of the ministry is a rejection of Jesus' call and gift to you.[Eph. 4:11]

Conclusion

One of the reasons for the United States' victory during WWII was that there were mighty men that believed in God and **believed in prayer**. During the war, even General George Patton would ask the Chaplain to write his prayer to God. Patton read the Chaplain's prayer out loud before the troops. If nothing happened, Patton asked for another Chaplain. He wanted a Chaplain that could reach Heaven. So, it was with many great men of fervent prayer that lead the victory. Hallelujah! There is no victory without faithful men standing at their assigned positions (standing in the gap[Ezek. 22:30]), fervently praying and earnestly reaching out to confront the enemy.

The church and many of its leaders live and walk as through the church is not at war. For shame! (Nevertheless, the spiritual warfare is worse than all human wars combined.) So, many prayers by leaders in the church are bankrupt in their prayer life. Prayer is nothing more than an appendage by some church leaders. Their prayers are like taking *stroll through the park*. Even worse, there is no aggressive follow-up and knocking on doors to win the battle.

Yet, many church leaders are not stupid. The leaders know intellectually there is deadly spiritual war going on. If they could spiritually see the war and chaos and havoc through the eyes of faith, their prayer might be more on target in their prayers and actions of faith.

Jude has given a brief but pungent introduction. This is wartime and the casualties and fatalities are very high. Unfortunately, many do not seem to realize the death and destruction that is occurring around them. There is no cry for help. There is no cry to Heaven for help.

Every church is doing its own things. There is little or no comradery helping another Pastors or churches. It is *sink or swim; you are on your own kid.* (Yes, some may give a little financial help, but there is no sharing of workers.) There is no laboring together. There are few looking to Jesus for help and guidance. Friend, do you truly believe we are in spiritual war, and the war is worse than all human wars combined?

The apostle writes to the church of Ephesus,

> For you were at one time darkness, but now you are light in the Lord. Walk as children of the light– 9for the fruit of the light consists in all goodness, righteousness, and truth– 10trying to learn what is pleasing to the Lord. 11Do not participate in the unfruitful deeds of darkness, but rather expose them. 12For the things they do in secret are shameful even to mention. 13But all things being exposed by the light are made evident. 14For everything made evident is light, and for this reason it says: "Awake, O sleeper! Rise from the dead, and Christ will shine on you!" 15Therefore be very careful how you live– not as unwise but as wise, 16taking advantage of every opportunity, because the days are evil. 17For this reason do not be foolish, but be wise by understanding what the Lord's will is. (Eph. 5:8-17 NET)

Let us learn to redeem the time because the days are evil.

Part Two

Vengeance is mine, I will repay, says the Lord

[5]Now I want to remind you, though you know everything once *and* for all, that the Lord, after saving a people out of the land of Egypt, subsequently destroyed those who did not believe. [6]And angels who did not keep their own domain but abandoned their proper dwelling place, *these* He has kept in eternal restraints under darkness for the judgment of the great day, [7]just as Sodom and Gomorrah and the cities around them, since they in the same way as these *angels*[a], indulged in sexual perversion and went after strange flesh, are exhibited as an example in undergoing the punishment of eternal fire.   (Jude 1:5-7 NAS)

[a]Note: the word "*angel*" in verse 7 is an insertion by the NAS (2020). The GK word "*aggelos*," *angel*, is not in the GK in verse 7.

CHAPTER 5

The Lord sustained Israel coming out of Egypt

Memory verse

Therefore let him who thinks he stands take heed that he does not fall. No temptation has overtaken you but such as is common to man; and God is faithful, who will not allow you to be tempted beyond what you are able, but with the temptation will provide the way of escape also, so that you will be able to endure it. (1 Cor. 10:12, 13)

Introduction

The Exodus of Israel coming out of Egypt is by far one the greatest miracles in the annals of human history. Three million people (and perhaps as high as six million) escaped the clutches of the Egyptian Army. There is no parallel or equal where God visibly sought a people in total bondage and declaring His plan of deliverance, and then rescuing the people unscathed as His people plunders the booty of Egypt.

Now the incredible Exodus miracle is being denied as some folklore or fairy tale today by many. Thus, calling God a liar. How evil is that? Others in disbelief allege that Israel was a war-like people, and Israel was able to deliver themselves by their own power and wit. In reality, such people are openly declaring God and His Word a lie. Friend, it is only a fool who dares declare God a liar!

There is no greater fool than anyone that is stupid enough to either declare God a liar or to declare God's Word is a lie!

> Do you see a man wise in his own eyes? *There is* more hope for a fool
> than for him.   (Proverbs 26-12 NKJ)

However, as Israel was to cross over into the promise land at Kadesh-Barnea, twelve men were selected from each of twelve tribes of Israel to spy out the land and give a report of what they seen. This took forty days to completely scout out the land. The land was everything that the Lord promised and even more,[Num. 13, 14.] Nevertheless, ten of the spies gave an (unbelievably) evil report that the people in the land were exceedingly large giants that inhabited and ruled the land.

> We even saw the Nephilim [lit. HEB, also the word *"giants"*] there—the descendants
> of Anak that come from the Nephilim [giants]! **We seemed like**
> **grasshoppers** in our own sight, and we must have seemed the same to
> them!"   (Num. 13:33 MSB)

Only Joshua and Caleb spoke the truth and declared exactly what they had seen and what God declared to everyone. Joshua and Caleb were confident that the land would be Israel's, and Israel would indeed inherit the promised blessings just as God promised. The people believed the evil report of the ten spies, and then, the people were even preparing to stone Joshua and Caleb who were encouraging the people to believe God and take possession of the land. Joshua and Caleb said to the people of Israel,

> Joshua son of Nun and Caleb son of Jephunneh, who were among those
> who had spied out the land, tore their clothes and said to the whole
> congregation of Israel, "The land we passed through and explored is an
> exceedingly good land. If the LORD delights in us, He will bring us into
> this land, a land flowing with milk and honey, and He will give it to us.
> Only do not rebel against the LORD, and do not be afraid of the people
> of the land, for they will be like bread for us. Their protection has been
> removed, and the LORD is with us. Do not be afraid of them!"
>
>   (Num. 14:6-9 MSB)

Due to Isreal initially believing the lie of the ten spies and refusing to take the land as God promised Israel, judgment fell upon Israel. As the result of disbelief, Israel would spend a year for each day they spied out the land, forty years wandering the wilderness.[Num. 14:34.]

Today, God has promised blessings to His people in Christ despite the adversities like the Anak. The churches needs only go forward as mighty warriors for the Lord.[2 Cor. 1:20; 1 Cor. 15:57, 58] We have the sure promises that Christ the Lord *will be with us forever* and *will never leave or forsake us.* [Mat. 28:20; Heb. 13:5]

Nevertheless, the church leaders are *faithless*, *fearful*, *rebellious*, *immoral*, and *love the world more* (a world that is to pass away, [1 John 2:17]). As the apostle Paul declares concerning our victorious walk of faith in Christ,

> Now thanks be to God who always leads us in triumph in Christ, and reveals through us the sweet aroma of his knowledge in every place.

> (2 Cor. 2:14 WEB)

If today there is any evangelism *door to door* by the church, the evangelism is nothing more than a *dribble* or a *drop-in-a-bucket*. Woefully, there is no *door to door evangelism*. Gimmicks or attractions have replaced evangelism. There is no more hard-hitting evangelism 7/24. (Evangelism is zero or near zero by many churches everywhere.) In addition, women and children are used instead of godly men to battle the enemy. Why? There are no men available. Where are the *"ish Elohim,"* men of God? The men are lazy and void any fire from on High.

Are there no men zealous for the Lord, men like Joshua and Caleb, men full of faith? As men attempt to declare the Gospel in an unbeliever's home today, some are presenting the Gospel like *women in labor*. Unbelievable, the Gospel is given with *soft words like a child*. Where are the men of God with spiritual backbone? Friend, without the Spirit of the living God and the fire from on High, there will be no great victories! The churches are acting like *paupers* (extremely poor), a beggar on *skid row*, or *even as a person living in a garbage dump-site*. Many are not living or walking like sons of the King. Where are the men of faith? Let us also remember what James says about faith. Faith without action (works) is dead; that is, faith without action is no faith at all.

A. Yet, many that did not believe, the Lord destroyed

Jude says in verse 5,

I will therefore put you in remembrance, though ye once knew this, how that **the Lord**,[b,1] having saved the people out of the land of Egypt, afterward destroyed them that believed not.	"I want to remind you, though you once knew this, that **the Lord**,[b,1], having saved the people out of the land of Egypt, afterward destroyed those who did not believe"	I will therefore admonish you, though ye once knew all things, that **Jesus**,[b,1] having saved the people out of the land of Egypt, did afterwards destroy them that believed not:	Now I want to remind you, although you once fully knew it, that **Jesus**,[b,1] who saved a people out of the land of Egypt, afterward destroyed those who did not believe.
KJV	Coptic	LAT/ENG	ESV

[b]Please see the notation #1 at the end of this chapter.

77

While there are more manuscripts that used "Jesus" instead of "the Lord," I am going concur with the BYZ and Coptic texts. (See note #1 at the end of this chapter.)

Let us also remember that God did ten astonishing mighty miracles before the Egyptians to demonstrate that the Lord is the only true God. The Egyptians were sternly warned: let Israel go or else the Egyptians shall indeed pay a dreadful price and the Egyptians would certainly regret their decision. The Egyptian Army was obliterated in the sea, but Israel had already crossed the sea as God split the water and Israel crossed over on dry ground.

Despite all the incredible signs, wonders, and mighty miracles, many Israel's leaders did not believe God. Like Israel, the church intellectually knows also the mighty miracles of God or ought to know. The faith of many saints today lacks coupling (uniting) *faith* with *action*. Yet, today, many leaders in the churches know with certainty,

> But without faith *it is* impossible to please *Him*, for he who comes to God must believe that He is, and *that* He is a rewarder of those who diligently seek Him. (Heb. 11:6 NKJ)

This is no faith in just believing the facts intellectually. Listen, believing the historical event, the natural man is able to acknowledge history as fact. Godly faith does what God declares in His Word. There is no godly faith unless it is coupled with action based upon *what God said* or *what God has done*. For example, Hebrews says,

> [16]And who was it who rebelled against God, even though they heard his voice? Wasn't it the people Moses led out of Egypt? [17]And who made God angry for forty years? Wasn't it the people who sinned, whose corpses lay in the wilderness? [18]And to whom was God speaking when he took an oath that they would never enter his rest? Wasn't it the people who disobeyed[c] him? [19]So we see that because of their unbelief they were not able to enter his rest. (Heb. 3:16-19 NLT)

> [c]Note: the GK word is *apeitheo* in v 18; the word meaning is to **disobey** and the KJV "*believe not*" is less favorable. In v 19, the word is *apistia*, **unbelief**.

Paul warns the church at Corinth that those in the church cannot continue to live wicked and immoral lives. As Christians, we **bear the name of Christ within us**. Living wickedly, we are bringing reproach and disgrace upon the name of the Lord. The Lord our God is holy and righteous God. He is blessed forever and ever! (Please read the Scripture below carefully.)

For I do not want you to be unaware, brothers and sisters, that our fathers were all under the cloud and all passed through the sea, ²and all were baptized into Moses in the cloud and in the sea, ³and all ate the same spiritual food, ⁴and all drank the same spiritual drink. For they were all drinking from the spiritual rock that followed them, and the rock was Christ. ⁵But **God was not pleased with most of them**, for they were cut down in the wilderness. ⁶These things happened as examples for us, so that **we will not crave evil things** [Num. 11:4] as they did. ⁷So **do not be idolaters** [Ex. 32:4ff], as some of them were. As it is written, "The people sat down to eat and drink and rose up to play."[Ex. 32:9] ⁸And **let us not be** [sexually] **immoral** [Num. 25:1], as some of them were, and twenty-three thousand died in a single day.[Num. 25:9] ⁹And let us **not put Christ to the test**,[Num. 21:5, 6] as some of them did, and were destroyed by snakes [serpents]. ¹⁰And **do not complain**,[murmur, Num. 16:41; 17:10] as some of them did, and were killed by the destroying angel. ¹¹These things happened to them as examples and were written for our instruction, on whom the ends of the ages have come. (1 Cor. 10:1-11 NET)

If a person is **not** genuinely saved, there will be no correction or discipline since they are without Christ. The Lord only disciplines those whom He genuinely saved.Heb.v12:5-8

Again, we must understand that belief, the acknowledgement of an intellectual truth as true is not biblical faith. This is intellectual faith only declaring the historical fact that is evident. Faith must be coupled with personal commitment of action to the facts. Biblical faith is putting into action upon what God declares or reveals in His Word. The acknowledgment that the historical facts are accurate and true is a declaration of an honest person. Yet, without acting on the facts given by God, there is no faith in the presence of God.

Today it is no longer Christianity! Today it is *churchianity* with perhaps a lot of *fan-fair or hoopla*, but there is little genuine substance demonstrating faith in obedience to God and His Word. There is often only timidness, indecisiveness, faithlessness, and infidelity. Even worse, there is discord within the clear commands or mandates of the risen Lord Jesus.

Instead, the many saints have given way to *division, dishonesty, lying, cheating,* and *wholesale wickedness* among the churches. Sadly, many Christians are bringing reproach and shame upon the blessed name of Jesus. There are no calls for people to come forward to receive Christ as Lord and Savior. Where is the attitude of quietness and serenity in preparing our hearts for worship of the King? Moreover, there is no confession of sin or the call for repentance, renewal, or revival. There is only disgrace and uncontrolled wickedness in the churches today.

Like Israel, the church is warned over and over again by God for their wickedness but to no avail. The apostle Paul warns the church that Christians cannot continue live immorally like they are doing or else the Lord will bring judgment upon them.

> Whoever, therefore, eats the bread or drinks the cup of the Lord in an unworthy manner will be answerable for the body and blood of the Lord. [28]Examine yourselves, and only then eat of the bread and drink of the cup. [29]For all who eat and drink without discerning the body, eat and drink judgment against themselves. [30]For this reason many of you are weak and ill, and some have died. [31]But if we judged ourselves, we would not be judged. [32]But when we are judged by the Lord, we are disciplined so that we may not be condemned along with the world.
>
> (1 Cor. 11:27-32 NRS)

When sin increases, God increases His grace and mercy all the more to save the sinners. Yet, the apostle asked a rhetorical question. (A question that needs no reply.)

> [20]But law came in, with the result that the trespass multiplied; but where sin increased, grace abounded [GK *huperperisseuo, super-increased*] all the more, [21]so that, just as sin exercised dominion in death, so grace might also exercise dominion through justification [*righteousness*] leading to eternal life through Jesus Christ our Lord. (Rom. 5:20, 21 NRS)

> [6:1]What then are we to say? **Should we continue in sin in order that grace may abound**? [2]By no means! How can we who died to sin go on living in it? (Rom. 5:20-6:2 NRS)

As humankind continue to increase in sin more and more, God continues to increase His grace and mercy all the more. God continues to increase His grace and mercy in order to save more sinners. The apostle asks another question,

> - do you show contempt for the riches of his kindness, forbearance and patience, not realizing that **God's kindness is intended to lead you to repentance**? (Rom. 2:4 NIV)

He did not increase grace and mercy so the saints could continue to sin more and more. This is the lie of antinomianism. This evil doctrine of antinomianism says that *there are no laws in the age of grace*; *do whatever you want.* Even worse, universalism teaches everyone will be saved, which is another lie.

B. The mixed multitude that did not genuinely believe

One of the things sometimes overlooked in the Exodus is the *mixed multitude* that accompanied Israel in their departure from Egypt. Among this *mixed multitude*, there were people continued to worship pagan gods of Egypt and likely had little or no genuine knowledge of the Lord our God. Many of these were people that were probably never in bondage by the Egyptians. Many in the *mixed multitude* were likely Egyptian themselves but associated with Israelites. The people in the *mixed multitude* had no genuine faith in the Lord. It is likely that some of *mixed multitude* had a little historical evidence and knowledge of the Lord our God. Hence, the *mixed multitude* had no connection or history with Abraham, Issac, Jacob, Joseph and tribes of Israel in whom God called out of darkness and sustained by His grace and mercy.

The same way with the churches: there is the *mixed multitude* among the saints. The *mixed multitude* in the churches only have an association with church, but they are without Christ and have no sure hope. They exhibit only at best *historical faith* of facts but without regeneration. The *mixed multitude* **do not know the Lord** as personal Savior. The *mixed multitude* are having a deadly effect on Christians and some of the saints living in sin.

This *mixed multitude* in the churches are even ignorant of the mighty deeds and blessings of God in Christ. (Regrettably, even many Christians are ignorant of Scripture especially the OT). The *mixed multitude* only know what they hear from others from the natural realm in the churches. The *mixed multitude* know little or nothing of God's power in their life. Is this why many only refer to the Lord as "god"?

The *mixed multitude* have no foundation in the faith. They only have a generic and worldly view of "a god." Shockingly, they know little concerning many of the great promises of God. Therefore, it is easy understand why many in the *mixed multitude* in the church are without genuine saving faith by the Spirit of God. The *mixed multitude* may profess faith, but they are void of genuine regeneration and being *born from above* by Spirit of the living God.[John 3:3-7]

As Isaiah the prophet said to Israel, and the same message applies to the churches today,

> Seek the LORD while He may be found, Call upon Him while He is near. Let the wicked forsake his way [*let them repent*], And the unrighteous man his [*flee his wicked*] thoughts; Let him return to the LORD [*let there be a revival*

among them], And He will have mercy on him; And to our God, For He will abundantly pardon. "For My thoughts *are* not your thoughts, Nor *are* your ways My ways," says the LORD. "For *as* the heavens are higher than the earth, So are My ways higher than your ways, And My thoughts than your thoughts."

(Isa. 55:6-8 NKJ)

The church is following and giving their attention to the *mixed multitude* in the churches rather than giving heed to God's Word. This is so very true among the so-called professors teaching in some of the seminaries. Some teachers in seminaries are void of genuine saving faith in Christ. They only possess a historical faith, and even their historical portion is alarmingly very distorted. We live in the world but the church is not to be part of the world.

Do not be unequally yoked with unbelievers [*don't marry an unbeliever*]. For what partnership has righteousness with lawlessness? Or what fellowship has light with darkness? ¹⁵ What accord has Christ with Belial [*a name for Satan*]? Or what portion does a believer share with an unbeliever? ¹⁶ What agreement has the temple of God with idols? For **we are the temple of the living God**; as God said, "I will make my dwelling among them and walk among them, and I will be their God, and they shall be my people. ¹⁷ Therefore go out from their midst, and **be separate from them**, says the Lord, and touch no unclean thing; then I will welcome you, ¹⁸ and I will be a father to you, and you shall be sons and daughters to me, says the Lord Almighty." (2 Cor. 6:14-18 ESV)

Christians have **Xmas** (*x'ed out*) Christmas, and "*Christ's*" name is removed from Christmas. Sat**na** is = to Sat**an**:

"*You better watch out, he knows if you been good or bad ... Satna is coming to town.*" This song is contributing honor to "*evil spirit,* which is right out of Hell."

So, playing Satna or playing the *Easter bunny* is robbing Christ of His rightful place in our hearts and minds. Laugh if you want, but know this for certain every one of us shall indeed give an account: "for every idle word we say."[Mat. 12:36] Friend, standing before the Lord will not be "a little chit-chat."

Listen to me, doing such things as "Satna" or the "Easter bunny" is a direct insult and mockery of our Lord. Friend, it is unwise to mock the grace and mercy of Christ Jesus the Lord. Get mad and deny it, but such actions will not be overlooked by God. Ignorance in actions demonstrates contempt for Christ the Lord whether one knows it or believes it. Ignorance is no excuse; it's only a cop out.

It doesn't matter, many Christians play idolatrous games with the world. Like little children, many Christians play like they are *ignorant of their actions and thoughts*. Oh, but yes, some Christians definitely lie even to themselves. How foolish is that? So, in this way, they have played the game. Yet, many Christians have played into the devil's hands. Some have been seduced again by the evil one without them knowing it. Their minds have *gone whoring into evil idolatry*. Yet, when warned or confronted of their actions, they will not listen or repent. Yeah, you've got it: they are offended and angry at being rebuked. Their love for the idolatrous world is more than they love the Lord.

Many Christians sadly omit church service on AM Sunday. Many churches no longer have evening service. Few people attend evening worship service even if the churches offer it. So, it is no surprise that there are many Christians that are unfaithful attending and worshiping the Lord. Little do some realize that they are storing up themselves for the day wrath. The Bible warns us,

> But because of your stubbornness and your unrepentant heart, you are storing up wrath against yourself for the day of God's wrath, when his righteous judgment will be revealed.   (Rom. 2:5 NIV)

> If any man's work is burned up, he will suffer loss; but he himself will be saved, yet so as through fire.   (1 Cor. 3:15)

Our association and friendship with the world rather than our love and faithful walk with the saints in church and the Lord Jesus will come with a very sad end. Let us return to the Lord. The Lord is gracious and He will forgive us of our sins. (Note this for certain: forgiveness, however, **does not** remove the consequences of sin.[Gal. 6:7]) Furthermore, intellectualism (believing the historical facts of the Gospel) does not bring about genuine regeneration by the Holy Spirit. Intellectualism of the faith in Christ only proves that the person is not stupid about who Jesus is, but believing the fact does produce genuine regeneration by the Holy Spirit. So, the acknowledgment the facts of Gospel are true is no assurance of genuine regeneration and being born again by the Holy Spirit.

Jude is warning, *examine your faith*:

Faith without regeneration by the Holy Spirit is **not** biblical saving faith. Similarly, just because some professes to believe the Gospel, this does not mean a person is genuinely born from above by the Spirit. As I have said many,

many times before: *a profession of faith in Christ* is *no assurance of possessing genuine saving faith* in Christ.

The Lord is holy and righteous God. A person had better be certain they are in the faith and *seek the Lord with a whole heart.* Jesus is not looking for our vote of confidence for faith. Our Lord is looking for wretched and wicked sinners deserving the wrath of God but sincerely searching forgiveness of sin and cleansing and to walk with Lord. We need to do as Jude says,

> Keep yourselves in the love of God, **LOOKING FOR THE MERCY of our Lord Jesus Christ** unto eternal life.   (Jude 1:21 KJV)

Are you looking for the mercy of the Lord unto eternal life through genuine commitment and trust in Christ the Lord?

Anyone that truly seeks the Lord our God, they shall indeed find Him. Yes, today some may make an intellectual confession of faith in Christ but without genuine commitment of whole heart and mind there is no genuine saving faith. There is only form without substance. Even worse, there are people that allege that they believe the Bible, but when probing their alleged belief, they actually do not genuinely and truly believe God's Word. Actually, they only have a *canned confession,* but their hearts and minds are not in it. The person only went through the motions or the mechanics of a *canned confession.* As I have already said, "their heart is not in it." As noted above, their profession of faith is absence of true "commitment of the heart and mind."

The apostle Peter warns about those that only have a *canned confession,* but without real regeneration,

> If people have escaped from the corrupting forces of the world through their knowledge of our Lord and Savior Jesus Christ, and then are again caught and conquered by them, such people are in worse condition at the end than they were at the beginning. It would have been much better for them never to have known the way of righteousness than to know it and then turn away from the sacred command that was given them. What happened to them shows that the proverbs are true: "A dog goes back to what it has vomited" and "A pig that has been washed goes back to roll in the mud."   (2 Peter 2:20-22 GNT)

There was no change in the person's thoughts and lifestyles. They have only made a *canned confession.* They remain unregenerate and on the road to Hell. (So, their confession of faith was not through the Holy Spirit.) They only had an intellectual acknowledgement of the historical truth. Most sorrowfully, they were void of genuine regeneration. They shall indeed perish in their sins without Christ the Lord as their only Redeemer. I say again:

> Put yourselves to the test to see if you are in the faith; examine yourselves! Or do you not recognize regarding yourselves that Jesus Christ is in you– unless, indeed, you fail the test!   (2 Cor. 13:5 NET)

Conclusion

After Jude's introduction (1:1-4) and shocking statement that wicked *men and women have entered the assembly of the redeemed undetected,* he warns of the *mixed multitude* that accompanied Israel in their amazing Exodus under the mighty hand of the Lord. He says,

> I will therefore put you in remembrance, though ye once knew this, how that the Lord, having saved the people out of the land of Egypt, afterward destroyed them that believed not.   (Jude 1:5 KJV)

The mixed multitude *paved the way* for corruption, disbelief and untold wickedness. The churches are filled with the mix multitude today. In the same way, corruption, disbelief and untold wickedness are with the mixed multitude.

In many so-called churches, Christ is no longer the center of life. Today, it is *churchianity* and no longer Christianity. It just a generic deity, *"god."* You will rarely hear the name of **the Lord** any more. Little do people realize that the removal "the Lord's name" may indeed be a clear sign of God's judgment. The Lord having removed His blessed name from their lips.

There are unfortunately many that only have profession of faith in Christ without a true regeneration of faith by Spirit of God. They profess to know Him, but their actions demonstrate and prove that they do not know the Lord as their Redeemer. They only give lip service.

They profess to love Jesus, but they rarely faithfully attend church. They profess to love Jesus, yet they give no willing active service to the Lord. The Day is coming for some who will experience the most dreadful *rude awakening*[2] because they had only profession of faith, but they were completely void of genuine commitment of faith. They are void of regeneration and saving faith in Christ the Lord.

85

Footnotes

1. Some GK MSS read "**the Lord**" and others read "**Jesus:**" All the translations which
    I frequently use except for the ESV prefer "**the Lord**." Only the ESV follows and
    uses the name "**Jesus**." Apparently, the textual manuscripts in Rome use the GK that
    tends to favor the name "**Jesus**." Even the Latin Vulgate favors "**Jesus**." However,
    this brings into question the reliability of the Vulgate in this particular situation. There
    are only three salient GK family texts: GK BYZ, Coptic, and Rome. There more GK
    MSS in Rome favoring "**Jesus**," but more GK text in one area (Rome) is not sufficient
    evidence to determine which word is preferred.

    There must be other aspects that must also be taken into account or considered
    as to which name is preferred in the GK texts. It is my opinion that the BYZ and the
    Egyptian (Coptic) texts use "**the Lord**" is stronger evidence for me based on the
    inherent context. Also, Bruce M. Metzger's A Textual Commentary on the GK NT
    concurs. (American Bible Society, Jude 1:5, 1971.) Other translations equally concur
    with "**the Lord**" are: GNV, KJV, ASV, NAS, NET, NIV, NRS, and CEB. (There other
    translations that agree with "**the Lord**" but are not mentioned).

    There are probably more GK manuscripts in Rome. Thus, it appears to be more
    favorable reading of "**Jesus**." Still, there are other things to consider in determining
    which word in the GK text is more credible. Below are reasons favoring "**the Lord**"
    as given in the KJV.

    a. *If the shoe don't fit, that not your shoe!* Well, in my mind before even reading
        Metzger GK commentary, the shoe did not seem to fit the context. Jude is
        discussing Israel coming out of Egypt, there is nothing in or surrounding the
        immediate text [Jude 1:5] supporting the name "**Jesus**." The word seemed out of
        place.

    b. *Does it have a true ring of genuineness?* People are fooled by fake diamond or
        what is sometimes referred to a "fool's gold." If a diamond has a hallow sound,
        it is likely fake. Gold and other precious metals can be given an acid test. If the
        metal bubbles up by acid on it, it is fake. In the same way here, the human name
        "**Jesus**" mentioned in [Jude 1:5] does not have the authenticity of gold to the context.
        If text does not have sense of genuineness, it is unlikely authentic. I would be
        very cautious in such a case. Unfortunately, there is no real acid test to give here.
        Desiderius Erasmus Roterodamus (known as Erasmus) suspected for example on
        text of '1 John 5:7' as forgery by the Roman Church. Still, he included it in the
        text though he suspected the text to be fraudulent. I think unfortunately the name
        "**Jesus**" [Jude 1:5] is a fraudulent text and is an insertion.

c. *Does it fit the context?* The increased number of GK texts in Rome with "**Jesus**" is impressive. However, the context suggest the name "**Jesus**" (our Lord's earth name) does not fit the context. So, if it does not fit context, it is a red flag for me. The name "**Jesus**" is unsuitable with OT context.

d. Similarly, *does the word(s) jell or mash with the historical setting?* The surrounding historical setting of events in Jude refers to the Exodus, sin of angels, and Sodom and Gomorrah [Jude 1:5-7]). Sorry, this just does mash with Jude's setting or circumstances in which he is writing? The historical surround does not support the name "**Jesus**." The context harmonize with the OT name "**the Lord**." If it does **not** mash with historical setting, it is likely not part of the text.

e. *The BYZ and Coptic Bible texts uses "**the Lord**." The Vulgate uses "**Jesus:**"* Jerome wrote and compiled the Latin Vulgate by the beginning of 5th century (383-404 AD). There are no early BYZ and Coptic Bible, but this still does not warrant ignoring evidence. This is still strong evidence supporting the BYZ and Coptic Bibles.

f. *The is no precedent establish in Scripture using NT name in OT history.* There is no Scripture support using "**Jesus**" in direct connection with Israel's history. Christ is the "Rock" that lead Israel [1 Cor. 10:4], but human name "**Jesus**" is not used in Israel history. Paul does use the name Jesus [Phi. 2:10], but the apostle's unique use fits the context. Keep in mind, Jude does not establish any bases or precedent of using "**Jesus**" during Israel history.

g. *Scholars such as Metzger should not be ignored.* I shall not go into Metzger's arguments of the use of "**the Lord**" instead of "**Jesus**." Nevertheless, Metzger is indeed a worthy scholar, and his choosing the name "**the Lord**" rather than "**Jesus**" should not be underestimated or easily dismissed.

    Therefore, though the use of "**Jesus**" may appear more favorable with some GK manuscripts, but there are other factors that ought to be taken into account. So, for the above reasons, I think that it is reasonable that the BYZ and Coptic GK texts and their use of "**the Lord**" is preferred over "**Jesus**."

2. *"Rude awakening:"* The terrifying realization in assuming a belief that is unfounded and without one shred of evidence of genuine saving trust in Christ Jesus as Lord and Savior. For example, a person believes he has genuinely trusted in Christ. The person realizes that he **never** genuinely repented and made a commitment and trusted in Jesus Christ. He does not possess genuine saving faith **nor** did he receive Christ as personal Lord and Savior.

CHAPTER 6

The fall of angels

(Who are the sons of God in Gen. 6?)

Memory verse

For You have made him a little lower than the angels, And You have crowned him with glory and honor. (Psa. 8:5 NKJ)

Introduction

These next two verses (Jude 1:6, 7) are so overrun with tradition and pagan interpretations that Jude's intention is less known in the churches. So, this section in Jude has been extended to examine the issues, and these issues shall be discussed in the next three chapters. However, friend, believe me that the gravity of these issues are far more complexed and important than few may realize. Here, unfortunately, tradition has definitely blinded many saints from the true biblical meaning!

Sadly, Jude's little Epistle is overlooked and not given much significance as to its overall importance to the doctrinal issues and inspiration and authority of Scripture. Yet, I am here to tell you that Jude's Epistle on canonistic issues and verbal and plenary inspiration and authoritative issues of all Scripture is of monumental importance. This is a battle for the Bible and its inherent authority is at forefront as we begin to probe this epistle. You may discover the necessity of reading through these chapters in the book more than once.

The legacy and future of these issues are transferred to you as you strive to transfer these issues to next succeeding generations. As the apostle Paul challenges young Pastor Timothy, we also have burden to deposit and commit to other faithful men.

> [1]You then, my son, be strong in the grace that is in Christ Jesus. [2]And the things you have heard me say in the presence of many witnesses entrust to reliable people who will also be qualified to teach others. [3]Join with me in suffering, like a good soldier of Christ Jesus. [4]No one serving as a soldier gets entangled in civilian affairs, but rather tries to please his commanding officer. [5]Similarly, anyone who competes as an athlete does not receive the victor's crown except by competing according to the rules. [6]The hardworking farmer should be the first to receive a share of the crops. [7]Reflect on what I am saying, for the Lord will give you insight into all this. (2 Tim. 2:1-7 NIV)

A. The sons of God in Gen. 6

Many expositors it seems link Gen. 6 to Jude's here. So, it is essential we begin with the discussion in Gen. 6. The question of *who are the sons of God in Gen. 6* will lay the foundation for these three chapters. The troubling problems lies with three major influences that have fostered a serious error that continues to misguide countless others entering into the fold. These three influences are: the flagrant errors in annals of _church history_, the pressures of ecclesiastical _tradition_, and even _pagan_ influences.

Unfortunately, many are unaware of such above influences upon their opinion or interpretation on the subject. The person's denial of not being influenced by the three above element changes nothing. The facts are that the above influences do greatly influence our interpretation of the Scripture.

Not all such influences are necessarily bad influences. Sometimes, such influences may actually steer in the right direction or properly steer us away from the potential error. Regrettably, church history, tradition, and pagan influences often then effect our thinking only deeper and perpetuate the error.

As we examine the question of *who are the sons of God in Gen. 6,* there are only three major interpretations:

1. The sons of God are the angelic beings.

2. The sons of God are the believers among the godly of Seth.

3. The sons of God are mighty or seeming powerful men.

Here is the text in Gen. 6.

> Now it came to pass, when **MEN** began to multiply on the face of the earth, and daughters were born to them, ² that the sons of God saw the daughters of men, that they *were* beautiful; and they [*sons of God*] took wives for themselves of all whom they chose. ³ And the LORD said, "My Spirit shall not strive with **MEN** forever, for he [*man*] *is* indeed flesh; yet his [*man*] days shall be one hundred and twenty years." ⁴ There were giants [HEB *Nephilim*] on the earth in those days, and also afterward, when the sons of God came in to the daughters of men and they bore *children* to them. Those *were* the **mighty MEN** who *were* of old, **MEN** of renown.
>
> (Gen. 6:1-4 NKJ)

Throughout the brief context, the entire emphasis is upon <u>human men</u>. There is nothing in the text suggesting "sons of God" were angelic beings. God's displeasure and anger is directed at mankind. There is absolutely nothing said or even alluding to *angels* here in Gen. 6. Therefore, there is nothing directly or indirectly in Gen. 6 referring *angels*. *Angels* ought to be ruled out in Gen. 6. There is nothing in Gen. 6 indicating that *angels* are even referred to in the text.

Yes, there are text that use the phrase "sons of God" as referring to angelic beings, but there is nothing in Gen. 6 suggesting or implying the "sons of God" are angels in Gen. 6.

Yes, there are texts in Scripture that refer to angels as "sons of God." Job says

> Now there was a day when the <u>sons of God</u> came to present themselves before the LORD, and **Satan came <u>also</u>** among them.   (Job 1:6 KJV)

The phrase is used again

> When the morning stars sang together, and all <u>the sons of God</u> shouted for joy?   (Job 38:7 KJV)

The expression "sons of God" certainly can apply to angels as noted in Job. However, there is nothing definitely or alluding to angels in Gen. 6. This is the simple facts which cannot be denied or refuted. That is, there no basis to conclude that angels are involved in Gen. 6.

This leaves only two possibilities as to the interpretations to who are the sons of God in Gen. 6. Either the phrase "sons of God" refers to the redeemed (which would then be the godly line of Seth), or the phrase "sons of God" refers mighty men of great strength, power, or authority. For those fixated and have leaned towards tradition, you are likely going to continue in assuming the phrase "sons of God" in Gen. 6 is angels.

In mocking towards the rulers in Israel, the Lord said,

> "You are gods [HEB *Elohim, pagan gods*], And all of you are sons[a] [HEB *ben, sons;* are *children* incorrect] of the Most High. Nevertheless you will die like men And fall like *any* one of the princes." (Psa. 82:6, 7)

> [a]Note: the word is not "*children*" (HEB *yeladim*); the HEB is "*ben*," meaning *son*. *Elohim* when referring the "**LORD**" is capitalized; otherwise, *Elohim* is uncapitalize since *elohim* refers pagan deity and not the Lord.

In the above verses in Psa. 82:6, 7, the Lord is mocking the rulers in Israel. The rulers had the power of life and death, and so, in this sense, the rulers were looked upon as the ultimate power over people. The meaning in Gen. 6 is like the redeemed, godly line of Seth. For example, the apostle says,

> For in Christ Jesus you are all sons of God through faith.

> (Gal. 3:26 NET)

Therefore, the evidence to me suggests the meaning in Gen. 6 is likely referring to the line of Seth, which was the godly line of the redeemed.

B. Grammatical and Historical Setting

Nowadays it seems popular to ascribe nearly any meaning you want to a text in the Bible. The context does not matter. A person just attributes any interpretation they want of Scripture, and this is done with the total disregard to contextual meaning. Friend, be careful judging others without checking yourself first.

I am sorry to say that many preachers and teachers are notorious to just grab any text to preach or teach on without any regards for the surrounding Scriptural context. The text is only used for a "*springboard*[1]" to launch their message. Politicians have long since used the *springboard* in running for office. However, politicians only come into second-place with preachers and teachers of the Bible. Friend, you may laugh, but I am afraid the joke is on you.

In my senior year in Bible college, some student said, "If Frank is taking to young people going swimming, he is the only man that would preach on *the floating ax*." While some student meant it as a sarcastic remark, I thanked the class and took as a compliment. (By the way, the floating ax was during prophet Elisha in [2 Kings 6:1-7].)

The point I am making is text being used ought to be the central core to the message of which you are preaching or teaching. However, I am sad to say many preachers seemingly give little or no regards concerning the context. Pastors that tend to use expository preaching are more apt to zoom in the context. Regrettably, many preachers use some text Scripture as I have said for nothing more than pretext[2].

When discussing the grammatical and historical setting in the study of Scripture, the context is 99.9% that important. If language means anything as to accurate communication and thought, context is priority #1 over everything else. Accurate and precise communication and understanding is an absolute necessity. This means that the literal meaning needs to be communicated if precise understanding is going to be properly understood.

What is the Grammatical and Historical Principle:

First importance here is that the meaning must be derived from the immediate surrounding context. Equally important, a person seeking the meaning of a text must never (I mean never) superimpose or interject outside source of the immediate context to determine the inherent meaning. We **must allow the central context to establish the intended meaning.** Allow the central context to determine its own inherent meaning is indeed the most sacred principle in the grammatical and historical interpretation. This principle should **never** be compromised or forfeited for any reason!

For example, when studying a controversial context such as Gen. 6, the most high priority must be given to the immediate context bar none. For instance, what is the root-word meaning to the word(s). There are three keys words that ought to be given priority in determining the meaning: a. verbs; b. nouns or subject; c. core-words.

    a.   Verbs are important because the verb describes the action taking place or the movement.

    b.   Noun or subject identifies upon whom or what the action is taking place.

    c.   Core-words help to clarify or increase the understanding of the thing being communicated.

In Gen. 6, the essential nouns are *sons of God, men, Nephilim, mighty men, men of renown,* and *120 years.* The central verbs are coupled with phrase *took wives* and *bore children*[3].

So, in the study of Gen. 6:1-4, the phrase must be derived from the immediate context. The noun phrase *"sons of God"* cannot be applied to angelic beings because there is nothing in the immediate context that warrants or justifies the use of "angels." This means that the noun phrase *"sons of God"* either refers to the <u>sons</u> <u>of</u> <u>Seth</u>, which could refer to the godly line, the redeemed. The only other option is that the noun phrase *"sons of God"* could perhaps refer to <u>mighty</u> <u>men</u> that metaphorically view so powerful men as *a god*.

In addition, this also confirms with the word or words as: <u>*men*</u>, <u>*mighty*</u> <u>*men*</u>, and <u>*men*</u> <u>*of renown*</u>. The very absence of any reference to angels only helps to seal tight and confirm the intended meaning by the biblical author.

The other word or phrases are: <u>*took*</u> <u>*wives*</u> and <u>*bore*</u> <u>*children*</u>, and <u>*Nephilim*</u> [or <u>*giants*</u> KJV]. Again, there is absolutely nothing said that angels took for themselves wives. (Remember, there is nothing in the context warranting "<u>*sons*</u> <u>*of God*</u>" meaning angels.) The only way angels can be applied is by superimposing a meaning that is not intended. The bearing of children is the natural result of the relationship implied in context between a man and a woman.

The word *Nephilim* or *giants* KJV clearly means human beings. The word Nephilim is plural HEB word. Nephilim probably suggests that these were people of large in size or statue. This further establishes that these were men large and strong. Hence, "mighty men which *were* of old, men of renown."[Gen. 6:1 KJV]

Lastly, is the phrase, "his days shall be one hundred and twentyyears."[Gen. 6:3] This is likely in reference to the time frame God set for the coming judgment upon mankind. This is important because "<u>if</u>" there was such catastrophic breach by angels: 1) There is implied <u>second</u> <u>fall</u> <u>of</u> <u>angels</u>. Was this alleged second breach by holy or unholy angels? 2) Where is the condemnation or judgment by God on angels in the context of Gen. 6:1-4. There is no judgment, and friend, if there is no judgment in the context, angels were not involved a second rebellion.

All this means is that the "sons of God" in Gen. 6:1-4 **cannot** **mean** or **refer** **to** **angels**. Many are still violating and robbing Gen. 6 of its right inherent and intended meaning. This is the grammatical and historical interpretation of Scripture and not eisegesis: reading your own meaning into the Bible.

C. Cohabitation of angels doesn't fit the paradigm

The fallacy in the argument the "sons of God" are angels in Gen. 6 overlooked the paradigm or design in creation. The Bible says,

> And the evening and the morning were the fourth day. [20]And God said,
> Let the waters bring forth abundantly the moving creature that hath life,
> and fowl *that* may fly above the earth in the open firmament of heaven.
> [21]And God created great whales, and every living creature that *moves*,
> which the waters brought forth abundantly, **after** **their** **kind**, and every

winged fowl **after his kind**: and God saw that *it was* good. [22]And God blessed them, saying, Be fruitful, and multiply, and fill the waters in the seas, and let fowl multiply in the earth. [23]And the evening and the morning were the fifth day. [24]And God said, Let the earth bring forth the living creature **after his kind**, cattle, and creeping thing, and beast of the earth **after his kind**: and it was so. [25]And God made the beast of the earth **after his kind**, and cattle **after their kind**, and *everything* that **creepeth** upon the earth **after his kind**: and God saw that *it was* good.

(Gen. 1:19-25 KJV)

Similarly, when God created man, the woman was no afterthought, but Eve (woman) was definite inherent design of making humankind.

And God said, Let us **make man** in our image, after our likeness: and **let THEM**[b] have dominion over the fish of the sea, and over the fowl of the air, and over the cattle, and over all the earth, and over every creeping thing that **creepeth** upon the earth. [27]So God **created man** in his *own* image, in the image of **God created he him; MALE and FEMALE created He THEM**[b]. [28]And **God blessed THEM**[b], and **God said unto THEM**[b], Be fruitful, and multiply, and replenish the earth, and subdue it: and have dominion over the fish of the sea, and over the fowl of the air, and over every living thing that *moves* upon the earth. [29]And God said, Behold, I have given you every herb bearing seed, which *is* upon the face of all the earth, and every tree, in the which *is* the fruit of a tree yielding seed; to you it shall be for meat [*be food for you*]. [30]And to every beast of the earth, and to every fowl of the air, and to *everything* that **creepeth** upon the earth, wherein *there is* life, *I have given* every green herb for meat [*food*]: and it was so. God saw all that He had made, and behold, it was very good. And there was evening and there was morning, the sixth day. (Gen. 1:26-31 KJV)

[b]Note: Man is refers to as "God created he him; MALE and FEMALE created He THEM."[v 27] Keep in mind God took from Adam's rib. See Gen. 2:21-23.

First, everything God created, He created, "**after his kind**." There is implied reproduction of all things procreating or reproducing "**after its kind**." This is in reference to genetics or biological genes in everything created. Unless the genes have a common source or origin in design, the genes will **not** line up to fertilize. This means reproduction is **impossible** between humans and spirit beings such as angels!

Also, please note that the woman was a definite part of the design of creation:

> And God said, 'Let us **make man** -- **let THEM** [*woman is included in the design*] have dominion --'   v 26

> "God **created he him** [*man*]; **MALE and FEMALE created he them**."

> v 27

> God **blessed THEM** [*man and woman* in design], and God said **unto THEM** [*man and woman* in design], Be fruitful, and multiply, and replenish the earth   v28

So, mankind also reproduces **after his kind**. Are we to suppose that God allowed the violation of His design of creation. That is, spirit being and flesh is able to cohabitate and reproduce a monster of half-human and half-spirit being. No! Perish the thought my brother.

D. Jesus' teaching of the resurrection

Our Lord taught that there is no marital or cohabitation relationships in Heaven. We belong to the Lord our God. Jesus declares the plain and simple truth about saints in Heaven. Jesus clarifies this issue in His discussion with the religious sect of the Sadducees.

The Sadducees reject all the OT except the first five books, books of Moses, Genesis through Deuteronomy. The Sadducees did not believe there is life after death. So, the Sadducees did not believe in any resurrection.

The Sadducees had asked Jesus a question concerning the resurrection. The question was a mockery since Sadducees did not believe in *an afterlife*. Sadducees asked Jesus, "If a woman remarries another man after her husbands' dies, 'Which man will be her husband in Heaven?'" Well, the question was to ridicule our Lord since He like the Pharisees believed all of God's Word, and there is truly an *afterlife* once a person's dies. Here is the dialogue:

> Then the Sadducees, who say there is no resurrection, came to him with a question. [19]"Teacher," they said, "Moses wrote for us that if a man's brother dies and leaves a wife but no children, the man must marry the widow and raise up offspring for his brother. [20]Now there were seven brothers. The first one married and died without leaving any children. [21]The second one married the widow, but he also died, leaving no child. It was the same with the third. [22]In fact, none of the seven left any children. Last of all, the woman died too. [23]At the resurrection whose wife will she be, since the seven were married to her?" (vv 18-23)

> [24]Jesus replied, "Are you not in error because you do not know the Scriptures or the power of God? [25]When the dead rise, they will neither marry nor be given in marriage; they will be like the angels in heaven. [26]Now about the dead rising— have you not read in the Book of Moses, in the account of the burning bush, how God said to him, 'I am the God of Abraham, the God of Isaac, and the God of Jacob'? [27]He is not the God of the dead, but [*the Lord is the God*] of the living. You are badly mistaken!" (vv 24-27) (Mark 12:18-27 NIV)

Our Lord rebukes the Sadducees by saying, "Are you not in error because you **do not know the Scriptures** or the **power of God**?"[Mark 12:24] Jesus uses the book of Moses, which Sadducees alleged to believe in the books of Moses.

> "Now about the dead rising— have you not read in the Book of Moses, in the account of the burning bush, how God said to him, **'I am the God of Abraham, the God of Isaac, and the God of Jacob'**? [27]He is not the God of the dead, but of the living. You are badly mistaken!"
>
> (Mark 12:26, 27 NIV)

There is the false doctrine that the redeemed waited in Hades (Abraham's bosom) until the resurrection of Jesus Christ arose from the dead. This is serious error formulated by some Dispensationalists and others who followed such faulty reasoning. Enoch and Elijah when to Heaven and certainly Moses and all believers go to Heaven at death. [2 Cor.5:8;Phi.1:32-23] To allege the OT redeemed resided in Hades until resurrection of Jesus Christ, this is totally absurd and completely ignorant of the Scripture. In addition, this following tradition void of and biblical basis.

Jesus also rebuke the Sadducees by saying,

> When the dead rise, they will neither marry nor be given in marriage; they will be **like the angels** in heaven. (Mark 12:25 NIV)

First, no saint in Christ shall be an angel! Angels were individually created by God. So, angels are **not** a race like Adam's posterity; **angels do not procreate** themselves. Therefore, angels are incapable of reproducing. There are many types of angels: some with wings and others without wings. Angels are spirit beings unlike humans; humans have bodies of flesh and blood. (The body of the redeemed are raised at resurrection. The body of the resurrection will be a glorified, and our bodies shall be similar to our Lord's resurrected and glorified body.[1 Cor. 15:51-56; Phi. 3:21]

In the resurrection, we shall be similar to angels in that we shall be celibates. As celibates, we shall belong unto the Lord and indeed holy to God.

(This is why God speaks of His redeemed and the marriage of the Lamb.) Angels are spirit beings, and angels are sexless creatures. There is no need to be able to procreate. Therefore, angels are incapable of sexual relationships. As noted already, angels are not a race unlike man. So, there is no need to be able to reproduce after their kind.

E. Origin of cohabitation of angels

The false doctrine that angels are able to cohabitate is from the erroneous books of Enoch which is a fictitious book, and the writings do not belong in the Bible. This is results of the predominate influence of centuries with such books of Enoch. Sadly, the perverted teaching has regained more popularity through movies alleging angels are able have relationships. Due to the internet and reprinted false books like the books of Enoch, these false notions have gained popularity.

It is even sadder when Christians are duped and lead astray from the sound teachings of Scripture. This departure from Scripture is the result of many things, but let me share with you three ways people get caught up with some these false teachings:

1. People are giving into the *earmarks of the last days*.

> For the time will come when they will not endure sound doctrine; but after their own lusts shall they heap to themselves teachers, **having itching ears**; And they shall **turn away** *their* **ears from the truth**, and shall be <u>**turned**</u> <u>**unto**</u> <u>**fables**</u>. (2 Tim. 4:3, 4 KJV)

So, many are lured into these unscriptural teachings. Once accepting such false teachings, it is nearly impossible to get them away from such perverted teachings.

2. Some people are deficient and lack a strong foundation overall teaching of the Bible.

> And He gave some *as* apostles, and some *as* prophets, and some *as* evangelists, and some *as* pastors and teachers, [12]for the equipping of the saints for the work of service, to the building up of the body of Christ; [13]until we all attain to the unity of the faith, and of the knowledge of the Son of God, to a mature man, to the measure of the stature which belongs to the fullness of Christ. [14]As a result, we are no longer to be children, **tossed here and there by waves and carried about by every**

97

> **wind of doctrine, by the trickery of men, by craftiness in deceitful scheming**; [15]but speaking the truth in love, we are to grow up in all *aspects* into Him who is the head, *even* Christ, [16]from whom the whole body, being fitted and held together by what every joint supplies, according to the proper working of each individual part, causes the growth of the body for the building up of itself in love. (Eph. 4:11-16)

Even if people are initially in a well-grounded church, unfortunately, some do not stay long enough in one church to be properly grounded in the Word. Even worse, some churches are bankrupt when it comes to teaching Scripture the whole counsel of God. Still other do not have a *teachable spirit*; they are too headstrong. Others do not even bother to read God's Words. Many people today are caught up with the *spirit of the age* and *have little time for the Bible study*.

3. Finally, some are actually lured or enticed by demon activity of the mind.

> The Spirit clearly says that in later times some will abandon the faith and **follow deceiving spirits** and things **taught by demons.**[ͨ] Such teachings come through **hypocritical liars**, whose consciences have been seared as with a hot iron. (1 Tim. 4:1, 3 NIV)

> [ͨ]Note: the KJV uses the word "devils." There is only one devil, Satan; the GK word is *daimonion, demons.*

Since their consciences have been seared, they are hardheaded and unable to see the truth of God's Word. It takes a humble and *teachable spirit* to say, "I am very sorry; I stand corrected. Thank you!" The god of this age, Satan, has blinded from truth.[2 Cor. 4:3, 4]

F. Second breach by angels questions God's Sovereignty

The capstone or the closing point is a so-called cohabitation of angels is the inference of a second breach by angels. Angels sinned shortly after the creations of mankind. Angels underwent a testing period like humans, except when angels rebilled there was no redemption for the angels that sinned. A second breach by angels is an outrageous proposition, it is ludicrous and an absolutely insane notion.

When angels and humankind were created, there was given a *probation under innocence* or *testing period* of choice and free-will. Adam's *testing period* was choosing to not eat of *"the tree of the knowledge of good and evil."*

> Then the LORD God took the man and put him in the garden of Eden to tend and keep it. And the LORD God commanded the man, saying, of every tree of the garden you may freely eat; but of the tree of the knowledge of good and evil you shall not eat, for in the day that you eat of it you shall surely die." (Gen. 2:15-17 NKJ)

As to the angels, Hebrews says, 'He makes his angels winds, and his servants a flame of fire.' [Heb.2:7 WEB] Furthermore, Job reveals all the angels saw some infinite power and greatness of God that Adam and Eve never knew. Angels witness some element of creation and His unleashing of His infinite and glorious power.

> When the morning stars sang together And all the sons of God shouted for joy? (Job 38:7)

Therefore, angels, like humans, were all created innocent and given freewill with the power of choice. We do not know the exact time frame when some angels rebelled and sinned against the Lord. Still, I think it is reasonable to imagine some angels sinned somewhere between the angels' creation and certainly before the fall of Adam.

Some theologians and expositors have surmised that when Lucifer (Satan an archangel, a ruling angel) saw Adam, he became very jealous, covetous, and envious of what Adam was capable possessing and awesome authority granted to humans. Note some of the qualities given to Adam. When you consider the authority given to humankind, the authority given to humankind (even in comparison to angels), man rule and authority over all creation is indeed most impressive! Man may seem frail and impotent as compared to Lucifer, a ruling archangel. Still, humankind was a special creation by God. The Lord created Adam in God's image. Man is given complete authority over everything:

- Adam is in likeness of God: 'Let Us make man in Our image, according to Our likeness.' [Gen. 1:26]

- Of Adam it is said: 'Yahweh [HEB LORD] God formed man from the dust of the ground, and [*God*] **breathed into his nostrils the breath of life**; and **man became a living soul**.' [Gen. 2:7 WEB]

- Adam was given complete rule over created things: 'let them [man and woman] rule over the fish of the sea and over the birds of the sky and over the cattle and over all the earth, and over every creeping thing that creeps on the earth.' [Gen. 1:26]

99

- Unlike Lucifer, Adam was given a mate: 'Then the LORD God said, "It is not good for the man to be alone; I will make him a helper suitable for him.' Gen. 2:18

- Adam and Eve are created in the image of God: 'So God created man in his *own* image, in the image of God created he him; <u>male</u> and <u>female</u> **created *He* them**.' Gen. 1:27 KJV

- God put forth a blessing upon Adam and Eve: 'And God blessed them, and God said unto them -' Gen. 1:28 KJV

- Adam and Eve were given the power and authority to procreate after Adam's kind, populate the whole earth: 'Be fruitful, and multiply, and replenish the earth.' Gen. 1:28 KJV

- Adam and Eve were given total authority which the Bible says: 'subdue it: and have dominion over the fish of the sea, and over the fowl of the air, and over every living thing that *moves* upon the earth.' Gen. 1:28 KJV

- Everything belonged to Adam and Eve: 'Behold, I have given you every plant yielding seed that is on the surface of all the earth, and every tree which has fruit yielding seed; it shall be food for you; 30 and to every beast of the earth and to every bird of the sky and to everything that moves on the earth which has life, *I have given* every green plant for food; and it was so.' Gen. 1:29, 30

- Adam was given authority to name every animal: 'Out of the ground the LORD God formed every beast of the field and every bird of the sky, and brought *them* to the man to see what he would call them; and whatever the man called a living creature, that was its name. The man gave names to all the cattle, and to the birds of the sky, and to every beast of the field, but for Adam there was not found a helper suitable for him.' Gen. 2:19, 20

- Adam's authority is summed up by King David with a possibility that may even include the entire creation, the entire universe- outer space:
  'When I consider Your heavens, the work of Your fingers, The **moon** and the **stars,** which You have ordained; 4What is man that You take thought of him, And the son of man that You care for him? 5Yet You have made him a little lower than God [*angels*, KJV], And You crown him with glory and majesty! 6You **make him to rule over the works of Your hands**; You have **put all things under his feet**, 7All sheep and oxen, And also the beasts of the field, 8The birds of the heavens and the fish of

the sea, Whatever passes through the paths of the seas. [9]O LORD, our Lord, How majestic is Your name **in all the earth!**' (Psa. 8:3-9)

[d]Note: King David description of man authority may imply even through the entire universe though the focal point is the earth.

I think initially, as humans, we do not fully realize the significance of the creation of mankind and mankind's God given ability endowed by man's Creator, which angels apparent do not possess. For example, Gen.11 at tower of Babel God said,

And the LORD said, "Look, they are one people, and they have all one language; and this is only the beginning of what they will do; **nothing that they propose to do will now be impossible** for them."

(Gen. 11:6 NRS)

Lucifer perhaps thought as God had made man that humans appeared inferior. Hence, Lucifer may have thought man was *weak, frail, feeble, fragile,* and insignificant compare an archangel with power and glory. As archangel (a ruling angel), Lucifer had many angels under his command. Then Ezekiel reveals this imagined which is likely a reference to Lucifer and his downfall.

"Son of man, take up a lamentation over the king of Tyre and say to him, 'Thus says the Lord GOD, "You had the seal of perfection, Full of wisdom and perfect in beauty. [13]**"You were in Eden, the garden of God**; Every precious stone was your covering: The ruby, the topaz and the diamond; The beryl, the onyx and the jasper; The lapis lazuli, the turquoise and the emerald; And the gold, the workmanship of your settings and sockets, Was in you. **On the day that you were created** They were prepared. [14]**"You were the anointed cherub** who covers, And I placed you *there*. You were on the holy mountain of God; You walked in the midst of the stones of fire. [15]**"You were blameless in your ways From the day you were created Until unrighteousness was found in you.** [16]**"**By the abundance of your trade You were internally filled with violence, And **you sinned**; Therefore **I have cast you as profane From the mountain of God.** And **I have destroyed you, O covering cherub,** From the midst of the stones of fire. (Ezek. 28:12-16)

Revelation may be hinting that Lucifer swept one-third of angels to follow him in his rebellion, see [Rev. 12:4]. All angels were holy and godly, but some of angels (one/third?) may have rebelled. Apparently, the rebellion of angels, though initially goodness and righteous, were stripped of all holiness and righteousness from God. Hence, all these fallen angels became pure evil and completely void of any redeeming value. The evil angels became totally worthless.

Hell was prepared for the angels that sinned.[Matt. 25:41] However, it seems evident most angels which sinned were willing to *"toe the line"*[4] (strictly obey the rules even though these angels sinned.) Therefore, the fallen angels were permitted limited amount of freedom to move and roam. However, it seems some other fallen angels refused to toe the line, which the Lord knew which evil angels that **would not** obey God's established limitations. Therefore, those evil angels that refuse to obey, those evil angels had to be imprisoned.

> And the angels who did not stay within their own domain but abandoned their proper dwelling—these He has kept in eternal chains under darkness, bound for judgment on that great day.   (Jude 1:6 MSB)

Lucifer and other fallen angels were given limited liberty. Still, no angels could make any movement or actions of any kind without direct permission from God. (Yet, with such limited movement by evil angels, this was to demonstrate that nothing in all creation cannot frustrate, alter, or hinder God plan for His creation.)

Job reveals the fallen have limited access even into the present of God.[Job 1:6; 2:1] God Himself or His abode of **Heaven cannot be corrupted**, **profaned**, or **tempted** since God and His angels are absolutely holy and righteous. "God cannot be tempted by evil, and He Himself does not tempt anyone."[James 1:13]

I have conclusively demonstrated cohabitation of angels and humankind is impossible to have occurred. The context in Gen.6 says nothing concerning angels. Yes, Jude refers angels fall of angels and even some were confined. There is no clear and conclusive evidence a so-called second breach by angels anywhere in Scripture. I say again, "A second breach or a second rebellion by angels is unconscionable."

It is even more convoluted that since the so-called breach by angels, "There is no evidence of second breach by angels *'holy* or *evil angels*?'" The Lord our God rules and completely governs all things accord to His holy and righteous will.[Rom. 11:33-36; Eph. 3:11] Yeah, the Bible says that God works all things "according to the purpose of Him who works all things according to the counsel of His will."[Eph. 1:11 NKJ Also see Rom. 8:28.]

Conclusion

I have taken time to clearly declare the error of a second breach by angels. The Scriptures are explicitly and conclusively clear. There was **no** second rebellion of angels that sinned and supposedly cohabited with human. The context of Gen. 6 does not allow such nonsense. However, tradition, pagan influence, carnal nature of man, the world, and the demonic forces caused people to give into the most preposterous and monsters lies. That is, there was allegedly a second breach by angels, and these angels cohabited with women. Then further stretch the lie and it even alleges spirit being and humans had offspring, which were freaks: half-human and half-spirit-beings. Here is the *kicker*: *all died in the flood.* Yet, we read, "And there we saw the giants, the sons of Anak, *which come* of the giants[HEB *Nephilim*]: and we were in our own sight as grasshoppers, and so we were in their sight."Num. 13:33 KJV If everyone died in the flood that was not in ark of Noah, there would not giants. Nephilim people that were very large, and this is why read of Nephilim in Numbers 13.

Even if the meaning that the offspring of angels and humans were mutation or freaks, why do we not see any more "*giants*." The HEB word Nephilim actually refers to people that are large in size or statue. The meaning is not some freak. Perish the taught. Friend, do not let tradition override the explicit and clear teaching of Scripture. Let us remain focused that Scripture inherently interprets Scripture. The Bible has the final say not tradition nor church dogma.

God bless those who live by the rule:

"The Word God stands on its own inherent authority, and the Scripture cannot be broken!" Hallelujah and glory to God forever and ever. Amen.

Footnote:

1. *Springboard* approach: the regular meaning refers a device where a person may *spring off a board* into the water. Metaphorically, *springboard* approach in preaching is where someone speaks on a particular topic but without any regards to the context of the reference. The text was only used to initially launch or *springboard* their message.

2. *Pretext*: "A pretext (adj.: *pretextual*) is an excuse to do something or say something that is not accurate. Pretexts may be based on a half-truth or developed in the context of a misleading fabrication. Pretexts have been used to conceal the true purpose or rationale behind actions and words. They are often heard in political speeches." Wikipedia Free Encyclopedia:https://en.wikipedia.org/wiki/Pretext

3. "Bore children:" the HEB (*yalad*) meaning give birth. The word 'bore', means "*to beget*" or "*to become the father*." However, "*children*" or "*offspring*" in Gen. 6:4 is the connotative implication.

4. *Toe the line*: "to do what you are <u>expected</u> to do without <u>causing</u> <u>trouble</u> for anyone." Cambridge Dictionary,

    https://dictionary.cambridge.org/us/dictionary/english/toe-the-line#google_vignette

CHAPTER 7

The fall of angels

(Consequences of sin against a Holy God)

Memory verse

For if God did not spare angels when they sinned, but cast them into hell[a] and committed them to pits of darkness, reserved for judgment-

(2 Peter 2:4)

[a]Note: hell is GK *tartaroo*. According to some, this is the word for the confinement for evil angels; *Tartarus* in ENG. This is not the Lake of Fire. The Lake of Fire is the final abode for all wicked angel and unregenerate. [Heb. 2:14-17].

Introduction

As we have already seen, *tradition* (whether long or short) seeks to rewrites biblical doctrine. In addition, even church *history* and *customs* (culture) within ethnic background may override or even pervert the plain teaching of Scripture. What many people are unaware that fallen humanity's psychic or mind is unfortunately very warps and distorts as to what he thinks he sees, hears, feels, and even smells.

Due to crippling effect within fallen man, we ought to be amazed if any accurate communication is actually achieved. Accurate communication is even less likely in the amidst of any form of hostility or strong negativism. For example, words become very distorted or misinterpreted when hostility or bitterness exists between people or even nations. As fallen humanity, we tend to "*re-filter*" or "*reinterprets*" what another said. We reinterpret people's words without realizing we are doing it.

"You don't believe it?" Well, psychiatrists, psychologists, and sociologists have known for some time that we as humans tend to *re-filter* things we see, hear, feel, think, and yes even smell.

For instance, a person might listen to something or an idea that they have negative feelings or strongly oppose. Yet, even if they like or affirm the person speaking or they are listening to, they distort the message. Amazingly and unbelievably, a person will inadvertently and unconsciously *reinterpret* what they hear very favorably even though they disagree with the conclusion. How crazy is that? The human mind just changes or *reinterprets* the meaning in a favorable light since they look very favorably upon the person speaking.

Conversely, a person who has strong negative feelings or thoughts against another person, as they listen to them speaking, their mind will also *reinterpret* the speaker's words very negatively even though they generally agree on the issue. Our minds change what we hear even when person actually fully agrees with the speaker. How warped is that? This just shows the wickedness of the human heart which we tend to deny concerning ourselves.

Well, I have sought to show the misunderstanding of the teaching in Gen. 6:1-4. Gen. 6 is not teaching that the "sons of God" are angels. This is serious error fostered by tradition, ecclesiastical doctrine, noncanonical books on the Bible, and even pagan influences. There is nothing in the ^Gen. 6 text concerning a second breach by angels. Angels are spirit beings. Angels do not procreate. The phrase "sons of God" refers either to the godly (e.g. line of Seth) or mighty or powerful men.

Now, we come to Jude who says,

> And the angels which kept not their first estate, but [sinned] left their own habitation, he [God] has reserved [the evil angels into] in everlasting chains under darkness unto the judgment of the great day. (Jude 1:6 KJV)

We read once again in OT,

> And it came to pass, when men [HEB *adam*, human beings] began to multiply on the face of the earth, and daughters were born unto them, ²That the sons of God [HEB ben Elohim] saw the daughters of men [human beings] that they *were* fair; and they took them wives of all which they chose. ³And the LORD said, **My spirit shall not always strive WITH MAN** [adam, human beings], for that he [man] also *IS* **FLESH**: yet his days shall be *a hundred* and twenty years. ⁴There were giants [HEB *nephilim*, giant people] in the earth in those days; and also after that, when the sons of God came in unto the daughters of

men, and they *bore children* to them, the same *became* mighty **MEN** which *were* of old, **MEN** of renown.   (Gen. 6:1-4 KJV)

Who are then the *"sons of God"* in Gen. 6?

As we noted previously, there are three basic views or interpretations. Many people are strongly influenced by *tradition, customs, church history, non-biblical writing,* and *pagan religions* handed down over generations. Here again are three basic interpretations of Gen. 6:

1. *The sons of God are* fallen angels that sinned.

2. *The sons of God are* the sons Seth that married ungodly (unbelieving women.)

3. *The sons of God are* men who viewed themselves as sons of God by their power or greatness.

Unfortunately, the predominate interpretation that still lingers is that *"the sons of God"* are angels. Wrong! Let us get a brief overview to summarize the issue to conclude Jude's statement on angels.

A. Angels that fell into sin

The general opinion concerning Gen. 6:1-4 has given way to tradition, church history, non-canonical books of the Bible, and even pagan religions. That is, the *sons of God* are supposedly evil angels, or even worse, these holy angels that breach with second rebellion. These are allegedly fallen angels that sinned and cohabited with human women. The problem here (as I have said) is that this interpretation is based on outside non-biblical writings. It is indeed dangerous to rely on tradition to build Bible dogma on outside sources rather than using the Bible as the primary source. Using outside sources rather than the Bible as the primary source of interpretation is seriously flawed.

The underlining premise seems to suggest there was a second breach by angels. That is, evil angels rebelled a second time. Even worse, there is also an inference that holy angel sinned or breached a second time. Such premise brings into question the sovereignty of God and His rule over His creation. (The interpretation is vague as to whether second breach were initially by holy or evil angels). I do not see anything in Gen. 6 that indicates that angels were involved in an intermarriage or cohabitation with the daughters of human women.

Where is the judgment upon angels in Gen. 6 if there is a breach by angels? There is nothing said concerning a judgment upon angels in the context. The fact is there is the omission of angels in the text. Where is the supposed cohabitation of angels and human women mentioned in the text? Where is there any concrete statement of a second breach by angels? Where in the text is implying a second rebellion by angels? A second breach by angels is unconscionable to me. In addition, the angels that had supposedly sinned, were they holy or evil angels? Whether holy or evil angels, there is nothing said against angels in the judgment in Gen. 6. So, how can there be a second breach by angels, but there is no judgment made upon angels for such a breach?

The interpretation gives way to tradition, going outside Scripture to supersede or have authority over God's explicit Word. Our Lord Jesus warns of such practices by the Pharisees.

> [*You Pharisees*] "- invalidating the word of God by your tradition which you have handed down; and you do many things such as that." (Mark 7:13)

Similarly, many follow the Roman Church that admits to using _oral_ or _written_ _tradition_ to establish their interpretation or doctrine. Thus, making Scripture subservient to tradition or manmade religions rather than allowing Scripture's inherent interpretation have the final meaning. So, in one breathe such above religions claim to believe all of Scripture, but in practice and in the next breathe there is the denial of the clear and unadulterated written Word of God. Thus, they conveniently set-aside the Word of God for the sake of their tradition. How wicked is that?

Biblically examining the meaning of "son of God"

The term in HEB is "*ben elohim:*" The etymology of the word "_elohim_" basically meant mighty or powerful. Hence, God is mighty or all powerful. Later, word _elohim_ was applied to God. Yet, _elohim_ is used to mean other things. For instance, _elohim_ is used of kings, rulers, judges, demons, angels, and strong people. Hence, _elohim_ can just refer to mighty or powerful people. The psalmist uses _elohim_ as a pun on the rules or judges. Even though word _elohim_ also refers to God of the Bible, the word was used in reference people. Note once again,

> They do not know nor do they understand; They walk about in darkness; All the foundations of the earth are shaken. [6]I said, "You are gods [HEB _elohim_], And all of you are sons [HEB _ben, sons_][b] of the Most High [*name for God*]. [7]"Nevertheless you will die like men And fall like *any* one of the princes." [8]Arise, O God, judge the earth! For it is You who possesses [b] all the nations. [e.g. *the universe belongs to the LORD and not fallen man*]   (Psa. 82:5-8)

ᵇThe HEB is explicit and definitive meaning "*son;*" the meaning is not *children.* "*Possesses,*" the connotation is better understood as the universe *belongs* to or *owned* by the Lord as given by NET and NRS.

Jesus quotes the above Psalm in John 10:30-34. But listen carefully my friend, humanity will never be "*a god.*" Erase this wicked thought from your mind forever! People at times may excise authoritative rule and power and even imagine themselves as though he/she is "*a god.*" There are those today claiming Evangelicalism or Fundamentalism. In their spiritual ignorance, they are worse than the Mormons, which allege they will be "*a god.*" Some Pentecostals and Charismatics are claiming to be *gods.* This is a doctrine right out of Hell. This is total ignorance. This is indeed a blatant lie. Such evil thought goes back to the temptation of Eve by the devil. The devil said,

> And the serpent said unto the woman, Ye shall not surely die: For God doth know that in the day ye eat thereof, then your eyes shall be opened, and **YE SHALL BE AS GODS** [*elohim*], knowing good and evil.
>
> (Gen. 3:4, 5 KJV)

Jesus did not mean that the rulers in Israel were *gods.*^John 10:30-34 Our Lord was mocking the Pharisees. This was because the Pharisees' were deficient in knowing and understanding the Scripture. How much more ignorance today among some people who do not know the Word of God. Their interpretation is based on depraved and fallen human nature. For shame!

Do you recall that the Sadducees did not believe many things written in the Scripture as they asked Jesus a question on the resurrection. For instance, the Sadducees denied the resurrection. Yet, the Sadducees' question was out of mockery on the resurrection. Our Lord "*turns the table on them.*¹"

> ²³On that day some Sadducees, who say that there is no resurrection [of the dead], came to Him and asked Him a question, ²⁴saying, "Teacher, Moses said, 'IF A MAN DIES, LEAVING NO CHILDREN, HIS BROTHER AS NEXT OF KIN SHALL MARRY HIS WIDOW, AND RAISE CHILDREN FOR HIS BROTHER.' ²⁵Now there were seven brothers among us; the first married and died, and having no children left his wife to his brother. ²⁶The second also [died childless], and the third, down to the seventh. ²⁷Last of all, the woman died. ²⁸So in the resurrection, whose wife of the seven will she be? For they all had *married* her."
>
> ²⁹But Jesus replied to them, "You are all wrong because you know neither the Scriptures [which teach the resurrection] nor the power of

God [for He is able to raise the dead]. [30]For in the resurrection neither do *men* marry nor are *women* given in marriage, but they are like angels in heaven [who do not marry nor produce children]. [31]But as to the resurrection of the dead--have you not read [in the Scripture] what God said to you: [32]'I AM THE GOD OF ABRAHAM, AND THE GOD OF ISAAC, AND THE GOD OF JACOB'? He is not the God of the dead, but of the living.'" (Matt. 22:24-32 CEV)

Also, I need to say a word concerning the false doctrine of *soul sleep*. The above text cannot be any plainer. Abraham, Isaac, and Jacob are very much alive in Heaven. In fact, Jesus testifies He saw and knows Abraham:

[51]"Timeless truth I speak to you: whoever keeps my word [e.g. *who genuinely believes in Christ*] **SHALL NEVER SEE DEATH**." [52]The Jews were saying to him, "Now we know that a demon is in you; Abraham is dead and The Prophets, and you are saying, 'Whoever keeps my words shall never taste [c] death.'" [53]"Are you greater than our father Abraham who died and The Prophets who have died? Who are you making yourself?" [54]Yeshua said to them, "If I glorify Myself, My glory is nothing; it is my Father who glorifies me, he of whom you say, 'He is our God.' " [55]"And you do not know him, but I know him, and if I had said that I did not know him, I Myself would have been a liar like you, but I do know him and I keep his word [e.g. *obey and do His Word*]." [56]"Abraham your father desired to see my day, and he saw it[c] and rejoiced." [57]The Jews were saying to him, "You are not yet fifty years old, and you have seen Abraham?" [58]Yeshua said to them: "Timeless truth I speak to you: Before Abraham would exist, I AM THE LIVING GOD." (John 8:51-58 ABPE)

[c]Note: "*shall never taste*" [v 52], meaning Abraham was alive in Heaven in his soul. Abraham "saw it and rejoiced" [v 56], meaning Abraham immediately went to Heaven, which is expressed in a Hebrew culture at that time referred to as *Abraham's bosom*. No redeemed person goes to Hades: hades is the unseen world.

Abraham, like other men of genuine saving faith, they too are alive and in Heaven. This is the plain teaching of Scripture.

Now, as to the nature of angels, the angelic beings neither marry or are given in marriage. In the same way among the redeemed, in Heaven. As I have already said, there are no marriages. Each saint belongs to the Lord. (Even more on this topic later.) Angels are incapable of procreating. So, angels are unable to reproduce or procreate. Even the text in Gen. 6, which we have noted, does not refer to angels. (Gen. 6 text clearly does not include angels.) Get it right. The angelic host are **spirit being**. Angels are **not flesh and blood**. So, it is impossible for angels to procreate. Hence, there is no such thing as "a hybrid:" *half spirit being* and *half flesh and blood*. Such thinking is ludicrous to say angels cohabited with women and had offspring. This is sheer nonsense!

B. Angels abandon their position

Because of tradition, church history, and pagan influences, some still assume ^{Gen. 6:1-4} refers to angelic being cohabited with humans. This is one of most outrageous biblical eisegesis ever. Eisegesis[3]: the act of reading into the biblical text with one's own ideas, biases, or cultural lens.

The HEB word *nephilim* (Gen. 6:4) can mean *"giant."* Nevertheless, all the so-called *giants, nephilim,* died in the flood. Therefore, we should not find any *nephilim* after flood. Right? Hello! However, *nephilim* are mentioned in Numbers. So, who are the *nephilim* that are mentioned in Numbers? These were *giants (nephilim)* people very large in size.

> "There also we saw the Nephilim [KJV giants] (the sons of Anak are part of the Nephilim); and we became like grasshoppers in our own sight, and so we were in their sight." (Num. 13:33)

Only eight people survived the flood. These were Noah, his wife, his three sons, and his sons' wives. How can there be *nephilim* when everyone died in the flood? There were no survivors; all perished in the flood.

Hebrews Epistle clarifies that angels are *spirit beings*; angels are not flesh and blood like humans. This is clearly noted in the NRS. The NRS has given an excellent translation by giving intended or connotative meaning in this text.

> Are not all angels^d spirits [*beings*] in the divine service, sent to serve for the sake of those who are to inherit salvation? (Heb. 1:14 NRS)

> ^dNote: the phrase means, *"angelic* spirits are for service; that is, to assist those who are heirs of eternal life." The GK phrase is *"leitourgikos pneuma."* The phrase literally means: *"serving spirits"* or *"ministering spirits."* The context bears out the emphasis that angels assisting and helping those that are to heirs of eternal life in Christ.

Therefore, angels are "spirit beings." Remember, angels are not flesh and blood. Also, as we note earlier, angels are sexless being and incapable of procreating. Still, even if angels are capable of procreating (which angels are incapable of procreating), angels are *spirits* and *not flesh and blood*. Do angels possess genes like creatures of flesh? I do not know if angels possess genes. If angels have genes or not does, it does not matter. The reason it does not matter is *how could spirits genes* (if angels have genes) line up properly with human genes of flesh and blood to fertilize and impregnate human genes? Such union is contrary to the design of creation. *Everything reproduces itself according to its kind*. There is no way a monstrous mutation would occur.

In Genesis one, the Scripture is clear-cut that each thing created according to its own kind. Hence, each thing created reproduced itself **according to their kind**! In the design of creation, there are separate and distinct things in their design. The genes of one kind cannot line up and unit another entirely different kind. Can one unite plant life with an animal life? No! In the same way, how can spirit being unite with flesh and blood? Spirit and flesh and blood cannot unite to create so-call hybrid; this is impossible due design in creation.

Tradition is superseding Scripture as noted before,

> [*Jesus said of the Pharisees*] "So you nullify the [authority of the] word of God [acting as if it did not apply] because of your tradition which you have handed down [through the elders]. And you do many things such as that."   (Mark 7:13 AMP)

When did the angels fall into sin?

Allow me reiterate again Gen. 6:1-4. Gen. 6 says nothing concerning angels nor the fall of angels as I have repeatedly declared! The judgment is upon humans and humans only. If angels sinned in Gen. 6, why is there no judgment mentioned on angels in the text? There is no such judgment mentioned in Gen. 6. *Tradition has taken over* the plain teaching of Scripture. Patient, please look at it again,

> Now it came to pass, when **MEN began to multiply** on the face of the earth, and **daughters were born to them** [*to MEN*], [2]that the **sons of God saw the daughters of MEN**, that they *were* beautiful; and they took wives for themselves of all whom they chose. [3]And the LORD said, "**My Spirit shall not strive with MAN** forever, for **he** [MAN] *is* **indeed flesh**; yet his days shall be one hundred and twenty years." [4]There were giants [HEB, *nephilim*] on the earth in those days, and also afterward, when the sons of God came in to the daughters of **MEN** and they bore *children* to them. Those *were* the mighty **MEN**[e] who *were* of old, **MEN**[e] of renown.   (Gen. 6:1-4 NKJ)

> [e]Note: the word "*man*" does not appear in parts the HEB text, but in the context, man is definitely implied. So, brackets "[]" are used to clarify the wording.

The error here is assuming the phrase "sons of God" refer to angels. (As I have said, even worse, there is the suggestion that angels got out of control and sinned a second time). In addition, Satan appears in Job, but Satan is never viewed or referred to as *son of God* in his fallen state. Sons of God refer to those belonging to the Lord and not evil beings. Perish the thought.

> Now there was a day when the sons of God[f] came to present themselves before the LORD, and **Satan came ALSO among them**. (Job 1:6 KJV)

> [f]Note: there is nothing in the text that says Satan is a "son of God." Satan means an adversary; so, how can an adversary (enemy) be a *son of God*? Impossible!

The same expression is used in Job 2:1. As I have already pointed out in Gen. 6:1-4, the judgment is only on humanity. There is no mention concerning angelic beings in the judgment. If there was such horrific breach by angelic beings, where is it mentioned in the judgment in Gen. 6? If there was such a breach by angels that had to be confined to a prison, where is it in Genesis 6? There is nothing given in the text of Genesis 6.

Well, would you know, some have theorized that it is in the text below. Let us check out the supposed text, and you can read for yourself.

[4]For if God did not spare angels when they sinned, but cast them into hell[g] [GK *tartaroo*, lowest level of the underworld, CEB] and committed them to pits of darkness, reserved for judgment; [5]and did not spare the ancient world, but preserved Noah, a preacher of righteousness, with seven others, when He brought a flood upon the world of the ungodly; [6]and *if* He condemned the cities of Sodom and Gomorrah to destruction by reducing *them* to ashes, having made them an example to those who would live ungodly *lives* thereafter. (2 Peter 2:4-6)	[6]And angels who did not keep their own domain, but abandoned their proper abode, He has kept in eternal bonds under darkness for the judgment of the great day, [7]just as Sodom and Gomorrah and the cities around them, since they in the <u>same way as these</u>** <u>indulged</u> in gross immorality and went after strange flesh, are exhibited as an example in undergoing the punishment of eternal fire. [see asterisks **] (Jude 1:6, 7 NAS 1995)

[g]Note: "hell," 'netherworld;' '--to be confined in Tartarus', held by many in the ancient world to be a place of torment hold in Tartarus 2 Peter 2:4. Danker, *Greek NT Lexicon;* from Bible Works 10.

** Most unfortunately, the NAS of 2020 and NET add the word "*angels*" in Jude 1:7 which is not in GK text:

ASV, 1901	NAS, 1977	NAS, 1995	NAS, 2020
And angels that kept not their own principality, but left their proper habitation, he hath kept in everlasting bonds under darkness unto the judgment of the great day. [7]Even as Sodom and Gomorrah, and the cities about them, having in like manner with these ** given themselves over to fornication and gone after strange flesh, are set forth as an example, suffering the punishment of eternal fire.	And angels who did not keep their own domain, but abandoned their proper abode, He has kept in eternal bonds under darkness for the judgment of the great day. [7]Just as Sodom and Gomorrah and the cities around them, since they in the same way as these ** indulged in gross immorality and went after strange flesh, are exhibited as an example, in undergoing the punishment of eternal fire.	And angels who did not keep their own domain, but abandoned their proper abode, He has kept in eternal bonds under darkness for the judgment of the great day, [7]just as Sodom and Gomorrah and the cities around them, since they in the same way as these ** indulged in gross immorality and went after strange flesh, are exhibited as an example in undergoing the punishment of eternal fire.	And angels who did not keep their own domain but abandoned their proper dwelling place, *these* He has kept in eternal restraints under darkness for the judgment of the great day, [7]just as Sodom and Gomorrah and the cities around them, since they in the same way as these ***angels*** indulged in sexual perversion and went after strange flesh, are exhibited as an example in undergoing the punishment of eternal fire.

** The double asterisk (**) shown the word "*angels*" does not appear in the GK text in Jude 1:7. This is an insertion by the translator.

The 2020 NAS and NET (and a few other translations) add the word "*angels*" in verse 7. However, "*angels*" is not in the GK text. Whether the NAS 2020 and NET are implying a reference to Gen. 6, is questionable. I think the added word "*angels*" is unwarranted. What do you think? There is no basis for the added word "*angels*" in Jude 1:7.

In the above texts in Gen. 6, there is nothing declaring angels sinned during Noah's day. The argument put forth that there was a second breach by angels in cohabiting with daughters of man is preposterous. As I have already said that a second breach by evil (or holy) angels is unconscionable and unthinkable. A second breach by angels brings to question the sovereignty of God. The Lord knew which angels would initially refuse to obey His commands in angels' initial fall. So, the Lord in the initial fall of angels had to confine certain angels. Here again, the text in Genesis 6 says nothing about angels. If angels sinned in Gen 6, why is the judgment just upon all humankind and nothing mentioned concerning angels sinning?

Neither Jude or Peter says when the angels sinned. It is only incorrectly assumed in the days of Noah.[2 Peter 2:5] The thoughts are not interwoven, but the thoughts are definitely separate and distinct. Peter refers to three judgments: angels [v 4]; Noah and the flood [v 5]; Sodom, Gomorrah, and surround cities [v 6]. The texts do not establish a second breach by angels.

C. God has kept some angels in spiritual-chains

In the initial rebellion of angels shortly following creation of man, perhaps some angels would have probably continued to transgress the limited restriction by God and rebel. Therefore, God confined those angels that refuse *toe the line*. However, to suggest a second breach by angels does not fit the divine design and sovereign rule of God over His creation. (Perhaps some peoples' God is too small!) Also, Satan was not foolish enough to not obey the Lord's limited parameters over them. Otherwise, Satan would have been confined in like manner.

Please keep in mind that angels, like humankind and all living creature, are extremely finite and totally dependent on God to exist. Even in Hell everything exists at the mercy of God. Everything that lives and breathes is confined to a creation by the Lord. The Lord is the only One that exist in or outside His creation. As the apostle Paul said,

> "For in him [*the Lord God*] **we live** and **move about** and **exist**, as even some of your own poets have said, 'For we too are his offspring[g].'"
>
> (Acts 17:28 NET)

[g]Note: word "*offspring*" or "*children*" is the GK "*genos*," but connotative implying "*created beings*."

We know in Job 1 and 2, Satan first had to be given permission to test Job. Satan could not test Job without permission by God. So, Satan had to be very careful to obey God's directive concerning the testing of Job. Satan knew disobeying God was futile. (Some do not realize this truth today.)

Satan is a created creature. He is finite and limited by God like all creatures. Yet, seemingly, some evil angels apparently overstepped their boundaries God established for angels that sinned. (This is the same as fools imagine they are "*gods*" or "shall be "*gods*.") God is sovereign in His rule.[Eph. 1:11] Satan was not stupid or foolish enough continue his open rebellion once he and the angels that followed him were giving strict limits by God. So, Satan was permitted to continue to deceive humankind, but he remains totally under the control and authority and power of God. Nevertheless, some angels that initially sinned seemingly went beyond the limits and had to be confined.

The same today, people that go too far in rebellion and wickedness, God will take their life or the person will wish God had taken their life. (Political leaders go too far like Nebuchadnezzar or Hitler in our day, God will kill them.) God sets the limit to how far a person or nation can live wickedly before God will judge them.

So then, some evil angels seemingly overstepped their bounds when angels initially sinned. Those evil angels went too far in the initial rebellion and had to be confined until the Judgment. The same today: some saints go too far in their sin or rebellion, and the Lord takes their life. Other saints' sin is so grievous God will take their life. Some saint are no judge immediately; their judgment follow them later [1 Tim. 5:24]. However, there may be some of these evil angels that are confined that may be unleashed near our Lord's Second Coming to earth. When these angels that are confined are released, this shall be a very terrifying ordeal for humankind but especially for unbelievers.

> Then the fifth angel sounded: And I saw a star fallen from heaven to the earth. To him was given the key to the bottomless pit. [2] And he opened the bottomless pit, and smoke arose out of the pit like the smoke of a great furnace. So the sun and the air were darkened because of the smoke of the pit. [3]Then out of the smoke locusts came upon the earth. And to them was given power, as the scorpions of the earth have power. [4]They were commanded not to harm the grass of the earth, or any green thing, or any tree, but only those men who do not have the seal of God on their foreheads. [5]And they were not given *authority* to kill them, but to torment them *for* five months. Their torment *was* like the torment of a scorpion when it strikes a man. [6]In those days men will seek death and will not find it; they will desire to die, and death will flee from them.
>
> (Rev. 9:1-6 NKJ)

When the evil angels were confined to prison, there is nothing said about when these evil angels sinned. As I have already said, alleging there was a so-called second breach by angels in Gen. 6 is unconscionable. Listen, there is nothing in text saying angels sinned Gen. 6. It is troubling to me that there are some that endorse this theory based upon tradition. Worse, some just follow others: *monkey see, monkey do*. So, based upon theory, some maintain there was a second breach. Some even use non-canonical writings to support their ungodly theory. Paul warns against such practices using non-canonical writing. [See Titus 1:14; 1 Tim. 1:4; 4:7; 2 Tim. 4:3, 4.] The apostle warns us not to given into such myths, but people still do it.

³As I urged you when I was on my way to Macedonia, stay on at Ephesus so that you may instruct certain individuals not to teach any different doctrines, ⁴**nor to pay attention to legends (fables,** ^[Jewish] **myths**) and endless genealogies, which give rise to **useless speculation** *and* meaningless arguments rather than advancing God's program *of instruction* which is grounded in faith [and requires surrendering the entire self to God in absolute trust and confidence]. ⁵But the goal of our instruction is love [which springs] from a pure heart and a good conscience and a sincere faith. ⁶Some individuals have wandered away from these things into empty arguments *and* useless discussions, ⁷wanting to be teachers of the Law [of Moses], even though they do not understand the terms they use or the subjects about which they make [such] confident declarations.   (1 Tim. 1:3-7 AMP)

Again the apostle warns of giving heed to Jewish myths,

¹³That testimony is true. For this reason rebuke them sharply, so that they may become sound in the faith, ¹⁴**not paying attention to Jewish myths** or to commandments of those who reject the truth. ¹⁵To the pure all things are pure, but to the corrupt and unbelieving nothing is pure. Their very minds and consciences are corrupted. ¹⁶They profess to know God, but they deny him by their actions. They are detestable, disobedient, unfit for any good work.

(Titus 1:13-16 NRS)

Some evil angels were confined to prison that is a fact. However, there is no evidence that there was a second breach by evil (or holy) angels. Some evil angels were permitted a certain amount of autonomy. Nevertheless, all evil angels were expected to fully obey or else suffer confinement in prison. However, there are no clear texts of Scripture confirming a second breach by angels and certainly not even in Gen 6. Tradition has superseded Scripture here. Scripture has the last word and not tradition.

Therefore, I find no conclusive evidence of second breach by angels. The evil angels breach or sinned only once. A second breach by angels (whether evil or holy angels) brings to question the sovereignty God.

Cohabitation by angels does not fit what Jesus taught on angels, and He has the final word on the subject. There is no conclusive evidence in Scripture of a second fall of angels or cohabiting with women. Biologically, spirit beings such angels and human of flesh and blood goes against the design of creation:

117

each reproduce according to their kind. However, angels do not reproduce or procreate. Angels are sexless creation.

Yes, some angels had to be confined or placed in confinement or prison. Yet, other evil angels were granted limited freedom and allowed a certain access to tempt humans. I think it is wiser to void using tradition or non-canonical writing to support one's biblical interpretations.

There is tradition as well as pagan religions that may suggest there was a second breach. However, I do not look to tradition or pagan religions to establish Scripture's interpretation. Scripture stands on its own inherent authority and interpretation. Is not Jesus' teaching against tradition's influence sufficient?

Conclusion

The phrase "sons of God" is used of the redeemed of men and women. "Sons of God" is used of holy angels. "Sons of God" is used of rulers or judges in Israel in mocking manner.[Psa. 82] I find no clear evidence that Satan or any fallen angels are referred as *sons of God*. Satan means adversary! So, how can an adversary of God be called "son of God"? Sons of God refers to those beings (human or angelic) that belong to the Lord. "Sons of God" is never used of fallen angels.

Even if evil angels cohabited in Gen. 6 (which is ludicrous), all the so-called offspring died out in the flood during the flood in Noah's day. So, how is that we find Nephilim (giants in the land) as in Num. 13:33? There were definite *giant*-like people as there are today. There are races that were apparently large in stature or size.

Scripture must have priority over tradition and certainly over pagan religions. I warn you and say again that I think it is very dangerous to use non-canonical material to establish any dogma. Some saints fail to connect Paul's warning "not to giving heed to Jewish myths." How can anyone give heed to such matters and especially when we are explicitly told don't do it? When we look to outside sources other than the Bible, we are superseding God's Word with tradition and even pagan sources. I think one problem is that people give too much attention to unreliable sources for truth. Even worse, some ecclesiastical bodies actually base their theology on tradition and outside non-canonical writings and supersede the authority of Scripture. The Bible must always be our primary source and not tradition or pagan religions.

Footnotes

1. *Turning the tables*: "If you **turn the tables** on someone, you change the situation completely, so that instead of **them** causing problems for you, you are causing problems for **them**." Collins Dictionary online:
https://www.collinsdictionary.com/us/dictionary/english/turn-the-tables#google_vignette

2. Sadducees and their doctrines.[Matt. 22:23-32] Let us clearly understand that Sadducees did **not** believe all of the Scriptures, and they had a humanistic view of the Bible. Sadducees were in some respects like the liberal element in church today. Some people profess faith in Christ. Yet ironically, at the same time, they actually deny cardinal doctrines of the Bible. The Pharisees believe the Scriptures.[Acts 23:8] There are three errors here by the Sadducees in [Matt. 22:23-32]. First error, there is no cohabitation in Heaven (no one is married in Heaven). Second error, the redeemed will not be angels. The saved in Christ will **not** be made angels. The Lord has already created all the angels He desired and needed. The point here is that the redeemed shall be unmarried; they will be celibate. The reason, we belong to the Lord. This is why the Bible refers to His redeemed as *"son," "wife,"* or *"bride;"* the redeemed have an intimate and personal communion with God. Third error, the dead are very much alive at death and in Heaven.[2 Cor. 5:8; Phi. 1:21-23] The resurrection is in reference to the transformation of the body.[1 Cor. 15:51-56]

3. "Eisegesis:" the word eisegesis means *reading into the text a person's own interpretation* rather than reading out the intended meaning given by the author. We need to practice "exegesis:" *read out of the Scriptures the intended and inherit meaning* of the biblical authors. This is sometimes referred to as the Historical and Grammatical Interpretation.

CHAPTER 8

Judgment upon Sodom, Gomorrah, and surrounding cities

Memory verse

He [*God*] condemned the cities of Sodom and Gomorrah to destruction by reducing *them* to ashes, having made them an example to those who would live ungodly *lives* thereafter   (2 Peter 2:6)

Introduction

The judgment of God upon Sodom, Gomorrah, and surrounding cities was indeed etched in history for time and memorial. The judgment fell upon Sodom and surrounding cities over five millenniums ago. The judgment was so severe that the area is still a wasteland. There is nothing that grows in that land to this very day.

> "And Lot lifted up his eyes and **saw all the valley of the Jordan, that it was well watered everywhere--** *this was* before the LORD destroyed Sodom and Gomorrah— **like the garden of the LORD —**"
>
> (Gen. 13:10)

Other than the judgment by God by the global flood in the day of Noah, there is no parallel or equal to the judgment upon Sodom, Gomorrah, and surrounding cities. The very name, "*sodomy*" exist to nearly every language. The word "*sodomy*" refers to the sexual perversion occurred in Sodom and Gomorrah, but the word still carries the same general meaning of wicked-ness occurring today. Shockingly nowadays, there are Pastors and teachers defending Sodom and Gomorrah. Unbelievable! These misguided and ill-fit teachers allege Sodom's and Gomorrah's sin was against the poor, according to the prophet Ezekiel, [Ezek. 16:48ff.] This is beyond ignorance; this is being *brain-dead.*

Wrong! Ezekiel the prophet is referring to Jerusalem (the capital of Judah and Samaria capital of Israel [10 tribes] as metaphors.) Ezekiel is **not** referring to literally Sodom and Gomorrah, the valley of the Jordan. Ezekiel is using a derogatory metaphor upon Judah and Israel.[e.g. Isa. 1:8; Rev. 11:10] The sin of Sodom, Gomorrah, and surrounding cities was an outrage against evil and grotesque sexual immorality of every kind. Read Genesis 19 carefully!

The sexual and immoral acts were borne out by the context:

> Before they had gone to bed [Lot, family, and angelic visitors], all the men from every part of the city of Sodom— both young and old— surrounded the house. They called to Lot, "Where are the men who came to you tonight? Bring them out to us so that we can have sex with them."
>
> (Gen. 19:4, 5 NIV)

Lot was even going send his two daughters out to the wicked men to spare his visitors of such evil.

> But Lot went out to them at the doorway, and shut the door behind him, and said, "Please, my brothers, do not act wickedly. Now behold, I have two daughters who have not had relations with man; please let me bring them out to you, and do to them whatever you like; only do nothing to these men, inasmuch as they have come under the shelter of my roof."
>
> (vv 6-8)

> "Out of our way!" they cried, and This man came to live here as a foreigner, and now he dares to judge us! We'll do more harm to you than to them!" They kept pressing in on Lot until they were close enough to break down the door. (v 9) (Gen. 19:6-9 NET)

This does not sound like sin against the poor. This is wickedness out of control. And to think Lot was offering his two virgin daughters to ravage. Lot was indeed vexed or a tormented righteous soul.[2 Peter 2:8]

Please hear me and pay close attention. Sin, when it reaches its full, the Lord shall judge that people. Man is allowed to establish its boundaries or establish its territory and rule, but know this for certain that when any individual or any group of people goes too far into the depth of sin, the Lord will judge that people. They have made themselves ripe for the wrath of God.

Friend, the wrath of God may be closer today in our generation than anyone might think.

Israel was to depart from Egypt and return to possess the promise land, the land of the Amorites and the other nations in the land. Once the Amorites' and other nations' sin reached it limit set by God, those nations were ripe for judgment.

> But in the fourth generation they (Israel) shall come hither again: for **the iniquity of the Amorites *is* not yet full**.   (Gen. 15:16 KJV)

The Lord sets a limit to how far humankind can live in abhorrent wickedness before the Lord will bring judgment on that people in any given area. This is the same with global wickedness. Sin shall increase in the world to a given point; then, the Lord will execute His judgment upon the whole world in righteousness.

The judgment of God applies even more so to the saints. God's will indeed judge the saints first, and this is because the saints bear His name within us. The present churches are a stumbling block to the unbelievers due to its wickedness. Friend, when the saints refuse to repent and turn from their wicked ways, the Lord may indeed judge His people. The saints bear the name of the Lord, and when saints live wickedly, this causes a stumbling block before the unbelievers. Unfortunately, today the hearts of many saints have been harden by sin.[Heb. 3:12-14] Many saints are unable to endure or hear the Word for correction and discipline from the Lord. Many believers have turned a deaf ear. Their hearts have become like granite stone.

Living in the age of grace is not a license for sin. God's Word continually warns us that if you deliberately persist in sin, especially in rebellion to His Word, we shall not escape the judgment of God. If anyone is not judged when they continue to rebel and live wickedly in sin, then, they had better reexamine the genuineness of their faith in Christ.[Rom. 8:9; Heb. 12:8] Such a person may still be unregenerate, and they are unquestionable without the Holy Spirit and on the road to Hell.

Jude refers to such people as.

> These people are divisive, worldly, devoid of the [*Holy*] Spirit.
>
> (Jude 1:19 NET)

Anyone that does not possess the Holy Spirit is **not saved**, and they do not belong to Christ the Lord.

A. Sodom, Gomorrah, and their cities that indulge in gross immorality

Jude 1:6, 7 says,

KJV	ASV	NAS 2020	NET
And the angels which kept not their first estate, but left their own habitation, he hath reserved in everlasting chains under darkness unto the judgment of the great day. ⁷ Even as Sodom and *Gomorrah*, and the cities about them in like manner, **giving themselves over to fornication, and going after strange flesh**, are set forth for an example, suffering the vengeance of eternal fire.	And angels that kept not their own principality, but left their proper habitation, he hath kept in everlasting bonds under darkness unto the judgment of the great day. ⁷ Even as Sodom and Gomorrah, and the cities about them, having in like manner with **these given themselves over to fornication and gone after strange flesh**, are set forth as an example, suffering the punishment of eternal fire.	⁶ And angels who did not keep their own domain but abandoned their proper dwelling place, *these* He has kept in eternal restraints under darkness for the judgment of the great day, ⁷ just as Sodom and Gomorrah and the cities around them, since they in the same way as **these *ANGELS* indulged in sexual perversion** and went after strange flesh, are exhibited as an example in undergoing the punishment of eternal fire.	You also know that the angels who did not keep within their proper domain but abandoned their own place of residence, he has kept in eternal chains in utter darkness, locked up for the judgment of the great Day. ⁷ So also Sodom and Gomorrah and the neighboring towns, since they indulged in sexual immorality and pursued unnatural desire in a way **similar to these ANGELS, are now displayed as an example** by suffering the punishment of eternal fire.

As noted previously, there is no reference to angels in verse 7. Jude gives a quick snapshots or portraits of various wickednesses. The insertion of angels in verse 7 is unwarranted. I see nothing in the GK text that justifies the insertion of *angels* in the contexts. So, I must leave this issue of the word "*angels*" in verse 7 to GK scholars settle this issue. The insertion of the word "*angels*" is not justified.

Jude is using a *triad*¹ layout in his style of writing, and the thoughts are not interwoven. Jude is giving three separate examples to substantiate his point. (Jude use triads through his epistle.) A person is mistaken if they are seeking to connect or link angels in verse 6 and again verse 7. For me, the NSA 2020 and NET are excellent translations, but in this situation, I must strong object and disagree. There is nothing here to warrant the word "*angels*" in verse 7. Jude is simply using a *triad* in verses 5-7 in his thoughts without interweaving his thoughts.

Melchizedek was a righteous priest and king in that region around the general area. Melchizedek's rule was no doubt well known in the surrounding nations or so it seems reasonable to me.

Some have theorized that Melchizedek was preincarnate of Christ based upon Hebrews statement:

> He is without father or mother or genealogy, having neither beginning
> of days nor end of life, but resembling the Son of God he continues a
> priest forever.   (Heb. 7:6 ESV)

Hebrews is not referring to Christ in the above verse. Hebrews says, "resembling the Son of God." Meaning that Melchizedek was a "*type*" but not Christ. Some have even conjected that Melchizedek was the king of Jerusalem in the days Abraham. but there is no conclusive evidence to establish this as a fact.

Melchizedek was a priest of the Most High God, and as priest of God, he likely preached and thought against immorality such that went on in Sodom, Gomorrah, and surrounding cities. Unfortunately, the people turned a deaf ear to his preaching if those cities heard of his preaching and teaching. (A deaf ear: *the person adamantly refused to listen or give heed to the other person's exhortation.*)

In the early days, when cities were being established, cities were ruled by "city king." Nations as people or ethnic as tribes were not yet commonly established, or so, it seems to me. The division of the various nations begin in Gen. 10 and 11, and immediately following, Abraham is called in Gen. 12:1ff.)

Long before Melchizedek, there was also the fervent preaching by Noah.

> And God did not spare the ancient world—except for Noah and the
> seven others in his family. **Noah warned the world of God's righteous
> judgment**. So God protected Noah when he destroyed the world of
> ungodly people with a vast flood.   (2 Peter 2:5 NLT)

God did not leave Himself without a witness. The flood in the days of Noah was God's judgment, but such judgment did change the wickedness of the human heart. Still, ancient history of people in many countries have knowledge of a global flood. This evidence of universal flood stands as witness to all humanity who wish to know the truth. Unfortunately and wretchedly, many so-called Evangelicals and even Fundamentalists deny a universal flood. How unconscionable is that?

So, we know that there was a global flood and not a local flood as some theorize. People wrote about the flood in the antiquity of human history. Mankind continues to rebel. Furthermore, mankind knew about God's judgment upon the world by a flood. Regrettably, humankind know about the judgment God and the flood, but even knowing about the flood, this did not cause mankind to fear God or repent and seek the Lord.

God calls Abraham out of paganism. Oh, but my friend, our father Abraham was "an *idolator*" like the rest of us, he was summed by God's grace and mercy. (Abraham was indeed a sinner like the rest of humankind.) Ezekiel uses metaphoric language to describe Abraham's and Sarah's call by God,

> [1]The word of the LORD came to me: [2]"Son of man, confront Jerusalem with her detestable practices [3]and say, 'This is what the Sovereign LORD says to Jerusalem: Your ancestry and birth were in the land of the Canaanites; your father was an Amorite and your mother a Hittite. [4]On the day you were born your cord was not cut, nor were you washed with water to make you clean, nor were you rubbed with salt or wrapped in cloths. [5]No one looked on you with pity or had compassion enough to do any of these things for you. Rather, you were thrown out into the open field, for on the day you were born you were despised [by people].
>
> (Ezek. 16:1-5 NIV)

Abraham married his sister Sarah, though Sarah had the same father as Abraham, she had a different mother,

> [*Abraham said to Abimelech*] yet indeed [*Sarah*] *she is* my sister; she *is* the daughter of my father, but not the daughter of my mother; and she became my wife. (Gen. 20:12 KJV)

The world in the days of Abraham was grossly wicked and seemingly maxed-out in idolatry. There was all kinds of violence and bloodshed. (Much like today!) Hello! It seems that violence was increasing. Apparently, people were made slaves by others. We know this because Abraham took his servants to rescue Lot and their two daughters out of slavery.[Gen. 14:14ff.]

The lesson we must learn and heed is that the Lord alone is God. There is no other God. Know for certain that the Lord rules His universe. Yeah, He rules this world! God's eyes cover all creation. Peter says,

> For the eyes of the Lord are on the righteous, and His ears are inclined to their prayer. But the face of the Lord is against those who do evil."
>
> (1 Peter 3:12 MSB)

Also, know for certain,

> Behold, the eyes of the Lord GOD *are* upon the sinful kingdom, and I
> will destroy it from off the face of the earth; saving that I will not utterly
> destroy the house of Jacob, saith the LORD.   (Amos 9:8 KJV)

My friend, if God's judgment falls upon Israel, then all the other peoples
of the world are *fair game* and the nations shall not escape His judgment! (By
fair game, everyone else is open for judgment.)

Eli the priest attempted to warn his sons and tell them that their sins will
bring judgment upon them, but his sons (like many in the churches today)
refused to listen and obey the Word of the Lord.

> If someone sins against another person, God can mediate for the guilty
> party. But if someone sins against the LORD, who can intercede?" But
> Eli's sons wouldn't listen to their father, for the LORD was already
> planning to put them to death.   (1 Sam. 2:25 NLT)

Let us be forever thankful for intercessory work of the Lord Jesus Christ
and the Holy Spirit when we pray. If we fail to pray, we also leave out the Holy
Spirit's and Christ the Lord's much needed intercessory work for us. The Holy
Spirit and the Son of God pray alongside us in our prayer.[Rom. 8:26-30]

Friend, we would do well to give earnest heed to the exhortation by the
Hebrews writer and his dreadful warning to every genuine believer in Christ
the Lord:

> [26]For if we deliberately keep on sinning after receiving the knowledge
> of the truth, no further sacrifice for sins is left for us, [27]but only a certain
> fearful expectation of judgment and a fury of fire that will consume
> God's enemies. [28]Someone who rejected the law of Moses was put to
> death without mercy on the testimony of two or three witnesses. [29]How
> much greater punishment do you think that person deserves who has
> contempt for the Son of God, and profanes the blood of the covenant
> that made him holy, and insults the Spirit of grace? [30]For we know the
> one who said, "Vengeance is mine, I will repay," and again, "The Lord
> will judge his people." [31]It is a terrifying thing to fall into the hands of
> the living God.   (Heb. 10:26-31 NET)

B. These indulged in even "going after strange flesh."

The NAS (2020), AMP (2003 & 2015), and LSB (2022 insert the word
"*angel*" in Jude 1:7. As noted earlier, I see **no** basis for the insert of the word
"*angels*."[Jude 1:5-7] Jude give separate and distinct thought as a triad as mentioned
earlier. I do **not** see any connection. The illustrates are separate and distinct.

Here it is again in Jude 1:5-7. This is the surrounding immediate context as given the NAS, NET, ESV, and NIV. There is no bases for the insertion of the word "angels" in verse 7.

NSA 2020	NET	ESV	NIV
[5]Now I want to remind you, though you know everything once *and* for all, that **the Lord**, after saving a people out of the land of Egypt, subsequently destroyed those who did not believe. [6]And angels who did not keep their own domain but abandoned their proper dwelling place, *these* He has kept in eternal restraints under darkness for the judgment of the great day, [7]just as Sodom and Gomorrah and the cities around them, since they in the same way as these **_angels_** indulged in sexual perversion and went after strange flesh, are exhibited as an example in undergoing the punishment of eternal fire.	Now I desire to remind you (even though you have been fully informed of these facts once for all) that **Jesus**, having saved the people out of the land of Egypt, later destroyed those who did not believe. [6]You also know that the angels who did not keep within their proper domain but abandoned their own place of residence, he has kept in eternal chains in utter darkness, locked up for the judgment of the great Day. [7]So also Sodom and Gomorrah and the neighboring towns, since they indulged in sexual immorality and pursued unnatural desire in a way similar to these **angels**, are now displayed as an example by suffering the punishment of eternal fire.	Now I want to remind you, although you once fully knew it, that **Jesus**, who saved a people out of the land of Egypt, afterward destroyed those who did not believe. [6]And the angels who did not stay within their own position of authority, but left their proper dwelling, he has kept in eternal chains under gloomy darkness until the judgment of the great day — [7]just as Sodom and Gomorrah and the surrounding cities, which likewise indulged in sexual immorality and pursued unnatural desire, serve as an example by undergoing a punishment of eternal fire.	Though you already know all this, I want to remind you that **the Lord** at one time delivered his people out of Egypt, but later destroyed those who did not believe. [6]And the angels who did not keep their positions of authority but abandoned their proper dwelling — these he has kept in darkness, bound with everlasting chains for judgment on the great Day. [7]In a similar way, Sodom and Gomorrah and the surrounding towns gave themselves up to sexual immorality and perversion. They serve as an example of those who suffer the punishment of eternal fire.

I certainly respect the NAS and NET and the other versions that add the word *angel* or *messenger* in Jude 1:7. Perhaps there is something in syntax in verse 7 I am missing. The LSV and the HCS also add the word *angel*, but I find no justification for the insertion *angel* or *messenger*. (*Messenger* is the meaning of *angel* in HEB and GK, and in LSV the word "messenger" is in brackets "[ ]".) Nevertheless, the word *angels* is omitted by ESV, NIV, and NRS in verse 7.

Why is sexual sin so severely judged? I suspect there are many reasons for the severity of God's judgment. (This is a question many have probably asked in their mind, but there are few unwillingly to openly put forth the question.) At any rate, allow me to share *five reasons* for the judgment of perversion of gross wickedness of sexual sins.

1. Sexual sins are against the design of the Creator.
2. Sexual sins are against a Holy and Righteous God.
3. Sexual sins are against the commandments of God.
4. Sexual sins can lead to the spread of diseases and death of a race.
5. Sexual sins are against humanity and lead to gross immorality and untold wickedness.

1. *Sexual sins are against the design of Creator.*

The Lord is the One that sets the standard and norm for His creation. Life exists at the mercy and will of God. *Man is dust, and to dust he shall return,* Gen. 3:19. Therefore, the chief purpose of all creation is:

> Let us hear the conclusion of the whole matter: **Fear God**, and **keep his commandments**: for this *is* the whole *duty* of man.   (Ecc. 12:13 KJV)

> And now, Israel, what doth the LORD thy God require of thee, but to **fear the LORD** thy God, to **walk in all his ways**, and to **love him**, and to **serve the LORD** thy God with all thy heart and with all thy soul,
>
> (Deut. 10:12 KJV)

As I have already said, every person can do whatever they want. Yet, know this, if one's sin is severe in God's eyes, then, God may indeed judge that person or nation. The Bible says that we should know this fact:

> But if you do not do so, behold, you have sinned against the LORD, and **be sure that your sin will find you out**.   (Num. 32:23)

Today the churches are in shambles and wickedness appears nearly everywhere. The church is a place where godliness and righteousness ought to be exhibited. Instead, there is wickedness and unbelief is everywhere. There is no calling for repentance. Shame on preachers today! The people in church have little or no fear of God today.

The churches are ripe for judgment. Again, hear me, "**The churches are ripe for judgment**." Only great and mighty spiritual awakening and revival with godly repentance will deliver the saints from God's awesome judgment. As the apostle concludes Romans one, he says,

> They know God's decree, that those who practice such things deserve
> to die—yet they not only do them but even applaud others who practice
> them.   (Rom. 1:32 NRS)

2. *Sexual sins are against a Holy and Righteous God.*

The Lord has established the standard! This standard is between husband
and wife, period! There is no other standard but the Lord's standard. When
the violation of God's standard is grossly and wickedly disregarded and mankind continues to rebel, knowingly or unknowingly, humankind have set themselves up for judgment by God.

Even the unlawful act of anarchy and revolt by a people against the government's rule can trigger judgment from God. United States was spared judgment because as a people we had no representative while under England. The
American Colonial Colony revolted. It was not because we were just people
(we are sinners like everyone else), it was unfair for England not to allow rep-
resentatives under colonial rule.

However, there were revolts in nations in which God seemingly may not
have judged. Why some nations are judged and other are seemingly not judged,
we must leave such a question rest in the merciful hands of God.

Israel's departure from Egypt was no revolt to overthrow the Egyptian rule.
Israel was under slavery by the Egyptians. God said to the ruling Egyptians
that they are to "Let My people go," *release My people Israel from the bondage.* The Pharaoh harden his heart against the Lord's command, and so, the
judgment of God was swift and very severe upon the Egyptians.

Just because sometimes people may appear to escape the judgment of God,
it does not follow or is always true that those peoples did escape His judgment.
Some peoples are indeed judged by God for their gross wickedness, but from
the human perspective, sometimes the judgment fell on certain peoples but not
on everyone. Why are some judged but others are not judged? I am not so sure
anyone knows why some are judged but others are similarly by-passed. God is
indeed just and holy. He alone chooses to reveal His reason(s) for judgment or
not reveal His reason(s). He need not give an answer to anyone. As the apostle
declares concerning His judgments,

> For God's gifts and his call are irrevocable. [30]Just as you who were
> at one time disobedient [as Gentiles] to God have now received mercy as a
> result of their [Israel's] disobedience, [31]so they too [Israel] have now become
> disobedient in order that they too may now receive mercy as a result of
> God's mercy to you. [32]For God has bound everyone [Israel and Gentiles] over to
> disobedience so that he may have mercy on them all [peoples].

[33]Oh, the depth of the riches of the wisdom and knowledge of God! How unsearchable his judgments, and his paths beyond tracing out! [34]"Who has known the mind of the Lord? Or who has been his counselor?" [35]"Who has ever given to God, that God should repay them?" [36]For from him and through him and for him are all things. To him be the glory forever! Amen.   (Rom. 11:29-36 NIV)

3. *Sexual sins are against the commandments of God.*

Some sexual sins may not be viewed as wickedness by some people or nations. Nevertheless, God alone set the standard for all creation. The Lord alone has the last word on the subject. Some people do not believe the Bible is the Word of God. It matters not if some people reject the Bible as the Word of God. The Bible is God's Word, and the Lord will surely judge humanity by the standard of His Word. So, it is a copout to say, "I do not believe the Bible is the Word of God." It does not matter if someone rejects His Word; humankind will pay severely for their rejection. So, God may indeed judge any people or nation for their wickedness anytime He chooses. It is madness when people foolishly declare God and His Word a liar.[1 John 5:10-13]

Others, even nations, do not believe that there is God, this does not change anything. God and His standard holds true and everyone is held accountable even if they deny the existence of God and His Word, the Bible. Any people or nation that reject the existence of an Eternal and Everlasting God the Lord is a fool. People will pay with the ultimate price. There are no atheists in Hell! (Their disbelief is dismissed by the reality of being in Hell.) Hello!

> The fool has said in his heart, "*There is* no God." They are corrupt, and have done abominable iniquity; *There is* none who does good. God looks down from heaven upon the children of men, To see if there are *any* who understand, who seek God. Every one of them has turned aside; They have together become corrupt; *There is* none who does good, No, not one.   (Psa. 53:1-3 NKJ)

The apostle says boldly,

> [4]Or do you show contempt for the riches of his kindness, forbearance and patience, not realizing that God's kindness is intended to lead you to repentance? [5]But because of your stubbornness and your unrepentant heart, you are storing up wrath against yourself for the day of God's wrath, when his righteous judgment will be revealed. [6]God "will repay each person according to what they have done."

[9]There will be trouble and distress for every human being who does evil: first for the Jew, then for the Gentile; [10]but glory, honor and peace for everyone who does good: first for the Jew, then for the Gentile. [11]For God does not show favoritism [partiality]. [12]All who sin apart from the law will also perish apart from the law, and all who sin under the law will be judged by the law. [13]For it is not those who hear the law who are righteous in God's sight, but it is those who obey[a] the law who will be declared righteous. [14](Indeed, when Gentiles, who do not have the law, do by nature things required by the law, they are a law for themselves, even though they do not have the law. [15]They show that the requirements of the law are written on their hearts, their consciences also bearing witness, and their thoughts sometimes accusing them and at other times even defending them.)   (Rom. 2:4, 5, 9-15 NIV)

[a]Note: The subdivisional context [(Rom. 1:18-3:20)] has one point: **all are guilty and under sin**. Paul quotes the psalmist that all sin.[Rom. 3:10-12] Scripture is explicit, "-we know that a person is justified not by the works of the law but through faith in Jesus Christ."[Gal. 2:16 NRS]

Again,

For the wrath of God is revealed from heaven against all ungodliness and unrighteousness of **people who suppress the truth** by their unrighteousness, [19]because what can be known about God is plain to them, because **God has made it plain** to them. [20]For since the creation of the world **his invisible attributes– his eternal power** and **divine nature–** have been **clearly seen**, because **they are understood** through what has been made. So **people are without excuse**. [21]For **although they knew God**, they **did not glorify him** as God or **give him thanks**, but they became futile in their thoughts and their senseless hearts were darkened. [22]Although **they claimed to be wise, they became fools** [23]and exchanged the glory of the immortal God for an image resembling mortal human beings or birds or four-footed animals or reptiles. [24]Therefore **God gave them over in the desires of their hearts** to impurity, to dishonor their bodies among themselves. [25]They **exchanged the truth of God for a lie** and worshiped and served the creation rather than the Creator, who is blessed forever! Amen. [26]For this reason God gave them over to dishonorable passions. For their women exchanged the natural sexual relations for unnatural ones, [27]and likewise the men also abandoned natural relations with women and were inflamed in their

131

passions for one another. Men committed shameless acts with men and received in themselves the due penalty for their error.

(Rom. 1:18-27 NET)

The apostle concludes as we noted earlier in this section in Romans this way,

Although they **fully know God's righteous decree** that those who practice such things **deserve to die**, they not only do them but also approve [*others*] of those who practice them.　　　(Rom. 1:32 NET)

There are others who may not practice wickedness on the same level as other people, but mankind still "- approve of those who practice them."[Rom. 1:32 NET]

4. *Sexual sins can lead to the spread of diseases and death of a people.*

The spread of sexual sins is very serious in the military. Such sins can lead to a court-martial: severe reprimand, unfavorable discharge from military, or even imprisonment. The spread of some sexual diseases can severely disable a strong army.

Who is to say that maybe the appearance of AIDS is a warning from God. Also, most a half-century after the discovery of AIDS, there is still no cure. There is likely will be no cure until the Lord in His infinite mercy allows a cure to be found.

Even sexual relationships among very close relatives can produce *grotesque, horrific deformities*, and *severe abnormalities* in their offspring. (This is a clear warning from God). The fact that countless millions are born with some very severe abnormalities due to close relatives ought to send *shockwaves across the bows of human consciousness*. But human consciousness has been seared as with a hot iron.[1 Tim. 4:2]

Wickedness in some churches is so pervasive that their sexual sins even shocked the State authorities in the USA. When I first moved to the NW, the State of Washington had to close one church's doors due extreme wickedness. In the church, the men threw their car-keys into a bowl. Then, the women frantically ran to grab a key to determine who they would sleep that night. This is the wickedness taking place in so-called churches. There is more shocking wickedness than this going in some churches. Why may we ask is such wickedness occurring in some churches? Friend, **there is no fear of God** today in many churches.

Please read the entire chapter 8 of Ezekiel, which is sometimes referred to as the *"hole in the wall." What is said, many Christians are no longer shocked when learning of such behavior by people.*

As we approach the last days, the Bible gives us this chilling and nerve-wracking portrait of human conduct,

> The Spirit clearly says that in later times some will **ABANDON THE FAITH** and **FOLLOW DECEIVING SPIRITS** and things **TAUGHT BY DEMONS** [*induced through the mind*]. 2 Such teachings come through **HYPOCRITICAL LIARS, WHOSE CONSCIENCES HAVE BEEN SEARED** as with a hot iron.   (1 Tim. 4:1, 2 NIV)

5. *Sexual sins are against humanity and lead to gross immorality and untold wickedness.*

When sexual sins are left unchecked, overlooked, or dismissed as nothing, then, that people will find themselves under the judgment of God. Moral character and godliness have collapsed in a society in some parts of the world. Therefore, wickedness runs wild. There will be little mercy for those people living such evil lives.

God's Word gives us this directive in life. Happy are the saints that live by this standard,

> And let the **peace of God rule in your hearts**, to the which also ye are called in one body; and **be ye thankful. Let the word of Christ dwell in you richly** in all wisdom; teaching and admonishing one another in psalms and hymns and spiritual songs, singing with grace in your hearts to the Lord. And **whatsoever ye do in word or deed,** *do* **all in the name of the Lord Jesus, giving thanks to God** and the Father by him.   (Col. 3:15-17 KJV)

For those who refuse to place their trust and saving faith in Christ the Lord, you had better be very careful how you live. For even in Hell, there are degrees and severity punishment. The more wicked one lives, the more severity punishment in Hell, and there is no escape from Hell. The less wicked a person lives, he will receive less punishment.

C. Sodom and other cities are set as an example for all

The judgment upon Sodom and Gomorrah stands as a warning to any people that exceeds in continual wickedness. No people or nation can continue to live in gross immorality and then imagine they will escape the mighty hand of Lord.

"Like the overthrow of Sodom and Gomorrah with its neighbors," says the LORD, "no one will live there, nor will a son of man reside in it."

(Jer. 49:18)

God and His Word are true and stand forever and ever. The psalmist says,

Forever, O LORD, your word is firmly fixed in the heavens.

(Psalm 119:89 ESV)

Young's literal translation reads,

Lamed. To the age, O Jehovah, Thy word is set up in the heavens.

(Psalm 119:89 YLT)

Jesus said concerning the Word of God,

"Heaven and earth will pass away, but My words will by no means pass away."   (Matt. 24:35 NKJ)

As the apostle Paul says concerning all acts and decision by God are true and there is no lie,

May it never be! Yes, let God be found true, but every man a liar. As it is written, "that you might be justified in your words, and might prevail when you come into judgment."   (Rom. 3:8 WEB)

Jesus is the **Pearl of Great Price**, He is the **Liley of the Valley**, and the **Bright Morning Star**. In Christ the Lord, there is life and life more abundantly.[John 10:10]

Jesus said plainly,

It is the Spirit who gives life; the flesh profits nothing. The words that I speak to you are spirit, and *they* are life. But there are some of you who do not believe." For Jesus knew from the beginning who they were who did not believe, and who would betray Him. And He said, "Therefore I have said to you that no one can come to Me unless it has been granted to him by My Father."

From that *time* many of His disciples went back and walked with Him no more. Then Jesus said to the twelve, "Do you also want to go away?"

But Simon Peter answered Him, "Lord, to whom shall we go? You [alone] have the words of eternal life. Also we have come to believe and know that You are the Christ, the Son of the living God." (John 6:63-69 KJV)

Therefore, Sodom and Gomorrah and those cities associated with their wickedness ought to serve as a *chilling reminder*. Gross wickedness shall be judged! There is no escape from the judgment of the living God. The Lord rules His universe with love, kind, grace, and mercy without end. However, know this for certain that anyone that refuses the love of God in Christ, they shall face the dreadful and furious wrath of God without end. There will be no mercy for the wicked who reject Christ Jesus. Jesus sternly warns all those who were given great light from God from the Lord. Friend, it is the utter most offense to reject Jesus as Lord. The Lord's dreadful wrath will fall upon all disbelievers. The Lord's wondrous mighty miracles are without number to those who want to know the truth. His teaching of the Word of God is wonderful and beyond amazement to those who truly know Him. God tabernacling in flesh to reach out to fallen and rebellious man is the greatest love and Light that has ever come to the human race. So, those who reject Jesus Christ will bring upon themselves the wrath of God unto the uttermost without end.

> "But I say to you that it will be more tolerable in that Day for Sodom than for that city. [13]Woe to you, Chorazin! Woe to you, Bethsaida! For if the mighty works which were done in you had been done in Tyre and Sidon, they would have repented long ago, sitting in sackcloth and ashes. [14]"But it will be more tolerable for Tyre and Sidon at the judgment than for you. [15]"And you, Capernaum, who are exalted to heaven, will be brought down to Hades. [16]"He who hears you hears Me, he who rejects you rejects Me, and he who rejects Me rejects Him who sent Me." (Luke 10:12-16 NKJ)

Conclusion

Today, many probably disregard the judgment upon Sodom, Gomorrah, and surrounding cities with mockery and doubt. Many people may either think it is fictitious or gross exaggeration. Listen, the judgment of these cities was catastrophic and horrific and unparalleled. Nothing grows in that area unto this day. Everything is dead. So, woe unto anyone that ignores the lesson upon God's judgment upon Sodom and the surrounding cities. God is on His Throne. Hallelujah! The Lord our God's rule is unreachable and fathomless in His universe. How much more then that the Lord judge the hearts of wicked mankind?

Isaiah says as to the greatness of the Lord our God,

> [12]Who has measured the waters in the hollow of his hand, or marked off the heavens [the entire universe] with the span of his hand? Who has held the dust of the earth in a basket, or weighed the mountains on a scale and the hills with a balance? [13]Who has directed the Spirit of the LORD, or informed

Him as His counselor? [14]Whom did He consult to enlighten Him, and who taught Him the paths of justice? Who imparted knowledge to Him and showed Him the way of understanding? [15]Surely the nations are like a drop in a bucket; they are considered a speck of dust on the scales; He lifts up the islands like fine dust. [16]Lebanon is not sufficient for fuel, nor its animals enough for a burnt offering. [17]All the nations are as nothing before Him; He regards them as nothingness and emptiness. [18]To whom will you liken God? To what image will you compare Him? [19]To an idol that a craftsman casts and a metalworker overlays with gold and fits with silver chains? [20]To one bereft of an offering who chooses wood that will not rot, who seeks a skilled craftsman to set up an idol that will not topple? [21]Do you not know? Have you not heard? Has it not been declared to you from the beginning? Have you not understood since the foundation of the earth? [22]He sits enthroned above the circle of the earth; its dwellers are like grasshoppers. He stretches out the heavens like a curtain, and spreads them out like a tent to dwell in. [23]He brings the princes to nothing and makes the rulers of the earth meaningless. [24]No sooner are they planted, no sooner are they sown, no sooner have their stems taken root in the ground, than He blows on them and they wither, and a whirlwind sweeps them away like stubble. [25]"To whom will you liken Me, or who is My equal?" asks the Holy One. [26]Lift up your eyes on high: Who created all these? He leads forth the starry host by number; He calls each one by name. Because of His great power and mighty strength, not one of them is missing.   (Isa. 40:12-26 MSB)

The churches had better heed the warning of the judgment upon Sodom and Gomorrah. Our God is a consuming fire.[Heb. 12:29] (When I say, "church or churches," I am referring to all genuine Christians regardless of the denomination or sect affiliation that are genuinely redeemed.) If a congregation finds itself under the judgment of God, there is no appeal. Remember Hebrews warning,

> How much worse punishment, do you think, will be deserved by the one who has trampled underfoot the Son of God, and has profaned the blood of the covenant by which he was sanctified, and has outraged the Spirit of grace? [30]For we know him who said, "Vengeance is mine; I will repay." And again, "The Lord will judge his people." [31]It is a fearful thing to fall into the hands of the living God.   (Heb. 10:29-31 ESV)

> Be not deceived; God is not mocked: for whatsoever a man soweth, that shall he also reap.   (Gal. 6:7 KJV)

Those who mock Calvary and Yehoshua as nothing more than a clown shall not escape the judgment. Disbelievers have been seduced and blinded by the power of darkness.

As the apostle Peter says,

> For the time *has come* for judgment to begin at the house of God; and if *it begins* with us first, what will *be* the end of those who do not obey the gospel of God? Now "If the righteous one is scarcely saved, Where will the ungodly and the sinner appear?"   (1 Peter 4:17, 18 NKJ)

As we close this section and chapter, may we remind ourselves once again,

> But if our gospel be hid, it is hid to them that are lost: In whom the god of this world hath blinded the minds of them which believe not, lest the light of the glorious gospel of Christ, who is the image of God, should shine unto them. For we preach not ourselves, but Christ Jesus the Lord; and ourselves your servants for Jesus' sake. For God, who commanded the light to shine out of darkness, hath shined in our hearts, to *give* the light of the knowledge of the glory of God in the face of Jesus Christ.
>
>   (2 Cor. 4:3-6 KJV)

Footnotes:

1. "Triad," dictionary.com definite the word as "a group of three, especially of three closely related persons or things." https://www.dictionary.com/browse/triad

Part 3

Rebellious and head-strong

[8]Yet in the same way these people also, dreaming, defile the flesh, reject authority, and speak abusively of *angelic* majesties. [9]But Michael the archangel, when he disputed with the devil and argued about the body of Moses, did not dare pronounce against him an abusive judgment, but said, "The Lord rebuke you!" [10]But these people disparage [*trivialize*] all the things that they do not understand; and all the things that they know by instinct, like unreasoning [*irrational*] animals, by these things they are destroyed. [11]Woe to them! For they have gone the way of Cain, and for pay they have given themselves up to the error of Balaam, and perished in the rebellion of Korah. [12]These are the ones who are hidden reefs in your love feasts [*the Lord's Supper*] when they feast with you without fear, *like shepherds* caring *only* for themselves [egoistic]; clouds without water, carried along by winds; autumn trees without fruit, doubly dead, uprooted; [13]wild waves of the sea, churning up their own shameful deeds like *dirty* foam; wandering stars, for whom the gloom of darkness has been reserved forever.   (Jude 1:8-13 NAS)

CHAPTER 9

Dispute over Moses' body with Michael and the devil

Memory verse

"Thou shalt not revile upon the Judges[1] [HEB Elohim], neither speak evil of the ruler of thy people." (Exod. 22:27 GNV)

Introduction

Jude says as given by NAS,

> Yet in the same way these men, also by dreaming, defile the flesh, and reject authority, and revile angelic majesties.[a] (Jude 1:8)

[a]Note: KJV is, "speak evil of _dignities_ [GK noun _doxa_]." Dignities, the GK word is _doxa_; it is the root word for "glory." As a noun and in this sense, _doxa_ literally meaning "glorious ones." It is a reference to an angelic host and their spender.

The particular sin Jude alludes to here is a sin that many are guilty of doing. In simply language, Jude is referring the sin of _slander_. _Sander_ is actually one of names for the evil one, GK _diabolos, slander_ or _accuser_. Satan is the _slandering one, accuser of the brethren_.[Rev. 12:10]

This is a dispute between Michael an archangel[2] and the devil who is Lucifer a fallen archangel, which we shall discuss later. Slandering other people is so pervasive that it is given little thought even in churches. Call it _gossiper_ or _gossipmonger, fault-finder, tittle-tattle_ or _backbite_ if you want, but it

141

is still *slander*! For example, rulers or governing powers are often *slandered* for their defective or careless lifestyle and/or rule. Still, any rule is better than no rule, which is anarchy. Kings and governors in NT time were pagan. Yet, the Word God says,

> I urge, then, first of all, that **petitions, prayers, intercession** and **thanksgiving be made** for[a] all people— [2]for **kings** and **all those in authority**, that we may live peaceful and quiet lives in all godliness and holiness. [3]This is good, and pleases God our Savior, [4]**who wants all people to be saved** and to **come to a knowledge of the truth**. [5]For there is one God and one mediator between God and mankind, the man Christ Jesus.   (1Tim 2:1-5 NIV)

[a]Note: "for" is the GK *huper*: to pray *on their behalf*.

If we were more on our knees for our leaders, we might be more thankful to God for the changes that might take place. Rulers help to establish peace and order. In many, many places in the world there is no godly rule. The demons influencing the world want disorder and the absence of peace and safety. Anarchy is when there is no kind of rule. Like in the days of the Judges,

> In those days *there was* no king in Israel; everyone did *what was* right in his own eyes.   (Judges 17:6 KJV)

Where there is no rule, there is anguish, fear, and life is not safe. Businesses are closed or at standstill. Farming is halted or in disarray. There is no life. The bare necessities of life are cut short. Famine, diseases, and sickness runs wild and out of control where there is no rule.

When evil runs roughshod over a people, there is no safety and life is a fleeing moment. Some seek death rather than life. It is for the reason noted above that most any rule is better than none.

A. The spirit of anarchy, refusing authority that is in rule

Jude introduces this section (1:8-13) with this statement:

> Likewise also these dreamers [*also*] defile the flesh, reject authority, and speak evil of dignitaries.[angelic majesties]   (Jude 1:8 NKJ)

Jude is pointing directly at the devil with his abusive language towards Michael the archangel concerning the body of Moses. (Jude uses non-biblical material on this subject. More on this later.) Jude reveals how *slandering* others is evil speaking, and such language ought to cease in the life of the redeemed. The saints should never speak evil or bring up accusations against other people with a slanderous intention.

One of the worse forms is speaking against another is speaking behind their back, which known as "backbiter" in the Bible. Another form which can be slanderous is when a person is an *informer*. Some *informers* enjoys telling or revealing others people faults or weakness. Such informers are known as "*tittle-tattle*." During war, those who turned against their own country were known as *informants*. In prisons, they are also called *informants*, but in prison if a person is discovered to be an *informant*, their life will be cut short by other prisoners. Judas Iscariot was an informant who betrayed Jesus.[Mat. 26:14-16]

Additionally, we ought to be praying for the good of our rulers and people. When we pray for others, let us avoid generalizing our prayers. Let us pinpoint or be specific in our prayer requests as much as possible. The problem is that many of us do not pray for others, but even when we pray on behalf of others, we certainly do not bother to pray specifically enough.

When we pray, let us pray for people by name as we pray the person. As I have said, let us be specific in the request for them. Interceding on behalf of others (for believers or unbelievers) is one of the most powerful arsenals given to us by God. **Do not** say: "Lord bless Pastor John." How do you desire God to bless Pastor John: bless sermon preparation; his evangelism; or the health of him and family. Let us be as explicit as possible. Our prayers will be more effective.

When asking people for prayer requests, the clearer and the more we are explicit in our prayers, the more effective will be our prayer life. We also ought to expect results when we pray. God always answers our prayer: *yes, no, or wait*. Don't just pray and forget it. Let us also expect a definite answer in your prayer. Do not forget to thank the Lord's answer in our prayers whether His answer is "*yes*" or "*no*."

When Jesus prays in John 17 or in the Garden of Gethsemane, His prayers were specific.

> [41][*Jesus*] -- knelt down and prayed, [42]saying, "Father, if you are willing, remove this cup from me. Nevertheless, not my will, but yours, be done." [43]And there appeared to him an angel from heaven, strengthening him. [44]And being in an agony he prayed more earnestly; and his sweat became like great drops of blood falling down to the ground. [45]And when he rose from prayer, he came to the disciples and found them sleeping for sorrow, [46]and he said to them, "Why are you sleeping? Rise and pray that you may not enter into temptation." (Luke 22:41-46 ESV)

Jesus' prayer asked the Father if there is some other way to save human-kind and keep Him from becoming the sin offering on the cross. Yet, He said,

> "Father, if you are willing, remove this cup from me. Nevertheless, not
> my will, but yours, be done."   (Luke 22:42)

Our Lord did not dread the cross. Jesus was going be our substitute; our Lord was going to bear our sins in His body.

> And He Himself bore our sins in His body on the cross, so that we might
> die to sin and live to righteousness; for by His wounds you were healed.
>
>   (1 Peter 2:24)

> God made the one [*Jesus Christ*] who did not know sin to be sin for us
> [*in our behalf*], so that in him we would become the righteousness of
> God.   (2 Cor. 5:21 NET)

Jesus is specific in His prayer. Ah, but also notice our Lord said, 'not My will, but Yours, be done.' God's will is always better than our will. Why is "God's will always better?" The Lord can see around the corner and see what is coming. The Lord knows what is the best solution or answer for us. Unfortunately, many of our prayers are petitioned to consume on our lust. James says that this kind of praying is wrong. "You ask and don't have because you ask with evil intentions, to waste it on your own cravings."James 4:3 CEB

What is Jude referring to when he says?

> Likewise also these *filthy* dreamers defile the flesh, despise dominion,
> and speak evil of dignities.   (Jude 1:8 KJV)

Jude is referring to people with an anarchy spirit. The bottom-line here is people with *an anarchy spirit* do not follow the establish rule of order. This is often exhibited by parents reflecting no respect for authority. Then, children or grandchildren see this disrespect towards governing authorities. "*Monkey see monkey do!*" Then, the children will follow the same pattern that they see and learn from their parents or grandparents or peers they admire.

This is obvious as children that do not follow the rules whether they are in school or in other situations. Parents sometimes split on which side: the children or the authority e.g. the school. Rather than split, the husband and wife ought to work together. The parents in most cases ought to take the side of the authorities. Similarly, let the parents avoid taking the side of the children, causing a division and discord in the home. Harmony and peace follow unity, but division and discord lead to a breakdown in the family unit. It is wiser when both parents stand together on the same issue even if one parent may disagree. Standing together on an issue gives stability and demonstrates unity. Parents splitting or remain divided on issues are teaching an evil practice to their children.

Again, Jude says,

> Likewise also these dreamers defile the flesh, reject authority, and speak evil of dignitaries [GK *doxa*, _glorious ones_, e.g. *angels*]. (Jude 1:8 NKJ)

When discord is evident, the same attitude or behavior may be evident in work place, among relatives or other associations, and other parts of life. Demons bring discord and conflict. Since many of the battles with demons are with the mind or inner thoughts, the apostle Paul says,

> — *we are* taking every thought *and* purpose captive to the obedience of Christ.　　　　　　　　　　　　　　　　　　　　(2 Cor. 10:5b AMP)

The apostle is exhorting the saints that even when a negative thought comes to mind, squash it immediately and submit to Christ who can take care of the bad thought. Remember, Satan will attack the mind,

> But I fear, lest by any means, as the serpent beguiled [*seduced*] Eve through his subtilty, so **your minds should be corrupted** from the simplicity that is in Christ.　　　　　　　　　　(2 Cor. 11:3 KJV)

Once the words come out of our mouth, the words cannot be withdrawn or taken back. Jude is revealing how people may at times show little respect or restraint in speech or action. Some people say whatever comes to mind, but they show no restraint or accept accountability for their words that may have been generated whether by *the world, the flesh,* or even *the devil.* This is why we need to be attentive to the Holy Spirit abiding in us in order to have better restraint with our thoughts and words.

James declares that we need to have control over our tongues.[James 3] Sometimes silence is worth more than ten thousand words.

> Look also at ships: although they are so large and are driven by fierce winds, they are turned by a very small rudder wherever the pilot desires. Even so the tongue is a little member and boasts [*of*] great things. [*Also*] See how great a forest a little fire kindles! And the tongue *is* a fire, [*and*] a world of iniquity. The tongue is so set among our members that it defiles the whole body, and sets on fire the course of nature; and it is set on fire by hell [GK _geenna_, e.g. _eternal fire_].　　　　　　(James 3:4-6 NKJ)

B. Challenge concerning Moses' body by Michael[2]

Let me first says, let us be very careful how we interpret Jude's use of Jewish *tradition*, myths, or *non-canonical writings* here. Paul rebukes such use of non-canonical writing, e.g. Jewish folklore. (Unfortunately, the less informed do not realize Jude is using non-biblical material or Jewish folklore.)

Jude uses the books of Enoch, which were typical Jewish fictitious writings especially after the secession or at the end of the writing prophets after 400 BC. Still, Jude gives an important principle that we do not want to overlook. Jude's quote is from first book of 1 Enoch.

> But when the archangel Michael, contending with the devil, was disputing about the body of Moses, he did not presume to **pronounce a blasphemous judgment**, but said, "The Lord rebuke you."
>
> (Jude 1:9 ESV)

The ESV is a little clearer. Michael is a ruling angel, and as a ruling angel, he has high ranking authority and power as an archangel. Michael came to the aid of an angel (likely Gabriel) that communicated divine revelation to Daniel the prophet, see Dan. 10:13. It is likely that Michael will have the authority and privilege to remove Satan and the other evil angels out of Heaven.[Rev. 12:7] So, Michael is likely one who shall cast Satan in to the Lake of fire.[Rev. 20:10] We have a similar rebuke upon Satan, which is similar to the rebuke upon demons by Jesus:[Mark 9:25]

> And the LORD [YHWH] said unto Satan, The LORD [YHWH] rebuke thee, O Satan; even the LORD that hath chosen Jerusalem rebuke thee: *is* not this a brand plucked out of the fire? (Zech. 3:2 KJV)

Here is how the ABPE translates the above verse,

> And the Angel of LORD[b] JEHOVAH said to Satan: "Satan, LORD JEHOVAH shall rebuke you, LORD JEHOVAH who has chosen Jerusalem shall rebuke you! This is a firebrand that was taken out of the fire!" (Zech. 3:2 ABPE)

> [b]Note: rather than just using the Lord twice [God's scared name, **YHWH**], ABPE use Lord and the Jehovah, same word in HEB. This is likely "the Messenger (or Angel of the Lord), a theophany. This is the preincarnate manifestation of the Messiah or the Christ. The Angel of the Lord also called the Angel (Messenger) of God or His Angel.

The point given by Jude is that **no** Christian has the intrinsic authority given to them to rebuke Satan. (This is a serious error of Charismatics and some Pentecostals.) Yes, Satan is finite compared to God as created being. Still, the devil is very high authority and power beyond any human comprehension. Satan is a ruling angel; he is an archangel. So, any person or church group that thinks they have authority and power over Satan and demons are very foolish and ignorant. They do not know the Scripture. Jesus granted the power and authority to the apostles over demons as well as seventy other.[Luke 9:1; 10:1ff] Nevertheless, Jesus alone retains the power and authority. Without Jesus, we cannot do anything[John 15:5]! Listen, we do not have the inherit power or authority to use Jesus name *carte blanche*. This is being foolish and ignorant of Scriptures.

Please be patient with this topic as we proceed; there is more. Now, we must discuss this text that is very, very controversial. Stay on track with me here.

> Even Michael, the chief angel, didn't dare to insult the devil, when the two of them were arguing about the body of Moses. All Michael said was, "The Lord will punish you!" But these people insult powers they don't know anything about. They are like senseless animals that end up getting destroyed, because they live only by their feelings.
>
> (Jude 1:9-10 CEV)

The text [(Jude 1:9, 10)] is severely misinterpreted and definitely misunderstood by many people. Only as we read carefully here and understand source of the material, we shall hopefully grasp and know the significance. We must be very careful handling the Word God with clear discernment in this text. This is especially true here. I am sorry for those who disagree with me and what is said here.

Some revealed their misunderstanding by give way to unbiblical sources: tradition, non-canonical sources, myths, and pagan influences that the Bible warns us. Some have unwarrantedly steamrolled over the biblical author and the Spirit God. They have given way to very serious errors of outside biblical influences. So, I beg you, please read carefully less you become an endorser of unbiblical teaching and misapply Scripture and remain ignore of the Holy Spirit that gives us the light.

Here is the text once again:

> [8]Nevertheless, these dreamers likewise defile their flesh, reject authority, and blaspheme glorious ones. [9]Yet Michael the archangel, when he was disputing with the Devil in a debate about Moses' body, did not dare bring an abusive condemnation against him but said, "The Lord rebuke you! " [10]But these people blaspheme anything

147

they don't understand. What they know by instinct like unreasoning [*irrational*] animals — they destroy themselves with these things.

(Jude 1:8-10 AMP)

Jude is quoting from the book of Enoch, 1 Enoch 1:8. Jude is **not** endorsing the books of Enoch, which are four books. Please erase such a thought from your mind that the books are inspired. The books of Enoch are a myth; they are not inspired by God. So, be patient as I explain below.

Jude is citing the material from a non-biblical source without giving any credence or endorsing the material. This was a typical practice by Jews and others writings during NT times (inter-testament period, 400 BC to the birth of Christ the Lord).

Jews used Jewish non-canonical writings and oral tradition but without endorsing the material. Again, Jude is citing from non-biblical material, but he is **not** endorsing, giving credence, or agreeing with such writers. Neither is Jude teaching the doctrine or giving credence to such philosophy of life. If you do assume Jude agrees with the book of Enoch is Scripture, you are committing a very serious and grievous error! I warn you God will not be pleased with such ignorance.

For example, the apostle Paul quotes outside sources as a well-educated Jew in his day. Still, neither Jude or Paul are endorsing these quotes. Jude and Paul are only establishing what was <u>acutely said</u>. I say again, Jude and Paul are not endorsing or giving credence or credibility to such statements. The things that the biblical authors write are accurate and the words are indeed acutely recorded. Nevertheless, the biblical authors are not implying inspiration or authority to the non-biblical authors or their words. If you are assuming that their use of such material equals or equivalent to endorsement as Scripture, you are sadly mistaken!

For example, Paul says,

> One of themselves, *even* a prophet of their own, said, The *Cretans are always* liars, evil beasts, slow bellies. (Titus 1:12)

Paul is not calling Cretans *liars, evil beasts, or slow bellies*. (*Slow bellies,* mean some is like pig: the person is more concerned about eating than doing the will of God.) More importantly, the apostle is not declaring the Cretans a biblical prophet. Paul is using the word prophet in a general or non-biblical sense. I say again, Paul is not belittling the Cretan people or referring all Cretans as "*always* liars, evil beasts, slow bellies." Paul is only citing the Cretan, which his audience would have understood.

Here is another example of Paul quoting a philosopher at the Areopagus (Mars Hill) in Athens. Paul is **not** referring to the poet or a philosopher as a genuine prophet. Paul is **not** saying that the poet is inspired. He is only citing their words of the poet. Speakers frequently cite people, even today, but this does **not** mean that they agree with the quote or in any way endorsing their words. Similarly, Paul quotes non-biblical source without endorsing the quote.

> Neither is [*God*] worshipped with *men's hands*, as though he needed *anything*, seeing *he gives* to all life and breath and all things, ²⁶And [*God*] *has* made of one blood all *mankind*, to dwell on all the face of the earth, and *has* assigned the seasons which were *ordained* before, and the *bounders* of their habitation, ²⁷That they *should seek* the Lord, if so be they might *have* groped after him, and *find* him though *doubtless* he be not *far* from *every* one of us. ²⁸For in him [*God*] we *live*, and *move*, and *have* our being, as also *certain* of your *own* Poets *have said*, for "we are also his generation."³ ²⁹Forasmuch then, as we are the generation of God, we ought [*to*] not *think* that ye [*the*] Godhead is like *unto* gold, or *silver*, or stone *graven* by *art* and the *invention* of man.

(Acts 17:25-29 GNV)

Paul is quoting non-biblical material source, but Paul is **not** agreeing nor giving credence to the statement. Just because the statement is quoted and given by a biblical author like Paul, this does not mean the statement is inspired. It just means that is what was accurately recorded by Paul.

Historically, Jerome tell us that Paul's quote in Titus 1:12, "that Paul is citing the *Oracles* (Chresmoi) of the Greek poet Epimenides."⁴

For instance, the Bible gives statements by the devil, but the Bible is **not** saying what the devil said is inspired nor free of error. The Bible just accurately records what the devil says, but the Bible is not giving inspiration to the devil's statements. God forbid!

The devil is a liar and the father lies.^John 8:44 The devil offered Jesus the kingdoms of the world, but Satan is a liar. The devil does not own the world, and he does not have authority to offer the kingdoms of this world to anyone. (Satan must be given permission by God before he can do such thing. Satan's authority and power is set by God.) Satan is a liar, and he is pure evil and incapable of declaring the truth! Jesus said of the devil, '- there is no truth in him.^John 8:44

The apostle John said: "*And* we know that we are of God, and the whole world lieth in wickedness [GK wicked one]."^1 John 5:19 KJV Newer versions add "the whole world lies in the power of the evil one,"^v 19 but the world does not

149

lie in the hands or power of Satan. The word power is **not** even in the GK. NKJ reads more accurately, "We know that we are of God, and the whole world lies *under the **sway** of* the wicked one."[1 John 5:19 NKJ] Satan has access to use the world, but he does not have power or authority over all the world. The Lord our God alone rules the entire universe. Make this abundantly clear in your mind now: the Lord is sovereign over His entire created universe and no one else! Some ignorantly put forth the false notion that Satan is able to usurp authority over God. How ignorant is that?

Read carefully and think with me please:

> Yet Michael the archangel, when contending with the devil he disputed about the body of Moses, durst not bring against him a railing accusation, but said, The Lord rebuke thee. But these speak evil of those things which they know not: but what they know naturally, as brute beasts, in those things they corrupt themselves. (Jude 1:9, 10 KJV)

The books of Enoch, from which Jude quotes, was written on or before beginning 300 BC. There were no writing prophets after 400 BC. There were no writing prophets in Enoch's day in Genesis. There were many writings after 400 BC by Jews and before the beginning of the NT, but these writings were **not** under the authority of the Holy Spirit and without the inspiration of a prophet or a prophet's authority. Evangelical Protestants do not endorse any other writings except the OT 39 books and the 27 books of the NT. The Catholic, the Church of England, Greek Orthodox, and Coptics add these books to the HEB Bible: Tobias, Judith, Baruch, other Ecclesiasticus writings, Wisdom, 1 and 2 Maccabees, and as well additions in Esther and Daniel. The Coptic Church even includes the books of Enoch as Scripture. The Coptics are Christians. Nevertheless, the Coptics are mistaken to endorse the books of Enoch and include them as Scripture.

These above books that have been added by Church of England are based upon oral and written of ecclesiastical tradition. In fact, the Church of England was pressuring Christians in early America to stop using Geneva Bible [(GNV)] which is an excellent translation by Puritans. England wanted the Puritans to use only the KJV. (England was money driven.) The Geneva Bible was in use in America for 200 years before using the KJV. Fact! The Puritans told England first, remove the Apocrypha books. Then, the Puritans told England that they would consider using the KJV. Keep in mind that the Geneva Bible was use for two hundred years before the KJV was in America. So then, the Geneva Bible was the official Bible by English speaking in early America.

Jude shall quote again from Enoch, which we shall note later. Jews often wrote fictitious material. People apparently enjoyed reading them, but these other writings were never considered Scripture then or now. So, these added traditional writing were never endorsed or given any credence by the prophets or apostles. As noted earlier, Paul spoke out against such endorsing.

> For there are many rebellious people, full of meaningless talk and deception, especially those of the circumcision group. ¹¹They must be silenced, because they are disrupting whole households by teaching things they ought not to teach-- and that for the sake of dishonest gain. ¹²One of Crete's own prophets has said it: "Cretans are always liars, evil brutes, lazy gluttons." ¹³This saying is true. Therefore rebuke them sharply, so that they will be sound in the faith ¹⁴and will **pay no attention to Jewish myths** or to the merely human commands of those who reject the truth. ¹⁵To the pure, all things are pure, but to those who are corrupted and do not believe, nothing is pure. In fact, both their minds and consciences are corrupted. ¹⁶They claim to know God, but by their actions they deny him. They are detestable, disobedient and unfit for doing anything good. (Titus 1:10-16 NIV)

Spiritual discernment is greatly needed in the church today. People are not well read or sufficiently versed in all the Scriptures. There are many preachers who are very deficient in knowledge and practice of Scripture. This is even more noticeable when people giving heed to *tradition, creeds, customs, church history,* and *pagan sources.* All these sources may be interesting to read. Let us rather give our priority and sole attention and authority to what we know is definitely Scripture.

Regrettably, many give credence to church history, which again is a serious mistake. (Church history is inundated or flooded with false doctrine, which is very much like the internet today.) Also, only the original Scriptural writings and in the original language of Scripture is inspired. Woe unto anyone that foolishly says that some translations are equally authoritative or inspired. Anyone alleging any translation (such as the KJV) is inspired is a fool!

The Catholic Church, the Church of England, and other churches give heavy credence to the Latin Vulgate. While the Latin Vulgate is indeed one of the most monumental works ever done in the last several millenniums, Jerome, the translator deliberately made unwarranted changes that was not in the GK text. This is why it is wise to read at least one new translation which is done by Fundamental or Evangelical scholars. I use the Latin Vulgate due the scholarly work in it. Still, I do not endorse Vulgate as reliable translation due the inherent serious defects. Still, it is important to note their particular perspective is to get a deeper understanding for ourselves in God's Word.

The books of Enoch discusses the body of Moses' at death, but unfortunately, the books of Enoch blurs information.[Deut. 34:5, 6] There is no biblical evidence concerning the devil arguing with Michael the archangel over the body of Moses. Those who blindly follow such non-biblical material do so at their own peril before the Lord. Accepting the material in the books of Enoch is being extremely *credulous*. Do not believe everything you hear or read. I warn you that the Lord will hold everyone accountable.

This is what Jesus meant when He said,

> "They [*the Pharisees*] are blind leaders of the blind. And if the blind leads the blind, both will fall into a ditch." (Matt. 15:14 NKJ)

Remember, Jesus said on the Day of Judgment,

> And I say to you that **every idle word** that men may speak, they will give for it a reckoning [*will full account to Him*] in day of judgment.
> (Matt. 12:36 LSV)

Sincerity does not count before the Lord. Truth is what counts. This is *the whole truth and nothing but the truth*. Please listen, **a half-truth is still a WHOLE LIE**! Woe to those who blindly follows their tradition, pagan influences, church history, or non-biblical material to supersede the Word of God.

As final note on the books of Enoch, there is a discuss on angels cohabiting with human women as well in Enoch. Again, there is no substance to the doctrine of angels cohabiting with humans Gen. 6. People who have "*itching ears*" want to feel the *tingle*. The *tingle* may have deadly venomous bite and you might regret it. The point we must understand and see here is that we are not to go beyond what is written in God's Word. (Stay away from speculations; avoid it like a plague.) Otherwise, we may be spreading untruths of God's Word. We may be even found perpetuating lies. Here is an axion to go by in teaching the Bible:

> *When the Bible is silent on a subject,*
> *the person teaching the Bible ought to also remain silent*!

Conclusion

Jude is a zealous Orthodox Jew in NT times. His readers understood his non-biblical material was not Scripture. Orthodox Jews then and even Orthodox Jews now would not conclude the writings in the books of Enoch as inspired or authoritative. Many Jews were fairly educated and well-read and wrote in more than one language. Jude is writing primarily to Jewish Christians which some scholars overlook today. Many of the Christian Jews were worshipping in the temple during writing of Jude. Many Orthodox zealous Christian Jews were observing many of the customs and traditions of the elders, which many are still doing today. (Should we do that today? No!) There were likely many clashes between NT Jews and OT Jews in and around Jerusalem and Judah, and in fact, there remains critical and dangerous divisions among the Jews even to this day. So, trying to keep peace remains very difficult in Jerusalem and Judah.

As late as the 4th century AD, there was a Syrian Judeo-Christian sect.[5] This sect believes the Gospels of the NT, but the sect still practices the Mosaic Law as means of righteousness. There are others in North Africa that practice Mosaic Law and grace. The apostle Paul said plainly,

> But if it is by grace, it is no longer on the basis of works, otherwise grace is no longer grace. (Rom. 11:6)

May the Lord give you peace with such a difficult text of Scripture. Nevertheless, let us not go beyond what is written in Scripture and its teaching. The Scriptures alone has final word!

Footnotes:

1. God, HEB "Elohim" Exodus 22:28: the KJV reads, "Thou shalt not revile the gods [*Elohim*]—" is an inappropriate rendering. GNV, "You shalt not *revile* [*curse*] *upon the judges*." The ABPE uses a similar translation as the GNV. The HEB meaning is, "You shall not curse **judges [which the leaders of Israel]**-" The HEB word for "*God*" is "*Elohim*," which is plural in HEB. But when "*Elohim*" is used of the God of Bible, it is capitalized and translated as a singular noun. (There is a singular in HEB for God, "El," and either are acceptable and translates as "God.") The HEB word "*Elohim*" has multiple meaning, and the context must determines the meaning. "*Elohim*" can refer to *judges* or *rulers* in mockery in Psa. 82:6, 7. **Even the Genva Bible, this evident with the HEB parallelism "judges" with "rulers," Exodus 22:28. (The word "judge" and "ruler" refers to the same person.)** Hence, some might conclude the word "*Elohim*" just means "*judges*." "*Elohim*" can mean: "*mighty one*." "*Elohim*" *refer to a pagan deity as god, goddess, gods, angels, and demons.* Though usual word for *angel* or *messenger* is

the HEB *"malak."* *"Elohim"* is used of *"angels"* in the GK OT, Psa. 8:5, **though many would probably disagree today.**

2. Archangels: I am aware of only three possible archangels in the Bible. *Michael* is considered a ruling or archangel. *Gabriel* is likely another archangel since he led battle against evil angels, and Michael came to assist Gabriel. Lucifer is likely an archangel but an evil archangel. "The Angel of the Lord" is not angelic being. These are theophanies and not angels. While outside sources, rather the Bible, allege there are twelve archangels, I only know possible three.

3. "Generation," Acts 17:28: the GK word is *genos*, which can mean: *race, offspring*, or even *children*. However, the connotative (not denotation) meaning of *genos* here is better understood to mean *"created by God."* Also, the spelling in the GNV Bible is in the old ENG, and the spelling has been updated and the word changes are in italics but no wording has been changed in the text.

4. A quote from Cretans: Paul is **not** claiming that the Cretan had a biblical prophet. Hear me, Paul is only quoting the material, and he is **not** endorsing the statement. Anyone teaching or speaking or orators in NT times would be referred to as a prophet, but such quotes are **not** prophets in biblical sense.
    https://www.christianstudylibrary.org/article/titus-112-%E2%80%93-cretans-are-always-liars

5. Sect of the Nazarene of the 4th century AD:
    https://www.google.com/search?q=sect+of+the+Nazarene&sca_esv=598432625&sxsrf=ACQVn09SSUxhu0zZ9W6l2_BgsQhcnCvXBQ%3A1705270691204&ei=o12kZc6GDNOy0PEP8fq0-AU&oq=philosophy+of+life&gs_lp=Egxnd3Mtd2l6LXNlcnAiEnBoaWxvc29waHkgb2YgbGlmZUUgAUABYAHAAeAGQAQCYAQCgAQCqAQC4ARLIAQD4AQbiAwQYACBBgs_ivs=1&sclient=gws-wiz-serp

CHAPTER 10

They slander what they do not understand

Memory verse

— behold, [*if*] you have sinned against the LORD, and be sure your sin will find you out. (Num. 32:23)

Introduction

At the very outset, Jude says forcefully,

> But these speak evil of those things which they know not: but what they know naturally, as brute beasts, in those things they corrupt themselves. Woe unto them! for they have gone in the way of Cain, and ran greedily after the error of Balaam for reward, and perished in the gainsaying of Core. (Jude 1:10, 11 KJV)

Allow me to paraphrase these verses:

> *But let me tell you these kind of people speak blasphemous words against things that they really do not understand. They are like wild, brute, and irrational animals without reasoning and headed for ruin. Woe to them: they have followed the path of Cain; they have run after the profiteering way of Balaam; and they perish in rebellion like Korah and their group.* (Jude 1:10, 11 paraphrased)

Reading old ENG is sometimes enjoyable, but it is not always easy to fully understand what is being said. So, we have to read and think carefully through the things that may seem to be a little difficult to fully grasp the meaning of the words. Jude writes to a small subculture, Orthodox Judaism Christians in Jerusalem (which is likely different from Galilee area Judaism). The Judaism in Jerusalem was likely a little more strict and legalistic, which may be difficult to fully understand nowadays.

Jude uses a triad again to illustrate the kind of people he is alerting us to here. Jude singles out three men that went too far into sinning against the Lord. Jude's emphasis is centered on one or two key words describing these men. Jude does not elaborate in detail concerning his three examples since his readers were thoroughly familiar with Jewish history and customs. These kinds of people Jude is citing bring with them trouble wherever they go. So, in *contending for the faith*, Jude is warning his readers that they must *watch-out* for such troublemakers.

The three people are: **Cain** who in *anger killed* his brother; **Balaam** a *money-grabbing* false prophet; and **Korah** (KJV Core, HEB Korah) a *leader of rebellion* against Moses. Unfortunately, the professing church today seems to have their full share of wicked people but professing faith. Yet, often their character is hidden within the heart. So, most of us are unaware of the evil lurking in their hearts or minds. There is a frightful increase in wickedness in the churches in our present day. (I say frightful because what I see is only "the tip of an *iceberg*¹;" it is probably worse.) This may be indication that we may be closer to *the last days* than we may realize? In addition, Jude's Epistle reflects gross wickedness that plagues many churches throughout the world in our day.

A. The sin of Cain

Cain, like all the rest of us humans, as sinners, but sadly, Cain's sins is not uncommon. Actually, Cain's sin had overtaken him before he slew his brother Abel. Jude, however, points to one main root of sin dominating Cain and many of us.

> At the designated time Cain brought some of the fruit of the ground for an offering to the LORD. ⁴But Abel brought some of the firstborn of his flock– even the fattest of them. And the LORD was pleased with Abel and his offering, ⁵but with Cain and his offering he was not pleased. So Cain became very angry, and his expression was downcast. ⁶Then the LORD said to Cain, "Why are you angry, and why is your expression downcast? ⁷Is it not true that if you do what is right, you will be fine? But if you do not do what is right, sin is crouching at the door. It desires to dominate you, but you must subdue it."

[8]Cain said to his brother Abel, "Let's go out to the field." While they were in the field, Cain attacked his brother Abel and killed him. [9]Then the LORD said to Cain, "Where is your brother Abel?" And he replied, "I don't know! Am I my brother's guardian?" [10]But the LORD said, "What have you done? The voice of your brother's blood is crying out to me from the ground! [11]So now, you are banished from the ground, which has opened its mouth to receive your brother's blood from your hand. (Gen. 4:3-11 NET)

Please notice again, "Abel brought some of the firstborn of his flock." Gen. 4:3 NET

I suspect that Cain may have had his own flock which he could have offered as a sacrifice. (Why didn't Cain also offer from his flock? We don't know, but I am certain he could have done the same.) The Scripture is silent on the subject. Scripture says of Cain's brother, 'Abel brought some of [*his own*] the firstborn of his flock.'[Gen. 4:3 NET] We have no information that Adam and Eve were told about offerings and sacrifices. The Scripture reveals that the Lord offered the first sacrifice, which very significant. From the offering, God covered Adam and Eve with the skin perhaps symbolizing forgiveness. Due to the immense importance of the sacrifice in Scripture, we ought to realize that Cain and Abel must have known what which animals were for sacrifices.

First fruits of harvest were acceptable as means of thanksgiving and praise to God, but the first fruits of harvest were for praise and thanksgiving but not for sin offering. However, in this instance, the Scripture does not reveal to us the full sequence of events. So, we must probe a little deeper. Likely, Cain became *enraged with jealously* with Abel and in jealously, he killed his own brother.

The seed of jealously takes on different forms. Jealously is often hidden because the person does not want to be detected or found out. The other person in whom he or she is jealous of would likely be shocked and stunned with disbelief if they were aware of their jealousy. They might think to themselves: *Why is he/she so jealous? I am insignificant in life.*

Sometimes Pastors get jealous of one another whether the congregation is small or large. So, in their hearts, they may be embittered or very resentful. The sin of jealousy left unchecked can fester. Their jealousy may lead to slandering the other, abusive language, discrediting the person, and turn to became their enemy.

Those who are overcome with jealousy or resentment can be destroyed by it. They need to repent and genuinely seek the Lord's forgiveness and cleansing and healing of the bitter jealousy. If repentance is **not** evident with any person of jealousy, they can become so embittered that they are engulfed by it. Then, they fail to seek restoration, forgiveness, and complete fellowship with the other(s). Listen, talking to the Lord in prayer in repentance is insufficient. True repentance seeks forgiveness, fellowship, and harmony and the end of hostility with the other person. There is a restoration of genuine fellowship and wholesome friendship again.

Jesus desires that the saints strive to maintain harmony and peace with one another since we are to be a testimony to the world around us. The saints are expected to be a model of peace-maker to the world. Harboring animosity, jealousy, and bitterness is the way the ungodly. This is how the wicked continually live. Jesus said,

> "You have heard that the ancients were told, 'You shall not commit murder' and 'Whoever commits murder shall be liable to the court.' "But I say to you that everyone who is angry with his brother shall be guilty before the court; and whoever shall say to his brother, 'Raca [*worthless fool or hollow-head*],' shall be guilty before the supreme court; and whoever shall say, 'You fool [GK *moron, e.g. ignorant moron*],' shall be guilty *enough to go* into the fiery hell. "If therefore you are presenting your offering at the altar [e.g. *under the OT*], and there [*you*] remember that your brother has something against you, leave [*immediately*] your offering there before the altar, and go your way; first be reconciled to your brother, and then come and present your offering. (Matt. 5:21-24)

Jesus sets the scene with three examples:

1. Verse 21, there is the *harboring angry* or resentment hidden in their hearts against their brother or sister. Left hidden, it festers and like fire consumes the person. The Lord expects the one we may have offended to seek forgiveness, reconciliation, and peace with the other person. Otherwise, in time, the anger may get out of control and destroy the person overcome with the angry.

There are at least three ways anger manifests itself.

a. First, there is _open_ and frontal aggression. The aggression can be aggression in words, physical action, and even harm against the person.

b. Second, there is _hidden_ and behind the back aggression (concealed), but the anger is known to perhaps to a selected few people or group. This is called *backbiting*.

c. Third, there is totally _suppressed_ and _harbored within_ a person's mind but just as deadly but unknown to anyone. Unchecked anger left untreated properly through theory, the person's in whom one is angry and without reconciliation is in a self-destructive mood.

Open and assaultive anger is very serious. Jesus is addressing those who have pretense of peace, but there are things hidden in the heart or mind that are within and no one realizes or knows but God. Our Lord desires that the saints seek forgiveness, reconciliation, and have harmony and peace. However, even hostility and brewing-anger towards the unregenerate is totally unacceptable to God.

2. Verse 22, the person belittles another person or persons (whether openly, concealed, or harboring in the mind) with his brother and angry for no reason. If he has reason to be angry, nevertheless, he is still expected to go and get reconciled, and seek restoration and forgiveness [Mat. 5:23f; 18:15-17]. The main emphasis is still striving for harmony and peace, and cease any jealousy or anger with one another.

3. Verse 22b, the use of the word Raca, meaning your brother is a _worthless fool_ or _hollow-head_. This is a brother in whom Christ died to save. Listen, Christ did not die for a _worthless fool_. We are precious in the eyes of the Lord. Everyone is created in image and likeliness of God. (This does not mean humans look like God or that God looks like a man, please read Deut. 4:12-20). There is the urgent need among the churches to demonstrate genuine repentance. The churches need to be forgiving, at peace, and seeking restoration with one another. I mean peace not just in each church, but let us exhibit more and more love toward one another churches that are fully Evangelical or Fundamentally sound.

Our Lord expects (the offender or the offended) to seek and strive for harmony and peace for the sake of Christ our Lord and His name and for the Gospel's sake.

> [23]"If therefore you are presenting your offering at the altar, and there [_you_] remember that your brother has something against you, [24]leave [_immediately_] your offering there before the altar, and go your way; first be reconciled to your brother, and then come and present your offering.

> (Matt. 5:23, 24)

For those who harbor angry, bitterness, or resentment towards others, they shall be dealt with by the Lord in time. Yes, and they shall regret their delay in seeking reconciliation with their brother. Listen, do not think that you can remain separate and aloof from your brother, but at same time, you can allege that you are now at peace with your brother. You are lying to yourself! If a person persists in gross wickedness, only then, we are just in separating and remaining unreconciled. God expects us to be reconciled since we bear His name.

One of the worse forms of angry is when anyone lies to himself. He may say, "I am not angry with him; let him go his way and I'll go my way!" The person has not sought or offered reconciliation and peace. You have lied to yourself. Therefore, such a person still harbors the bitterness, but he is in denial of his own resentment towards his brother or sister. Listen, harboring *anger* or *bitterness* are internal-seeds of self-destruction.

Cain harbored his anger, and perhaps his anger was hidden or suppressed in his mind. Still, though his anger may have been concealed towards Abel, his anger was in his mind. Cain's hidden anger was just as deadly. Anger of Cain destroyed Abel, and anger destroyed Cain. The church needs to be careful with people who tend to harbor or suppressed angry towards others. This is especially true of those who are unforgiving and refuse to seek peace and reconciliation. 'If a house is divided against itself, it cannot stand.'[Mark 3:26 MSB]

B. The profiteering greed of Balaam

Balaam is a portrait of modern electronic ministries and their grotesque lifestyle today. The so-called *Balaamism* and their lifestyle today reflects the low ebb to which the so-called professing clergy have arrived. As I have said, this may be indicative of the last days, [1 Tim. 4:1-3; 2 Tim. 3:1ff; 2 Peter 2:1; 3:3] Jesus foretold the rise of counterfeit or false ministers and false ministries.[Mat.24:5ff] There are false *miracle-workers,* [so-called *healers*] money-grabbing *evangelists*, carnal and wicked *Pastors*, and fake *ministries*. Remember, a half-truth is still a whole lie! Deception in the end times will be so bad, Jesus said,

> "For false Christs and false prophets shall rise, and shall *show* signs and wonders, to seduce, if *it were* possible, even the elect."
>
> (Mark 13:22 KJV)

Many believers have *itching ears* today and have given heed to evil spirits, which is the teachings of demons. _Sound doctrine_ with godly living is given way to _seductive evil spirits_. Even among believers today, many can no long distinguish counterfeiters from genuine believers. Friend, this is no joke. How much more then people are unable to distinguish the genuine minister from a wicked and fake minister or fake ministry? Many have *wholesaled-out* for a plastic peace. (*Plastic*, mean natural man generated.) There is no unity of "faith" without a solid foundation. The foundation must be the Fundamentals and Essentials of the truth in God's Word. This must be *sound doctrine* and *godly lifestyle*. Unfortunately, many of the saints are just too naïve.

Like Balaam, these counterfeiters know that the Lord is the one and only true God. But nowadays, the Lord is preached as a genic *"god."* Often the Lord's name is omitted to appeal more to the public or to a carnal and wicked world at large. Foolishly, some are attempting to preach the Gospel without being offensive. It matters not that they offend the Lord our God with their *watered-down* Gospel. Listen, in giving the Gospel, the Gospel is an offense to the natural man. The general public does not want to hear the Gospel.

Friend, the preaching of the Gospel is indeed very offensive to the unre-generate.[1 Cor. 1:18-24] People are offended when confronted with their sin. So, many so-called Fundamental churches are preaching and teaching a genic name, *god*. Churches are attempting to be non-offensive with the Gospel. With the genic name *god*, each person is left to fill in their *god* of their choosing. Liberals, other religions, politicians, and false teachers have used the genic name *god* long before now.

The genic name *god* is so pervasive that little do many actually know that the Lord is God's name forever.[Exodus 3:13-15] The Bible emphasis is indeed the **Lord** rather *God* is strongly taught and revealed in both OT and NT.[Deut. 6:4-5; Phi. 2:9-11] The change from *"Lord"* to *"God"* gradually began in the forties or early fifties in the USA. (Yet, the change had already been pervasive for a long time in the world.) Even Jews have opted to use the genic name *God*. Those who ground in the Word ought to know better. The emerging and mixing of languages (as world travel continues to expand) has only helped to foster the genic name rather than Lord. (Yes, we know it is **YHWH**, but **LORD** is an excellent word to identify the true God of the universe.)

There is no warning given to people as to pending terrifying wrath of God. Yes, the love of God is offered to all. But all humanity is presently under the unending and horrific wrath of God without Christ as their personal Lord and Redeemer. God's love is available to all but only through Christ Jesus. Without Christ, the wrath of God continually remains over unregenerate.[John 3:36]

Likewise today, Balaam was a *soothsayer* that hired himself out to anyone able to pay his price. The fact that Balaam was not from the line of prophets as declared by Moses in [Deut. 18:15ff] makes him a false prophet. (Hear me, Balaam was a false and wicked prophet; he was not prophet patterned after Moses.) Balaam was pagan *soothsayer*, and only as pagan *soothsayer*, he is called a prophet. Yes, Balaam even received revelation from God. This does not change anything; he was still a false prophet like many false prophets today.

Yet, Balaam was no fool; he did not want to lock horns with the Lord, the living God. This is exactly what he did. Balaam showed the Moabites how to bring in beautiful pagan women from among them, this would lead Israel to indeed sin and God's judgment upon the nation of Israel.[Num. 25:1ff]

I had a friend allege that because Balaam was used by the Spirit (prophesied by the Spirit), that he was saved and a genuine biblical prophet. I laughed and said, "Listen friend, Balaam's donkey spoke by the Spirit of God. So, was his donkey saved?"[Num. 22:21-39] Balaam's donkey was **not** saved even though the donkey also spoke by the Spirit. Being used by the Spirit is **no** assurance of regeneration. (I say again, *"Being used by the Spirit is no assurance of regeneration."*) Many fail to realize that being used by God is no assurance of being redeemed. This is not yet comprehended by naïve and the less informed. The high priest Caiaphas prophesied through the Holy Spirit concerning Jesus going to the cross,[John 11:49-52] but Caiaphas was certainly not saved. God uses the unregenerate people or nations to bring judgment on Israel, but God still judged those people or nations that brought judgment upon Israel.

Those who follow the footsteps of Balaam (money grabbing *soothsayer*) may try to *lean* or *straddle* the fence of orthodoxy. However, like Balaam (who wanted to die the death of the righteous [Num. 23:10]), died among the wicked. He perished in his sin. So will the soothsayers today shall also indeed perish in their sin.[Mat. 7:21-23] They profess to know God, but by their works they deny Him.[Titus 1:16] Some of these soothsayers today among the churches are so self-deceived that they believe their own lies. How foolish is that?

It is not the possession of money that brings ruin; it is the <u>*craving-love*</u> for it. This means that most of us are non-exempt.

> And constant friction among people who are **DEPRAVED IN MIND** and **DEPRIVED OF THE TRUTH, imagining that godliness is a means of gain.** But godliness with contentment is great gain, for we brought nothing into the world, and we cannot take anything out of the world. But if we have food and clothing, with these we will be content. But those who desire to be rich fall into temptation, into a snare, into many senseless and harmful desires that plunge people into ruin and destruction. For **the <u>LOVE</u> <u>OF</u> <u>MONEY</u> is *the* root of all kinds of evils.** It is through this **CRAVING** [for money] that some have wandered away from the faith and pierced themselves with many pangs.
>
> (1 Tim. 6:5-10 ESV)

Again, it is **not** the possession of money that is the root of evil:

> For the **LOVE OF MONEY** is the root of all evil: which while some
> **coveted after, they have erred from the faith**, and pierced themselves
> through with many sorrows. (1 Tim. 6:10 KJV)

Balaam ran after money from any people that had plenty of it. Balaam was a Midianite. Midian was a son Keturah the wife of Abraham after Sarah died. There is no evidence that Balaam possessed genuine saving faith. Though I am certain that Abraham taught all the children and servants under Keturah about true faith in the Lord our God.

C. Perishing in the rebellion of Korah

The sin of Korah is where certain men decide to *justify* themselves and override the authority of the appointed leader(s) and their rightful position of authority and rule. Revelation 2 and 3, for example, establishes the Pastor has supervising authority and rule over the congregation. (While there are likely multiple Pastors in a church, there is a *ruling* or *presiding* Pastor over an assembly.) The Pastor is held responsible over the care of church much like the husband is responsible over the family. Regrettably, today various takeovers in churches are extremely pervasive in many Protestant churches. Due to the sinfulness of the human heart, adverse takeovers exist among of denominational churches, but such takeovers are often concealed.

Underneath the veneer of even soft-spoken words, the excuses used to perpetrate this sin seems like there is no end to such actions. Scripturally, there is no excuse for taking over a godly man's pastorate. Underneath, the excuse of pretense the rebellious might say, *We are looking for good of all the people.* Many buy into this fabricated lie. There are also trumped up charges (*which are most frequently false*) that make the leader guilty even though he may innocent.

Before we get too far, the sin of Korah and those appointed with him in the delegation were Dathan, Abiram, and On. Perhaps Korah was the chief spokesman for the group. The group sought to usurp Moses' position and authority. [Num. 16:1ff] In simple language, these men were appointed chief men to lead a rebellion! Rebellion is a form of anarchy where there is no rule. Rebellion is the sin of witchcraft.[1 Sam. 15:23] The Lord is a God of order. He is not a God of disorder and lawlessness. Where there is no established rule, there is the absence of harmony and peace.

KJV uses the word *"gainsaying"* in Jude 1:11, which is difficult to understand the meaning in today's language. The root word means for <u>gainsaying</u> is from the GK *"<u>antilogia</u>." Antilogia* implies to *"to speak in opposition against another"* or *"speak against another."* The inference is to slander. But the context around Jude is deeper in meaning. Jude is actually referring to the act of **rebellion, to speak out to overthrow another**. This is the sin of Korah and the group that is associated with those who follower him, two hundred and fifty men and their families. *Rebellion* runs wild throughout many churches today with intent of adverse takeovers. There seems that there is no end in sight among Fundamental and Evangelical (*Protestant*) denominations, fellowships, and churches. Roman, Eastern Orthodox, and Coptics are less known to the public, but it is often hidden from the public. Still, it is just as prevalent. Rebellion is due to the bent of the human heart. Wickedness of such sins are equally present among the churches.

Such takeovers like Korah and his group may appear initially as just cause. (This is because Satan appears or approaches the mind to set the seed.) Yet, under the innocent inquiry is the real reason which is to gain control. In time, those who help to set this up will even lie to themselves. It's true. They imagine they are standing for truth, love, peace, and harmony for all. Nice platitude of words.

It is bad when someone lies to you or lies to others. Ah, but it is even more grievous *when one lies to himself.* Here the real capstone is when **you lie to God**. The one who deceives himself and lies to God is indeed "the fool of fools" when he **begins to believe the lie himself!** When one lies to God who knows your heart and mind, you are indeed the worse of fools. The greatest fool is one that stupidly attempts to lie to God and he even believes his own lie!

The charge that was put forth against Moses is that all Israel was holy unto the Lord. (Same word *holy* also means *dedicated* or *saint.*) Moses knew Israel was whole priest unto the nations. Korah and their group concocted the lie that Moses was exhausting himself over the people. Truth was Moses was approaching 120 old. If Moses had not interceded for Israel, the Lord told him that He would destroy Israel and start with him to create a new nation. (Although the Lord was only testing Moses, God would have never destroyed Israel.)

Many Israelites and especially *the mix multitude* became impatient when Moses was on the mountain receiving the Law. So, Aaron made golden calf to worship at the whim of the people. Aaron was supposedly to lead Israel in godly worship of the Lord, the true God.[Exodus 32:1ff]

And the LORD said to Moses, "I have seen this people, and indeed it *is* a stiff-necked [*stubborn*] people! [10]"Now therefore, let Me alone, that My wrath may burn hot against them and I may consume them. And I will make of you a great nation." [11]Then Moses pleaded with the LORD his God, and said: "LORD, why does Your wrath burn hot against Your people whom You have brought out of the land of Egypt with great power and with a mighty hand? [12]"Why should the Egyptians speak, and say, 'He brought them out to harm them, to kill them in the mountains, and to consume them from the face of the earth'? Turn from Your fierce wrath, and relent from this harm to Your people. [13]"Remember Abraham, Isaac, and Israel, Your servants, to whom You swore by Your own self, and said to them, 'I will multiply your descendants as the stars of heaven; and all this land that I have spoken of I give to your descendants, and they shall inherit *it* forever.'" (Exod. 32:9-13 NKJ)

The Lord was not going destroy Israel. As I have already said that God was testing Moses to manifest the greatest of Moses and his humbleness of heart and mind.

What we must see here is that Korah and his group reflect an unstable and unfaithfulness of the human heart. We as humans easily drift off the path of righteousness like a leaf driven constantly by wind.

There is no victory when a church or group of churches splits. Divisions, fractions and cliques unfortunately exist and will continue to exist. Splits are not God's will or plan. Unfortunately, due the fickleness of the human heart, God in his mercy allows such practices.

The church is in furious war, and no war can be won with divisions or splits in place. Pride and arrogance step into and muddy the waters. Sometimes, the parties involved in the fractions want to have their way or no way. (Some, if they cannot have it their way, they would rather see the various fractions be destroyed.)

When the flesh gets control, things just begin to fall apart. Walking humbly before the Lord is the only way. Humbleness is the responsibility of all the saints. However, we are so full of *"useless hot air"* we have difficulty keeping our feet on the ground. Some of us have our heads so high in the clouds that we *can no longer see where are going.*

Solomon said,

The highway of the upright is to turn away from evil; One who watches his way protects his life. Pride *goes* before destruction, And *a* haughty

spirit before tumbling. It is better to be humble in spirit with the needy
Than to divide the spoils with the proud. (Proverb 16:17-19)

Conclusion

Jude warns his listeners against people like Cain, Baalam, and Korah.
Did Jude's listeners heed his words? No! It was not very many years later
Jerusalem was leveled to the ground by Titus and his mighty army in 70 AD.
Unfortunately, Israel was set by God for judgment and no one could stop it.

The churches have only become more and more corrupt. The leaders are
abandoning Jesus' mandates and *only doing what seems right in their own eye*.
Jesus and the apostles gave us a blueprint (plan), and our Lord and His apostles
have given us the examples to follow. We are not doing what His Word is
teaching us to do, and this is especially in the epistles.

The churches are not calling people forward to receive Christ. Are we just
to assume the elect come marching in the church without going out after and
seeking the lost? There is an urgent need in churches to **preach repentance** or
renewal in our day. Even with hard and forceful preaching, many saints cannot endure sound doctrine and the correction. We are too full of self, stubborn,
and self-willed. We have turned a deaf ear to the Word and Holy Spirit. Don't
say, "Not me!" We as saints also stand guilty before a holy and righteous God.
Sorrowfully, we have given ourselves over to **itching ears**. Oh yes, we want to
feel the tingle. Many us are unable to endure sound doctrine and reproof and
discipline!

Jude revealed the case of the human heart. Jude hit at the root cause of the
problem, which Satan's attacks, and the churches lack spiritual maturity void
of godliness and spiritual discernment.

My friend please read Psalm 136, and let us get on our knees to worship
the Lord. Let us give thanks for His infinite mercy endues forever.

O give thanks unto the God of heaven: for his mercy *endures* forever.

(Psa. 136:26 KJV)

Footnotes:

1. "Iceberg:" when I use the word *iceberg* here, I mean most of the danger is unseen; the
    danger is beneath the water and hidden. Like an iceberg that destroyed the Titanic ship.
    The iceberg was hidden under the water. The ship hit the iceberg cutting a gigantic
    hole in the side of the ship causing the ship to sink. In the same way, there are *icebergs*
    among the churches causing serious damage and destruction among the saints.

CHAPTER 11

These are hidden reefs among your love-meal

Memory verse

Now as Jannes and Jambres[a] withstood Moses, so do these also resist the truth: men of corrupt minds, reprobate concerning the faith.

(2 Tim. 3:8 KJV)

[a]Note: the two men Paul mentions above were the magicians that opposed Moses before the Pharaoh.

Introduction

Jude's next group is not named. He characterizes this group with *image* or *portrait* rather using names. He does not point to any particular person or group in Israel's history. He is pointing to their character or lifestyle, which was apparently existing in the church. These men were portrayed hidden or concealed like *reefs in the sea*. These men in the church pave a path leading to destruction and doom. Jude says,

These are **spots in your feasts of charity**, when they feast with you, **feeding themselves without fear**: clouds *they are* without water, carried about of winds; trees whose fruit *withered*, without fruit, twice dead, plucked up by the roots; Raging waves of the sea, foaming out their own shame; wandering stars, to whom is reserved the blackness of darkness *forever*.	These men are **dangerous reefs at your love feasts, feasting without reverence, feeding only themselves**. They are waterless clouds, carried along by the winds; autumn trees without fruit—twice dead, uprooted; wild sea waves, spewing out the foam of their shame; wayward stars for whom the utter depths of eternal darkness have been reserved.
Jude 1:12, 13 KJV	Jude 1:12, 13 NET

There are at least two distinct portraits Jude seems to paint here. The first is those sharing in the *Communion* or Lord's Supper. The next image of a *hollow or empty shell* with no substance in their spiritual life. Jude saying plainly that these men's real character is obvious for those who have spiritual discernment.

Jude describes these men as though they were unregenerate. Have these men masked themselves with pretense or charade, but were some of these men leaders in the assembly? Yet, these men's inner-core is rotten? Are these men spiritually dead with no life from Christ? Do they carry within them a *rotten stench* but somehow hid their unregenerate stench? Shockingly, these are men absent of any real spiritual depth. Unbelievable! Perhaps these men only have a thin-layer or veneer-covering of the faith, but these are people void of any biblical foundation. Like today, are these people getting their degrees or ordination from *mail-ordering-houses*? (I use the saying as a pun.) Death and ruin is their path and anyone that follows them. Friend, Jude's portrait certainly fits the churches of today!

Like others we have noted by Jude, these people may profess faith in the Lord, but seemingly, these are people without regeneration by the Spirit of God. They may have an intellectual acknowledgment of faith in Christ, but some of these people are certainly unsaved. Their faith in Jesus is only at best an historical acknowledge to the truth but without genuine saving faith in Jesus Christ. They are without any true concrete and solid commitment to Jesus Christ in relationship to the church. Christ is not the Lord and Redeemer ruling in their life. There is little or no evidence in their life of worship or service for the King. They may be actually absence of genuine trust in Christ as Lord and Savior. Hence, they may have never been born from above.[John 3:3-7] They may have gone through the motion of profession of faith, but they are without genuine regeneration by the Spirit of God. Woe!

These are people that may indeed believe the historical fact of the Gospel, professing to intellectually believe in the Gospel and the Bible. Yet, are these men without Christ and void of genuine hope in Christ? Their inner-character or core suggest that they are utterly lost in sin and sit for the judgment.[John 3:36]

A. Common love-meal and celebrating the Communion

Jude is discussing the Communion, the Lord's Supper, or what he refers to as Feast of Charity[KJV], which is the *love Feast*. Unfortunately, the Lord's Supper is so frequent, commonplace, and very ordinary today. The Lord Supper is observed and finished in minutes in a congregation of 200 or 250. There is no time for sharing or testimonies any more during observance of Communion.

The Communion services is very contemporary and streamlined. Communion is "short and sweet" but with a brief moment of meditation.

Peter might be alluding to the Communion in his second epistle, but he does not use the phrase "Feast of Charity."[GK, *feast of love*, Jude 1:12] Peter uses the regular word for feast, "*suneuocheo*," which means, "feast together with you."

> [12]These false teachers are like unthinking animals, creatures of instinct, born to be caught and destroyed. They scoff at things they do not understand, and like animals, they will be destroyed. [13]Their destruction is their reward for the harm they have done. They love to indulge in evil pleasures in broad daylight. They are a disgrace and a stain among you. They delight in deception even as they eat with you in your fellowship meals [*suneuocheo*b]. [14]They commit adultery with their eyes, and their desire for sin is never satisfied. They lure unstable people into sin, and they are well trained in greed. They live under God's curse. [15]They have wandered off the right road and followed the footsteps of Balaam son of Beor, who loved to earn money by doing wrong. [16]But Balaam was stopped from his mad course when his donkey rebuked him with a human voice.   (2 Peter 2:12-16 NLT)

> bTranslation of *suneuocheo*, the meaning is just simply, "feasting with you" as given by KJV. NAS phrase "*carouse with you*" is incorrect.

The early churches practiced sharing a common meal before celebrating the Lord Supper.[1 Cor. 10:14-11:22] The Lord's Supper may have been more closely associated with the Passover meal than many of us actually realize today. The association to the Passover was probably soon dropped or omitted in the early churches due to connection with Israel and the Law and Jewish celebration. In Luke's Gospel, there is the observance of the Passover [Luke 22:15-18] and immediately following is the observance of the Lord's Supper.[Luke 22:19, 20 [see 1 Cor. 11:23-26]] Luke seems connect the two observances closely together. (However, Luke does not seem to set his Gospel as chronologically as Matthew and Mark.) Today, there is a strong disassociation of the Old Covenant and the Exodus and with no mentioning or reference in many churches. For shame! Communion is the celebration of redemption; but still, in this sense of redemption, there is a connection of the Passover and with the New Covenant Jewish Christians and their assemblies.

I am not so sure Communion was to be practiced so frequently as it is today. Some churches observe Communion weekly or monthly. (Sacramental churches nearly every worship service.) Whether the common meal was tacked-on early on in the church services, this is a debatable issue. Perhaps the practice is probably left to the churches to choose the format for the Lord's Supper.

Today, there are four interpretations (not just three) among the professing churches. Two interpretations follow the sacramental practice. The Roman Catholic view is Transubstantiation. Here it is believed that the elements are _changed_ into Christ's blood and body. Hence, it is known as Transubstantiation. It is believed to be the literal presence of Christ in the Communion. This Communion is observed as a sacrament for cleansing and forgivingness. The clergy or appointed overseer alone drinks the cup (wine) which is said to have be transformed into the blood of Christ. When Christ initiated the Communion, 'This is My blood of the covenant, which is being poured out for many':[Mark 14:24 NKJ] did our Lord drink His own blood; or did He mean the cup was only a symbol?

The other sacramental viewed is Consubstantiation. In the interpretation of Consubstantiation, the elements are present of _the bread_ and _the cup_, but it also believed that Christ's _blood_ and _body_ are equally present. Consubstantiation teaches there are four elements present: the bread (1), the wine (2), the blood (3), the body of Christ (4). Consubstantiation was put forth by Dr. Martin Luther. Unlike Transubstantiation which provides forgiveness of sin, Consubstantiation interpreted the elements as a means of grace to the believer, but the true believers' redemption is already complete in Christ.

The two non-sacramental interpretations are the _Spiritual Presence_ of Christ and the _Memorial_ (or _Celebratory_) interpretations. John Calvin established the view that Christ was _spiritually present_ during Communion, the Spiritual Presence of Christ. Calvin held that there were spiritual benefits in taking the Lord's Supper, but Calvin's view of "the spiritual benefit(s)" are unclear to me. Calvin held that Christ is Present during Communion service but not necessarily present in the element of the bread or cup. Yes, our Lord certainly is present during worship service, as noted below. So then, if our Lord is present during worship services (which He is definitely present), then, Christ is present during Communion.

> "These things says He who holds the seven stars [a reference to the _Pastors_] in His right hand who [_Christ_] **WALKS IN THE MIDST** of the seven golden lampstands [which is _the seven churches_]."　　　　　　(Rev. 2:1 NKJ)

Additionally, in Revelation, our Lord is examining each of _our inner motives_ during worship and observance of Communion, 'I am He who searches the **MINDS** and **HEARTS** [_inner most being_].'[Rev. 2:23] Our Lord is examining our _attitude_ and our _thoughts_ and _mindset_. What is our _attitude_ and _thinking_ towards Him and our brethren in church? In this instance, we need to be very much aware of our mindset even when we supposedly think our minds are blank or empty. Friend, let us be forever conscious of our Lord's presence as He is examining our thoughts of Him and others in the church and even those outside the church.

As I have said, it is difficult to clearly understand Calvin's complete view of Communion. John Calvin is a very important person to note especially due to his strong influence, particularly in reference to Evangelical Theology. (Calvin's influence is far greater than many realize and rightly so if I may add.) He definitely is worthy of studying more carefully. Unfortunately, Calvin is misunderstood and unfortunately overlooked by some extreme Evangelicals and Fundamentalists. Shame on those who bypass him.

Ulrich (or Huldrych) Zwingli a Swiss reformer during Reformation held what has been referred to as the Memorial view, which I prefer calling Celebratory view. A memorial tends to remind me of the departed dead. Friend, Christ the Lord is very much alive and risen. Hallelujah! (Hence, I refer to this interpretation as the Celebratory view in my practice.)

Did you know that Zwingli actually agreed with Luther in his doctrine? True, he only disagreed over the teaching of Communion. Otherwise, Zwingli generally agreed with Luther. Zwingli may have held that there were *spiritual benefits* in Communion as a reformer during Reformation, but this point is not clear to me on this point on Zwingli. Most Bible churches have followed Zwingli's interpretation of Communion; that is, it is a Memorial.

If grace is given through Communion, the Bible is silent on the issue. Grace might be communicated through prayer, but whether it is even proper speak of special blessing such as grace through the Lord's Supper or even in prayer, I would rather think we ought to be careful in imagining such an idea. I tend to be a little cautious with such assumptions since the Scripture is not explicit concerning this issue on Communion. Caution should be used in discussing such things since, "greater is He [*the Holy Spirit*] that is in you, than he that is in the world." [1 John 4:4 KJV] As believers, Christ is indeed within us by the Holy Spirit. There is nothing greater to have than having the presence of the Holy Spirit within us! So, how could we have more grace with the Holy Spirit abiding in us?

A few key words to note in Jude 1:12, 13:

Jude uses several words with the association of "Feast of Charity." a) *spots in your* Feast of Charity. b) *feast* [GK, *suneuocheo*] *with you without fear.* [NKJ] c) feeding themselves without fear.

a) *Spots in your Feast of Charity* [KJV]: the GK word *spilas* is for "*spots.*" The meaning of the word *spilas* is actually "*rocks in the sea:*" meaning "*hid-*

171

den reefs" and not "*spots.*" The Friberg Analytical GK Lex says concerning the GK word *spilas*: "ungodly people who wreck the lives of others before danger is suspected *hidden danger.*"[1]

b) *Feeding themselves without fear* [KJV]: void of fear or reverence for God. For sure, there is very little fear of God it seems among the saints today. The churches' leadership set the trend for worship service, attitude, actions, and activities in the church. So, how the Pastor(s) and spiritual leaders behave in the church shall be held accountable before God. Certainly, the leadership ought to set the pace and norm in the worship service and other activities.

The church leadership set pace and norm with their *demeaner, dressing down or flamboyant dress, behavior, attitude,* and other things. After all, are we not entering a building sanctified for worshiping the Lord Almighty? Has it escaped your notice, friend, that there are angels present observing our worship? The King Himself is present. There are man, woman, or children watching the leaders. Families notice if there is less reverence for the Lord in or just outside. The people will pattern themselves after the leaders that are in charge of church and all activities.

c) *Feeding themselves without fear:* [KJV] the word *feeding* is the root word for shepherding (GK, *poimaino*). The same word "*feed*" [KJV] in [John 21:16]. *Poimaino* means to shepherd by *watching* the sheep, *feed* or *feeding* the sheep, *caring* for the sheep, and *guarding* the sheep. Friberg says of the word *poimaino*:

"- as one who takes care of a group of animals, especially shepherding a flock *tend, feed, pasture* (Luke 17.7); metaphorically, of administrative and protective activity in relation to a community of believers; *guide, care for, look after* (Acts 20.28); with emphasis on the governing aspects of administration *rule* (Rev. 2.27)"[2]

Paul warns the church at Corinth in their ungodly behavior.[1 Cor. 1:10-13; 3:1-4; 5:1ff; 10:14ff; 11:18-22, 27-30] In chapter 11:30, "For this cause many *are weak* and *sickly* among you, and many *sleep.* "[actually = *many died*] The Lord took the life of some believers because they were living very immoral lives. Woe! How much more even among the churches today? There is very little fear of God among the saints today. This is unfortunately even among the leadership. For shame! If the Lord continued the same judgment as He did in 1 Cor. 11:30 today, there might be even more empty seats.

B. Hollow shell, void of spiritual life, and casting off their shame

Next, Jude uses ungodly characteristics to describe the lifestyle of the some of the people among the church. This is unbelievable! Note the phrases associated in each portrait:

a. They are *clouds without water*: Jude uses farming image to illustrate the character of the ungodly which also worship in the church. Clouds is a good sign to the farmer. Clouds are hope for the need of rain for his planted crop. However, these clouds Jude refers to bring no rain or blessing. Clouds symbolize rain that is very necessary for watering or nutrition for the crops. In the same way, these men may be actual Elders (or supposed leaders in the church); but these Elders provide no spiritual nutrition for the saints. Let me tell you I have seen such leaders in churches, and yes, they were spiritually lifeless; believe me, they were **spiritually dead**. Friend, I mean they were indeed **spiritually dead**!

And why may we ask that these men *provide no spiritual nutrition for the saints*? There is no spiritual-life within these spiritual leaders. They are not only wicked but may be unregenerate and without Christ as Lord and Savior. Oh yes, they profess to know Jesus Christ as Lord, but as noted earlier, they are liars and unsaved.

1) *Carried about by the winds*: Like the clouds that are motionless and unable to move on their own. These clouds Jude is referring to drift by the winds of the *flesh*, the *world*, and *evil ones*. Their sermons are without any substance, no power, and void of spiritual truth or depth. Their doctrine of God is empty, completely bankrupted.

In addition, these false teachers are driven by the winds: as such, they are driven by the impulse of the *lower nature*. Hence, they are as Jacob said of his son Reuben, 'unstable *and* reckless *and* boiling over like water [in sinful lust]-' Gen. 49:4 AMP.

b. *Late autumn trees without fruit*: Autumn is the time when the fruit trees are harvested. Yet, these men bear no fruit. There is little or no evangelism. They do not know even how to give an invitation to receive Christ as Lord and Savior. How bankrupt it that? Our Lord said, 'Wherefore by their fruits ye shall know them,' Mat. 7:20 KJV. These men are spiritually barren and fruitless. Why, they are spiritually barren, and as our Lord said, 'without Me you can do nothing,' John 15:5.

(1) *Twice dead, plucked up by the roots*: Wow! Here the imagery is not only trees that are completely dead, but these trees are completely unrooted, laying on the ground. Shockingly, like trees uprooted, these are trees that in absolutely no way can they produce any fruit. These are so-called ministers, which is a farce. These ministers are completely lifeless, no life. They have

no life of Christ in them. Hence, they are *twice dead, plucked up by the roots*. Yeah, these trees that may look sound or good for at least firewood. However, these trees are laying down on the ground. These trees after examining the tree on the ground are totally rotten through and through. Even the wood is not good for firewood. So, it is with these counterfeit or worldly Elders; they are useless. You might as well just *chuck them* or *pitch them*. I mean *get rid of them*. Regrettably, for many churches, there will be no "cleaning house."

c. *Raging waves of the sea*: Here Jude uses the picture of the waves of the sea crashing into the shore. **Raging waves**, perhaps destructive and having no benefit to anything or anyone. The *crashing waves* erode the much needed soil, and the *crashing waves* bring destruction and ruin with them.

(1) *Foaming up their own shame*: Jude goes one step further, some of these men may have been so openly immoral that their shame is evident to those with spiritual discernment. (Unfortunately, there is little spiritual discernment today.) Paul describes false teachers this way,

> Having a **form of godliness**, but denying the power thereof: from such turn away. For of this sort are [these type of people] they which creep into houses, and lead captive silly women laden with sins, led away with divers lusts [evil desires, NIV], Ever learning, and never able to come to the knowledge of the truth. Now as Jannes and Jambres withstood Moses, so do these also resist the truth: men of corrupt minds, reprobate concerning the faith. But they shall proceed no further: for their folly shall be manifest unto all *men*, as theirs also was.   (2 Tim. 3:5-9 KJV)

d. *Wandering stars*: Jude is not referring to stars in universe. Stars are suns and very huge. Mostly likely Jude means *asteroids* [asteroids look like stars to human eye.] Asteroids serve very little purpose. Asteroids move through space at a high rate of speed. If asteroids hit anything in their path, they will crash into whatever is in front of them. If anything is in their path, the *asteroids* will destroy it and itself. So, if anyone adheres to or follows these false teachers, they are headed for their own doom along with the false teachers.

(1) *For whom is reserved the blackness of darkness forever*: Jude is saying that the Lake of Fire will be their final abode. Some may laugh at Hell (the Lake of Fire), and they remark, "Well, I will have a lot of company." No! In Hell, you cannot even see your hand in front of you even though a person is in his resurrected body. Friend, in Hell, a person is all alone. There is no one near you. Hell is more than dark. Hell is void of any light; it is utter darkness. There is nothing but gloom and total despair. All alone, hopeless, and totally dejected. Hell is pictured as a place of unimaginable and endless suffering and despair.

Today, the churches are flooded with charlatans, counterfeiters, false teachers, and fake healers. These charlatans are fleecing people of their money. These charlatans are *ripping off and fleecing the saints that belongs to the Lord.* They ignorantly tell people, "If you have enough faith, you will be healed." What a lie! Jesus said if we have the faith the size of a mustard seed to the apostles who had authority to heal,

> The apostles said to the Lord, "Increase our faith!" And the Lord said, "If you had faith like a grain of mustard seed, you could say to this mulberry tree, 'Be uprooted and planted in the sea,' and it would obey you." (Luke 7:5, 6 ESV)

Sadly, the above text is robbed of its rightful context. The healing was the authority granted to the apostles as signs of true prophet or apostle.[Heb.2:4; Rom. 15:19; 2 Cor. 12:4, 12] The Jews looked for signs of genuine prophet or apostle.[1 Cor. 1:18] This is like saying that the apostles had the mind of Christ. Thus, ignorantly alleging that the church has the mind of Christ [1 Cor. 2:16]. The notion we have the mind of Christ is totally ludicrous. The carnal church at Corinth certainly did not possess the mind of Christ. Hear me, neither do we possess the mind of Christ today. This is *eisegesis* in the worst form!

The promise of healing was directed to the apostles and those specially endowed by Christ the Lord. (Signs and wonders accompany them.[Matt. 10:1ff; Heb. 2:3, 4]) There is for sure spiritual application. By application, our prayer must first be in line with God's will.

> And this is the boldness we have in him, that if we ask anything according to his will, he hears us. [15] And if we know that he hears us in whatever we ask, we know that we have obtained the requests made of him. (1 John 5:14, 15 NRS)

Healing was a sign, wonder, and miraculous miracle that were proofs that these men were men of God (*ish Elohim*). Yeah, these were indeed prophets or apostles or especially gifted by God. God heals, amen, but He heals according to His will,

> In Him also we have obtained an inheritance, being predestined according to the purpose of Him **who works all things according to the counsel of His will**. (Eph. 1:11 NKJ)

Erase such foolishness from your mind forever. We cannot manipulate the Lord like He is some stone idol or lifeless imagine. The Lord is the Living God, and He rules His universe according to His sovereign and holy will. Praise the Lord!

Those who espouse that it is God's will to heal any and all who exhibit sufficient genuine faith in Christ are in very grievous error and void spiritual discernment and enlightenment. Some forget that the death rate is the same among believers and non-believers. There is no OT or NT text that teaches wholesale healing for anyone if they have sufficient faith. This is spiritual ignorance, and it is a preposterous lie. Prayer is not mean to move God or manipulate Him to do our will. The Lord can add years to our lives by His infinite mercy and will like He did with King Hezekiah.[Isaiah 38] Nevertheless, I am reminded that Solomon said,

"There is a time to be born, and there is a time to die." (Ecc. 3:2)

Similarly, Solomon said,

Do not be excessively wicked and do not be a fool; otherwise you might die before your time.   (Ecc. 7:17 NET)

Conclusion

It is shocking to me that Jude appears to be referring to Pastors or Elders which are supposed to be spiritually uplifting and guiding the church. Jude is giving "a tip of the iceberg." The churches are incredibly worse today. Sadly, these are corrupt and counterfeit leaders which were already working through the early churches. Satan was busy early on in the churches corrupting and misleading the minds of people. How much more in our day? Friend, we ought to weep and be horrified.

These men Jude refers to may possess an intellectual knowledge and even have gone through a *"canned profession"* of faith in Christ. Yet, this is very questionable and stretching the point. What Jude says though certainly parallels the churches across the world today. Yes, this is shocking but true. The professing churches across the world are inundated (flooded) with counterfeits, false teachers, charlatans, and deceitful and phony miracle workers. These are men morally and spiritually **bankrupt**. Unfortunately, few are willing to call them what they are: these charlatans seemingly without Christ as Lord and Savior.

Jude seems to suggest that these men have no consciousness as to what they say or do. They are even liars. Yes, you read me correctly; these are liars. These are wicked men living depraved lives. Wow! Their wickedness is very evident to anyone who has sufficient spiritual discernment. Unfortunately, the churches are void of spiritual discernment.

They are as the apostle John says,

> They went out from us, but they didn't belong to us; for if they had belonged to us, they would have continued with us. But they left, that they might be revealed that none of them belong to us.
>
> (1 John 2:19 WEB)

The churches today, like the early churches in Jude's day, needed not only to have a *good house cleaning*, but the churches also needs desperately a *revival*, a spiritual *renewal* and have a godly *awaking* that can only come by the Holy Spirit of God. How desperately and earnestly we need a dynamic and explosive awakening from on High. The churches are spiritually bankrupt!

The promise of God has this assurance and spiritual application waiting for those churches that are genuinely humble and seek the Lord with a whole heart while He may be found:

> If my people, which are called by my name, shall humble themselves, and pray, and seek my face, and turn from their wicked ways; then will I hear from heaven, and will forgive their sin, and will heal their land.
>
> (2 Chro. 7:14 KJV)

The risen Lord Jesus said to the church of Laodicea,

> Because *you say*, I am rich, and increased with goods, and have need of nothing; and knowest not that thou art wretched, and miserable, and poor, and blind, and naked: [18]I counsel thee to buy of me gold tried in the fire, that thou mayest be rich; and white raiment, that thou mayest be clothed, and *that* the shame of thy nakedness do not appear; and anoint thine eyes with eyesalve, that thou mayest see. [19]As many as I love, I rebuke and chasten [*correct, discipline*]: be zealous therefore, and **REPENT**. [20]Behold, I stand at the door, and knock: if any man hear my voice, and open the door, I will come in to him, and will sup with him, and he with me. [21]To him that *overcomes* will I grant to sit with me in my throne, even as I also overcame, and am set down with my Father in his throne. **[22]He that hath an ear, let him hear what the Spirit saith unto the churches**. (Rev. 3:17-22 KJV)

otnotes:

1. "*Spots*," Jude 1:12, GK *spilas*, *hidden reefs* or *dangerous reefs*: Friberg Analytical Lexicon, Bible Works 10.

2. "*Feeding*" GK, *poimaino*, Jude may have in mind an Elder or presiding Pastor(s) that is caring for himself with no concern the sheep.

Part Four

The Judgment of God is coming

[14]*It was* also about these people *that* Enoch, *in the* seventh *generation* from Adam, prophesied, saying, "Behold, the Lord has come with many thousands of His holy ones, [15]to execute judgment upon all, and to convict all the ungodly of all their ungodly deeds which they have done in an ungodly way, and of all the harsh things which ungodly sinners have spoken against Him." [16]These are grumblers, finding fault, following after their *own* lusts; they speak arrogantly, flattering people for the sake of *gaining an* advantage.   (Jude 1:14-16 NAS)

CHAPTER 12

The Prophecies of Enoch

Memory verse

And in *their* greed they will exploit you with false words; their judgment from long ago is not idle, and their destruction is not asleep.

(2 Peter 2:3)

Introduction

This is one of the texts that shall challenges most students of the Sacred Scriptures. Jude says,

> And Enoch also, the seventh from Adam, prophesied of these, saying, Behold, the Lord cometh with ten thousands of his saints,[a] To execute judgment upon all, and to convince all that are ungodly among them of all their ungodly deeds which they have ungodly committed, and of all their hard *speeches* which ungodly sinners have spoken against him.

> (Jude 1:14, 15 KJV)

> [a]Note: "*saints*," GK is *hagios*, plural meaning "*holy ones*." *Hagios* refers to holy things, e.g. in the temple. The word is used of holy angels and redeemed of God. Preferred translation is "*holy ones*."

Jude's quote is from the books of Enoch, but his quote is only in part. Jude is only *alluding indirectly* to the books of Enoch. It is likely not a direct quote. There are some that think Jude is not even quoting from the books of Enoch. While it is probable that Jude is quoting from the books of Enoch, he and his audience are very aware his source is non-canonical and not Scripture. Jude is using the books of Enoch to illustrate a simple truth, *the judgment of God is coming*. Friend, indeed, God's judgment is coming! Listen, Jude is **not** using the books of Enoch as Scripture. I say again, Jude is definitely **not** using the books of Enoch as authoritative Scripture. He is using the text from Enoch only as an illustration. The books of Enoch are fictitious writings, which Paul calls fables or myths.[2 Tim. 4:4; Titus 1:14]

Please listen! There are some churches that may think of the books of Enoch is Scripture. For instance, the Coptic Church in Egypt view such writing as the books of Enoch as Scripture. The material was probably written between 200 to 300 BC according to some scholars. The Lord ceased all prophetic writings by 400 BC. The canon of Scripture remained sealed closed until the arrival of John the Baptist and the Messiah. Malachi was the last prophetic book written in the HEB Bible. Malachi prophesied concerning the forerunner for Messiah, which was John the Baptist.[Mal. 4:5, 6; Mat. 11:14]

The books of Enoch are **not** inspired. The books of Enoch are **not** authoritative Scripture. Furthermore, I do not recommend it for reading since the material is filled with corrupt, false, and even evil doctrines. Accepting the books of Enoch as Scripture as the Coptic church has done is a serious and ill-informed error. Jews sometimes tended to use outside or non-biblical material. Jews **did not** consider such material as Sacred Scripture and neither should we.

As noted previously, even Paul quotes pagan philosophers,[Titus 1:12; Acts 17:28] but he does **not** endorse or agree with their writings. Paul is merely using the material much like Jude.

The Scripture declares that the devil offered the kingdoms of the world to Jesus. (Jesus was tempted in His human nature, but our Lord in His Divinity as God cannot be tempted.[James 1:13]) Christ is the Creator and Maker and Owner of all things. The world belongs to Christ who created everything.[John 1:1-3, 10; Col.1:16f] Nevertheless, the temptation of our Lord in His human nature was definitely genuine. Yet, the temptation by Satan was an enigma since the devil is a liar. So, the temptation is indeed a paradox to the finite mind of man.

So, Satan's offer of the kingdoms of the world was something in which he had no authority to give. Satan's temptation was legitimate since our Lord possessed a human nature. Listen, we must keep in mind that the devil is a liar. Satan is the father of lies, and as our Lord said, 'there is no truth in him.'. What paradox that exist with evil one! Our *Lord know all things,*[1 John 2:24; 13:3; 16:30; 21:17]

> He is the image of the invisible God, the firstborn of all creation [Preeminent One over all creation]. [16]For by him all things were created, in heaven and on

earth, visible and invisible, whether thrones or dominions or rulers or authorities— all things were **created through him** and **for him**. ¹⁷And he is **before all things** [He is Eternal], and in him all things hold together. [*sustained and maintained*] (Col. 1:15-17 ESV)

So, the bottom line, Satan has no real authority over the universe or the world. Devil is able to manipulate the world as though he controls the world but only to a limited degree. Remember, Satan is a liar. He may seem to have a lot of power and authority permitted to him by God. Friend, the world belongs to God alone and get that fact cemented in your mind forever.

Let us keep in mind that the devil is limited and finite. Yes, he is powerful and a ruling angel, but still, he is a created being and limited in power and authority. He is therefore finite and limited power as permitted by God. As a created being, he is limited in movement and action. Satan exists only because God allows him to exist. Satan cannot offer legitimately the kingdom of the world to anyone he chooses. Satan can only do what the Lord permits him the authority to do.

As King Hezekiah said in his prayer:

And Hezekiah prayed to the LORD: "LORD, the God of Israel, enthroned between the cherubim, you alone are God over all the kingdoms of the earth. You have made heaven and earth. (2 King 19:15 NIV)

As we learn from Job 1 and 2, Satan can only do what God <u>allows</u> him to do. Therefore, please hear me: Satan is limited and limited in power and authority that God granted him. However, do not be a fool; Satan is very powerful compared to fallen humanity. He is a ruler over other evil angels.

A. Prophecies of Enoch, seventh from Adam

What is overlooked is that the books of Enoch are non-canonical source (*not Scripture*). The writings are being used by Jude as folklores **not** as Scripture nor authoritative. Furthermore, Jude is probably paraphrasing Enoch as a general statement which he himself borrows or partially quotes. Enoch is maybe even *embellishing or* giving an over-exaggeration of his material. Still, he is not quoting from Scripture. Erase the thought from your mind that the books of Enoch are Scripture. Jude is **not** quoting Scripture!

Here is the actual paralleling from book of Enoch and the epistle of Jude. Note that they are similarities, but there are certainly unique distinctions and different.

Book of Enoch 1:9	Jude 1:14, 15 KJV
And behold! He cometh with ten thousands of His Holy ones[b] to execute judgment upon all, and to destroy all the ungodly:	And Enoch also, the seventh from Adam, prophesied of these, saying,
And to convict all flesh of all the works of their ungodliness which they have ungodly committed,	Behold, the Lord cometh with ten thousands of his saints [GK *hogios* = *saints, holy ones*][b],
	To execute judgment upon all,
And of all the hard things which ungodly sinners have spoken against Him.	And to convince[b] [GK *exelegcho, convict*] all that are ungodly among them of all their ungodly deeds which they have ungodly committed, and of all
Book of Enoch[2]	their hard *speeches* which ungodly sinners have spoken against him.

[b]Enoch was originally written in Aramaic. Holy one may refer to angels or the saints, but the meaning likely means *holy angels*. The GK *exelegcho*, means here to *reprove* or *convict* John 8:46; 16:8 **not** convince. (*Convince* is a Roman Catholic view, but *convict* is the biblical view.) GNV Bible uses "*rebuke*," which means to correct.

The books of Enoch omits the use of the name "**Lord**," which is unusual for an Orthodox Jew to omit the name of the Lord especially during this period. Jude refers to God as the "Lord." Jude does not use a pronoun, "*he*."

The expression, "cometh with ten thousands" is GK "*murias*," which can mean: "ten thousand, thousands, innumerable hosts, and myriads and myriads." (Comes with "ten thousand_s_" is an old ENG spelling.) "*Ten thousand*" is an expression used in Scripture.

> The **LORD came** from Sinai, and rose up from Seir unto them; he shined forth from mount Paran, and **he came with ten thousands** [or *ten thousand*] **of saints**:   (Deut. 33:2 KJV)

> The chariots of God **are ten thousand** fold, thousands of rejoicing ones: **the Lord is among them**, in Sina, in the holy place. (Psa. 68:17 LXE)

> — **ten thousand** times ten thousand stood before him: the judgment was set -   (Dan. 7:10 KJV)

> "— the number of them was **ten thousand times ten thousand**, and thousands of thousands."   (Rev. 5:11 KJV)

The phrase "*ten thousand*(s)" is a common phrase, whether the phrase is a metaphor or literal is debatable. The meaning intended is "*an innumerable number*." The similarity between Jude and Deut. 33:2 is significant enough to note. It is likely that the author of books of Enoch is borrowing from Deuteronomy, a typical phrase. Jews were very familiar with such phrases in the Bible. It may be that Jude is indeed alluding to the books of Enoch. The reference to the coming judgment is common enough that Enoch is likely borrowing the idea from Deut. 33:2. The books of Enoch are simply exploiting the material in the Bible. The books of Enoch is not prophetic. The books of Enoch are mythical or fictitious. Personally, I think of Jude's quote of Enoch as nothing more than simple reference to a general truth that God's judgment is dreadful.(e.g. Heb. 12:29) Yes, God will judge the world. However, the books of Enoch are bogus writings. Its theology is found defective and wanting. Anyone endorsing these false books of Enoch as biblical prophecy is in grievous error. Unfortunately, even some translators have been misled by the phony writing.

Therefore, while it is likely Jude is using the first book of Enoch, Jude is like Paul using pagan source but without endorsing their expressions.Titus 1:12; Acts 17:28 Jude is not quoting the books of Enoch as Scripture. Jude is just citing the thought without giving any agreement or endorsing the alleged books of Enoch as Scripture. Early on Christians did not endorse the books of Enoch as Scripture. Friend, neither should we use such material as Scripture. I am sorry to say the Coptic Church is wrongly included the books of Enoch with other false Jewish writings which are non-canonical.

I know this is indeed a sharp distinction to make since Jude is using the books of Enoch. However, quoting from a source does not mean to given agreement or endorsement. Please be very careful and avoid assuming Jude is using Enoch as Scripture. Jude is **not** using his source as Scripture.

In my mind, I am certain that Jude is referring to the books of Enoch. Still, Jude's use of this material in the earlier unfolding the church, probably in Jerusalem. However, many make a serious error today if they are assuming that Jude is citing the material as Scripture. I have no doubt cults and liberals are quick to conclude Jude is citing the books of Enoch as Scripture. Liberals and cults have erroneous interpretation as Scripture, and they are wrong. So, it is not surprising to note that such groups may endorse the books of Enoch as Scripture. The standard for a writing prophet in Scripture is very stringent!

Also, the naïve, the novice, gullible, credulous, and immature Christians are ill-equipped spiritually might assume the books of Enoch are genuinely inspired. Some these same people may assume that such books were lost but now found. Listen please: there are **NO** lost books of the Bible. Even the epistle of Laodicea which Paul refers to is likely the epistle of Ephesians. Paul says in his closing of his letter to the Colossians,

Greet the brethren who are in Laodicea and also Nympha and the church that is in her[c] house. When this letter is read among you, have it also read in the church of the Laodiceans; and you, for your part read **my letter *that is coming* from Laodicea.** (Col. 4:15, 16)

[c]Note: some MSS read in the masculine "his house," but the GK is definitely in the feminine, "in her house."

Paul's letters were circulated among the churches early on. Paul was fully aware that his writing were inspired by the Holy Spirit.[1 Cor.2:4, 13; 2 Thes. 3:14] Some of Paul's letters did not always have the church's name on the letters when his letter were recirculated to even more churches. So, some scholars think that Ephesians is indeed the original Laodicean letter. (I warn you **not to smack** or **snare** at such conclusions since the Lord is watching and reading our minds and hearts.[Rev.2:22, 23]) The Laodicea name was likely dropped, which was not uncommon for circulated letters to find the name omitted. The Laodicean letter is likely now the Ephesian letter. Again, if you smirk at this observation, I warn you again that you shall be held accountable for every sneer to Jesus.[Mat. 12:36]

Paul's letters were well guarded throughout the churches in the Roman world. Paul's letters were well guarded because the Roman Government sought destroy all the NT manuscripts. The first three hundred years, Roman Government sought to destroy any NT manuscripts during this period. So, NT manuscripts would be indeed a very rare find during the first three hundred years. Even individual letters and fragments were also rarely found among the early period under 300 AD. The Roman Government destroyed all the NT manuscripts they could find.

As to counterfeit writings like the books of Enoch, Paul reveals even during his ministry people were apparently writing bogus letters and put his name on the letters. These bogus writers used the various apostles' names in an attempt to mislead people.

[1]As to the coming of our Lord Jesus Christ and our being gathered together to him, we beg you, brothers and sisters,[d] [2]not to be quickly shaken in mind or alarmed, either **by spirit** or **by word** or **by letter, as though from us**, to the effect that the day of the Lord is already here. [3]Let no one deceive you in any way; for that day will not come unless the rebellion [GK *apostasia, apostasy* or *falling away*] comes first and the lawless one is revealed, the one destined for destruction. (2 Thess. 2:1-3 NRS)

[d]Note: GK is "*brethren.*" The phrase "*brothers and sisters*" is due to the feminine movement worldwide.

Paul is telling his readers that there are no so-called *"spirit,"* or *spoken words* from him, or *written letter* by him that the Day of the Lord has arrived. As such claims, Paul is saying the letters are fake. Paul is very clear that he did not write such letters. So, Paul's warns them to watch out! Those endorsing books of Enoch as Scripture, they had better watch out as well. The books of Enoch have false and serious enormous doctrines in them.

Paul alerts us in three ways fake messages might be received:

1. The phrases: "**by spirit**" is uncertain to the precise meaning, but Paul is probably referring to someone aware of the church or someone outside the church falsifying the claim of a *message from a spirit.* Whether *by spirit* means an angelic being, some person, or even Holy Spirit. "By spirit" is unclear here.

2. The phrase: "**by word**," perhaps someone speaking up in the assembly or someone claiming to receive information directly from Paul. Some translate "**by word**" (GK *logos*) as *message.* Whether it is translated *word* or *message*, the meaning is likely a reference by *word of mouth*, which was necessary among Jewish believers, [Deut. 19:15; 2 Cor. 13:1.]

3. The phrase: "**by letter**," is likely a counterfeit letter alleging from the apostle Paul. (A forged or fraudulent letter.) The early church was flooded with fake letters. The Pastors and Elders believers had to be very astute and wise with critical discernment. Regrettably, critical discernment is seriously lacking in the churches today across the world. This is one of reason for Paul signing his name to his letter. Thessalonian letters were likely Paul's first epistles written. So, early on the church faced such difficulties with fraudulent claims.

At Miletus, [Acts 20:17] Paul warns the Elders of Ephesus that after his departure that the church in Ephesus needs to be prepared for battle. (We shall note this issue momentarily.) Unfortunately, there are many immature, unskilled, and lack well-rounded personal study to properly deal with such issues in our day. Many leaders just lack in depth of study in *all the Scripture*, OT and NT. Still others lack in study on material on various subjects, e.g.; subjects on Christian doctrine. Yet, others are *out of touch* (too much into the world or themselves) weigh or ponder on Bible doctrine. Some people are oblivious to any attack or battle with evil spirits. To them, *it is out sight, and it is out of the mind.* It is indeed incredible but the evil one is deceiving many from the truth. Listen to me, the devil is producing counterfeit preachers and teachers by thousands with their errors.

Today, the churches are greatly deficient with godly men (Spirit filled or Spirit guided men). Some churches have men, but many such men are little children and immature and unprepared for battle with evil spirits. Like little children, everything they attempt to do is: *childish* and it is hence *out of sight and out of mind*. If they can't see it, feel it, or carnally experience it, it is non-existent. Worst of all, there are few men in the church with **spiritual backbone to speak out** against such wicked error. Churches have fallen short in following Jesus' mandates. For example, Jesus said, '**Follow Me**, I will make you fishers of men,' [Mat. 4:19]. Some Pastors and leaders in the churches are too lazy to go out at night to reach the lost for Christ. (We must go out at night if we desire to genuinely reach men for Christ.) Furthermore, some leaders do not take Jesus' words serious enough: '**Follow Me, I will make you fishers of men**.' Jesus is specifically referring **men** and no *women, youths,* and *children*. More importantly, our Lord is referring **married men**.[1 Tim. 3:1-7; Titus 1:6-9] (The churches need men married with family demonstrating "managing this household well.")

Here me now! Here is Paul's warning [Acts 20:27ff] to the Elders at Ephesus. Friend, this is what we shall definitely experience if we are not out **all week long and even at night knocking on doors. We must reach out to men** for Christ. Let us remind ourselves that we are working for the King. **Therefore, we must equip other men for the work of the ministry**. This is an **urgent mandate** from the risen Lord. Paul says,

> [27]For I did not shrink from declaring to you **THE WHOLE COUNSEL OF GOD** [e.g., *in 3 years*]. [28]Pay careful attention to yourselves and to all the flock, in which the Holy Spirit has made you overseers, to care for the church of God, which he **obtained with his own blood**. [29]I know that after my departure **fierce wolves will COME IN AMONG YOU** [*from the outside*], not sparing the flock; [30]and from **AMONG YOUR OWN SELVES** [*men within the church*] **will arise men speaking twisted things**, to draw away the disciples after them.   (Acts 20:27-30 ESV)

In the first 300 years, the churches selected faithful individuals to hold on to portions of an epistle from the apostles. Some people may not have been given the whole letter but part of the letter. There was a fear that Romans might find the letter(s) and destroy the letter(s). Furthermore, as I have said, there were counterfeit or bogus letters with the apostles' names used. So, early on in the churches, Paul started signing his name to his letters to ensure that the genuine writings were from him.[1 Cor. 16:21; Gal. 6:11; Col. 4:18; 2 Thes. 3:17; Phm. 1:19]

It is amazing that with all the fragment and pieces of letters discovered of the NT (there were hundreds), the variances are only about half a page, or 2%. So, even skeptics consider this as 100% find. Whereas, writings like Homer, Socrates, Plato, and others Greek writings are missing 40 to 60%. There is little variances in the manuscript, and there is no major doctrines effected. This is indeed amazing to the ardent scholars and cynics. The same with the HEB Bible, the OT; the variances are nearly zero!

B. The Lord is coming to execute judgment

The theme of the coming judgment of the Lord is frequently mentioned in Scripture. However, the actual man Enoch, Gen. 5:23, 24, he was no prophet. Though for certain, Enoch definitely stands out in Scripture as a mighty man of God and indeed a godly man. Enoch and Elijah are the only two men ever translated direct to Heaven without experiencing death. Please pay attention: men who receive revelation from God before Samuel were referred to as "seers" (in olden times). The word seer means, *one who sees*. That is, the seer saw or heard divine revelation from the Lord our God. Samuel says,

> (*Before time* in Israel, when a man went to inquire of God, thus he *spoke*, Come, and let us go to **the seer**: for *he that is* now *called* a Prophet was beforetime called a **Seer**.) (1 Sam. 9:9)

The Enoch in Gen. 5: was **not** declared a prophet though for certain he was indeed a unique *man of God*. Therefore, how could Enoch prophesize if there were no prophets in that day, seventh from Adam? The books of Enoch were written no later than 300 BC. The books of Enoch are bogus writings. Jews did **not** consider the books of Enoch as genuine or authentic and neither should we. As for me, I am certain, Jude is inspired of God. Still, Jude would not make such serious error concerning books of Enoch. Jews in Jude's day would have laughed at him for using the books of Enoch as Scripture. So, the books of Enoch are fake books.

As I have said earlier, Jude is using the material of the books of Enoch much like Paul quoting outside biblical material. Except in Jude's case, he is using the material from his own culture, but he gives no credence or endorsement as Scripture. He does not give any authority to it. Therefore, be careful what you say about the books of Enoch! If you do not heed this warning, it will all fall upon your own head because you have been duly warned. So now, you had better heed my warning.

There are some people that are naïve, and there are others simply too egotistical. Some do not have *teachable spirits*! "All you need is the Bible," which is true. If you only have your Bible, then this will be sufficient for the ministry. However, you imagine that the Spirit shall teach you the rest: fine but you better do as John says, "**Test the spirit**."[1 John 4:1-4] You shall discover the truth at the judgment Seat of Christ,[2 Cor. 5:10] which shall be unfortunately *to your own chagrin.*

Many godly men, faithful servants of Christ, all they have is their own Bible. Some can only quote Scripture since having a complete Bible is very difficult to possess in some hostile countries against Christians, the church, and the Gospel. So, possessing books to help study the Bible are even harder to come by nowadays. This is one of reasons I have been laboriously writing to help fill in the gap.

So, anyone may fall into ignorance for lack of knowledge. Sorrowfully, some are so egocentric and arrogant even when people carefully explain things to them, they still ignore the warning. Yet still, some may not listen. There are people who are just too stubborn and *bull-headed.* This is like Korah and those who follow him in the rebellion. Korah and his group refused to listen. I mean they are headstrong and refuse to listen to reason. These people have gone on in their own stubborn and obstinate ways. I promise you that those with such an attitude will surely regret it.

What do you think Paul means to Timothy when he said to him: "when thou come, bring *with thee*, and the books, but **especially the parchments**"?[2 Tim. 4:13 KJV] If all you have to work with is the Bible, be thankful to God you have a Bible. However, if there are study helps to guide and educate you even more, then use them to the full glory of God.

If you have opportunity and access to study helps, but think you only need the Bible; I am sorry you are too arrogant and self-centered for me. I have studied long and hard to fight the fight for Jesus' Kingdom. I would gladly do it again if the Lord allowed. In fact, I wish I had studied the original languages even more to be better prepared for this day!

Unfortunately, there are too many men already supposedly in the ministry that are very *headstrong* and *hardheaded* and *self-willed* and *too full of self* to even listen to the Spirit of the living God.

Remember, Jesus said to all seven churches of Revelation (which is a very important application to us today.) He said,

> He that hath an ear, let him hear what the Spirit saith unto the churches-
>
> (Rev. 2:7, 11, 17, 29; 3:6, 13, 22 KJV)

The Hebrews writer warns against **hardening our hearts against the Holy Spirit** (Heb 3:7ff, 15; 4:7ff). The church has hardened its heart! So, how can there be a revival, renewal, and a spiritual awakening? There will be none with unrepented hearts and without a *godly-turnaround* and *cleansing* by the Holy Spirit. As David said,

> Purge me with hyssop, and I shall be clean; wash me, and I shall be whiter than snow. [8]Let me hear joy and gladness; let the bones that you have broken rejoice. [9]Hide your face from my sins, and blot out all my iniquities. [10]Create in me a clean heart, O God, and renew a right spirit within me. [11]Cast me not away from your presence, and take not your Holy Spirit[e] from me. [12]Restore to me the joy of your salvation, and uphold me with a willing spirit. [13]Then I will teach transgressors your ways, and sinners will return to you. [14]Deliver me from bloodguiltiness, O God, O God of my salvation, and my tongue will sing aloud of your righteousness. [15]O Lord, open my lips, and my mouth will declare your praise. [16]For you will not delight in sacrifice, or [*else*] I would give it; you will not be pleased with a burnt offering. [17]The sacrifices of God are a broken spirit; a broken and contrite heart, O God, you will not despise. [18]Do good to Zion in your good pleasure; build up the walls of Jerusalem; [19]then will you delight in right sacrifices, in burnt offerings and whole burnt offerings; then bulls will be offered on your altar.
>
> (Psa. 51:7-19 ESV)

> [e]Note: David was not referring to losing his salvation, "take not your Holy Spirit from me."[v 11] David enjoyed the roll as a prophet in which he was guided by the Holy Spirit. He did not want lose his position as prophet. No genuine believer will lose the Holy Spirit or lose his salvation.[John 6:39]

If your friend such as me is unable to tell you to "**watch out what you read** or **things you hear**," how in the world are you going to ever listen to the Holy Spirit Whom you cannot see or hear with an audible voice?

May the Lord be gracious and merciful in helping you to hear the Lord's directive whether it is from other people you need to listen to or read or from the blessed Holy Spirit.

> Therefore, just as the Holy Spirit says, "Today if you hear His voice, **Do not harden your hearts**.   (Heb. 3:7, 8)

Conclusion

My friend, this is one of the most difficult writings I have had to do since I must use strong words to warn you. I want to encourage you. However, this is a time for sharp rebuke for those who are stubborn and tend to resist spiritual correction! Many cannot hear the gentle wooing of the Holy Spirit though they tell themselves, "Yes I can." Many have their ears or eyes fixated on the radio, TV, videos, music, cell phones, and other electronic devices blasting away. Tell me, "How can you the hear the Lord? 'Be still, and know that I am God. I will be exalted among the nations. I will be exalted in the earth.'[Psa. 46:10 WEB]

Jude's use of the books of Enoch is **not** as an endorsement or agreement as though Jude is using the books as Scripture. (This is the mistake made by the Coptic Church.) Watch out that you are not deceived by the evil one. Do not give heed to the books of Enoch. These books of Enoch seventh from Adam are fake and **not inspired**.

The Bible warns of the last days.[2 Tim. 4:1ff] I do not know if we are in the last days. However, the events occurring today suggest that we may indeed be closer to those Days than many fully realize. Friend, it is only going to get worse. More and more people shall certainly be deceived. Watch out!

If you think the material Jude refers to is Scripture particularly the books of Enoch (seventh from Adam) prophesied the coming of the Lord, then you have been deceived. Sorry, I cannot help you. May the Lord be merciful to you.

Footnotes:

1. "Lord know all things:" when discussing the two natures of Christ, His Deity and human (hypostatic union), we must be very careful. Our Lord's two natures were never mixed, united, confounded, or collated. The two natures remain separate and distinct in order to be High Priest of God.[1 Tim. 2:5; Heb. 2:14-18; 4:14-16] So, in the hypostatic union, Jesus reveals His Deity by His power and authority by the things He did and said. Yet, in His humanity, sometimes our Lord cloaked or veiled His Deity by not knowing certain events.[Mark 13:32] Hence, the apostle says,

   > "By common confession, the **mystery of godliness is great**: God[f] appeared in the flesh, was vindicated by the Spirit, was seen by angels, was proclaimed among the nations, was believed in throughout the world, was taken up in glory."   (1 Tim. 3:16 MSB)

   [f]Note: some GK MSS use a pronoun "He" rather than "God."

2. Book of Enoch 1:9
https://www.ccel.org/c/charles/otpseudepig/enoch/ENOCH_1.HTM

CHAPTER 13

Fault-finders craving after evil and exploiting people

Memory verse

For the time will come when they will not endure sound doctrine; but wanting to have their ears tickled, they will accumulate for themselves teachers in accordance to their own desires (2 Tim. 4:3)

Introduction

Jude now sums up his brief subdivision and discussion in this section as given by the NAS,

These are grumblers, finding fault [*faultfinder*], following after their *own* lusts; they speak arrogantly, flattering people for the sake of *gaining an* advantage. (Jude 1:16)

The King James gives it this way as the NAS follows the KJV,

These are murmurers, complainers [*faultfinder*], walking after their own lusts; and their mouth *speaks* great swelling words, having men's persons in admiration because of advantage. (Jude 1:16 KJV)

Jude actually warns us as he readily knew just how these deceivers will attempt to deceive and exploit and take advantage of us today. Amazing and awesome indeed! God's Word is warning us with the deceiving words of those that will attempt exploit and take advantage of saints. When the Lord gives us such clarity of warning, we had better take full heed of the warning; otherwise, we shall certainly be exploited by them.

Only God's Word can give us such amazing and wonderful clarity and accuracy. There is no other book that can give us such "word or word" predictions and be right on target. Just think: the world around us, believers and nonbelievers, are continually being exploited by religious leaders claiming to be servants of God. Hear me, even though these religious leaders appear so godly and innocent, these people are ravenous wolves, evil, and wicked to the core.

Unfortunately, many of the saints today are void of *spiritual discernment*. Yes, sad but true, there are saints lacking spiritual discernment and very credulous. Why are they without *godly discernment*? Many of the saints are following the tune of the world and being lured with lust of the lower nature. Worst of all Satan is deceiving and blinding them with childish ways among the carnal churches today.

What is so amazing is some of the saints imagine themselves a notch above others. I know, it is unbelievable but true. Some of the churches today are similar to the church of Laodicea,

> "You say, 'I am rich; I have acquired wealth and do not need a thing.'
> But you **do not realize** that **you are wretched, pitiful, poor, blind and naked.'"** (Rev. 3:14 NIV)

The risen Lord is saying this to the Laodicean church from Heaven: "Laodicea, you need a good **old-fashioned revival** and **spiritual awaking**." Friend, the churches are like the Laodicean church whether we realize it or not. The churches today do not even know that they are indeed '*wretched, pitiful, poor, blind and naked.*'

We might say, "Well, it can't get any worse." Oh but my brother, it is getting a lot worse. Why will it get worse? "The saints are *too satisfied with our present spiritual condition and walk*! Friend, when the churches are '*wretched, pitiful, poor, blind and naked,*' but satisfied with their own spiritual condition and walk, they are chronically and spiritually sick and nearly dead in their faith in Christ.

Let us therefore give heed to God's Word and the warnings, least we become victims of the exploiters and fault-finders and becoming easy prey to our lower natures, the world around us, and spiritual forces.

A. These are people driven by the old nature

One of the childish ways among the churches is when the saints just assume everyone that names the Name of Christ is a true Christian. Not everyone that names the Name of Christ is saved. Even worse, not everyone that names the Name of Christ is genuine but a fraud.

Sincerity without Christ will only guarantee a person's abode in Hell. Ironically and unbelievably, some of these people that are popular in the electronic churches are nothing more than thieving charlatans who exploit others. These charlatans do not even realize that they are in reality laboring for the evil one. How sad is that? They are *twice dead and plucked up by the roots*, and they are *triple-blinded*: (their spiritual eyes are blind, hearts are blind, and their minds are blind). They actually believe they are servants of Christ, but they are servants of Satan.

Wait, it is even worse! It is worse because some initially knew the righteous way of the Lord, but they turn from the righteous way of the Lord. What Peter says as given by the Amplified Bible concerning such false teachers is slightly long but very important to note.

> [17]These [false teachers] are springs without water and mists driven by a tempest, for whom is reserved the gloom of black darkness [a reference to *Hell*]. [18]For uttering arrogant *words* of vanity [pompous words disguised to sound scholarly or profound, but meaning nothing and containing no spiritual truth], they beguile *and* lure *using* lustful desires, by sensuality, those who barely escape from the ones who live in error. [19]They promise them liberty, when they themselves are the slaves of depravity—for by whatever anyone is defeated *and* overcome, to that [person, thing, philosophy, or concept] he is *continually* enslaved. [20]For if, **after they have escaped the pollutions of the world by [personal] knowledge of our Lord and Savior Jesus Christ, they are again entangled in them and are overcome, their last condition has become worse for them than the first. [21]For it would have been better for them NOT to have [personally] known the way of righteousness, than to have known it and then to have turned back from the holy commandment** [verbally] handed on to them [e.g. *they been instructed*]. [22]The thing spoken of in the true proverb has happened to them, "THE DOG RETURNS TO HIS OWN VOMIT," and, "A sow is washed only to wallow [again] in the mire." (2 Peter 2:17-22 AMP)

Yes, these are people who have known the righteous way of the Lord and His blessings, but they have been lured by the *love for the world*. Other are drawn away by *sensual pleasure of the carnal flesh*. Still others, they were deceived by *master illusionist, Satan* and the evil forces.

195

Friend, I cannot say this strong enough, please hear me: we are *fighting the greatest spiritual war since the beginning of the ages.* As I have said many times, this war that the saints are in is more dangerous than all the human-wars of mankind since the beginning of time. We cannot see the enemy. We do not always know who the enemy is. Our enemy comes from all directions: the mind, multi-media, friends or neighbors, and a host of other methods. Our only defense is our total **commitment to Christ** and **to His Word**, and a **decisive walk in the Spirit**, and **taking up of the shield of faith**, and "**praying without ceasing!**"

If some of the saints were not so blinded in our present generation, they could sense the warfare going on all around them. The bombs are falling everywhere. Sadly, many saints are unaware what is really going on around them. The casualties are extremely high everywhere, but because our lack of sensitivity to the Word of God and the wooing of the Holy Spirit, it is as though: *I see nothing, I hear nothing, I know nothing, and all is well.*

The apostle Paul says (as we noted in the past),

> As I have told you many times and now say with deep sadness, many people live as enemies of the cross. Their lives end with destruction. Their god is their stomach, and they take pride in their disgrace [*behavior*] because their thoughts focus on earthly things.
>
> (Phil. 3:18, 19 CEB)

Many have it so wrong: they live as Heaven is only a dream someday, but life here on earth is forever. They are making no preparation for Heaven.

Note some of our attitudes and behavior today:
We rarely talk to the God in prayer.
We rarely pray to God for others.
We rarely read and study the Bible, expect to hear sermon or prepare a sermon for teaching.
We rarely attend church faithfully.
We are rarely involved in Bible study group.
We rarely fellowship with other saints in in the church.
We rarely do any service for God through church.
We rarely give sacrificially, faithfully, and financially.
We rarely give Christ much thought throughout the day.
We rarely (if ever) share the Gospel and ask for decisions.
We rarely giving thanks to God for His being over our lives.
We rarely (if ever) ask what is God's will is for our lives.

We rarely (if ever) pray faithfully and regularly for family and friends.
We rarely (if ever) pray for our Government leaders.
We rarely pray for loved-ones and their needs.
We rarely (if ever) give to the poor or the unfortunate.
We rarely (if ever) respond to the Holy Spirit wooing.
We rarely (if ever) discuss Christian issues with leaders.
We rarely (if ever) keep Christ the center of our lives.

There are many, many other such things we fail to do. Christ is not the center of our lives even among the genuinely saved. For many of us, we are like a little child, "Out of sight, out of the mind." Only as we fall from some seriously situation or injure then we _might_ call upon the Lord for help in time of need. How ungodly is that?

Now, do you see my brother how we are so easily overcome with the things in this world, our carnal nature, and the forces of darkness? This is why we are so much like the Laodicean church? This is why we need confession of sin and repentance in our daily lives. This is why we need a _revival from on High_. This is why we need a godly spiritual _renewal today, right now_. We are spiritually impotent to serve the Lord, but oddly enough, we are unaware of our desperate condition just like Laodicea. Even when we are warned or realized our condition, we do not believe it. Neither do we listen. Solomon said it well,

> Do you see a man [who is **unteachable** and] **wise in his own eyes** _and_ **full of self-conceit**? There is more hope for a fool than for him.
>
> (Prov. 26:12 AMP)

Therefore, let us keep our _heads up_, our _ears perked_, be _tentative to listen_, keep a _tender heart, minds clear and open_, and _have a willing spirit ready_ to do the King's business. We have only one life to live, and that life ought to be for Christ and Him alone. Let us make it count!

Do not let this happen to you as given below:

> 'I was hungry and you didn't give me food to eat. I was thirsty and you didn't give me anything to drink. [43]I was a stranger and you didn't welcome me. I was naked and you didn't give me clothes to wear. I was sick and in prison, and you didn't visit me.'
>
> [44]"Then they will reply, 'Lord, when did we see you hungry or thirsty or a stranger or naked or sick or in prison and didn't do anything to help you?'

[45]Then he will answer, 'I assure you that when you haven't done it for one of the least of these, you haven't done it for me.'

(Matt. 25:42-45 CEB)

Listen carefully: we do **not** do good things to get to Heaven, Jesus alone paid for our redemption with His precious blood and death on the cross. We do good things for Christ and His glory because we are His redeemed and already citizens of Heaven. Hallelujah!

B. These are people looking for ways to exploit others

Many find themselves caught up with *nonsensical hoopla* and carnal *emotional appeal* at the moment. Little do they realize that they have been manipulated and lured into a plastic sensualism to get into their pocket and pick their wallet or purse empty. Like the slick barker in a circus, carnival, or sideshow, people are drawn into the net, and then, they are pick clean to the bones as by vultures.

These are counterfeit workers of Christ promising to make you rich and heal all your diseases. In reality, the truth is that they will strip you of your hard-earned money. These charlatans shall in an instant abandon you and abandon your loved-ones. They shall forsake you in your hour of urgent need with your chronic and fatal illness. These false prophets will leave you or your loved-ones on the death bed and hopelessness.

Why do these false teachers abandon you? They are liars without any power and without Christ. They are deceivers without any hope and certainty in this life and in the life to come. They are completely void of the fear of the true and living God due to the ignorance and utter darkness that is in them. They are servants of the evil one and not servants of the Gospel of Christ. They are spiritually bankrupt from the get-go. The righteous way of the Lord they have never known.

Many come from long distance in total desperation seeking help and healing for their loved-ones. These desperate people attempting to get in line for the so-called healing, but these charlatans quickly shuffle them out the side door. Oh, but yes, they do my friend! The chronically ill are crying and begging for help as they are pushed to the side and shutout. As I have said, the chronically and fatally ill are actually escorted briskly, quickly, and quietly out a side door. The chronically and fatally ill are discarded like a sack of garbage or as an unwanted thing and left alone on the street. How wicked is that?

Friend, I am not exaggerating. These are the shameful things that these evil charlatans are doing today. This is done to untold thousands upon thousands of desperate people. While inside, these charlatans have their fake *"pretenders to be chronically ill"* standing by to claim miraculous and instant healings. They are liars of the worse kind!

In the meanwhile, these charlatans have their ushers lined up with their *big buckets* to cash in on the money flowing in like an overflowing river of money pilling up. So, many saints and unbelievers that follow are all being fleeced.

The stars of the charlatans' shows and their fake performances even surpass the great magician: "Now you see; now you don't." Hollywood could not put on a better production. Still, the stars of the charlatans' act are *all fakers* (*yes you read me right, "all fakers"*). There is no truth in them; they are *liars and evil doers*. Unbelievable, but they are indeed counterfeiters of the Gospel and liars with their false Gospel. They have no fear of the living God. They are heralders of a fake Gospel. They have become self-deceived and even seduced and lead astray by evil spirits. Yes, they claim to be servants of Christ. Ah, but these self-deceived liars will find that our Lord already has His word for them:

> Not everyone that saith unto me, Lord, Lord, shall enter into the kingdom of heaven; but he that doeth the will of my Father which is in heaven. Many will say to me in that day, Lord, Lord, have we not prophesied in thy name? and in thy name have cast out devils? and in thy name done many wonderful works? And then will I profess unto them, I never knew you: depart from me, ye that work iniquity.
>
> (Matt. 7:21-23 KJV)

Listen to me my brother: our Lord does not say that He once knew them but He does not know any longer. Our Lord says to them, "**I NEVER KNEW YOU**: depart from me, ye that work iniquity.'"Matt. 7:23 KJV

Many of these co-workers among the charlatans' show will finally come to realize that they have been following a lie! These co-workers shall regrettably realize that they have been helping a false Gospel, and they have become liars of the Gospel.

Friend, this is the message of Jude. They shall not escape wrath of God. Sincerity means nothing when you are servants of a false Gospel. They may say, "Lord, we didn't know; we were sincere and honest men." Jesus' word will be,

> And then will I profess unto them, I never knew you: depart from me, ye that work iniquity. (Matt. 7:21-23 KJV)

Friend, *the road to Hell is paved with sincerity*. Yes, and amen, the door to Heaven is open to all. However, once you open the one or the other doors into eternity, there is no reprieve or turning back. It is too late! Friend, there are only two doors in eternity, death is not the end, it is only the beginning. There is the one door into eternity which is into Heaven. Dreadfully, there is the other door into eternity that leads into Hell and that is forever and ever. A person's fate has been cast once a person enters the door into eternity. Friend, I am telling you, there is no turning back. The workers of the fake Gospel shall sadly follow their charlatan leaders right into Hell.

You think I am over exaggerating, then hear our Lord's words,

> Go in through the narrow gate, because wide [is] the gate and broad the way that is leading to the destruction, and many are those going in through it; how narrow [is] the gate and compressed the way that is leading to life, and **FEW ARE THOSE FINDING IT!**
>
> (Matt. 7:13-14 LSV)

These false teachers have deceived and mislead their hearers. Regrettable, these slick barkers of a false Gospel have deceived and mislead their own co-workers that followed them. Like the cow that is petted just before the stroke of the ax; so it will be with the co-workers of the false Gospel. The ax of destruction awaits them though they are being petted now by false and evil soothsayers. The co-workers of the false Gospel also have been exploited, and their fate for eternity has been sealed forever.

Conclusion

I am sorry to say that Coptic Church has been deceived by the books of Enoch and other non-canonical books. The Coptic's have added many of these writing into their Canon of Scripture. While the books of Enoch have not been accepted or endorsed as Scripture by the majority of Evangelical Christians, there are many things in the books of Enoch that people are ignorantly follow-ing and teaching. Such false teachings have found their way in the churches and even major Evangelical and Fundamental Bible schools, Bible colleges, and well-known seminaries. This luring error has found its way throughout the entire Christian community. The deception is very, very great.

I am begging you to please, please hear me: Jude's warning is necessary for the churches across the world today. Friend, I am imploring you to listen to me, you had better watch out. Satan is a master illusionist. I am warning you, he works on the minds and even the emotions of people.[2 Cor. 11:3; Col. 2:8] The devil and evil spirits come as though they are illumining light from God.[2 Cor. 11:13-15] However, Satan and the demons are deceiving liars headed for Hell. Satan and demons will seek to deceive and destroy you and your love-ones. Again, I beg you to please listen to me, sincerity is not the measurement with God. Truth is the only measurement. Make certain you are in Christ and in His truth!

Part Five

Pressing forward
in your high calling in Christ

[17]But you, beloved, ought to remember the words that were spoken beforehand by the apostles of our Lord Jesus Christ, [18] that they were saying to you, "In the last time there will be mockers, following after their own ungodly lusts." [19]These are the ones who cause divisions, worldly-minded, devoid of the Spirit. [20]But you, beloved, building yourselves up on your most holy faith, praying in the Holy Spirit, [21]keep yourselves in the love of God, looking forward to the mercy of our Lord Jesus Christ to eternal life. [22]And have mercy on some, who are doubting; [23] save others, snatching them out of the fire; and on some have mercy with fear, hating even the garment polluted by the flesh.

(Jude 1:17-23 NAS)

CHAPTER 14

Earmarks of the Last Days

Memory verse

'And it shall come to pass in the last days, says God, That I will pour out of My Spirit on all flesh; Your sons and your daughters shall prophesy, Your young men shall see visions, Your old men shall dream dreams.'

(Acts 2:17 NKJ)

Introduction

As we have noted earlier, many people today have "*itching ears.*" That is, people have what might be characterized as wanting to have their *ear tickled* so to speak. Many people want to hear about prophecies concerning the final end of all things. It is a luring subject. Satan uses such prophecies to lure and entice people away from the truth of the Gospel and our service for the Lord.

Actually, the study of prophecy tends to stifle the study and stifle godly living and walking with Christ. Such study tends to put godliness *on the back-burner* of our lives. The study of prophecy, generally, does not promote or stimulate or motivate spiritual growth and service for Christ. You might initially think that the studying prophecy might challenge us to live more godly lives and do service for the Lord when hearing things about the *last things* or *the end times*. Unfortunately, prophecy studies will at times draw big crowds and even sometimes increase revenue. However, the study of the end times does not promote or challenge us to live more godly lives and serve the King.

In the same way, this why many people of the world like going to fore-tellers, seances, reading tarot cards, reading the palm of the hand, reading tea leaves, horoscopes (Zodiac signs), crystal balls, and a host of other ungodly things.

Ignorant or ill-informed Christians are naïve or oblivious to the dangers of such things as foretellers and other such things. People who do such things are playing with <u>deadly fire</u>. Some have dabbled into such things unaware of the grave dangers. As a result of such deadly dabbling, some have been ensnared by demonic attractions and lured into a maze or web of evil forces through these various things mentioned above. Such inquiry and dabbling have drawn them into a nightmare with demons when they step into such webs. As a result of such entrapment, they were locked in and unable get out or free themselves of such evil clutches. Friend, I am not joking; I am serious!

If you think such things happening to people are funny, friend, get on your knees right now and ask the Lord to forgive you for your stupidity. This is worse than being held *captive* or taken as a *prisoner*. There is no military or government with all their power that is able to free people from Satan's grip on a person. Hear me! Only the power of Christ can deliver anyone from such evil forces.

I hope I have your full attention now! The issue of the end times may be interesting to many people. However, the topic of the "**end times**" is far more complex and very difficult than most people fully realize. So, let us proceed with holy caution and with the tentativeness of spiritual discernment of the Spirit of the living God and His Word.

The elder Jude says,

> But you, beloved, must remember the predictions of the apostles of our Lord Jesus Christ; for they said to you, "In the last time there will be scoffers, indulging their own ungodly lusts."   (Jude 1:17, 18 NRS)

A. In what sense have the last days begun?

Please note at the outset, Jude is clear that he **does not regard himself as an apostle.** (Get it right, Jude does not identify himself as one of the apostles.) Hear me again, Jude does not include himself as an apostle. In fact, Jude does not even address himself as an Elder. He is a servant, bondservant, or slave of Christ the Lord. (Out of great respect for Jude, I honor him with title Elder.) In addition, Jude points to the authority of the apostles in establishing his point.

> But you, beloved, must remember **THE PREDICTIONS OF THE APOSTLES** of our Lord Jesus Christ; for they said to you, "**In the last time there will be** scoffers, indulging their own ungodly lusts."
>
> (Jude 1:17, 18 NRS)

Hopefully, now it more obvious why Jude does not consider himself as an apostle or even an elder. Jude does not even say anything that suggests he is a leader in church. Ecclesiastical tradition has sadly blinded many people and even some scholars.

Let me *clear the deck*. (Remove all obstacles.) I want one thing very, very clear. So, please listen and get this deep down into your soul. Our Lord said clearly and unequivocally concerning the **end times** and **His return,**

Matt. 24:36 KJV	Mark 13:32 KJV
But of that day and hour *knows* **NO MAN,** no, **NOT THE ANGELS** of heaven, but my **FATHER ONLY.**	But of that day and *that* hour *knows* no man, no, not the angels which are in heaven, **neither the Son**, but the Father.

First, Jesus is abundantly clear concerning anyone that declares that he/she knows where we are today as to the end times. Listen, *no one knows the Day of our Lord's coming*. Second, our Lord said,

> "— **NOT THE ANGELS** which are in heaven, **NEITHER THE SON**, but [*only*] the Father." (Mark 13:32 KJV)

Let us examine the last thought first. The doctrine Christology is priority one! Our Lord said, '—not the angels which are in heaven, neither the Son, but the Father.'[Mark 13:32]

There are those that are quick to deny Christ's eternal deity. In the depravity of our carnal faith, we often live like withered leaves blown by the wind. So, we should not be dumbfounded why there is so much of a defective view of Christ and such great error as to Christ's absolute Sovereign Deity as Eternal and Everlasting God. Nevertheless, **Christ is the Creator**. He is the **absolute Sustainer of all things.**[John 1:1-3; 10; Col. 1:15-17] **Christ existed from all eternity,** [1 Cor. 8:6]. We know **the Father, the Son, and the Spirit are One.**[John 10:30; 17:21-23] Even in Christ's humanity, the Bible is lucid and explicit that **Christ the Lord knows all things**.[Mat. 9:4; John 2:24; 21:17] Finally, **Christ is in the Father and the Father is in Christ**.[John 14:10, 11]

Jesus said,

> "If you had known Me, you would have known My Father also; from now on **you know Him**, and **have seen Him**." Philip said to Him, "Lord, show us the Father, and it is enough for us." Jesus said to him, "Have I been so long with you, and *yet* you have not come to know Me, Philip? **He who has seen Me has seen the Father**; how do you say, 'Show us the Father'? (John 14:7-9)

207

The problem lies with the fault-finders that hate Jesus Christ and hate the Gospel. The haters of Jesus seek to hinder and distort of God's Word. (Oh yes, make no doubt, there are many people that actually hate Jesus Christ.) They spend their time looking for what they think are errors or mistakes in the Bible. This is because the Bible (in their mind) is simply of human origin and full of errors. Little do they realize they are being manipulate by the prince of darkness.

So, what is the answer to Mark 13:32 or Matt. 24:36? There are times Christ the Lord decides to "*cloak*" His eternal deity for reasons we do not always know. Nevertheless, know this for certain that the Lord Jesus Christ is the Eternal God blessed forever and ever. He is without beginning and end. He is the Life-Giver and Sustainer for all things from all eternity. Therefore, be very careful what you say or even think concerning Him. Everything in creation shall stand before Him, and listen, when people stand before the Lord Jesus, there is no appeal for those who charge our Lord with error.

Let us now step back and look at the first issue which our Lord makes known to us concerning the last days. He said,

> But of that day and *that* hour *knows* no man, no, not the angels which
> are in heaven-   (Mark 13:32a KJV)

"But of that day and *that* hour *knows* no man"

Some like to speculate concerning prophecy, even after we just read what Jesus said, 'But of that day and *that* hour *knows* no man –' Such speculators of prophecy like to climb through the back-window so to speak concerning predictions since Jesus said, of '*that* hour *knows* no man.' These *ticklers of our ears* will say, but "We can examine the signs." While this is very true, we need to watch out and be extremely careful least we trip into the hole which we may have created in our carnal ravenousness appetites.

Now *the ticklers of our ears* have us in their grasp; or do they readily have us in their grasp? We are not in their grasp because such prophecies happen to have *multiple examples* and *many, many applications*. Hold on for a moment! More importantly, and please, please get this one down: we are all **void of divine revelation** from the Lord today. We are void of fully and clarifying comprehending the exact and precise meaning of the prophecy or prophecies. We do not know where we are in the prophetic clock of events as they unfold. The reason we lack precise insight into prophecy and world events is that we are without a genuine biblical prophet on the scene today as established by Moses' pattern in [Deut. 18:15ff]. So, without a genuine biblical prophet established by Moses, how can we ever hope to know where in the prophetic timeclock? We don't!

So then, we have **no idea where we are in the time frame** of any prophecy. Friend, we are simply unable to know where we are in reference to a particular prophecy being fulfilled today. Think with me now! Prophecy is like *riding a bus*; we may have passed similar scenes on the bus, but though the scenes may look the same, it is not the same scenes we have seen in the past on the bus. Therefore, we must be very careful to watch out in coming to some conclusion(s) on prophetic prophecies in the Bible. This is especially true since the **Scripture declares** that **prophecy has been sealed** by God. Hello!

Prophecy is sealed? Yes, Daniel is one of the clearest prophecies concerning the **end times**. Yet, Daniel is told that all prophecies have been sealed. There are no prophets today in the classical sense like Moses [Deut. 18:15ff] with us regardless of what some people claim or predict. Daniel says,

> "Seventy weeks have been decreed for your people and your holy city [e.g. *Jerusalem*], to finish the transgression, to make an end of sin, to make atonement for iniquity, to bring in everlasting righteousness, **TO SEAL UP VISION AND PROPHECY** and to anoint the most holy *place*. So you are to know and discern *that* from the issuing of a decree to restore and rebuild Jerusalem until Messiah the Prince *there will be* seven weeks and sixty-two weeks; it will be built again, with plaza and moat, even in times of distress. Then after the sixty-two weeks the Messiah will be cut off and have nothing, and the people of the prince who is to come will destroy the city and the sanctuary. And its end *will come* with a flood; even to the end there will be war; desolations are determined."

(Dan. 9:24-26)

'**TO SEAL UP VISION AND PROPHECY**' means there are no biblical prophets or apostles present today to interpret the events. So, we cannot know nor interpret some particular event as to whether a particular event that occurred or is occurring might be in the movement of prophetic prophecy. So, we can only note what may seem similar scenes (like traveling on a bus), which might suggest that a particular prophetic prophecy is being fulfilled.

If the prophecy has been sealed since the arrival and crucifixion and ascension of the Messiah (which it has been according to Daniel's prophecy), then the understanding of the Messiah's return to earth in reference to Israel **cannot** be completely understood or known. This means that there is left only human *speculations, notions,* and *conjectures*; but there is nothing substantial or concrete concerning fulfillment of prophecies.

Therefore, let us be very careful about anyone thinking that they know approximately just when Jesus will return. Jesus was explicit:

"But as for that day and hour **NO ONE KNOWS IT**–"

Matt. 24:36 NET)

"[*But of that day and that hour*] not the angels which are in heaven [*know*]-" When it comes to angels, our Lord does not classify whether He is referring to holy angels or whether He is referring fallen angels. (That is, neither holy or evil angels do not know the exact time frame of His return to earth and the prophecies concerning Israel.) I think we need to keep in mind particularly that it is evil angels that will attempt to entice people. Demons will use predictions by humans to lure us. However, even holy angels do not know the time of Jesus return, but holy angels will **not** try to deceive humans.

Our Lord is definitely including evil angels (demons) since they would attempt to deceive us through false prophets. (Got it?) Evil angels will attempt to seduce us through the false prophets, and demons will use the mind to deceive us. The method used by demons is wide open to every possible means as noted above. This is especially true since demons will seek to place an idea or thought into a person's mind and seduce them without the person realizing it. This is because Satan and the evil angels will give the idea or make the thought known in the mind, as though the thought was actually from God. For instance, evil angels will use Scripture to mislead people and put the idea into peoples' minds. This is what Satan did to the apostle Peter, remember?

> From that time Jesus began to show His disciples that He must go to Jerusalem, and suffer many things from the elders and chief priests and scribes, and be killed, and be raised up on the third day.
>
> Peter took Him aside and began to rebuke Him, saying, "God forbid *it*, Lord! This shall never happen to You."
>
> But He turned and said to Peter, "Get behind Me, Satan! You are a stumbling block to Me; for you are not setting your mind on God's interests, but man's." (Matt. 16:21-23)

Apparently, Satan or one the demons suggested to Peter the negative response to Jesus to not go to the cross which seals our redemption. Satan certainly used a similar approach with Eve [2 Cor. 11:3]. Satan used Peter by putting the thought into his mind. Listen friend, if Satan is able to use Peter even with Christ presence, then, we are easy prey.

We have an example of demons insertion of thoughts in the minds of humans. This example is what might be called a *classic example* of "demonic induced thoughts." (This is classic; so, "**chisel this in your mind**.") The prophet Micaiah was asked by King Ahab and King Jehoshaphat whether Israel should go against the King Syria (or Aram) to regain the territory of Ramoth Gilead. In mockery, Micaiah initially says "yes," but the prophet says it in a way that Ahab apparently realizing that Micaiah is mocking him.

Ahab was enraged at the prophet Micaiah for mocking him. Then, Ahab instructs Micaiah to tell him the truth, as through Ahab was somehow interested in the truth all long which he was not seeking the truth of God. Here is where we get an amazing glimpse into the works of demons. "Read carefully," this is because this is happening everywhere throughout the churches today.

> Micaiah said, "That being the case, hear the word of the LORD. I saw the LORD sitting on his throne, with all the heavenly assembly standing on his right and on his left. [20]The LORD said, 'Who will deceive Ahab, so he will attack Ramoth Gilead and die there?' One said this and another that. [21]Then **a spirit stepped forward** and stood before the LORD. He said, '**I will deceive him**.' The LORD asked him, 'How?' [22]He replied, '**I will go out** and **BE A LYING SPIRIT IN THE MOUTHS OF <u>ALL</u> <u>HIS</u> <u>PROPHETS</u>**.' The LORD said, 'Deceive and overpower him. Go out and do as you have proposed.' [23]So now [Micaiah says], look, the **LORD has PLACED A LYING SPIRIT IN THE MOUTHS OF <u>ALL</u> THESE <u>PROPHETS</u>** of yours; but the LORD has decreed disaster for you." [24]Zedekiah son of Kenaanah approached, [*and he*] hit Micaiah on the jaw, and said, "Which way did the LORD's spirit go when he went from me to speak to you?" [25]Micaiah replied, "Look, you will see in the day when you go into an inner room to hide." [26]Then the king of Israel said, "Take Micaiah and return him to Amon the city official and Joash the king's son. [27]Say, 'This is what the king says, "Put this man in prison. Give him only a little bread and water until I safely return."'[28]Micaiah said, "If you really do safely return, then the LORD has not spoken through me." (1 Kings 22:19-28a NET)

The Lord permitted an evil angel (*a spirit*, [v 21f]) to entice or lure Ahab into battle. Most likely, the evil angels or evil spirits may have limited access and limited duration while into Heaven. Evil angels cannot do anything they want (especially to the redeemed). Evil angels must have authorization or permission from the Lord before they can do anything. The Lord is in control of His entire creation. Even Ahab's case: the "spirit" could do nothing until the Lord granted permission or gave *the go-ahead*. 'Thou shalt persuade *him*, and prevail also: go forth, and do so.'[1 Kings 22:21 KJV]

211

So, there are scenes that occur as though it is the last days unfolding when the Messiah shall arrive. This is because the focal point or all the prophets pointed to this day of the Messiah. This is the day upon which the Messiah first arrived. The arrival includes at His crucifixion and resurrection, of which all the prophets spoke concerning the Messiah or the Christ.

B. In what sense are the last days approaching us today?

Peter, on the day of Pentecost said concerning the prophecy of Joel 2:28ff,

> But Peter, standing with the eleven, raised his voice and addressed them, "Men of Judea and all who live in Jerusalem, let this be known to you, and listen to what I say. [15]Indeed, these are not drunk, as you suppose, for it is only nine o'clock in the morning. [16]No, this is what was spoken through the prophet Joel: [17]'In the last days it will be, God declares, that I will pour out my Spirit upon all flesh, and your sons and your daughters shall prophesy, and your young men shall see visions, and your old men shall dream dreams. [18]Even upon my slaves, both men and women, in those days I will pour out my Spirit; and they shall prophesy. (Acts 2:14-18 NRS)

If you recall the illustration of riding a bus and passing by scenes you may have thought you had seen before but you know the scenes were jut similar but not the same, this is how prophetic prophecy may seem to us.

For example, during WWII, prophecy speakers were maintaining that Adolf Hitler was the beast, Benito Mussolini was the false prophet, and Emperor of Japan, Hirohito was worshiped as god by the Japanese. So, Hirohito was supposedly the antichrist. Keep in mind, Satan and none of demons know when Christ is returning. Nevertheless, demons are definitely able put false and misleading ideas into the minds of people as we noted earlier.

So, anyone thinking he/she is teaching fulfillment of prophecy they had better watch out. Let us also keep in mind that demons have the ability to make themselves appear as though they are angels or messengers from God even as illuminating light from God.[2 Cor. 11:13-15] Many of these false teachers of prophecy can be easy targets by demons. So, these misguided teachers can be seduced by demons without them knowing they have been deceivingly seduced. Wake up time my friend!

Please stay focused with me now. If Satan is able to deceive and even put things into the apostle Peter's mind even with the presence of Christ, then certainly as I have already said, *we are easy targets* by demons to deceive us through prophecy speakers, Pastors, and teachers of the Bible. Remember, sincerity does not count; it is only truth that counts before God.

Furthermore, there have been very many men in the last two thousand years claiming to be the Messiah, the Christ, or the Anointed One of God. There have risen many religious leaders claiming to have unique insight into the prophecies of the end times. Thus, they claim revelational insight (divine insight) by God.

Some men and women that were allegedly proficient and even profound experts in the original biblical languages in which the Bible is written cannot unravel the mystery of Bible prophecy. Others may be even well-versed history and biblical theology and doctrine, but they are void of divine revelation. Nevertheless, Jesus explicitly declared: 'But of that day and hour no one knows, not even the angels of heaven, nor the Son, but the Father alone.'^{Matt. 24:36}

Therefore, there shall be events which may **seem** to verify certain biblical prophecies. Nevertheless, we need to watch out and be very careful least we are sucked into what may appear as some fulfillment of Scripture. Such observations and conclusions may only be "a scene that looks like a fulfillment" regardless of so-called clarity. Yet, the scene is only something **similar** but definitely **not a fulfillment** of prophecy. Are you with me?

Let me give some excellent instances today which **may appear as fulfillment**, but watch out that you do not get sucked into the illusion. (Yes, the example might be a sign of fulfillment, but the sign is really only just a portrait of the coming fulfillment of prophecy.)

Illustration 1: **Israel is back in the land**. Yes, Israel is now a nation fully recognized since May 14, 1948. Good example, but Israel could be displaced and out of the promise land by unforeseen events. If that happens, there is nothing to discredit the actual prophecy concerning the nation of Israel's return to the promise land. For Israel shall indeed return to the land upon the Lord's appointed time and not man's time. Then, such return to the land will be a fulfillment of Scripture.

Illustration 2: **Hebrew language** was a dead language, but now, Hebrew is a live and living language. Hebrew's spelling, pronouncing, and speaking of Hebrew was uncertain for centuries. The language is much more precise and distinct due to similar languages in Mid-East. Hebrew is in some ways much like Aramaic. This is a marvel to say the least. Still, we need to be cautious on this sign. While this is significant, this does not signal any fulfillment or deter the fulfillment of any prophecies being fulfilled.

<u>Illustration</u> 3: Jesus declared **believers would undergo or experience perse-cutions** and lawlessness will increase ^{Mat. 24:9-12}. As noted earlier, let us realize such prophecies have endless scenes duplicated, but similar scenes of prophe-cies are not necessarily a fulfillment.

<u>Illustration</u> 4: (this is a *biggie*) the destruction of Jerusalem and in particular the **destruction of the temple** in Jerusalem. This is especially in reference to Paul's prophecy.^{2 Thess. 2:3-12} Jesus prophecy of the fall of Jerusalem and the destruction of the temple ^(Matt. 24:1-3) may be only a *type*, *prototype*, or *portrait* by Titus in 70 AD, but the destruction of Jerusalem is **not** an actual fulfillment of Jesus' prophecy. Paul's prophecy in ^{2 Thessalonians 2:1ff} is prophecy yet to be ful-filled. The temple Paul has in mind is when Israel leaders will <u>build</u> <u>the</u> <u>temple</u>. Yes, the temple in Jerusalem shall indeed be built.

Still, caution is exhorted since there are no prophets like Moses to clarify that such events are a fulfillment of Scripture. Yes, there are many claiming to be a prophet or an apostle, but these are **liars** and **frauds** and **self-deceived**. These people are not genuine biblical prophets or apostles patterned after Moses.^{Deut. 18:16ff}

There are other prophecies that could be noted to illustrate the point here of prophecies being fulfilled. So, the examples above are sufficient to illustrate the point. Still, there are similar signs: disturbance in the heavens. (Translated as "stars" of the heavens are likely asteroids.) We also see the increase of earthquakes, drought, climate changes, increase in diseases (pestilences), and wars and rumors of war. All the above and many more are like scenes that you had already seen before, but the scenes are similar but <u>not</u> necessarily the actual fulfillment. Are you getting the point? Only a genuine prophet who receives divine revelation would know if it was a fulfillment or just only a type. There are **no** prophets or apostles in the classical sense patterned after Moses today. Biblical divine revelation has been slammed sealed. And friend, I do mean **slammed sealed**.

There is no genuine prophet or apostle today. Those with *itching ears* are leaving themselves opened to demon illusion. First, a prophet or apostle must come under the strict pattern established by Moses.^{Deut. 18:15ff} Second, the prophet or apostle must be a Hebrew according to biblical pattern and not a Gentile. Third, version and prophecy (revelation from God) is sealed.^{Dan.9:24ff} Fourth and finally, Jesus Himself declared concerning that day:

> **But of that day and *that* hour KNOWS NO MAN** ^[when Jesus return to earth], no, not the angels which are in heaven, neither the Son, but the Father.

> (Mark 13:32 KJV)

There is still more! Here again the proponents and speculators on the coming of Christ climb through the back window so to speak by saying: the church is a *mystery* or *secret* before Christ return. The inference implied is that the mystery of the rapture preempts (comes before Christ returns to earth.) Friend, this only double-seals in cement.

Listen, if we do not know when Christ is coming to judge the world, how can we ever actually know when our Lord is coming for His church? Such speculations are senseless and fallen off into the abyss to the unknown. No, we are unable to know when Jesus is coming for the church. Unbelievable, but there are still very many wild and crazy schemes that people speculate to *tickle the ears*.

The prediction on the coming of our Lord Jesus is so muddled, fumbled, and misconstrued because these *speculators of the end times* mix and confuse prophets that belong exclusively to Israel or exclusively to the church. So, many of these prophecies do not belong to the church. There are other prophecies that address exclusively to the church. In other words, these speculators get their prophecies confused between Israel and the church. This is like many teachers today who mix Law and Grace in the present age or present the administrative plan of God. There are others with the crazy notion that there are two simultaneous programs co-existing today: the Gospel of Circumcision and the Gospel of Uncircumcision. This idea of two Gospels is most insane idea I have ever heard. So, I say, "Hog wash!" There is but one Gospel, and this is the Gospel of the Grace where Jesus died for sinners, He was buried, risen, and coming again for His church He purchased with His own blood. Hallelujah!

For certain the Four Gospels confirm Jesus' promises to Israel:

> For I say that Christ has become a servant to the circumcision on behalf
> of the truth of God to **confirm the promises** *given* **to the fathers**.

> (Rom. 15:8)

Jesus' teaching was under the Mosaic Law and the Prophets,[Mat.5:17, 18] which means Jesus centered on the Law and its meaning and practice. The twelve apostles were worshipping and living under the Law after Calvary. Hello! Paul is a key theologian to the NT bar none, but the other apostles are also equally key elements to understanding the revelation of God. The book of Acts is actually a transitioning from Israel and the administration under the Law and into the church and the Gospel grace. Keep in mind Jewish Christian believers were still worshiping and obeying the Law even after Paul was arrested and sent to Rome.[Acts 21:20]

As I have already pointed out, some are so confused that they allege the theory that there are two Gospels whereby we can be saved today. How convoluted is that? So, some incorrectly allege that today there are two Gospels in which we can be saved. There is the so-called Gospel of the Circumcision, and there is the Gospel of the Uncircumcision. As I have said, such theological jargon is utter nonsense. Friend, this is absolute insane thinking!

Even text like 2 Tim. 2:15 is seriously abused, misused, and misunderstood. Still, the principle of *"rightly dividing Word"* or **properly handling the Word of Truth**, is necessary when studying the Bible. This is where *Postmillennialists* and *Amillennialists*, spiritualize Scripture. Such groups allege the promises in the OT and NT to Israel as a nation are gone forever. Therefore, these *spiritualizers* say the promises are now fulfilled in the church. What preposterous and ignorant error. There is no just basis or foundation for such wild conjecture. The Lord is faithful, and that my friend is why the Lord will surely call Israel as His covenant people when the time comes.

Wait, there is more. Conversely to the other two theological groups mentioned above, there are some Dispensationalists that make such dichotomy between the *church* and *Israel* that they allege that the church is not under the New Covenant. Such Dispensationalists maintain that Paul only means a New Covenant. Some hyper-dispensationalists even allege Hebrews Epistle is not for the church. How weird is that? Other hyper-dispensationalists even allege that the general epistles (Hebrews through Revelation) are the circumcision epistles (only Jewish believers in future) and not for the church. Paul's epistles are the only epistles for the church.

While it is true that Paul is a chief theologian for the NT, this does not mean to cast away the rest of the NT or the HEB Bible, the OT. This is the confusion that many are working through today. Some are so ignorant that they only preach and teach the NT. How wacky is that? It is no wonder why there is such confusion and chaos in the theological world. At the core of this confusion is not just the carnal flesh and the world's influence, but demons are helping to fill the minds! Further confusion exists because there are just many *deficient* in Scripture, *without spiritual discernment*. Some have never read through the OT or even the NT once. Friend, this sick! Still others, they have concocted *mindboggling and mad speculations* running incredibly wild.

Therefore, please be cautious when studying or hearing people speak as experts on biblical prophecy. There are many similarities to what appears as fulfillment, but similarities are not necessarily fulfillment. We can only know with certainty with a genuine prophet or apostle on the scene today. However, **there are NO biblical prophets or apostles today**. Biblical prophecies have been sealed! So, there are many people that have been unknowingly **deceived by evil spirits**. Yes, there are people that are no doubt sincere, but listen, they are in very grievous error.

Watch out also because Satan indeed will use *"things to come"* in prophecy to lure people away from the Gospel. Yes, I say again, Satan will use *future events in prophecy* to lure people away from the Gospel. The evil one will use prophecy to draw even the saints away from living godly lives and actually keep them from serving our Lord Jesus. Friend, I am warning you, you had better watch out.

Conclusion

Prophetic study is not as clear and simple as some proponents of prophecy may imply. Prophecy in Scripture is very complex and difficult. More importantly, there are no true prophets or apostles in classical sense today. A biblical prophet or apostle as established under Moses are very strict and stringent. Furthermore, overlooked, the Lord will allow the false prophet to actually appear as fulfillment even using miracles to deceive people. But listen, the Lord is testing His people and their faithfulness to Him and His Word. Listen, the Lord maybe even testing our spiritual discernment. Watch out!

> "If there arises among you a prophet or a dreamer of dreams, and he gives you a sign or a wonder, and the sign or the wonder comes to pass [e.g., is fulfilled], of which he spoke to you, saying, `Let us go after other gods'— which you have not known— `and let us serve them,' you shall not listen to the words of that prophet or that dreamer of dreams, for the LORD your God is testing you to know whether you love the LORD your God with all your heart and with all your soul. (Deut. 13:1-3 NKJ)

Today, it is easier to deceive. Today, the name of the Lord is removed! The person's *"god"* is left unnamed to filled in the blank. The omission of "the **Lord**" as God and the generic use of *"god"* has opened the *Pandora's Box* for people to be led astray. This is especially true of those who *soft-peddle* the Gospel to avoid offending their *audience* or *constituency*. Here in is the problem today: there is just too much soft-pedalling of the Gospel to avoid offending people. The name of the Lord is nearly out of the equation today.

Well, "Do you just preach a generic *'god,'* or do you preach Jesus Christ as Lord?" Let me use Open Bible Ministries' overall theme verses,

> For we do not preach ourselves but **CHRIST JESUS AS LORD**, and ourselves as your bond-servants for Jesus' sake. For God, who said,

> "Light shall shine out of darkness," is the One who has shone in our hearts to give the Light of the knowledge of the glory of God in the face of Christ. (2 Cor. 4:5, 6)

Therefore, *caution* is the watch word. It is easy to be led into the maze but difficult to find your way out. Let us be very careful least you are lured in the web of demons rather than God. You may be in a web in which you cannot get out. Don't laugh; friend, I am *dead serious*.

There are many prophecies some people are alleging that are being fulfilled today. However, whether such alleged prophecies are only a type or fulfillment, there is no genuine prophet or apostle present today to confirm or reject the alleged event. Daniel declares upon the time of the Messiah that prophecy has been sealed closed by the Lord our God. I am warning you so you do not get taken in or lured by some smooth talkers of prophecy.

Take heed of Jesus' warning:

> Be ye therefore ready also: for the Son of man cometh at an hour when ye think not. (Luke 12:40 KJV)

> Keep awake therefore, for you do not know on what day your Lord is coming. [43]But understand this: if the owner of the house had known in what part of the night the thief was coming, he would have stayed awake and would not have let his house be broken into. [44]Therefore you also must be ready, for the Son of Man is coming at an unexpected hour.
>
> (Matt. 24:42-44 NRS)

CHAPTER 15

Characteristics accentuating our day

Memory verse

However, you are not in the flesh but in the Spirit, if indeed the Spirit of God dwells in you. But if anyone does not have the Spirit of Christ, he does not belong to Him. If Christ is in you, though the body is dead because of sin, yet the [*human*] spirit[a] is alive because of righteousness [*of Christ*]. But if the Spirit of Him who raised Jesus from the dead dwells in you, He who raised Christ Jesus from the dead will also give life to your mortal bodies through His Spirit who dwells in you. (Rom. 8:9-11)

[a]Note: Paul is referring to human spirit, which both saved and unsaved possess.

Introduction

Jude lays out three (triads again) distinct traits or earmarks of potential trouble makers we may encounter around the church or actually existing in the church. Jude says,

These are the ones who cause divisions, worldly-minded, devoid of the Spirit. (Jude 1:19)

Just because a person attends a church or becomes a member of a church that professes Christianity, this does not mean that a person is indeed a genuine Christian and born again in true biblical sense. A Christian is a person that is

219

truly born from above [John 3:3-7] by Spirit of the Lord and now in Christ and a citizen of Heaven.[Phi. 3:20] Yes, there might be even unsaved that is a member in an Evangelical church. Even if the person intellectually believes the Gospel, this does not mean he is actually regenerated and in Christ in biblical sense. The intellectual acknowledgment concerning the facts of the Gospel is by no means a proof that someone is actually saved. It just means they are not stupid, but they may not necessarily be saved and in Christ.

As I have repeatedly said, intellectual assent or an intellectual confession of historical faith in Christ is by no means an assurance or genuine evidence that a person is truly born from above by the Holy Spirit. Jesus said to Nicodemus who believed the Bible, a scholarly teacher of the Bible, and even a high-ranking ruler in Israel,

> Jesus answered him, "Very truly, I tell you, no one can see the kingdom of God without being **born from above**." [4]Nicodemus said to him, "How can anyone be born after having grown old? Can one enter a second time into the mother's womb and be born?" [5]Jesus answered, "Very truly, I tell you, no one can enter the kingdom of God without being born of water[b] and Spirit. [6]What is born of the flesh is flesh, and what is born of the Spirit is spirit. [7]Do not be astonished that I said to you, 'You must be **born from above**.' (John 3:3-7 NRS)
>
> [b]Note: Jesus does not mean by 'being born of water,' _water baptism_. The thief on cross believed, and he was saved without _water baptism_. Cornelius and his household received the Spirit before _water baptism_. [Acts 10:44f] The "water" Jesus is referring to is the Word of God.[Eph. 5:26; Titus 3:5]

Water baptism does not save anyone. _Water baptism_ will get you wet, but **water baptism will not save you** from your sins. The thief on the cross believed in Jesus, and he was saved by personally trusting in Jesus Christ as the Lord. The thief was never even water baptized. Jesus said to the thief on the cross due his faith in Christ, 'Jesus said unto him, "Verily I say unto thee, _Today_ shalt thou be with me in paradise."'[Luke 23:43 KJV]

Similarly, as noted above, Cornelius and all in his household believed and received the Holy Spirit before being water baptized.[Acts 10:44ff] This conclusively establishes that a person is saved without being _water baptized_. If water baptism was necessary for salvation, Cornelius and his household would have to be water baptized before receiving the Holy Spirit. However, they all received the Holy Spirit before being _water baptized_.

Paul and Silas told the Philippian jailer how to receive eternal life and become genuinely redeemed in Christ. Paul and Silas said to the jailer who asked how to have eternal life,

> Then he [*the head-jailer*] called for a light, and sprang in, and came trembling, and fell down before Paul and Silas, And brought them out, and said, Sirs, what must I do to be saved? And they said, Believe [trust] on the Lord Jesus Christ, and thou shalt be saved, and thy house.
>
> (Acts 16:29-31 KJV)

Those who adamantly teach that water baptism is required to be saved, though they are zealously sincere, friend, they are in serious error and **deadly wrong**. This is because Jesus paid the full price for our redemption with His shed blood and death on the cross. It is all by grace.[Eph. 2:8-10] As the hymn writer said, "Jesus paid it all, All to Him I owe; Sin had left a crimson stain, He washed it white as snow."[1] Yes, Jesus paid it all, and friend, **eternal life is all by grace** *plus nothing*. Trust in the Lord Jesus, and He will indeed save you to the uttermost.[Heb. 7:25]

To be genuinely saved by the Holy Spirit, we must **place our personal trust and commitment upon Jesus Christ as the Lord** *trusting* with all our whole heart and soul that the Lord Jesus died on the cross for sins and arose again.[1 Cor. 15:3,4] Therefore, to receive eternal life, just **call upon the Lord Jesus right now**, confess that you are a sinner, and **call upon the Lord to save you**. Tell Him you want to **receive Him (Jesus Christ) by faith as the Lord of your life** right now.[Rom. 10:9-13] The promise is guaranteed, "But to all who have received him– those who believe [*truly trust*] in his name– he has given the right to become God's children."[John 1:12 NET]

Jesus said, as translated by Common English Bible,

> "This is why I told you that you would die in your sins. If you don't believe that **I Am**[c], you will die in your sins."   (John 8:24 CEB)
>
> [c]Note: there is no "*he*" in the GK, and the "**I AM**" is the literal name for the Lord. "**I AM**" is the eternal Name for God.[Exodus 3:13-15]

If anyone is relying anything else other than **trusting** and **receiving** Jesus Christ as their personal Lord and Savior, they will certainly perish in their sins. Jesus alone is the only way into Heaven. Listen to me, there is no church that can give eternal life; Jesus as Lord is the only One who can give eternal life. There is no other name given whereby we can be saved from our sin and have eternal life in Heaven.[Acts 4:12] Jesus said when we truly believe the Father who sent Him as Lord,

> Very truly, I tell you, anyone who hears my word and believes [*trust in*] him who sent me has eternal life, and does not come under judgment, but has passed from death to [*into eternal*] life.   (John 5:24 NRS)

If you do not recall when you passed from death into eternal life, you should make sure *right now* by calling on Jesus and receiving right now!

Yes, the church has fallen away from the mandates of Christ. Yes, the church in many ways has corrupted itself and has become carnally minded. Yes, Yes, the church has been caught up and entangled with the world. Still, the church is the only origination that Jesus established. Listen, the church Jesus started and established is invisible. The church is not organization. (The church is made up of all the redeemed.) The church is not perfect, but we serve a Perfect Savior. Jesus did not start a church of people of His own. The church is everyone genuinely saved and in Christ. The church is invisibly made up of all the people that genuinely trust in Jesus Christ as Lord and all Savior.

> Be on guard for yourselves and for all the flock, among which the Holy Spirit has made you overseers [*bishops*], to shepherd [*pastor*] **the church of God which He purchased with His own blood.**   (Acts 20:28)

True, the word "church" in the NT 85% of the time refers to the local church. However, the other 15%, the word "church" refers the Body of Christ, all believers. Anyone alleging the church only refers to the local church is in **serious error**. To say the word church always means the local church is superimposing their church doctrine or tradition into the clear teaching of the Scripture, which is eisegesis and not exegesis.

A. They have difficulty walking in harmony with others

Jude first earmark of those who might tend to incite trouble is: "These [*are them*] who **separate themselves**."[Jude 1:19 KJV] The meaning as it is used here in Jude, GK *apodiorizo*, has the connotative sense that these are people that are **divisive**. Divisive, meaning they are likely to be **contradictive** with others. Contradictive: they tend to oppose or resist certain truths. (The word contradiction means conflict: *to say* or *do the opposite*.) Also, it can imply, "asserting the contrary or opposite; *contradicting*; inconsistent; logically opposite: *contradictory statements*."[2] So, do not confuse contradictive with contradiction.

These are people who separate or have a click in the church or separate group around them. Though the meaning can mean in a sense to isolate themselves. The meaning probably implies causing *division*. Such people may have their own group that they associate with rather than just fellowship with the whole church and not to be a part of the whole assembly.

For example, Korah and his group would be an example which Jude mentions earlier.[Jude v 11] Jeroboam who helped lead the revolt against King Rehoboam. Jeroboam became king of the ten tribes of Israel.[2 Chron. 10:2ff]

Unfortunately, many Fundamental churches are divisive due to "*party spirit*." (By *party spirit*, I mean they tend to be contradictive towards one another and often arguing over doctrinal issues.) However, the doctrinal issues are often minor and not major doctrinal issues. For example, some insist only in contemporary hymns. Yet, others group very adamant demanding only traditional hymns. Still, both groups agree on strong doctrinal hymns. The issue is unable to work in *harmony together* and *being of one mind*.

So, what really is the culprit? Really, some people are **insisting on having everything their way**. Often such people will give the sense that they are being faithful to God and doctrine. In reality, they have difficulty accepting other opinions other than their opinion. Working in harmony with others of difference in opinions is difficult for some people. They have one way of doing things and that is "their way or no way." Thus, some people just have contentious mindset.

Jesus said, 'a house divided against a house will fall.'[Luke 11:17 MSB] We should never compromise God's Word for peace. We need to be faithful to the Lord and His Word. Yet, there are issues that are foolish and carnally minded having nothing to do with faith in Christ. Some people split (separated over) what color should be the new rug in the church. Such separation is ungodly and foolish. However, there are issues where we ought to stand our ground. For instance, the Bible is clear that women are **not** permitted to be chief Bishop or Pastor of the assembly of believers. The position of ruling Pastor is a husband of one wife (married once) and manages his home well.

> So I want the men to pray in every place, lifting up holy hands without anger or dispute [*dissension*]. [9]Likewise the women are to dress in suitable apparel, with modesty and self-control. Their adornment must not be with braided hair and gold or pearls or expensive clothing [*avoid being flamboyant*], [10]but with good deeds, as is proper for women who profess [*godliness*] reverence for God. [11]A woman must learn quietly with all submissiveness. [12]But I do not allow a woman to teach or [*nor*] exercise authority over a man. She must remain quiet [e.g., *no talking, man or woman in worship*]. [13]For Adam was formed first and then Eve. [14]And Adam was not deceived, but the woman, because she was fully deceived, fell into

transgression. [15]But she will be delivered through childbearing, if she continues in faith and love and holiness with self-control.

(1 Tim. 2:8-15 NET)

Many focus on the issue of a woman Pastor, but they tend to ignore or overlook the exhortation of modest dress and behavior for a godly men and woman. (What is said of women's dress equally applies to men: avoid being *flamboyant*.) Paul is exhorting godly behavior of all in worship. As to be silent in church, please see 1 Cor. 11:10; 14:34. Nowadays, people wear most anything and even eat and drink during worship. Unfortunately, many people fail to realize this during worship: 1) **angels** are present and watching. 2) **the King** is present and watching in the worship service. Listen, if the saints could see the King and angels present, I believe people would be more careful with dress, action, and attitude. How insensitive otherwise is that to Christ and angels? Well, is the King present in worship?

No military can fight a battle when the leadership is divided nor how the military should proceed with their war plans. A marriage will have difficulty working together when people insist on having it their way. No basketball team can win without working in harmony and together. The same is with the leadership in the church, people must work together as one man.[Phi. 2:1-4] In times of war, the country's leaders must agree on a plan to gain the victory.

Paul addresses the Corinth church due its divisions in the church and for its *carnality* and *party spirit* (cliques within the assembly).

God is faithful, by whom you were called into fellowship with his son, Jesus Christ our Lord. [10]I urge you, brothers and sisters, by the name of our Lord Jesus Christ, to agree together, to **end your divisions**, and to be **united by the same mind and purpose**. [11]For members of Chloe's household have made it clear to me, my brothers and sisters, that there are **quarrels among you**. [12]Now I mean this, that each of you is saying, "I am with Paul," or "I am with Apollos," or "I am with Cephas," or "I am with Christ." [13]Is Christ divided? Paul wasn't crucified for you, was he? Or were you in fact baptized in the name of Paul?

(1 Cor. 1:9-13 NET)

Again, the apostle says to the church at Corinth,

And I could not *speak[d] unto* you, brethren, as *unto spiritual* men, **but as unto carnal**, even as unto [mere] babes in Christ. [2]I *given* you *milk* to *drink*, and not meat [solid food]: for *you* were not yet able to *bear* it, neither yet *now* are *you* able. [3]For *you* are yet *carnal*: for whereas there is among you *envying*, and strife, and *divisions*, are ye not *carnal*, and *walk* as men? ⁴For when one *saying*, I am *Paul*, and another, I am Apollos, are *you* not *carnal*? ⁵Who is Paul then? and who is Apollos, but the ministers [*servants*] by *whom you believed*, and as the Lord *gave* to *every* man? ⁶I *have* planted, Apollos *waters*, but God *gives* the increase.

(1 Cor. 3:1-6 GNV)

ᵃNote: words were upgraded to conform to the present ENG spelling, but no words are changed or added except the word in brackets "[ ]" for clarity.

The various churches of the same fellowship are stronger if they work together in complete harmony. Unfortunately, due to jealousy, envy, carnality, and strive, many churches are unable to work together. This is the sad condition of many churches today. So, many churches cannot agree on how to fight the battle and win the war for our Lord in their area. This leaves the local churches in disarray, and individual congregations as well as fellowship of churches seem to split due party spirit. In addition, sheep stealing and other ungodly behavior exist among the churches.

B. They are given over to their animalistic appetite

The KJV uses one word, "*sensual.*" This is the GK *psuchikos*, implying "*the natural man*" or "*the unspiritual man.*" (From the root word meaning the *soul of man*.) NAS, translates the word *psuchikos* as "*worldly-minded.*" Hence,

[These are the ones who] *worldly-minded*   (Jude 1:19b)

[These be they who] *sensual*   (Jude 1:19b KJV)

For example, Paul says,

But the natural man [*psuchikos*] *receives* not the things of the Spirit of God: for they are foolishness unto him: neither can he know *them*, because they are spiritually discerned.   (1 Cor. 2:14 KJV)

Again, the apostle says,

It is sown a natural [*psuchikos*] body, it is raised a spiritual body. There is a natural [*psuchikos*] body, and there is a spiritual body. And so it is written, "The first man Adam became a living being." The last Adam [*Christ Jesus*] *became* a life-giving spirit.   (1 Cor. 15:44, 45 NKJ)

225

As noted earlier, Paul had to say with tears concerning some workers in the church who drifted off into the world and have become enemies of the Gospel,

> For many walk, of whom I told you often, and now tell you even weeping, as the enemies of the cross of Christ, whose end is destruction, whose god is the belly [e.g. sensual appetite], and whose glory is in their shame, who think about earthly things. For our citizenship is in heaven, from where we also wait for a Savior, the Lord Jesus Christ, who will change the body of our humiliation to be conformed to the body of his glory, according to the working by which he is able even to subject all things to himself. (Phi. 3:18-21 WEB)

We need to keep our focus on the things of Heaven in Christ. As the apostle says, this ought to be our daily aim in our walk with Christ the Lord. (Did you catch it? This is not a walk in Christ; this ought to be our walk **with Christ**.)

> Therefore if you have been raised up with Christ, keep seeking the things above, where Christ is, seated at the right hand of God. [2]Set your mind on the things above, not on the things that are on earth. [3]For you have died and your life is hidden **with Christ** in God. [4]When Christ, who is our life, is revealed, then you also will be revealed with Him in glory. (Col. 3:1-4)

So, Jude is saying these are men who walk according to the ways of the world and give little thought to the Word and godly walk with Christ. These are men given over to their sensual appetites. As a Pastor or leader in the church, watch out, you can **expect trouble from the sensual man**. The natural mind is more focused on the things of this world rather than the things of Christ, the Word of God, or Heavenly things.

This does not mean he is unsaved though he might actually be unregenerate. If this person made a good confession of faith, then, treat the person as unspiritual and immature but love him as a brother in Christ. However, if you suspect that the person is unregenerate and lost, Pastor take him aside and talk to him, and tell him you think he might be unsaved.

You will probably have to explain the difference between confession of faith and the possession of genuine saving faith in Christ.

Confession of faith: this is anyone that intellectually believes the historical facts of the Gospel [e.g. 1 Cor. 15:3, 4], but remains unregenerate and lost in sin. The person has **not** personally and truly trusted in Christ's work on Calvary for salvation. He/she needs to receive Jesus Christ as their Lord and Savior. To be saved, a person must be truly relying on the shed blood and death of Jesus Christ as Lord and Savior for his sin.

Possession saving faith: this is a person that has genuinely called upon the Lord to save him. He is truly born from above by Spirit and exhibits evidence of regeneration in his life. Yes, he has definitely received Christ as his personal Lord and Savior. His reliance for Heaven is that he has made a definite commitment to Jesus as His Lord and Savior, and there is evidence in their life. He is solely trusting in Jesus who died in his place for sin and arose again the third day. He knows when he called upon the Lord to save him.^John 1:12, 13; Rom. 10:9-13 If anyone does not recall calling upon the Lord to save him, he may still be unsaved. This is unfortunately the condition of many in the churches today. There are people that only *possess intellectual assent to the Gospel*. They have never genuinely called upon the Lord to save them and make them a child of God by faith in Christ. (Yes, there some who only went through emotions or historical confession without genuine regeneration of saving faith.)

Keep in mind at this point, Jude may not be saying the person is unsaved. However, the person is not walking as a godly saint in Christ. So, he may be too much into the things of this world to profit spiritual correction. (A person caught up by the world will have serious difficulties in receiving spiritual correction.) Some saints are void of a godly walk in Christ. In addition, such person may be weak in spiritual truths, especial in Scripture and Bible doctrine. They may still remain a babe in Christ though they have been saved for a number of years. Here is a clue to the spiritual maturity and walk:

1) Many things in Scripture seems to be a mystery to them.

2) Their thinking is too much like unregenerate.

3) They have little desire to attend church; church is too boring.

4) They demonstrate that they have little or no desire to serve the Lord Jesus in anything.

These are babes or carnal believers that need a spiritual ***renewal*** and to ***rededicate*** their lives. They need to surrender to the Lordship and Kingship of Christ to rule in and over their lives.^Col. 3:15-17 They need to have serious commitment to Christ and His Kingdom. Such people need more *time in the study and submission to the Word* of God under proper leadership. (They will have difficulty submitting to spiritual leadership over them.)

They need to study especially Paul's Epistles and the General Epistles (Hebrews through Revelation.) They need to develop a <u>fervent</u> and <u>continual</u> *prayer life*. They need to develop the practice of <u>confessing</u> and <u>repenting</u>

of <u>sins</u> in their daily walk with Christ. They need to be a regular and *faithful witness* in evangelism. They need to get more *involved in serving* and *giving* through the church. (Here is a biggie), their **families must come first** in all that they do. They need to strive to be a godly example caring for their family and loved-ones. Listen carefully: **never** sacrifice your family for service. Such service is not pleasing to the Lord.[1 Tim. 3:4, 5; 5:8] You can make sacrifices only if you were never married or father of children and free of any personal obligation responsibility. A divorcee **is not free**; he has obligated himself to his family for life! No divorcee is ever to abandon or forsake his responsibilities to his family. Listen, if you cannot be faithful to your family, how in the world can you allege to be faithful to God whom you cannot see? **It cannot be done!**

There are **no** short-cuts in the Christian walk. I say again, "*There are no short-cuts in the Christian walk.*" **If** Christ is on the throne of our life, then a person is indeed ready for the King's service. You cannot continue with the attraction of world and claim you love Jesus.

> No servant can serve two masters: for either he will hate the one, and love the other; or else he will hold to the one, and despise the other. Ye cannot serve God and mammon.[Aramaic: *wealth, riches*]   (Luke 16:13 KJV)

Nevertheless, our loving Jesus Christ must be given priority #1![Deut. 6:4, 5; Matt. 10:37] After our love to Jesus, He expects our family must come first in our service Him! Jesus expects total commitment to Him and total commitment to the family. Yet, Jesus **DOES NOT** expect or desire that we (particularly the husband, the responsible head) sacrifice our family for service. A person's service will not be pleasing to God.

> But if any provide not for his own, and *especially* for those of his own house-*hold*, he hath denied the faith, and is worse than an infidel.
>
> (1 Tim. 5:8 KJV)

What Paul says is the Christian standard for Elders in the church ought to be the **standard for all** spiritual and godly men and women in Christ. This is not a standard just for a leader. This is indeed the standard for all who will live godly in Christ Jesus. (However, no woman is permitted the authority to Pastor or be an Overseer of a church!)

> — [*he*] must be above reproach, **THE HUSBAND OF ONE WIFE**, temperate, prudent, respectable, hospitable, able to teach, [3]not addicted to wine or pugnacious [not a *bully*], but gentle, uncontentious, free from the love of money. [4]*He must be* **ONE WHO MANAGES HIS OWN HOUSEHOLD WELL**, keeping **his children under control** with all

dignity [5](but if a **MAN DOES NOT KNOW HOW TO MANAGE HIS OWN HOUSEHOLD**, how will he take care of the church of God?); [6]*and* not a new convert, lest he become conceited and fall into the condemnation incurred by the devil. [7]And he must have a good reputation with those outside *the church*, so that he may not fall into reproach and the snare of the devil.   (1 Tim. 3:1-7)

C. They remain unregenerate and without the Holy Spirit

Finally, Jude says this concerning potential problem that the saints may face in the church.

> These be they who — having not the Spirit.   (Jude 1:19c KJV)

By the word *spirit*, Jude is definitely referring to the Holy Spirit. The Holy Spirit indwells in every genuine believer and there is no exception to the standard. All the genuinely saved in Christ have the Holy Spirit. This is important to note since anyone without the Holy Spirit is <u>unsaved,</u>

> But ye are not in the flesh, but in the Spirit, if so be that the Spirit of God dwell in you. Now if **any man <u>have</u> <u>not</u> the Spirit of Christ, he is none of his** [Christ]. [10]And if Christ *be* in you, [though] the body *is* dead because of sin; but the Spirit *is* life because of righteousness.[e] [11]But if the Spirit of him that raised up Jesus from the dead dwell in you, he that raised up Christ from the dead shall also quicken [will make alive] your mortal bodies by his Spirit that dwelleth in you.   (Rom. 8:9-11 KJV)

> [e]Note: this is not our righteousness; this is Christ's imputed righteousness.[2 Cor. 5:21; Phi. 3:9]

To have the Spirit of Christ, this is the same as possessing the Holy Spirit. This is because the blessed Trinity share in one essence of being. (An extremely important doctrine.) Jesus said as literally translated by the Aramaic Bible,

> "I and my Father, **<u>WE</u>**[f] are One."   (John 10:30 ABPE)

> [f]Note: the "**<u>We</u>**" is indeed in the GK text, but the "**<u>We</u>**" is not generally translated in the ENG. However, the GK is very explicit and meaning is definitely that the presence of Christ and the Father, but each person within the Godhead of the blessed Trinity is separate and distinct.

There are multiple and serious defects concerning the interpretations of the Trinity. (However, I cannot discuss all of the errors of this doctrine here.) Below are a few examples of the more common errors of interpretations concerning the blessed Trinity. For example, the serious errors that the Father does not share in the same essence being with Christ and the Holy Spirit. This view divides the person of the One God. God is one in essence of being, but God is in three persons: the Father, the Son, and the Holy Spirit. Jesus said emphatically,

> "If you had known Me, you would have known My Father also; and from now on you know Him and have seen Him." Philip said to Him, "Lord, show us the Father, and it is sufficient for us." Jesus said to him, "Have I been with you so long, and yet you have not known Me, Philip? He who has seen Me has seen the Father; so how can you say, `Show us the Father `?   (John 14:7-9 NKJ)

Jesus is not alluding to the false doctrine of the "oneness doctrine," which denies the Trinity. As we just read above, Jesus said, 'I and my Father, **WE ARE ONE**.'John 10:30 ABPE

Jesus did not mean that Jesus is the Father nor is the Father Jesus. Though the Trinity share in the one essence of being, the Father and the Son, and the Holy Spirit, each Person is within the Trinity of God. The Persons within the Trinity are separate and distinct. There is but one God but in three Persons: the Father, the Son, and the Holy Spirit. Jesus is declaring He and the Father and Holy Spirit share in one and only one essence of being.

Another heresy alleges that Christ and the Holy Spirit *proceeded* or *came from* the Father. Thus, there is an inference that the Son and the Holy Spirit originated or proceeded from the Father, which further implying the Father is the only one without beginning or end. The Bible is very clear declaring the Trinity. The Trinity is **co-eternal, without beginning or end**. The Trinity co-exist and share in the same one and only one essence of being. To allege the Son and the Holy Spirit proceeded from the Father is illogical and heresy, and it implies the denial of the unity and co-eternality of the Trinity. Christ is the Creator and Sustainer of all things that have come in being or came into existence.John1:1-3, 10; 1 Cor. 8:6; Col.1:16, 17; Heb.1:2 (Yet, the blessed Trinity were all active in creation.) Furthermore, all the fullness of God dwells in Christ.Col. 1:19, 2:9; John1:14; 2 Cor.5:19; 1 Tim. 3:16; Heb.1:3 To see the Son is to look into the face of the Father.John 14:7-9

Therefore, it is imperative that we understand and fully comprehend that the Father, the Son, and the Holy Spirit share in only one essence of being. Otherwise, the unity and oneness of God is fractured. There is but One God, the Lord God Almighty.Deut. 6:4; Isa.44:5; Rom. 3:30; 1Cor.8:4, 6; 1 Tim.2:5 God is One, but He is in three persons the Father, the Son, and the Holy Spirit!Matt. 28:18-20

Back again to Jude's statement:

These be they who — having not the Spirit.　　　(Jude 1:19 KJV)

Jude is definitely referring to the unsaved, those without Christ and remain lost in sin. The unregenerate possess **no life** or **light** from God other than as a natural man, which is available to everyone.[John 1:4, 9] The unregenerate though they unaware of the thoughts and actions they are simply groping through this world. The unsaved are in darkness and enslaved to the evil one. If the unsaved only knew that they were being overran by Satan, believe me, they would be running and crying after Christ the Lord.[2 Cor. 4:3, 4; Eph. 2:2-3]

The unsaved are not stupid, but the unregenerate are being led by the course of this world. They being energized by the prince of darkness, Satan.

> And you *He made alive,* who were dead in trespasses and sins, in which you once **walked according to the COURSE OF THIS WORLD, according to THE PRINCE OF THE POWER OF THE AIR, THE SPIRIT** [evil spirit, devil] **who NOW WORKS IN THE SONS OF DISOBEDIENCE**, among whom also we all once conducted ourselves in the lusts of our flesh, fulfilling the desires of the flesh and of the mind, and **WERE BY NATURE CHILDREN OF WRATH**, just as the others.　　　(Eph. 2:1-3 NKJ)

The Lord Jesus has delivered the believers from the power of darkness and placed us into the Kingdom of the Beloved Son of God.

> Giving thanks to the Father, who has qualified us to share in the inheritance of the saints in light. For He delivered us from the domain of darkness, and transferred us to the kingdom of His beloved Son, in whom we have redemption, the forgiveness of sins.　　　(Col. 1:12-14)

Not only are the unsaved void of light from the Lord, but their thinking is also under the world's influence and mindset, which is totally alienated from God. What a paradox or conundrum: God gives light to everyone, some more and some less, but Satan seeks to distort and blur the Light. Praise the Lord he cannot overtake the Light which is given the redeemed who walk in the Light.

> The light shines in the darkness, and the darkness did not overcome it.
>
> (John 1:5 NRS)

The unregenerate's affection is centered in the things of this world, and their affection is not on things above in Heaven, where Christ is. They can only imagine some religious after-life since they are void of eternal life in Christ.

As noted all the above, the unregenerate are unaware or blind to the fact that Satan is energizing through them.[2 Cor. 4:3, 4] The Bible says, as noted above,

"— the ruler of the power of the air, the [evil] spirit that is now at work among those who are disobedient [e.g. who have not trusted in Christ]."Eph. 2:2 NRS The unregenerate are powerless to free themselves from the evil demons. And even worse, they do not even know they are in bondage to do his will.2 Tim. 2:23-26 There is no power in this natural world that is able to rescue people from the power of Satan. No, not one! Listen, Jesus is the only Person who can deliver or rescue people from the powers of darkness of the evil forces. And yes, praise the Lord who set us free.

If mankind really and truly realized and comprehended his total importance,Rom.5:8 perhaps many more people would be more eager or ready to hear and receive Christ. Christ Jesus did not come to take us from life. Friend, Jesus came to give life.John 10:10 Our Lord is ready and willing to indeed deliver anyone from dominion of darkness, and He will surely transfer them into His marvelous Light. Jesus is the only One that can free us. As Jesus said,

> "If therefore the Son shall make you free, you shall be free indeed."
>
> (John 8:36)

So then, the unregenerate are under a **three-fold bondage**. Yes, it is true. The unsaved are under the **bondage to the world**. The unsaved are under the **bondage to the carnal flesh** (the old nature). The unsaved are under the **bondage to the evil one** energizing through them. Without Christ, they have struck out!

Conclusion

These three characteristics or traits have the potential to cause serious problems in the churches. These are exhibited among the carnal Christians as well as the unregenerate. The Bible is clear that if anyone is genuinely in Christ he is indeed a new creation. He is a new creation right now. The genuine saved in Christ has been born from above and indwelt by the Holy Spirit:

> For Christ's love compels [engulfs, surrounds] us, because we are convinced that one died for all [believers], and therefore all died [that are believers]. And he died for all [Christ died in particular for all believers], that those who [now] live should no longer live for themselves but for him [Christ] who died for them and was raised again. So from now on we regard no one from a worldly point of view. Though we [even] once regarded Christ in this way, we do so no longer. Therefore, if anyone is in Christ, **the new creation has come**: The old has gone, **the new is here!** All this is from God, who

> reconciled us to himself through Christ and gave us the ministry of
> reconciliation: (2 Cor. 5:14-18 NIV)

Nevertheless, the Christian still continues to battle with the old nature (the natural man within) that resides with new nature within him, [Gal. 5:14-18]. Therefore, Paul says,

> If we live in the Spirit, let us also walk in the Spirit. Let us not be
> desirous of vain glory, provoking one another, envying one another.
>
> (Gal. 5:25, 26 KJV)

Let us be certain, as far as humanly possible, that people do not only profess faith in Christ but they possess definite evidence of genuine saving faith in Christ and walking in and with the Holy Spirit of God.

Footnotes:

1. Jesus Paid it All, the chorus to the song: written by Elvina M. Hall
   https://hymnary.org/text/i_hear_the_savior_say_thy_strength_indee

2. "Contradiction," http://ww.dictionary.com/browse/contradictary

CHAPTER 16

Building your faith

(Section 1: *building up in your holy faith*)

Memory verse

As you have therefore received Christ Jesus the Lord, so walk in Him, rooted and built up in Him and established in the faith, as you have been taught, abounding in it with thanksgiving.   (Col. 2:6, 7 NKJ)

Introduction

Now, Jude shifts to exhort the saints as he is preparing to move into his benediction and blessing in his letter, which is the last two verses. As in his earlier exhortations in his brief letter, he does not waste any words. His message is short and direct as he encourages the saints to "*earnestly contend for the faith*!" Jude moves rapidly through his letter. So, watch for key words that accentuate his message.

Jude singles out four things in this section. In this chapter, we will focus his emphasis on "building up in your holy faith." In this chapter, we shall examine three areas, and then, we shall examine his fourth exhortation in the next chapter.

a. *Building up in your holy faith*

b. *Praying in the Spirit*

c. *Abiding and walking in the love of God*

d. *Eagerly anticipating the merciful return of the Lord Jesus*

Jude's four things seems simple enough, but let us not underestimate the battle that Jude warns us and indeed rages against the saints. *The world* is hostile to the proclamation of the Gospel. *The old nature* we are to reckon or consider dead.^{Rom. 6:11} We must rely on our new nature within us, the Holy Spirit. Still, we ought to fully realize that the *old nature* is **not dead**, but the old nature within the believer is very much alive. Finally, we contend with the e*vil forces*, which we are unable to see. So, let us stand fully alert to battle the enemy as we draw upon the power of Christ for the sure victory; yet, also, encourage one another in the faith as we press forward to <u>win souls</u> for Christ, <u>establish</u> them <u>in the faith</u>, and <u>equip</u> them <u>for the work</u> of the ministry.

> Finally, **be strong in the Lord** and **in the strength of his might.** ¹¹**Put on the whole armor of God**, that you may be able to stand against the schemes ^[*cunning trickery*] of the devil. ¹²For we do not wrestle against flesh and blood, but against the rulers, against the authorities, against the cosmic powers over this present darkness, against the **spiritual forces of evil** in the heavenly places. ¹³Therefore **take up the whole armor of God**, that you may be able to withstand in the evil day, and having done all, to stand firm. ¹⁴Stand therefore, having fastened **on the belt of truth**, and having **put on the breastplate of righteousness**, ¹⁵and, as shoes for your feet, **having put on the readiness given by the gospel of peace.** ¹⁶In all circumstances **take up the shield of faith**, with which you can **extinguish all the flaming darts** of the **evil one**; ¹⁷and take the **helmet of salvation**, and **the sword of the Spirit**, which is **the word of God**, ¹⁸**praying at all times in the Spirit**, with all prayer and supplication. To that end keep alert with all perseverance, making supplication for all the saints,   (Eph. 6:10-18 ESV)

Many interpret Paul as referring to the Roman soldier dressed for battle. I am not sure, but he may have in mind the spiritual dress for battle in the OT.^{e.g. Isa. 11:6; 22:21; 59:17; 61:10} Paul uses the above example of being fully dressed for the spiritual warfare in other epistles he has written.^{e.g. Rom. 13:12; 2 Cor. 6:7; 1 Thess. 5:8} Whether Paul is referring to the Roman soldier or Israelite preparing for battle is unclear to me. The point is that the saints in Christ, **WE ARE IN A WAR!** I say again, the **SAINTS ARE IN A DEADLY WAR**. The enemy is real. The war is real. The casualties are real, and the casualties are very high. This is a real war, a war that is worse than all human wars combined. Sadly, many churches are not preparing the troops for warfare. Even many of the leaders are not prepared for battle. Yeah, some leaders do not know how to prepare for war. Others do not even sense or fully realize the deadly war going on around them. How bad is that?

Paul's point here is to prepare for battle with the enemy. The war is here and now. Some do not even realize that enemy is attacking the command post, which is the church. So, let us be ready for battle and actively engage the enemy, Satan. Let us go out into the **highways and byways and compel them to enter** the Kingdom of God while there is still time.

Beloved, building up in your holy faith

Let us keep in mind Jude's overall theme: *"Earnestly Contend for the Faith."* While Jude's theme includes personal saving faith in Christ, his overall emphasis is, "-- **earnestly contend for the faith** which is the truth of the Gospel and declaring the Christian Faith which has already been handed down to the saints," [Jude 1:3].

As I have already noted, there are at least three things that we shall examine in this chapter. Jude is referring to:

A. *The body of doctrine* that has been entrusted to us in the NT along with the OT.

B. Equally important, Jude *reminds us of the need to be faithfully teaching*. Let us faithfully proclaim the true message, the true teaching that goes with the body of doctrine.

C. Lastly, there is necessity to *put into practice and do* as the NT teaches. Let us be undergirded solely by Scripture, which is the solidarity and unity of the OT and NT.

A. The body of doctrine

Nowadays, we are blessed with the internet, which has access to libraries of faithful Christian literature that is both new and from years gone by. The internet is a marvel and a blessing. However, wickedness and false doctrines are also easily accessible and with deadly pitfalls for the naïve, unsuspecting, and immature.

Therefore, also, keep mind that the internet is a minefield filled with booby-traps[1] and extremely dangerous. The internet is **not** for *children*, most *youth, the naïve, unsuspecting,* and *immature*; do not leave such people unsupervised. (Shame, shame on you if you leave them unsupervised; the internet is too dangerous.) I say again, the internet is a blessing, but the internet is also inundated or overrun with every unimaginable evil and wickedness that is unparalleled in history of mankind. For this reason, some people are better off if they stay away from personally accessing or using the internet.

The internet provides access to excellent materials which are helpful in the ministry. The internet is also like Pandora's Box; it can open to all sources of evil and false doctrines that can lead people astray. There are many fake and fraudulent writings that lead many people into counterfeit and erroneous doctrines. I was able to locate and find a copy of the books of Enoch. Enoch is a fraudulent book claiming to be written by Enoch Seventh from Adam, which Jude alludes to in his epistle. I say again, Jude is not endorsing the material in the books of Enoch.

In addition, both the internet and TV-internet and regular TV are flooded with every kind of so-called lost books of the Bible. Listen and pay very close attention as I say once again: **there are NO lost books of the Bible**! Anyone telling you there are lost books of the Bible is either a *boldface liar* or *a fool*.

A fool may stumble on to some program claiming to have found a lost book of the Bible. There are **no** lost books of the Bible. There are **many liars** making fools out of people who are now reading these counterfeit books, like Enoch, but they are not reading God's Word. They have fallen prey to fraudulent books induced by the evil one and through modern-day marketing. (These are fraudulent writings that claim to be God's Word.) As I have said earlier, the early church had to contend and fight a host of false speakers and false writing that claimed to be even authorized by some of the apostles.[e.g. 2 Thess. 2:2, 3; 2 Tim. 2:18f; 1 John 4:1] So, listen, **DO NOT BELIEVE IT**. There are **no** lost books of the Bible.

Equally important, let me underscore and emphasize that we need men who will be faithful to the body of doctrine and the instructions given us through God's Word by the apostles. First, there is no new teaching given. There are no new apostle or prophets today. There is but one church, this is church built by Jesus. Jesus is the one foundation that has **already been laid** and **built on the apostles** and **prophets**, and **Jesus is the one foundation**.[1 Cor. 3:9-11; Eph. 2:20; 4:11, 12]

The Canon of Scripture and its revelation is **completed** and **sealed** by the Holy Spirit. There is no more added revelation since the NT of the apostles and prophets. If anyone attempts to add to the Bible, they have called a curse upon themselves. Yes, you heard me correctly. Anyone following such a group claiming newer revelation is following a lie. In fact, they have called a curse upon themselves. Let me give the NET translation, which is a shocker but very true and plain,

⁶I am astonished that you are so quickly deserting the one who called you by the grace of Christ and are following a different [GK *heteros, not the same gospel*] gospel – ⁷not that there really is another gospel, but there are some who are disturbing you and wanting to distort the gospel of Christ. ⁸But even if **we** [*as apostles*] (or **an angel** from heaven) should preach a gospel contrary to the one we [*have already*] preached to you, let him be condemned to hellª![GK *anathema, cursed to hell*] ⁹As we have said before, and now I say again, if anyone is preaching to you a gospel contrary to what you received, let him be condemned to hell!　　　　　　　　　(Gal. 1:6-9 NET)

ªNote: though actual word is *anathema*, "*cursed*;" the end result is being cast into the Lake of Fire, which is hell! Here is the Gospel in a nutshell, nothing more and nothing less, ¹ Cor. 15:3, 4.

The apostle John gives us this chilling warning of anyone adding or taking away from the Word of God which is already completed and lacking nothing. This applies to anyone thinking he/she has found a lost book of the Bible.

¹⁸I testify to everyone who hears the words of the prophecy of this book: if anyone adds to them, God will add to him the plagues which are written in this book. ¹⁹and if anyone takes away from the words of the book of this prophecy, God will take away his part from the tree of life and from the holy city, which are written in this book.

²⁰He who testifies to these things says, "Yes, I am coming quickly." Amen. Come, Lord Jesus.

²¹The grace of the Lord Jesus be with all. Amen.　　　(Rev. 22:18-21)

Let us therefore remain ever faithful to the Word of God. I would sternly warn you to stay away from any such counterfeit books that claim authority as Scripture. In reading such books that claim to be lost, you may be opening yourself to the luring influence of demons. (Friend, I am not joking; I am dead serious!) Furthermore and similarly, watch out for the cults and churches that have departed from the plain teaching of the Bible. There are many, many denominations, fellowships, groups, and churches that have already forsaken cardinal doctrines of the faith. This is especially true with churches, groups, or individuals that claim to have received special revelation from God. They are either ill-deceived or liars. The Bible is complete. We do not need anything else.

B. Remain and be faithful to the teaching

Here we need to be watchful for anyone alleging something new that they have allegedly discovered. Listen, the hymn writer was right that says,

Tell me the old, old story[2]

-1-
Tell me the old, old story,
Of unseen things above,
Of Jesus and His glory,
Of Jesus and His love;
Tell me the story simply,
As to a little child,
For I am weak and weary,
And helpless and defiled.

- refrain-
Tell me the old, old story,
Tell me the old, old story,
Tell me the old, old story,
Of Jesus and His love.

-4-
Tell me the same old story,
When you have cause to fear
That this world's empty glory
Is costing me too dear;
And when the Lord's bright glory
Is dawning on my soul,
Tell me the old, old story:
"Christ Jesus makes thee whole."

The danger here, as I have repeatedly said, is "*having itching ears.*" But friend, this is the fickleness of the human heart looking for something *new* and *different*. I do not mean we cannot have various types of music or style of music or various styles in our preaching and teaching, or even possess a new translation. The Spirit of God will raise up men and women gifted in music and other areas of the ministry. The Lord will put the new song in the minds of people who love the Lord. Do you know how to determine if a new song is worthy of the Lord? Well, the song shall be fruitful. The song will glorify Christ and His redemption.

Now listen carefully: the music and the preaching and teaching, whether old or new style, **_must_** bring glory, honor, and praise to Christ the Lord and *His work on Calvary.* (The song **is NOT** based popularity.) If the song or message is sound in doctrine, then, the song shall exalt and glorify Christ as

239

Sovereign Lord. It ought to indeed draw people closer to Him in adoration, worship, and service for the King. The song or message will declare that Jesus is worthy of our total commitment and surrender to His Lordship. We do not worship a generic *god*, which is occurring right now in many, many churches today. Listen: we worship **the LORD our God Almighty** who lives forever and ever, amen! This is what the Bible teaches, and this is what we are to declare.

Early Christians died for that declaration. In Rome, the pagan religions declared Caesar is Kurios, GK for **LORD**. Christians adamantly declared boldly, NO! **Jesus is Kurios. Jesus is Lord** or **Jesus is Kurios**. In HEB, our Lord would be addressed as **Yehoshua, YHWH**.[Phi 2:9-11] (The old pronunciation was thought to be Joshuah, but today a more accurate rendering is **Yehoshua**.) If you do not believe that **Yehoshua** [Jesus Christ] is **YHWH**, you will surely die in your sin.[John 8:24]

There are atrocious or horrible songs. There are some songs that unfortunately tend to be too generic, and these songs are unworthy for Christ and His glory and praise. These unworthy songs have **no** Gospel message in them! There are many songs that are poor choices for Christian hymns or spiritual songs. These songs say **nothing** concerning Christ the Lord. Here is an example of a song that is indeed popular today, the song "Amen" is bankrupt spiritually. The song "Amen" **says nothing** or **declares nothing** concerning Christ the Lord and His redemption.

There are many such songs that repeat the same phrase over and over again. Many repetitious songs are unworthy and give no glory and honor to Christ. These songs are unworthy for worship of our Lord. Yet, these songs are appealing especially to the **nature man** (unsaved) and many immature Christians I am sorry to say. Many of these songs do not properly exalt and glorify Christ our Lord or His work on Calvary. Many songs for worship are simply bankrupt and putrid. Sorry but such songs **STINKS**!

There are songs about the virgin Mary. Friend, I tell you that you are practicing idolatry if you sing song Mary, any saint, or any man like Joseph Smith. Even worse if one looks to Mary as an intercessor, while others even worship Mary, your idolater. How wicked and idolatrous is that? Friend, such acts are not only wrong, but this is also wicked and pure evil. Read about Ezekiel and the hole in the wall, Ezek. 8:7ff.

Another such hymn is "I Believe." The song "I Believe" appeals to the nature man because the unregenerate imagine of "god" of his own depraved and wicked mind. (Yes, this appeals to the babe in Christ, but some Christians just do not see where it is wrong. Woe!) The songs like "I Believe" say nothing to the mature man in Christ, the new man in Christ. The song says nothing to honor Christ the Lord. The song "I Believe" appeals to the natural man. The song appeals to unregenerate because he is believing in a generic "*god*" that he has manufactured or conceived in his carnal mind. Even the atheist believes what he calls "*mother nature*" or nowadays, "*the force;*" this all since the days of the Stars Wars movies.

Some churches have songs for *rebaptizing* believers who have already been properly water baptized by immersion. The song is, "*Take Me to the Water.*" Out of deep respect for by brethren in Christ who use this song, I shall not give any more detail. Nevertheless, friend, I am sorry but you cannot go back. This why we have repentance. We also such not rebaptize any who is properly baptized. Listen baptism is a portrait of Christ's work, [Rom. 6:1-11]. Shall we insult the Spirit of God who has spiritual ingrafted (baptized every believer in Christ?[1 Cor. 12:13])

The worse song I have ever heard in church is "The devil is a liar!" Yes, the devil is indeed the father of lies. However, God forbid that any fool would write a song about the devil. This is being brain dead!

The early church, the first 300 years, did not cry out (as noted above), "We believe in God." No! The Roman world at that time were worshiping many so-called gods and lords. The early church cried out loud, "**JESUS IS LORD**."[Phi. 2:10, 11; Ex. 3:13-15] The early Christians were totally committed to Jesus Christ as absolute Lord and the only Sovereign. The Christians were willing to die for that cry: **Jesus Lord**. Is Jesus Lord of all in your life, or is Jesus, while He is indeed Lord, is He just someone in your life? Does Jesus as Lord truly rule your life, or are you the king ruling your life? Maybe you recognize Jesus as King, but Jesus is not the King over your life.

Therefore, the paramount or supreme doctrine, even in music, must center around Jesus Christ and His Sovereign Lordship and the redemption our Lord accomplished on the cross as the Risen Savior. As the apostle Paul says,

> And let the peace of **God RULE in your hearts**, to the which also ye are called in one body; and be ye thankful. Let the ***WORD*** **of Christ dwell in you richly** in all wisdom; teaching and admonishing one another in **psalms** and **hymns** and **spiritual songs**, singing with grace in your hearts to the Lord. And whatsoever ye do in word or deed, ***do*** **all in the name of the Lord Jesus, GIVING THANKS to God** and the Father by him. (vv 15-17)

And whatsoever ye do, do *it* **HEARTILY, as to the Lord**, and not unto men; Knowing that of the Lord ye shall receive the reward of the inheritance: for ye serve the Lord Christ.

(vv 23, 24) (Col. 3:15-17, 23, 24 KJV)

So, to many churches, Jesus is just a sidebar to the church worship service and its ministry. Listen, many say Christ is the center; but most sadly, today personal so-called experience is priority #1. What a shame. Christ is no longer the focal point, the center of worship. Hear me, everything we do ought to glorify and praise the name Jesus. Remember, JESUS in HEB is YEHOSHUA: meaning the LORD WILL SAVE or the Lord saves.

Salvation is found in no one else, for there is no other name under heaven given to mankind by which we must be saved." (Acts 4:12 NIV)

For the unbelievers, ignorant, the fools, or the liars that teach Jesus is not the way only into Heaven or teach that Jesus is just *one of the ways* into Heaven, Hell is awaiting and opened for you.

C. Put into practice, doing what Scripture teaches

There are various ways that churches have departed from the truth of God's Word. The departure is collectively and openly denying orthodoxy or truth of the Gospel. The churches have departed from biblical Evangelicalism or the major doctrines of Fundamentals of the Faith. "Evangelicalism" just means the Gospel or Good News.[GK *euaggelion*] Friend, here is the complete Gospel in a nutshell, which is 1 Cor. 15:3, 4. In addition, there are *churches* that may deny, in part or whole, the absolute authority of Scripture as fully inspired and inspired without error. Many churches have abandoned the mandates of our risen Lord. Some, unfortunately, do not even know what the mandates of the Christian walk are. What a shame!

The first obvious denial: there is an *overt* rejection of mainstream Evangelicalism. (Evangelical or Evangelicalism just means that a person believes in the Good News, Jesus died on the cross in our place for sin, He is risen, and coming again.) I mean to say plainly that there is a clear and deceptive declaration of the rejection the Gospel or Scripture. Oh yes, they may claim to cling to the Gospel, but they have deceived themselves because they have actually denied the Gospel. They are lying to themselves, and they no longer speak the truth. They speak with *two tongues*. (One tongue alleges to speak the truth, but with the other tongue, they are *bald-faced liars*.)

For instance, denominations or churches may openly declares they do **not** believe Jesus is the Eternal Creator and Sustainer of all things. There are others that openly *deny of the virgin birth*. Yet, disgustingly, they accept homosexuals as simply a different lifestyle. Well, I am here to tell you that the Bible categorically condemns homosexually and other sexual perversions. Like the cults, these people reinterpret the Bible to their ungodly standard.

Yet, ironically, they may give a "tongue in cheek" professing to believe the whole Bible and that the Bible is the Word of God. Yet, on the other hand, these opponents say that the Bible only contains the Word of God. Hence, the Bible in its totality is not the Word of God. Amazingly, there are still other denominations or churches that deny the *plenary* and *inherent* and *infallibility* of Scripture. (The fail to realize that in so doing, such groups have *set themselves* as the final judge over the Word of God.) Here is the kicker: in the same breath they have allowed *tradition, ecclesiastical bodies, church history,* or *other outside influences* (*even pagan influence*) to determine the truth and meaning of Scripture. Nevertheless, the Scripture stands forever, and Scripture cannot be broken!^{John 10:35b}

In addition, there are the less obvious groups. These are the covert or hidden and undeclared groups, but they are just spiritually bankrupt and corrupt. These are churches or individuals that deny or **refuse to practice** certain mandates even though ordered by Christ or even explicitly stated doctrines in the Scripture. This is again a *tongue in cheek* approach. This is because while they profess to believe God's Word, they ***DO NOT DO*** or ***DO NOT*** *put into practice* what God's Word plainly commands. Again, they set themselves up as the final or ultimate authority and superimpose their own authority. Their tradition or church dogma override the plain and explicit teaching of Scripture.

For instance, the first 300 years, the early church practiced believer's water baptisms by *immersion*, which is a fact. Many are ill-informed and do not actually know that water baptism was the OT practice by Orthodox Jews then and today. True! Jesus continues water baptism by immersion, though our Lord's mandate of water baptism is the New Covenant water baptism. Scripture is clear that John the Baptist practiced under the OT water baptism by *immersion*. Oh, but yes, John the Baptist's water baptism was under the Old Covenant. Yet, Paul saw the solidarity between the two.^{see Acts 19:1-7} John the Baptist definitely practiced water baptism by immersion under the Old Covenant of Circumcision and Law of Moses. The New Covenant water baptism by the apostles was water baptism by immersion. Ecclesiastical leaders changed it by the fourth century AD.

243

Since there is little spiritual backbone by godly men today in the church, such leaders look the other way or *tongue in cheek* and allege that they believe all the Bible. Yet, my friend, they actually in reality do not practice it. Listen, if you do not practice it, how then can you say you believe it? *If you do not practice, then you do not believe it*!

In the fourth century, a church council decided on their human authority to change water baptism from immersion to sprinkling. In addition, infant baptism became center stage (became predominant) and replaced believers' baptisms. There was no warrant to cease believers' water baptism by immersion. There is certainly no Scripture basis for infant baptism. Here ecclesiastical tradition overrode the plain and explicit teaching of Scripture.

The same church council falsely declared that water baptism washes away sin. (However, early on Paul declared how people departed from the faith.[Gal. 1:6-9]) Water baptism does not wash away our sin. Only Jesus' **shed blood** and **death** alone cleanses us from all our sins. We are sanctified, baptized, and sealed by Holy Spirit.[1 Cor. 6:9-11] Our Lord has cleansed us through faith in Him and His sacrifice for our sins on the cross. Thus, many churches have superimposed their tradition and ecclesiastical teaching over the plain teaching and authority of Scripture. God's Word, the Bible, has the last word. Unfortunately, there are few men with godly backbones with spiritual maturity that will stand boldly and speak out against such evil. They are afraid of men. Moreover, some like the praise of men more than praise of God. How shameful is that? For those who attend such churches, they look the other way. Meanwhile, many faithful churches struggle, but the above people do not attend the struggling churches because they cannot get their ears tickled. Friend, we will all stand before the Lord,[2 Cor. 5:10] and we shall not be able to look the other way.

Next, many churches have ceased giving *altar calls* and give the invitation to receive Christ. **<u>Triple shame</u>**! There is no conviction of sin any more. What, no one sins anymore? There is no more a call for people to come forward to receive Christ. There is no one calling upon people to repent. Calling people to the altar is **GONE**! Jesus never ceased such mandate. Therefore, we are not to cease in giving altar calls. Altar calls is when asking the unbeliever to come forward to confess and receive Christ. Ah, but altar calls also ought to be included to ask the saved, the Christian, to come forward to confess their sins and get in proper fellowship with Christ and their walk with the Lord.[1 John 1:8-10] Nevertheless, our Lord Jesus gave us this command,

> He said to them, "Thus it is written, that the Christ would suffer and rise again from the dead the third day, and that **<u>REPENTANCE</u>** for

FORGIVENESS OF SINS would be **PROCLAIMED** in His name to
all the nations —"   (Luke 24:46, 47)

In simple language, the churches are expected to be evangelistic throughout the world including through the churches in the community. Hello! The
problem is that many leaders say to themselves, "I know all my people, and
they are saved."

Well, I am here to tell you, "**NO**! You do not know your people. You certainly do not know their hearts and minds." But, pay attention, the risen Lord
said,

> "I am He who **searches the minds** and **hearts** [the innermost thoughts,
> purposes]; and I will give to each one of you [a reward or punishment]
> according to your deeds."   (Rev. 2:23b AMP)

The truth is that preachers are fearful. At the same, preachers want to soft-
peddle the Gospel. They want to appeal to the natural man. This is why many
preachers use "God" instead of properly using "Lord." Well, you are going
offend one side or the other. Please hear me: We shall either offend modern
(the natural man) or wakeup call: the other side, to water down the Gospel and
we shall indeed offend the Lord our God who gave us the Gospel to proclaim.
Which shall it be for you?

There are still many faithful churches preaching and giving the invitation to receive Jesus Christ right now. It is a shocking shame there are not
a lot more! So, there are some churches executing *aggressive evangelism*.
(*Aggressive evangelism* is going door to door **at night** and even **on the streets**
compelling people to come to Christ before it's too late.) What is so sad, as I
have said, some preachers don't even know how to give an invitation. They
do not know how to draw in the net. (Some Bible Colleges and Seminaries do
not teach how to give salvation invitations in Homiletics.) This is deplorable.

They either never knew how to give an invitation to receive Christ or
to repent, or they have regrettably lost touch with Christ's mandate or have
become *anesthetized* (totally insensitive) to the Spirit of God. They **do not**
even know how to present the Gospel so a person can be saved. They are
unable to properly call people forward to receive Christ Jesus as Lord and
Savior. Even far worse, there is **no follow up** or **equipping the saints** for the
work of the ministry.[Eph. 4:12] Where is the individual or collective evangelism?
Where is the whole church continuing to evangelize throughout their area?
It is gone! This is why we must by necessity include the starting multiple
churches in their area, and please let us do it right, let us follow our risen
Lord's mandates.

The churches also need to **continue** *recruiting* and *training in evangelism and as I have said follow ups*. The churches are for the most part seemingly "fearful" going out. Friend, I am not joking. True! I had more than one Pastor tell me, "The people are not interested in his area." Of course, people are not interested, they need to be saved first. Yes, the churches are fearful for going to share the Gospel with others. Yet, Jesus has promised, *'I will be with you always.'* Matt. 28:18-20 Maybe they do believe it!

Other churches are simply totally **IGNORANT** or just **OPENLY DISOBEDIENT to Jesus command**. They just do not evangelize. And as I have said, they do not even give altar calls in church. Other churches are too withdrawn. Some churches are like Laodicean church: they are neither hot nor cold. Still other churches, as I have said, theologize around the command based upon the *misunderstanding* with the *doctrine of election*. "The elect," God will just bring people into the church. So, in essence, God will save people and bring the saved into the church. But my Bible says,

> So then faith *comes* by hearing, and hearing by the word of God.
>
> (Rom. 10:17 NKJ)

Even if people should come into the church, there is no call to repent or call to receive the Gospel. The churches are using *lures* and *attractions* and *attention getters*. Friend, we do not invite people to church. What is the matter with you? We are to invite people to receive Christ.

The apostle Paul goes on explaining that the Gospel has gone out into the world for example to the Jews, but many of the Jews did not believe. Nevertheless, the Gospel needs go forth,

> How then will they call on him in whom they have not believed? And how are they to believe in him of whom they have never heard? And how are they to hear without someone preaching? [15]And how are they to preach unless they are sent? As it is written, "How beautiful are the feet of those who preach the good news!" [16]But they have not all obeyed the gospel. For Isaiah says, "Lord, who has believed what he has heard from us?" [17]So faith comes from hearing, and hearing through the word of Christ [or *through the hearing of the Word of God*].
>
> (Rom. 10:14-17 ESV)

Hence, missionaries is at a low Ebb today. Missions are especially low to bring people under conviction of sin and the need for repentance. Many men refuse to go, but many are fearful of the government or other religious groups. There are few men willing to answer the call to serve Christ at any cost. There are fewer willing to answer the call to missions. Many of the Pastors, its leaders, and church groups **hog all the money** with big fat salaries. So, if anything is left for missions, it is only a dribble or a drip in a bucket.

Even worse, many families, especially men, are adamantly refusing to go to the mission field even though they admit that God is calling them. They could go on a short-term missions for a month or less. These are men just simply disobedient and refuse to go. Other men refuse to go out and knock on doors to do evangelism. Others *"salve their conscience"* by saying, "I never felt called." Listen and let this indelible be branded in your mind forever: missions are not based on a *feeling of the natural man*. Missions are based upon a **COMMAND** to the new spiritual man in Christ. Hello! Like church of Laodicea, many men's love for the Lord Jesus is neither hot nor cold; it is *putrid, stagnant, stale, and repulsive.*

Jesus illustrates this point of evangelizing going everywhere in a parable, A Royal Banquet Dinner.^{Matt. 22:1-14; Luke 14:16-24} The parable can be summed up in one verse,

> And the lord said unto the servant, **Go out into the highways and hedges, and COMPEL** *them* **to come in, that my house may be filled**.
>
> (Luke 14:23 KJV)

Please pay attention and listen to me: unfortunately, many churches are just *openly in total disregard* concerning Christ's mandates. Churches are no longer going out to knock on doors or compel people at night. Many churches are sitting still! Many churches like many saints, are *stagnate* and *dead*! There is no evangelism from the pulpit. Some are just *ignorantly disobedient*. While still others disobey through their *theological gymnastics*. That is, as noted above, they assume God will just bring in the elect. Still other, they are simply fearful. Regardless, how you put it in words, churches are not going out to "compel people to come."

We have three witnesses in the closing of Revelation. Yes, I said three; so get right. First, we have the **witness of the Son of God calling** people to come,

> He said to me, "I am the Alpha and the Omega, the Beginning and the End. **I WILL GIVE FREELY TO HIM WHO** [*WHOEVER*] **IS THIRSTY FROM THE SPRING OF THE WATER OF LIFE**."
>
> (Rev. 21:6, 7 WEB)

The risen Lord Jesus is giving an invitation from Heaven to come and receive now and become a citizen of Heaven today. Hallelujah!

Next, we have two witnesses: the **witness of the Holy Spirit** and the **witness of the bride** (the believers in Heaven). The Holy Spirit and believers already in Heaven are making the appeal and telling people they need to come and receive Jesus **now** and **receive** eternal life,

> The Spirit and the bride say [GK is plural. *saying*], "Come." And let the one who hears say, "Come." And **let the one who is thirsty come; LET THE ONE WHO WISHES TAKE THE WATER OF LIFE WITHOUT COST.** (Rev. 22:17)

Friend, there is no accident that we have three witnesses: the **risen Christ**, the **Holy Spirit** among us, and the saints that have gone into Heaven before us which is the **bride** saying, "come." This is because the Word of God teaches us that in the mouth of two or three witnesses let every word be established or confirmed.^{Duet. 19:15; John 8:17; 2 Cor. 13:1; 1 Tim. 5:19} This is definitely the principle being applied here.

Friend, the call for repentance and to trust and receive Jesus Christ as your Lord and Savior is the call to do it right now.

> While God has overlooked the times of human ignorance, **NOW HE COMMANDS ALL PEOPLE EVERYWHERE TO REPENT**.
> (Acts 17:30 NRS)

Did you know the word "repent" is no longer in many preachers vocabulary? It is gone. However, our risen Lord in his message to each of the seven churches (it is the same even to two churches that needed no challenge to repent.)

> 'He who has an ear, let him hear what the Spirit says to the churches.'
> (Rev. 3:13)

Do you have ear to hear the Holy Spirit? If you are continually on the cell phone, video, game, TV, internet, Xbox, etc., then you cannot hear Him. I don't care what you say; still, you cannot hear Him.

Know this also which we previously noted, repentance is not just for the unsaved. Scripture declares repentance and confession are also for the saints in Christ.^{James 5:16; 1 John 1:7-10} Friend, this is not just repentance; this is a **call for renewal, revival, restoration** and **cleansing**. The churches need more than reviving; the churches need a renewal and restoration and cleansing. Well, let me ask you very plainly: "When was the last time you *repented your sins*?" "Well, when was the last time you asked the Lord to forgive you of your sins?"

If we are honest with ourselves, we probably do not remember repenting of your sins. Woe unto the churches today.

Conclusion

Building oneself up in their holy faith is staying with the one and only foundation which is Jesus Christ. Yea, we have this assurance:

> In whom [*Christ*] are hid all the treasures of wisdom and knowledge.
>
> (Col. 2:3 KJV)

Listen my brother, put Christ Jesus first in your life in all you say or do. If the Lord Jesus is first in your life, you will not be able to count the blessings. Ah, but you had better expect trouble with the world, the flesh, and the devil. However, trouble will come sadly even with other Christians. Jesus wants to walk with you through this world of sin and woe. He will bless you when you walk in accordance to His Word and you truly seek His will. Put Jesus first. Please listen, **the Lord Jesus is your greater Friend** who loves you and who will genuinely care for you. He has all the power and authority to care for you and your family. He has your best interest in mind. I know: "I've been there and I'm doing that-"

> And let the peace of God rule in your hearts, to the which also ye are called in one body; and be ye thankful. Let the word of Christ dwell in you richly in all wisdom; teaching and admonishing one another in psalms and hymns and spiritual songs, singing with grace in your hearts to the Lord. And whatsoever ye do in word or deed, *do* all in the name of the Lord Jesus, giving thanks to God and the Father by him.
>
> (Col. 3:15-17 KJV)

Many churches and denominations and fellowships have departed in one form or another from the faith. There will be more that are continuing to depart from the faith in Christ. Instead, many churches are following the footsteps of tradition, ecclesiastical amalgamation, church history, and outside material for their authority. Listen, the Bible is the only authority! But if you say, "I believe in the Bible," but you do not what it says, what kind of faith is that?

Jude says that the truth in God's Word has already been handed down to us. Let us stay faithful to those teachings handed down to us. Let us find faithful men who will continue to fight for the faith: "earnestly contend for the faith which was once delivered unto the saints."[Jude 1:3 KJV]

249

Let us do and not just say we believe God's Word. Let us do what Jesus said, "Go out into the highways and hedges, and **compel** *them* **to come in**, that my house may be filled."Luke 14:23 KJV

Going to the mission field is not based on feeling or some sense of calling. Friend, mission and evangelism is a command from the risen Lord Jesus!

CHAPTER 17

Building your faith

(Section 2: Eagerly anticipating Christ Jesus' coming)

Memory verse

Spirit Himself testifies with our spirit that we are children of God,

(Rom. 8:16)

Introduction

In some respects, our spiritual life in Christ here on earth parallels taking care of our body. We *need to eat* a good and well-balanced diet to maintain our optimum health. Ah, but we also need a good and *rounded exercise* to keep our body at its optimum function level. To top it off, we need *proper rest and relaxation*. I have been more aware of this fact as senior citizen.

What is said about the individual physical bodies has some application to a godly and Christ-centered assembly in community where it exists. The diet is of course biblically sound *preaching and teaching* which encompasses declaring the whole counsel of God.[Acts 20:27] Declaring the "whole counsel of God" must include as priority one, constant *fervent and zealous* **evangelism** and **equipping saints**. There is the **personal study** in the Word and devotional **quiet time in prayer** as well.

Paul was able to give the whole counsel of God in three years. Awesome! To accomplish the whole counsel of God, he taught night and day. He taught, "-publicly and from house to house."[Acts 20:20] There are very few professionals, e.g. doctors, making house calls today. In the same way, there are few Pastors or Christian workers in the churches making house calls. (Visiting the homes of people ought to be priority #1 for our Lord.) That is, going "house to house" and persuading people to come to Jesus as Lord and to enter the Kingdom of God. Also, let us persuade the saints "press onward in our high calling in Christ Jesus."[Phi. 3:14]

It is a pity that there are few churches preaching for commitment to Christ today. I mean to actually call people forward publicly. Additionally sad, there are fewer churches that have the Bible class, Sunday School. Unfortunately, there are fewer people willing to commit themselves to early morning Sunday Bible class before church hour or even after the worship hour. My friend, Bible class hour is where we learn and grow in Christ. At 86 now, I enjoy attending and participating in the Bible hour. If we are not open to learn through having a Bible class hour, how shall we have an ear to hear the wooing of the blessed Holy Spirit? Too many churches have become spiritual sluggish and apathetic in their walk of faith in Christ! Like a basketball game: *Everything has to be slam dunked in an hour in church*!

The Lord did not establish a day of rest, the Sabbath, for nothing. Yes, yes, we are not under the Law, but a day of rest in is an imprint of creation for all humankind. A day of rest is an imprint by Creator, and sadly, few today understand this biblical principle. A day of rest, my friend, is one of the wonderful gifts to the saints in Christ. For Jesus said:

> Come unto me, all *ye* that *labor* and are heavy laden, and I will give you rest. Take my yoke upon you, and learn of me; for I am meek and lowly in heart: and **ye shall find rest unto your souls**. For my yoke *is* easy, and my burden is light. (Matt. 11:28-30 KJV)

Jesus said the above because many religious leaders then, and even now, laid heavy religious burdens upon people with their traditions and church doctrine. Many Pastors of these electronic churches are demanding many things: fat-salaries, expensive cars, homes, and even private jet plans. Truth of the Gospel is that our Lord said, *come as you are*. Yes, the wonderful grace of Jesus will surely gladly receive you, clean you up, and even change your life for the better in the here and now. Praise the Lord, He shall wonderfully change your life to glorify His blessed name. Jesus is the greatest Friend you'll ever have in this life and in the life to come.

A. Continue to pray in the Spirit

As we continue with Jude's exhortation, he says,

> But you, beloved, building yourselves up on your most holy faith, **praying in the Holy Spirit**, keep yourselves in the love of God, looking for the mercy of our Lord Jesus Christ unto eternal life.
>
> (Jude 1:20, 21 NKJ)

"Praying in the Holy Spirit" [Jude 1:20] is where many stumble and trip into erroneous doctrines and false teachings. This is because they misunderstand what Scripture is declaring. They are missing the point as they practice eisegesis, *reading their error into Scriptures*. Let us rather practice exegesis, *reading out of the Scripture the intended meaning* of the biblical authors. The Bible stands upon its own inherent declaration. Thus, it is the job of the saints to grasp and proclaim the precise and intended meaning by the biblical author.

"Praying in the Holy Spirit," the Elder Jude is **not** referring to some pagan *ecstatic utterance, some chant,* or some *spirit-altering experience*. Praying in the Spirit is **simply striving to earnestly pray in the will of God**. Unfortunately, some suppose *"praying in the Holy Spirit"* is some *ecstatic utterance* or *spirit-altering experience*. Some even suppose *"praying in the Holy Spirit"* is a means of manipulate the Lord God like some pagan gods of the world. Perish that evil thought my brother.

Paul says,

> What is *the outcome* then? I shall **pray with the spirit** and I shall **pray with the mind** also; I shall **sing with the spirit** and I shall **sing with the mind** also. (1 Cor. 14:15)

Even the verse above, many have stumbled and tripped over this section due their "eisegesis reading." Even if several volumes were written on the subject, many are too fixated upon alleged personal experience rather than hearing and understanding the truth. Let those who base their life on *feeling* (which is driven by *lower nature*) do so, but let us continue our walk of faith in Christ based upon what is **plainly written in Scripture**.

Let us note two similar texts (and the misunderstandings) that might cause some to stumble or *trip* over what Jude is saying, "praying in the Holy Spirit."

> Likewise the Spirit helps us in our weakness; for we do not know how to pray as we ought [to pray], but that very **Spirit intercedes with sighs too deep for words**. And God, who searches the heart, knows what is the mind of the Spirit, because the Spirit intercedes for the saints according to the will of God. We know that all things work together for good for those who love God, **who are called according to his purpose**.
>
> (Rom. 8:26-28 NRS)

Again, the apostle says,

PRAYING always with **all prayer** and **supplication IN THE SPIRIT**, and watching thereunto with all perseverance and supplication for all saints. (Eph. 6:18 KJV)

There are people so adamant that they imagine that "*'praying in the Holy Spirit'* is some *ecstatic utterance* or *spirit-altering experience.*" Some imagine "praying in the Spirit" is an action that **is not cognitive thought**. Some may even say within themselves, "I do not care what others say, *I know what I have experienced.*"

Friend, I must tell you, "**No**; you do not know what you have experienced." You only know what **you think** you may have experienced. The reason being, Satan is a deceiving <u>counterfeiter</u>, a <u>liar</u>, and a <u>fabricating illusionist</u>. The evil one works upon the natural man, and he especially works on their *emotions* and *mind*.[2 Cor. 11:3, 13-15] Satan can deceive the natural man outside Christ without them knowing it. The natural man give way to the emotions of his carnal nature. Please hear me, remember, the devil is even able to deceive apostle Peter concerning the cross.[Mat. 16:22f] Friend, if Satan can deceive Peter with Christ present, he can certainly deceive you or me!

What does Paul mean in Rom. 8:26ff? First, Paul does **not** mean in Rom. 8:26ff that we are unable to know what to pray for in our prayers. Listen, if someone is deadly sick and we were asked to pray for them, we **know exactly** what to pray for concerning the person. So, Paul does **not** mean we are unable to know what to pray in our prayers.

So, what is the meaning Rom. 8:26ff? Here is Paul's point: we **do not know** what is **the will of God** in given situation. So, for example, we pray for the sick as godly saint in Christ, but the decision rests in the Lord and not with us. This is why we ought to be *praying for the will of God*. God's will is what matters because His will shall be done. Hallelujah! If you think it is the will of God to heal all sickness, I am sorry but you are **<u>WRONG</u>**! You have failed to recognize that the death rate is the same among Charismatic and Pentecostal healers and none healers! Hello! (All Christians believe in healing, but it is not the will of God to heal everyone in this age.)

Christian Science (which is neither Christian nor science) claim the power to heal all diseases. Listen, Christian Science is a deceiving cult and a liar! Christian Science is unable to heal. Besides, Christian Science does not know the Gospel! They can only proclaim their false teaching.

In addition, it is important to realize that the Holy Spirit aids us in our prayers. The Holy Spirit assists the believers in their prayers. The Spirit of God assists us through being like holy *Intercessor-filter*. The Holy Spirit takes our prayer to Christ Jesus. Then, our Lord intercedes in Heaven unto the Father.[Eph. 2:18]

The Holy Spirit is going to filter out all the carnal and ungodly things we might foolishly put in our prayers from the natural man. One such foolish or childish prayer is, "God I pray for all the sick people in the hospital." Such a prayer may sound sincere and well-meaning to the natural man. But the mature saint he/she ought to know better than to make such petition. There is no prayer like that anywhere in God's Word. Besides, our access to the Father is only through Jesus blood and His righteousness. Let all the saints say, "Amen!"

This is why the apostle says,

> And we know that all things work together for good to them that love God, to them who are the called according to *his* purpose.
>
> (Rom. 8:28 KJV)

Friend, Paul did **not** mean that *all things work for good to them that love God*. WRONG! Please get it right: don't forget to include the rest of the verse: "we know that God causes all things to work together for good to those who love God — to **them who are the CALLED ACCORDING TO *HIS* PURPOSE**." This means we ought to be **seeking the will of God in ALL MATTERS**. God's will is always better.

The same applies when Paul says, "Praying always with all prayer and supplication in the Spirit."[Eph. 6:18] The Holy Spirit knows what is in the mind of the blessed Triune God. We do not counsel God. Listen, only a fool would dare think such carnal thing. (There are certainly many "*toddler* Christians today but bankrupt in Scripture.) Paul says as he quotes the OT,

> Oh, the depth of the riches both of the wisdom and knowledge of God! How unsearchable *are* His judgments and His ways past finding out! "For who has known the mind of the LORD? Or who has become His counselor?" "Or who has first given to Him And it shall be repaid to him?" For of Him and through Him and to Him *are* all things, to whom *be* glory forever. Amen. (Rom. 11:33-36 NKJ)

And again, the apostle says,

> In Christ[b] we have also obtained an inheritance, having been destined according to the purpose of him who **accomplishes all things according to his counsel and will**. (Eph. 1:11 NRS)

255

[b]Note: while the express is "In whom" KJV, the NRS clarifies and reminds us that it is **in Christ** that "accomplishes all things according to his counsel and will."

Friend, Jesus is not our servant. We are Jesus' servant forever if you are saved. Have you failed to realize you are Jesus' *servant* or *slave* if you are truly saved?

B. Abiding and walking in the love of God

Jude says, "Keep yourselves in the love of God, looking for the mercy of our Lord Jesus Christ unto eternal life." [Jude 1:21 KJV] While it is likely these two phrases are woven together and supplement each other, let us take each phrase as piece meal, one by one. Let us look at these two phrases in *reverse order* and in paraphrase:

> *As we eagerly anticipate our Lord return, let us keep our guard up and remain vigil by abiding and walking in the Lord's love.*

> (Jude 1:21 paraphrase in reverse order)

First, Jude is not referring to our love for the Lord, which is finite, fragmentary, fickle, and impotent. Jude is definitely referring to **God's love working in** and **abiding in each of us**. In other words, let the Spirit of God's love radiate in and through us. The flesh's love is generated by the natural man. The natural man is carnal, ego-centric, and most of all it is depraved. The natural love of humans is of short duration. The natural man's love is ruled by *impulse*, *emotions*, and *carnal reasoning*. Similarly, the apostle Paul says,

> [13]You however, brethren, were called to freedom. Only do not turn your freedom into an excuse for giving way to your lower natures [natural man]; but become bondservants to one another in a spirit of love. [14]For the entire Law has been obeyed when you have kept the single precept, which says, "You are to love your fellow man equally with yourself." [15]But if you are perpetually snarling and snapping at one another, beware lest you are destroyed by one another. [16]This then is what I mean. Let your lives be guided by the [Holy] Spirit [new man], and then you will certainly not indulge the cravings of your lower natures [natural man]. [17]For the cravings of the lower nature [natural man] are opposed to those of the [Holy] Spirit [new man], and the cravings of the [Holy] Spirit [new man] are opposed to those of the lower nature [natural man]; because these are antagonistic to each other, so that you cannot do everything to which

you are inclined. [18]But if the [*Holy*] Spirit [*new man*] is leading you, you are not subject to Law. (Gal. 5:13-18 WNT)

The reality is that we struggle with the natural man within us, the old nature. There is text that illustrates this very point. It is slightly long, but the NRSV does an excellent job clarifying the struggle within the believers. Perhaps the unregenerate may have some struggles within himself, but the unregenerate is totally consumed by the old nature. The unregenerate does not have Christ within to empower or strengthen him; that is, "do the good that he would."

While some allege that Romans 7 is Paul before he was saved, the apostle is actually relating the reality of the struggle within the believer that is seeking to please God.

> For we know that the law is spiritual; but I am of the flesh,[*carnal*] sold into slavery under sin. I do not understand my own actions. For I do not do what I want, but I do the very thing I hate. Now if I do what I do not want, I agree that the law is good. But in fact it is no longer I that do it, but sin that dwells within me. For I know that nothing good dwells within me, that is, in my flesh.[*the carnal nature*] **I can will what is right, but I cannot do it.** (vv 14-18)

> For I do not do the good I want, but the evil I do not want is what I do. Now if I do what I do not want, it is no longer I that do it, but sin that dwells within me. So I find it to be a law that when I want to do what is good, evil lies close at hand. For **I delight in the law of God in my inmost self**, but I see in my members another law at war with the law of my mind, making me captive to the law of sin that dwells in my members.[*the carnal nature*] Wretched man that I am! Who will rescue me from this body of death? Thanks be to God through Jesus Christ our Lord! So then, with my mind I am a slave to the law of God, but with my flesh I am a slave to the law of sin. (vv 19-25) (Rom. 7:15-25 NRS)

The above is exactly why we need to be **tuned-in** with an attitude of prayer, *praying without ceasing.*[1 Thess. 5:17] "*Praying without ceasing*" is like having the radio on and being "*tuned-in*" while you do your work. For instance, a mother or wife is preparing breakfast, but she *tuned-in* to the dialogue or conversation that is taking place at kitchen table. In the same way, we should be ever conscious of the Lord's presence within us: keep ourselves in *an attitude of prayer* throughout your day *whether home alone, in school, work,* or *play.*

We do not stop what we are doing. But we just simply talk to the Lord; He is our very best Friend. "*The Lord is turned-in to us every moment, but we must be turned-in to the Lord throughout the day.*" We talk to Him in whatever

257

we are doing as though He was sitting very near us and as though we could see Him.

The problem is that we do not talk to Him throughout the day. We actual change channels so to speak, and we tuned Him out. Even worse, we do not expect the Lord to respond when we are talking to Him. So, our spiritual ears are **not** tuned-in. I do not mean that we are able to hear the Lord audibly, but He speaks to our mind or heart as we sense His presence within us. However, we need to be very, very careful here. The evil angels will counterfeit God presence, and demons come to our minds like this happened to Peter. Compare Mat. 16:22f to 2 Cor. 11:3, 13-15; 1 John 4:1-4.

"Keep yourselves in the love of God" is *abiding in the presence of God while walk in the love of God.* (Remember, not walking in our carnal love for God, but we are to walk in the power of God's love within us, the Holy Spirit.) This is not passive mindset, while our minds are supposedly a *blank,* or our minds *drifting off* somewhere, or we are just *daydreaming.* This is taking a definite and conscious effect to *"stay tuned-in."*

We stay *tuned-in* by talking to the Lord or just remembering someone in need of prayer and taking a moment and pray for the request. We do not even have to pray audible. We do not need to stop whatever we are doing. Just pray in your mind silently, and the Holy Spirit shall pray with you. Hello again! Friend, this is a vibrant and living relationship that is indeed reality with the risen and glorified Lord of Glory. Hallelujah. Yes indeed, our Lord is living God that desires we have vibrant relationship with Him throughout our day. It's true! Friend, this is truly real!

A Pastor was in debate with the atheist Madame O'Hara, as she asked the Pastor, "Well, how do you know there is a God?" "Madame O'Hara," he said, "Well, I just talked with Him this morning. All is well with Him." This friend is in a *living* and *vibrant* relationship with the Eternal God! Friend, this is much more than being in some special physical position with our body, e.g. *on our knees.* We just have a little talk with Jesus; and He will make right. Below is some of lyrics:

Just a Little Talk with Jesus[1]

I once was lost in sin but Jesus took me in
And then a little light from heaven filled my soul
He bathed my heart in love and He wrote my name above
And just a little talk with Jesus makes me whole

Now let us have a little talk with Jesus
Let us tell Him all about our troubles
He will hear our faintest cry
And He will answer by and by

I may have doubts and fears
My eyes be filled with tears
But Jesus is a friend who watches day and night
I go to him in prayer
He knows my every care

And just a little talk with Jesus makes it right
Now let us have a little talk with Jesus
Let us tell Him all about our troubles
He will hear our faintest cry
And He will answer by and by

If you will talk with Jesus as your best Friend, you will soon learn, *"Yes, He will speak to your heart by and by."*

C. Eagerly anticipating the merciful return of the Lord

We needn't be anxious. I do not think this is what NAS is attempting to declare that we are anxiously waiting our Lord's return. The NAS 2020 revision follows the KJV and ASV, "looking forward". The word "looking" KJV or "anticipating" *prosdechomai*: we ought to be looking for the mercy of the Lord Jesus. Perhaps we might better say, *we eagerly anticipate our Lord Jesus' return.* For example, Paul says similarly,

> Looking for that blessed hope, and the glorious appearing of the great God and our *Savior* Jesus Christ.   (Titus 2:13 KJV)

We are eagerly looking forward to seeing our Lord Jesus face to face with joy as the apostle Peter says,

> Blessed be the God and Father of our Lord Jesus Christ, who according to his **great mercy** caused us to be born again [new birth] to a living hope through the resurrection of Jesus Christ from the dead, to an incorruptible and undefiled inheritance that doesn't fade away, reserved in Heaven for you, who by the power of God are guarded through faith for a salvation ready to be revealed in the last time. In this you greatly rejoice, though now for a little while, if need be, you have been grieved in various trials, that the proof of your faith, which is more precious

than gold that perishes, even though it is tested by fire, may be found to result in praise, glory, and honor at the revelation [*the coming*] of Jesus Christ— whom, not having [*physically seen or met Him*] known, you love. In him, though now you don't see him, yet believing, you rejoice greatly with joy that is unspeakable [*indescribable*] and full of glory, receiving the result of your faith, the salvation of your souls.   (1 Peter 1:3-8 WEB)

Jude does **not** mean we sit and wait for Jesus' coming. We should rather be eagerly anticipating His coming, which ought to challenge us to maintain an *active* worship and service towards our Lord. He is coming for His church which He has purchased with His is own blood. He has washed and cleansed us as Paul says,

For we ourselves were also once foolish, disobedient, deceived, serving various lusts and pleasures, living in malice and envy, hateful and hating one another. But when the kindness and the love of God our Savior toward man appeared, not by works of righteousness which we have done, but **according to His mercy He saved us**, through the **washing of regeneration and renewing of the Holy Spirit**, whom He poured out on us abundantly through Jesus Christ our Savior, that **having been justified by His grace** we should become heirs according to the hope of eternal life.   (Titus 3:3-7 NKJ)

Again, as the apostle gives an exhortation to the duty of the husband in the marriage, Paul uses our Lord's wonderful intimate relation with the church as an example,

As Christ also loved the church and gave Himself up for her, so that He might sanctify her, **having cleansed** her by the **WASHING OF WATER**[c] **WITH THE WORD**, that He might present to Himself the church in all her glory, **having no spot or wrinkle** or any such thing; but that she **would be holy and blameless**.   (Eph. 5:25b-27)

[c]Note: Carefully read my brother, there **is not** one drop of water implied here. All the water in the world cannot remove sin. This is the work of the Holy Spirit.

As Paul says to the carnal church at Corinth,

[9]Have you not known that the unrighteous will not inherit the Kingdom of God? Do not be led astray; neither whoremongers, nor idolaters, nor adulterers, nor effeminate, nor sodomites,[d] [10]nor thieves, nor covetous, nor drunkards, nor revilers, nor extortioners, will inherit the Kingdom

of God. [11]And certain of you were these! But you were **washed**, but you were **sanctified**, but you were **declared righteous**, in the **Name of the Lord Jesus**, and **in the Spirit of our God**.　　(1 Cor. 6:9-11 LSV)

[d]Note: homosexual, GK *arsenokoites*, "one who engages in same-sex activity, sodomite." Gingrich GK Lex., Bible Works 10.

My friend, there is none worthy of Heaven. The prophet Isaiah literally describes the repulsive and wicked stench of humankind so-called righteous acts,

And we are as unclean—all of us, And all our righteous acts [are] as garments of menstruation; And we fade as a leaf—all of us. And our iniquities take us away as wind.　　(Isa. 64:6 LSV)

Did you know that some ecclesiastical tradition in churches have the wicked gall to teach that their church has a *"Bank of Merit."* The so-called "Bank of Merit" is where people supposedly so worthy before God went directly to Heaven based on their so-called good works. These so-called people have been canonized as "saints." These "saints" did so many good works that their good works were deposited into the *Bank of Merit* in Heaven. Thus, these people were canonized "saints" by their ecclesiastical dogma because of the overabundance of good works. What a preposterous and evil lie. Hence, everyone else who is not a saint (based on good works) has to suffer in purgatory for eons and eons. What preposterous fabrication and insult to the shed blood and death of our Lord Jesus Christ.

The apostle Peter says,

Now "If the righteous one is **scarcely saved**, Where will the ungodly and the sinner appear?"　　(1 Peter 4:18 NKJ)

Peter is quoting from the GK OT, the Septuagint. (This is why NAS capitalizes the words in their version to indicate it is quote from the OT.) Let me give you the Septuagint translation from which Peter quotes. The ENG Septuagint translation is a little shorter:

If the righteous scarcely be saved, where shall the ungodly and the sinner appear?　　(Prov. 11:31 LXE)

Listen, Solomon in Proverbs does not mean that there is anyone righteous. There are none righteous; no, not one.[Rom. 3:10ff] We are only made righteous because the Lord has cleansed us from inside out by Holy Spirit and the work of Christ on Calvary. Friend, the Lord Jesus took our place; Christ Jesus bore our sins in His body; He died in our place for sins.[2 Cor. 5:21; 1 Peter 2:24]

Now, you know and understand better why Jude says,

— looking for the **MERCY** of our Lord Jesus Christ unto eternal life.

(Jude 1:21 KJV)

Again, do not get offended but pay close attention: do you recall why the apostle Paul said above? Repetition is good for learning; so, let look at his words once more:

For we ourselves were also once foolish, disobedient, deceived, serving various lusts and pleasures, living in malice and envy, hateful and hating one another. But when the kindness and **the love of God our Savior toward man** [all of humanity] appeared, not by works of righteousness which we have done, but **ACCORDING TO HIS MERCY He saved us**, through the **washing of regeneration and renewing of the Holy Spirit,** whom He poured out on us abundantly through Jesus Christ our Savior, that **having been justified by His grace** we should become heirs according to the hope of eternal life. (Titus 3:3-7 NKJ)

The Lord saved us *according to His mercy*. It is by His mercy and grace all the way. Hebrews writer says,

Therefore, in all things He had to be made like *His* brethren [Christ becoming human], that He might be a **merciful** and **faithful** High Priest [*Jesus*] in things *pertaining* to God, to make propitiation for the sins of the people. For in that He Himself has suffered, being tempted, He is able to aid those who are tempted. (Heb. 2:17, 18 NKJ)

Again,

Since, then, we have a great high priest who has passed through the heavens, Jesus, the Son of God, let us hold fast to our confession. For we do not have a high priest who is unable to sympathize with our weaknesses, but we have one who in every respect has been tested as we are, yet without sin. Let us therefore **approach the throne of grace with boldness,** so that we **MAY RECEIVE MERCY** and **FIND GRACE TO HELP** in time of need. (Heb. 4:14-16 NRS)

What a paradox! As sinners, we are wretched and wicked and spiritually bankrupt and dead in sin before the Lord our God. Nevertheless, the Lord has reached down to **ALL OF HUMANITY** out of His infinite mercy and grace to save any and every one that will just put their trust and commitment in Jesus Christ as their Lord and Savior. Trust Jesus right now: His shed blood and death is available for righteousness. (Without Jesus as our Savior we are all condemned and remaining under the infinite wrath of God.[See John 3:18, 36]) Believe and receive Him right now. He is waiting on you to call upon His Name.

> He came to what was his own, and his own people did not accept him. But to all who received him, who believed in his name, he gave power to become children of God, who were born, not of blood or of the will of the flesh or of the will of man, but of God.   (John 1:11-13 NRS)

Will you trust in Him right now? He is waiting for you to call upon Him now.

Conclusion

Jude's letter is indeed brief, but it is not lacking in teaching us to "earnestly to contend for the faith has been entrust to us." Will you be faithful with the Deposit, the Word of God? Friend, will you *earnestly contend for the faith that has been entrust to us*?

> Dear friends, although I was very eager to write to you about the salvation we share, I felt compelled to write and **urge you to contend for the faith that was once for all entrusted to God's holy people**.
>
> (Jude 1:3 NIV)

Yes, let us with eager anticipation look for the blessed hope.

> Looking for that blessed hope, and the glorious appearing of the great God and our Savior Jesus Christ.   (Titus 2:13 KJV)

But you, beloved, build yourselves up on your most holy faith; pray in the Holy Spirit; keep yourselves in the love of God; look forward to the mercy of our Lord Jesus Christ that leads to eternal life. (Jude 1:20, 21 NRS)

Footnotes:

1. "Just a Little Talk with Jesus," written by Rev. Cleavant Derricks in 1937.

CHAPTER 18

Keeping busy in the service of our Lord

Memory verse

And the LORD passed by before him, and proclaimed, The LORD, The LORD God, merciful and gracious, longsuffering, and abundant in goodness and truth, Keeping mercy for thousands, forgiving iniquity and transgression and sin, and that will by no means clear *the guilty*; visiting the iniquity of the fathers upon the children, and upon the children's children, unto the third and to the fourth *generation.*

(Exodus 34:6, 7 KJV)

Introduction

As we closed on this section, we noticed the emphasis of "looking or eagerly anticipating the **mercy** of our Lord Jesus Christ." Jude continues with the thought that the saints also should exhibit "*mercy*" to others even if they are unworthy. The saints need to be equally merciful towards all people. Mercy needs to be given to people whether it is sharing the Gospel to the unregenerate or towards a brother or sister in Christ. We need to be merciful even towards saints that are wayward or drifting "*in*" or "*from*" the faith. Unfortunately, some <u>Christians</u> become so ensnared by the world, the flesh, or the devil that they are impotent to free themselves.

So, the same mercy the Lord has shown to us, the believers are expected to be ever merciful towards others. Jesus teaches a parable on being merciful to others in this world of woes. The Lord continues to be merciful towards all mankind. The saints must be exhibiting mercy towards others in need for this is the example of Lord. He called or referred to every one as "*friend*," whether they were cordial or foe. Our Lord addressed people as friend. Let us note Jesus' parable which is slightly long, but it highlights the portrait being merciful towards others.

> [21]Then Peter having come near to Him, said, "Lord, how often will my brother sin against me, and I forgive him—until seven times?" [22]Jesus says to him, "I do not say to you until seven times, but until seventy times seven.

²³Because of this was the kingdom of the heavens likened to a man, a king, who willed to take reckoning with his servants, ²⁴and he having begun to take account, there was brought near to him one debtor of a myriad of talents[a],[ten thousand talents] ²⁵and he having nothing to pay, his lord commanded him to be sold, and his wife, and the children, and all, whatever he had, and payment to be made. ²⁶The servant then, having fallen down, was prostrating to him, saying, Lord, have patience with me, and I will pay you all; ²⁷and the lord of that servant having been moved with compassion released him, and the debt he forgave him. ²⁸ And that servant having come forth, found one of his fellow-servants who was owing him one hundred denarii[a], and having laid hold, he took him by the throat, saying, Pay me that which you owe. ²⁹His fellow-servant then, having fallen down at his feet, was calling on him, saying, Have patience with me, and I will pay you all; ³⁰and he would not, but having gone away, he cast him into prison, until he might pay that which was owing. ³¹And his fellow-servants having seen the things that were done, were grieved exceedingly, and having come, showed fully to their lord all the things that were done; ³²then having called him, his lord says to him, Evil servant! All that debt I forgave you, seeing you called on me; ³³did it not seem necessary to you to have dealt kindly with your fellow servant, as I also dealt kindly with you? ³⁴And having been angry, his lord delivered him to the inquisitors, until he might pay all that was owing to him; ³⁵so also My heavenly Father will do to you, if you may not forgive each one his brother from your hearts their trespasses."

(Matt. 18:21-35 LSV)

[a] Note: Jesus uses a *hyperbole* to illustrate His point. The LSV is correct and very literal. ESV notation v 24, a talent is = 20 years for a common laborer, which means "myriad of talents:" 10,000 x 20 years, impossible to pay back. In v 28, hundred denarius is = a common laborer day's wages.

Some are so cold and void of mercy and compassion that some might say concerning the wicked, "If they don't want Jesus, let them go to hell." Similar attitude is towards those that are ensnared by sin even towards their brethren in Christ. Shame on you!

Paul, who refers to himself as the worse of sinners, said, as given by NRS,

And the Lord's servant must not be quarrelsome but kindly to everyone, an apt teacher, patient, correcting opponents with gentleness. God may

> perhaps grant that they will repent and come to know the truth, and that they may escape from the snare of the devil, having been held captive by him to do his will. (2 Tim. 2:24-26 NRS)

The point that Jude is exhorting is that the Christians are to reach out to the lost that are without Christ. (This is the fruit of the Holy Spirit and walking in the Spirit.) In the same way, the mature saints are to equally reach out to the wayward Christian caught in sin. Christ Jesus came to buy back (to **redeem**) and **deliver** the sinner and the saint from the slavery of their bondage. That is, the saints are expected to lead the sinner to genuinely seek and receive the Lord Jesus. Jesus will rescue the unsaved, and how much then will our Lord rescue the saint ensnare by sin? Our Lord Jesus came to deliver us from the power of Satan [Col. 1:10-14]. For we were ourselves were once enslaved to elements of this world, but Jesus set us free. [John 8:36; Titus 3:3-5] Hallelujah!

A. Being merciful to the wavering

Jude says as given by NRS,

> And have mercy on some who are wavering; save others by snatching them out of the fire; and have mercy on still others with fear, hating even the tunic[a] defiled by their bodies. (Jude 1:22, 23 NRS)

> [a]Note: "tunic" is the literal meaning, but the word "clothing" or "garment" closer to the idea here. "Tunic," implying "clothing" or "garment."

Maybe you are one of the very strong in the faith. So, you stand your ground unwavering. Well, if you are, then PTL. Unfortunately, some of us in Christ become entangled in the web of the world, and getting ensnared by the world can happen to anyone in the faith. For those weakened by *the world, the lower nature*, or *evil forces* we ought to reach out to help others when we are able. It matters not *how* or *why* they are entangled. Please hear me, for the love of the Lord, we ought to reach out in *mercy* to them. As the apostle Paul says,

> Brethren, if a man be suddenly taken[-*over*][b] in any *offense,* [*trespass*] ye which are spiritually,[*mature in Christ*] restore such one with the spirit of *meekness*, considering thy *self*, least thou also be tempted.
>
> (Gal. 6:1 GNV)

> [b]Note: old ENG spelling is update but no words are changed except for the added brackets [ ].

266

Let us then reach out in mercy to help those entangled by the world when possible. The Lord reached out to each of us out of His infinite mercy, grace, and love, which we do not deserve. The Lord does not reach to only a select few. The Lord is not willing that any perish but that all should come to repentance and receive Him.[2 Peter 3:9] Therefore, let us reach out to others in mercy as the Lord reached down from Heaven to rescue us from the life of sin by His mercy.

Do you recall what the apostle Peter asked the Lord how many times should he forgive his brother or sister in Christ who sins against him? Look again, Jesus says:

> Then Peter came up and said to Him, "Lord, how many times shall my brother sin against me and I *still* forgive him? Up to seven times?" Jesus said to him, "I do not say to you, up to seven times, but up to seventy-seven times.ᶜ" (Matt. 18:21, 22)

> ᶜNote: the reading can be either 77 times or seventy times seven; the KJV and ASV are correct in the biblical sense, "seventy times seven." Hence, implying forgiven your brother or sister every time they sincerely repent and asked for forgiveness. Our goal ought to be restoration and complete fellowship, but if there is no repentance, forgiveness is futile.

Some just assume to go ahead and forgive a person whether the person repents or asked forgiveness or not. While it is admirable to be forgiving of others, how have you helped those who refuse to repent? The person who sinned or committed offense against us, we have not helped them into biblical repentance leading to *restoration* and *complete fellowship.*

This is the point: we want to attempt to lead a person with the desire to do the right thing before God. We ought to encourage people that have offended or sinned against others to seek restoration, fellowship, and especially renewal through repentance. If there is no repentance, then, there is no desire for restoration and fellowship. The person may still be "gloating" over their sin, or they may be still harboring bitterness or resentment, which means there is no repentance. If the person remains *gloating, bitterness and unrepented,* how does forgiving them help lead them towards godliness, restoration, and renewed fellowship?

(To gloat means: "*dwelling* on one's own success or another's *misfortune* with *smugness or malignant* pleasure." Oxford Dictionary)

Unlimited forgiveness or *carte blanche* without leading a person to repentance is to endorse their wrong-doing. There is the failure without leading them to repentance and restoration and regain fellowship again. What spiritual benefit is there in forgiveness if the brother or sister remains unchanged in their wrong-doing? None!

Nowadays, there is seemingly little or no call for repentance in the church. What, people do not sin anymore? Repentance just means the call to change the mind and acknowledgement of the wrong doing and to do the right and godly thing. Thus, the person seeks forgiveness, restoration, and wholesome fellowship once again. The churches are long overdue for a call to repentance. The churches are missing out on the big one: the call for *repentance, restoration, renewal,* and good old fashion spiritual *revival.* Check out, repentance is the repeated theme of the Bible!

"Have mercy on some, who are doubting-"[Jude 1:22]

Jude is exhorting the believers to reach out to people that falter in the faith. Do not wait until they come to you or the church since many will not reach out to you or the church. So, Jude says, "*on some have **mercy**,*" and on others "*who are **doubting**.*" KJV, reads, "- some have compassion, making a difference."[v 22] Unfortunately, the KJV is a little unclear in today's ENG. Jude is appealing to reaching out to people, but let us be merciful since they may be entangled with a web in the world. The word "difference" [v 22 KJV] is the GK word *diakrino* which means that they have "*poor judgment,* (lack of discernment)" and this is especially true in **deficient in making godly spiritual decisions and discernments**. They lack maturity in their knowledge of God's Word and their walk of faith.

Today, many churches are flooded with Christians that *lack spiritual discernment.* Meaning: their judging concerning spiritual things are very poor. They lack godly insight in what do. They may go to places that are *worldly, carnal, or luring attractions* by the evil one. These are things we ought to avoid, but the naïve and immature are unable discern the danger of such place.

If anyone is desirous to reach out to some of these people Jude is referring to here, they had better first watch out for themselves. This is a ministry for the **very mature** and **well-grounded** and very strong spiritually in the faith. This is **NOT** for the immature in the faith. The godly need a **lot of training** with **much supervision**. This type of ministry is **not** for everyone and especially *new* or *babe* or *immature* and especially those with **poor discernment** least they fall prey to the natural or carnal man that also resides within us. This is just common sense, but those without spiritual discernment may walk into such places very naïvely and obliviously to the many dangers all around them.

For example, sending an immature and ungrounded believer into a place that is a *bar* or *house of ill repute,* is a disaster waiting to happen. Anyone taking on such ministry without training and calling by the Lord is underestimating the luring power of sin of the world, the frailty or weakness of the flesh, or ignoring the power of Satan. If you get near fire, you are likely to be burned.

A word to the wise, **No one** is above falling into sin.[1 Cor. 10:12] Yes, we want to help others towards restoration and a godly walk in Christ. Yes and amen, but **DO NOT** put yourself or your loved-ones "*in harm's way.*"[1] For example, **DO NOT** bring wicked strangers into your house to reach them for Christ. "Would you bring the devil into home to be in the presence of your wife or children?" **DO NOT** be a fool! Otherwise, the wicked may destroy one of your loved-ones or even destroy your home. Then, you will be held accountable for the destruction of your loved-one or family due your ignorance in bring the wicked into your home. Some have done this due to their lack of spiritual discernment. Like I said, if we handle fire or put fire in front of our family or love-ones, then, likely someone will indeed get seriously burned. Then friend, God will hold you responsible for putting your love-ones in harm's way.

B. Rescue some as though snatching them out of the fire

Jude's next phrase varies slightly in the text and translations and where to place the emphasis.

And others **save with fear**, pulling *them* **out of the fire**; hating even the garment spotted by the flesh. KJV	But others **save with fear**, pulling them **out of the fire**, hating even the garment defiled by the flesh Coptic	and **some save, snatching them out of the fire**; and on some **have mercy with fear**; hating even the garment spotted by the flesh. ASV	**save others, snatching them out of the fire**; and on some **have mercy with fear**, hating even the garment polluted by the flesh. NAS

Note: the BYZ and Coptic texts have the "fear" at beginning the sentence, but word "fear" appears in the next clause in other texts: "save others, snatching them out of the fire; and on some have mercy with fear—"[v 23 NAS].

There is slight variance in the order texts. It is certainly prudent to have some *fear* when helping people in bondage among the wicked. *Playing house* with the world, flesh, and the devil, you are likely going get scorched. That is, you or your loved-ones might get seriously *mauled*.

The word fear might belong to the next clause. The variance in the text as to whether "fear" belongs in first or second clause. Note the parallel and variance again:

And others **save with fear**, pulling *them* out of the fire; hating even the garment spotted by the flesh.	And some save, snatching them out of the fire; and on some **have mercy with fear**; hating even the garment spotted by the flesh.
KJV	ASV

In either case, the two clauses supplement each other. That is, helping those in bondage of sin, whether the world, the flesh, or the devil. However, the servants of the Lord helping had better be careful themselves. As I have already said, caution is necessary since you might get charred yourself.

But to the rest of the clause, "pulling *them* out of the fire," what does Jude mean here? Sin of the world, the flesh, or devil is a fire. James says this about the carnal use of the tongue,

> And the tongue *is* a fire, a world of iniquity. The tongue is so set among our members that it defiles the whole body, and sets on fire the course of nature; and it is set on fire by hell. (James 3:6 KJV)

Isaiah gives this thought,

> Woe to those who are wise in their own eyes and clever in their own sight. Woe to those who are heroes in drinking wine and champions in mixing strong drink, who acquit the guilty for a bribe and deprive the innocent of justice. Therefore, as a tongue of fire consumes the straw, and as dry grass shrivels in the flame, so their roots will decay and their blossoms will blow away like dust; for they have rejected the instruction of the LORD of Hosts and despised the word of the Holy One of Israel. Therefore the anger of the LORD burns against His people; His hand is raised against them to strike them down. The mountains quake, and the corpses lay like refuse [*dung*] in the streets. (Isa. 5:21-25 BSB)

Jesus said,

> But I say to you that everyone who continues to be angry with his brother *or* harbors malice against him shall be guilty before the court; and whoever speaks [contemptuously and insultingly] to his brother, 'Raca (You empty-headed idiot)!' shall be guilty before the supreme court (Sanhedrin); and whoever says, 'You fool!' shall be in danger of the fiery hell. (Matt. 5:22 AMP)

While the meaning is difficult to know with any certainty, it is possible that Jude is sayings, "Proceed with caution when helping your brother or sister ensnared by sin. Paul says,

Brethren, if a man be overtaken in a fault, ye which are spiritual, restore such *a* one in the spirit of meekness; considering thyself, lest thou also be tempted. ²Bear ye one another's burdens,[e.g. *overload*] and so fulfil the law of Christ. ³For if a man think himself to be something, when he is nothing, he *deceives* himself. ⁴But let every man prove his own work, and then shall he have rejoicing in himself alone, and not in another. ⁵For every man shall bear his own burden.[e.g., *normal load in life*] ⁶Let him that is taught in the word communicate unto him that *teaches* in all good things. ⁷Be not deceived; God is not mocked: for whatsoever a man soweth, that shall he also reap. ⁸For he that soweth to his flesh shall of the flesh reap corruption; but he that soweth to the Spirit shall of the Spirit reap life everlasting. ⁹And let us not be weary in well doing [*doing good*]: for in due season we shall reap, if we faint not. ¹⁰As we have therefore opportunity, let us do good unto all *men*, especially unto them who are of the household of faith.   (Gal. 6:1-10 KJV)

C. Careful with some engulfed by the carnal flesh

Let us note the whole issue once again as given by NAS:

And have mercy on some, who are doubting; save others, snatching them out of the fire; and on some have mercy with fear, hating even the garment polluted by the flesh.   (Jude 1:22, 23)

Let us parallel the last phrase here in Jude.

- hating even the garment spotted by the flesh. v 23 KJV	- hating even the garment polluted by the flesh. v 23 NAS

Here Jude even addresses the stench or rottenness that is associated with clothing of those enslaved to wickedness of the world, flesh, and the evil one. It is easy to observe those who are enslaved to alcohol or drugs. Their whole waking hours are given-over to some stimulus until they pass out or fall unconsciousness.

Such above person has no concern for nutritious food for the body. Good hygiene is alien word since they live for their next fix. Even animals are repulsed by their body-odor, and even the stench of their cloths are putrid to anyone. Sleep is whatever street, alley, or garbage dump will do just fine. So, it is no wonder their clothing is only good to be burned; their lack of up-keep on clean cloth is beyond being washed or repaired. As the Proverbs says of those enslaved,

> You will say, "They have struck me, but I am not harmed!˟ They beat me, but I did not know it! When will I awake? I will look for another drink." (Prov. 23:35 NET)

> ˟Note: the meaning is that the person so inebriated that the person could not feel it when they were *struck*.

The scene of an alcoholic or drug addicted person's life soon come to ruin; their life is cut short. Some do not realize they are enslaved to sin, or they are in denial. They shall come to dreadful and terrifying ends. Only the Lord Jesus is able deliver such persons from their vices. The same can be said of those addicted to *gambling* or *playing the lottery*. Such a person bases their life on "*luck*" or "*chance*." Life is more rewarding and precious when we walk with the Lord and His Word.

Jude says, "- hating even the garment polluted by the flesh."[v 23c] Friend, when you come to genuinely know and walk with the Savior, *as I've said many times before*, "He cleanses you up from the inside out." Ah, but friend, our Lord also "cleanses you on the outside" as well when you remain obedient to His Word.

Jesus changes our ways of thinking when we truly know Him and walk in His Word. The change ought to be evident if the person is truly *in Christ* and walking *sound doctrine* being taught and challenged. Everyone needs to be faithfully reading and walking in the light of His Word. In so doing, we are being obedient in all things we say and do.[Col. 3:15-17, 23] Amen, our Lord shall indeed clean you up to do His will. Christ Jesus does just clean up "to go on your merrily way." Our Lord gets us cleaned up to do His will!

Well, think with me for a moment. Look at India with their thousands of gods and goddesses. Look at any country where paganism rules, the people suffer and some do not even have clothing for their back. This is the condition of the pagan world without the True biblical Christ Jesus, risen, glorified, and hallelujah coming again.

Even in the communist countries, many people have nothing. (Though nowadays, China may appear or look *good with the present veneer they have built*, but without the Lord, they will come up short.) Many Russians are driven to find their peace in a bottle of vodka.

Where the *Gospel has free course* and the *saints are walking godly* and *churches are faithful and obedient*, that country will progress by His grace and mercy. Regrettably, those who follow the path of the wicked world of the ungodly will indeed be like Jude says, "- hating even the garment polluted by the flesh."[v 23 NAS]

The stench and smell of the clothing of the ungodly ensnared by the endless vices of the world will have difficulty keeping clean. Yes, the saints will bath in clean water and be fresh and presentable in the presence of the Lord our God. This my friend is what the genuine Gospel of the Lord Jesus will do. So, Jude exhorts us to reach out to "*the up and out*" as well "*the down and out.*"

The next time you see someone enslaved to alcohol, drugs, or some kind stimulus, those specially gifted and called of God can reach out to such people enslaved. Yes, enslaved because the world, flesh, or the evil one has them in bondage.

Let us look at the text again we noted previously. The text appears contradictory (compare v 2 with v 5). The old ENG is not as clear. We will compare it from the KJV and MSB which both only use the Byzantine text.

Brethren, if a man be overtaken in a fault, ye which are spiritual, restore such *a* one in the spirit of meekness; considering thyself, lest thou also be tempted. [2]Bear ye one another's burdens, and so fulfil the law of Christ. [3]For if a man think himself to be something, when he is nothing, he *deceives* himself. [4]But let every man prove his own work, and then shall he have rejoicing in himself alone, and not in another. [5]For every man shall bear his own burden. (Gal. 6:1-5 KJV)	[1]Brothers, if someone is caught in a trespass, you who are spiritual should restore him with a spirit of gentleness. But watch yourself, or you also may be tempted. [2]Carry one another's burdens [*help with their overload*], and in this way you will fulfill the law of Christ. [3]If anyone thinks he is something when he is nothing, he deceives himself. [4]Each one should test his own work. Then he will have reason to boast in himself alone, and not in someone else. [5]For each one should carry his own [*normal*] load. (Gal. 6:1-5 MSB)

The meaning is everyone is responsible to carry their regular load or normal burden in this life, v 2. In v 5, those that have extra larger load (overload) or burdened-down not part regular of a person's load of life, we are to help our brother when they are weighed down. We ought to help them with extra heavier load which has them burdened down. For example, some have *lost their jobs*, become *seriously ill*, or had *death in the family*. These are times of an overload. When we are able, let us reach out are to help even the unbeliever as well.

Conclusion

Jude hits a sensitive nerve here in this section. Some may say, "Let them wallow in mud, they enjoy the company of the pigs." Those enslaved to the vices of the world, flesh, or the devil often realize their enslavement. Unfortunately, they may often feel powerless in themselves to free themselves from such bondage. Some have given up on life and feel powerless to do anything. The Gospel and with follow up and getting them grounded in the Word of God will change a person. (Others want nothing to do with Jesus Christ will drop you like *burning wood on fire*.) Nevertheless, God's Word declares,

> As ye have therefore received Christ Jesus the Lord, *so* walk ye in him: Rooted and built up in him, and stablished in the faith, as ye have been taught, abounding therein with thanksgiving. Beware lest any man spoil you through philosophy and vain deceit, after the tradition of men, after the rudiments of the world, and not after Christ. For in him dwelleth all the fulness of the Godhead bodily.   (Col. 2:6-9 KJV)

Did you know that the natural man, the unregenerate, has alcohol and drugs programs run and managed by the unregenerate? Unfortunately, the percentage of those who attend such programs by the government produce a recovery of only about 6%. Yes, you read me correctly only 6% are delivered their drug addiction.

In Seattle, for example, where the Gospel is given and strict Bible study and doctrine in Christ is Lord of the life for two years commitment, the recovery is 97%. This is the power of Christ the Lord. There is no change where Christ is not preached and taught that Jesus Christ must be absolute Lord over the life. This is not churchianity; friend, this is genuine **biblical Christianity**.

However, there are few Pastors or Christian workers willing to preach and expect commitment. They soft-peddle the Gospel with generic "god." The saints and churches are too carnal or too immature in the faith. Yes, many churches are too self-centered. So, how in the world will the churches have any impact in the community or surroundings in their location? There will be none! This is because the churches like the Laodicean church is too satisfied with the "*status quo*." The churches' impact is only "*a dribble*; *a dripping faucet*." Christ alone is able deliver people enslaved. Regrettably, many, many churches lack spiritual foresight and fortitude in their walk with Christ the Lord to even attempt such needed outreaches.

There is lack of zeal for the Lord today. Friend, we **need fire from on high by the Holy Spirit** that will burn away chaff. Know this for certain as John the Baptist said, so our blessed Lord will do because like Israel, the churches have been unfaithful.

"His winnowing fork is in His hand, and He will thoroughly clear His threshing floor; and He will gather His wheat into the barn, but He will burn up the chaff with unquenchable fire."   (Matt. 3:12)

Footnotes:

1. "In harm's way:" If someone is put in harm's way, they are caused to be in a dangerous situation. Collin's Dictionary,
    https://www.collinsdictionary.com/us/dictionary/english/in-harms-way#:~:text=phrase,full%20dictionary%20entry%20for%20harm

Part Six

Presented Faultless in God's Presence, Jude 1:24, 25

[24]Now to Him who is able to protect you from stumbling, and to make you stand in the presence of His glory, blameless with great joy, [25]to the only God our Savior, through Jesus Christ our Lord, *be* glory, majesty, dominion, and authority before all time and now and forever. Amen.

(Jude 1:24, 25 NAS)

CHAPTER 19

The Doxology that is beyond Time and Immortal

(Section one, "Doxology of joy")

Memory verse

Now may the God of peace who brought up our Lord Jesus from the dead, that great Shepherd of the sheep, through the blood of the everlasting covenant, make you complete in every good work to do His will, working in you what is well pleasing in His sight, through Jesus Christ, to whom *be* glory forever and ever. Amen. (Heb. 13:20, 21 NKJ)

Introduction

Jude sums up his epistle with an amazing, awesome, and incredible doxology. There are many wonderful such doxologies or benedictions and invocations of blessings in Scriptures. These wonderful doxologies ought to lighten us up like brilliant Christmas trees. Since many of us in Christ lack of a spiritual thirst today, sadly, "Who would care?"

Let me tell you even if you do not care to read such terminus doxologies, you are missing out on some of the most wonderful Scriptures. Many of us may read through such doxologies but without giving much if any ponderous of thought. We just zoom through giving them little thought. What a shame! Our goal is to read through the Bible and not *cogitate* and *deliberate* through what we are reading. There is zero contemplation.

So, please give me your complete and undivided attention. **It is such**

glorious doxologies that is what Heaven is all about. Yes, my friend, we shall indeed be singing, praising, and giving thanksgiving to the Lord our God. The Lord alone is worthy of all our worship, and to Him alone belongs all the glory and honor now and forever more. Let all the saints and church say, "Amen, hallelujah!"

My friend, if you still lacking enlightenment, let me direct you to Revelation chapters four and five. Read the text below, and read it slowly, *hang on every word* because it is a glorious text to the Lord our God, our Redeemer. Yes, it is more than a praise; the text is a song of worship, yea an anthem of praise. The entire universe will quake at the singing of the hymn in Rev. 5.

> When He [*the Lamb*] had taken the book, the four living creatures and the twenty-four elders fell down before the Lamb, each one holding a harp and golden bowls full of incense, which are the prayers of the saints. [9]And they sang a new song, saying,
>
> "Worthy are You to take the book and to break its seals; for You were slain, and purchased for God with Your blood *men* from every tribe and tongue and people and nation. [10]You have made them *to be* a kingdom and priests to our God; and they will reign upon the earth."
>
> [11]Then I looked, and I heard the voice of many angels around the throne and the living creatures and the elders; and the number of them was myriads of myriads, and thousands of thousands, [12]saying with a loud voice,
>
> "Worthy is the Lamb that was slain to receive power and riches and wisdom and might and honor and glory and blessing."
>
> [13]And every created thing which is in heaven and on the earth and under the earth and on the sea, and all things in them, I heard saying, "To Him who sits on the throne, and to the Lamb, *be* blessing and honor and glory and dominion forever and ever."
>
> [14]And the four living creatures kept saying, "Amen." And the elders fell down and worshiped. (Rev. 5:8-14)

Wake up my brother! This is what Heaven is all about. So, as we examine Jude's doxology, please approach it with a sense of worship and awesome praise. Jude declares one of the most incredible doxologies ever penned by fallen and depraved humanity. Let us enjoy this wonderful praise to God. The doxology is so awesome that it must be examined in two chapters, and even then, the two chapters are insufficient to do justice to this breath-taking doxology.

A. Now to Him who is able

To whom is Jude referring in the pronoun "Him?"[Rev. 5:8] The pronoun is uncapitalized by many translations except the NAS, NKJ, and few others that are so minded. Well, if you are unsure to whom the pronoun belongs, let us see it again as given by NAS,

> Now **to Him** who is able to keep you from stumbling, and to make you
> stand in the presence of His glory blameless with great joy, (Jude 1:24)

In Revelation chapter five, the praise(s) and song(s) belongs to Jesus Christ our Lord. Christ the Lord is the Designer, Creator, Sustainer, and Executor over the entire universe and all life; yeah, all creation. Let all who love the Lord Jesus say, "Amen, Hallelujah, and glory to God!" Christ the Lord is the One from whom all things came into being. Hence, **"to Him"** refers to Christ the Lord that belongs all glory and praise now and forever more.

The heretics with their cancerous and deadly doctrine that *"Christ is begotten not made"* which still lingers and looms over the church like a dark cloud, misleading countless millions. This heresy is so pervasive throughout the church that many remain chained to the evil doctrine, oblivious and completely blind by the power of darkness.

Listen: there is but one God who is eternal and is without beginning or ending. Yet, the Lord our God is in three Persons: the Father, the Son, and the Holy Spirit. Logically therefore, the blessed Trinity share in one and only one essence of being. Those who reject the declaration that there is only One God but in three Persons are committing spiritual suicide for all eternity in Hell.

Anyone espousing such ignorant teaching that the Son of God and the Holy Spirit were begotten in time have been blinded by ecclesiastical tradition and false doctrine through the forces of darkness. That is to allege, "begotten" in the sense that the Son and Holy Spirit originated from the Father. The blessed Trinity is co-eternal and without beginning or end. There is no second generation of "gods." Such teaching implying a "second generation of gods" is utter madness.

Furthermore, to assert that the Father has a different essence of being than the Son of God and the Holy Spirit is completely theologically erroneous and a lie from Hell. There is one God and sharing in one essence of being. Jesus was very clear and explicit: Christ and the Father "We **are** one."^John 10:30 To see the Son is to look upon the Father.^John 14:8-11

Hear me: there is but One true God. The Bible declares without any ambiguity and with total clarity that there is but One God; yet, in the mystery of God, the Lord is Triune or Trinity of God. No one in creation is able understand or explain it except the Eternal God Himself. We believe it because God's Word declares it, but we do not have to comprehend or explain it in order to believe it.

The term "only begotten" refers to the Lord our God who Himself tabernacles in flesh, which was prophesied.

> I will declare the decree: the LORD hath said unto me, Thou *art* my
> Son; this day have I begotten thee.   (Psa. 2:7 KJV)

David who wrote the above psalm is not declaring the beginning of the Son, but the prophetic prophecy which declares that the Messiah is the Eternal and Everlasting God. Christ the Lord tabernacles Himself into human history and lays down His life on the cross to redeem sinful humanity. As the apostle Paul clearly declares to Israel in a synagogue.

> And we bring you the good news that what God promised to the fathers,
> this he has fulfilled to us their children by raising Jesus, as also it is
> written in the second Psalm, "'You are my Son, today I have begotten
> you.' 34 And as for the fact that he raised him from the dead, no more to
> return to corruption, he has spoken in this way, 'I will give you the holy
> and sure blessings of David.'"   (Acts 13:32-34 ESV)

Paul declared how the Lord Himself came into the world as the Redeemer, laying down His life on the cross and rising the third day.^1 Cor. 15:3, 4 The meaning in Psalm two is not begotten *as to have a beginning*, but the Messiah [the Anointed One] tabernacles Himself in flesh, became man.^John `1:14; 1 Tim. 3:16 He laid down His life on the cross for our sins. This my friend, is the meaning of the word "*begotten*" in the context.

Furthermore, the word "*son*" does not mean offspring as referring children in the context. The meaning "*son*" implies relationship within the Triune God, Who is forever and ever.

Let me illustrate the point. Holy angels of God are referred to as "*sons of God*." Holy angels are "*sons*" of God *by personal relationship* to their Creator. Holy angels were *made* holy by God. God made the holy angels that did not sin His own possession. So, the holy angels that remained faithful and did not sin were confirmed with absolute holiness and righteousness by God. This is in contrast to angels that sinned. The angels that **did not remain faithful** to God but sinned; these angels that sinned were stripped of all holiness and righteousness from God. These angels that sinned were sealed forever in their unholiness and unrighteousness. These angels that sinned became the *wicked* and completely *evil angels* or *evil spirits*. Therefore, the holy angels are now known as "sons of God."[Job 1:6; 2:1; 38:7] Evil angels are **NOT** sons of God because they are without a personal relationship to God. Holy angels are **not** offspring of God. Holy angels are "sons of God" *by relationship* to God.

In the same way concerning humans. Men and women that are redeemed of God are also referred to "*son*." ("Son of God" is used of both men and women.) In this sense, "*son*" does not mean or refer to a particular gender as *male* or *female*. In addition, "*son*" does **not** refer to physical descendants of God, but rather "*son*" (similar to holy angels) refers to personal relationship with the Lord our God. Moreover, "*son*" implies to all the redeemed of God that they are now heirs of God. For instance, the Bible says concerning the redeemed,

> For **you are ALL SONS**[a] **of God** through faith in Christ Jesus. For all of you who were baptized[b] into Christ have clothed yourselves with Christ. There is neither Jew nor Greek, there is neither slave nor free man, **there is neither MALE nor FEMALE**; for **you are all one in Christ Jesus**. And **if you belong to Christ**, then **you are Abraham's descendants**, heirs according to promise. (Gal. 3:26-29)

> [a]Note: the KJV uses the word "children;" however, the GK word "*huios*" is literally "*sons*" and not children. *Huios* is the root word for "adoption" (GK **huio**thesia), *the placing as sons*. Hence, referring to male and female.

> [b]The *baptism* is not water baptism; this is the baptism of Holy Spirit.[1 Cor. 12:13] Water baptism cannot place anyone in Christ. Only the Holy Spirit can place us in Christ's death, burial, and resurrection.[Rom. 6:1-10]

Again, Paul says,

> But when the fullness of the time came, God sent forth His Son, born of a woman, born under the Law, [5]so that He might redeem those who were under the Law, that we might receive the **adoption** [GK *huiothesia*] **as sons**. [6]Because you are sons [GK *huios*], God has sent forth the Spirit of His Son into our hearts, crying, "Abba! Father!" [7]Therefore you are no longer a slave, but a son; and if a son, then an heir through God.

> (Gal. 4:4-7)

Therefore, get it right: the phrase "Son of God" refers to **relationship** within the blessed Trinity. In the same way, "son" is used of holy angels and humans (male and female), "sons" by relationship to God. However, Christ the Lord is "Son of God" because of **His eternal relationship** within the blessed Trinity. The Christ is the Son of God by His "Co-eternality" within the Triune God. So then, the word Son as it is use of the Messiah does not mean offspring nor having origin nor having a beginning! Christ is the Creator, and He is forever and ever!

Now we know to whom Jude is referring to here, Christ Lord, but notice also, Jude says,

> Now unto him that is <u>able</u>   (Jude 1:24 KJV)

The word "*able*" (GK *dunamai*): "capacity or ability *be able, be capable of, can, have power to*; and with an infinitive, implies what one is able to do,"[1] e.g. Mat. 3:9.

"*Able*" is from the same root word (GK *dunamai*, the noun *dunamis*) used when Jesus denounces the Sadducees.

> Jesus answered and said unto them, Ye do err, not knowing the scriptures, nor the power [GK dunamis] of God.   (Matt. 22:29 KJV)

The power of God is infinite and immeasurable and who can know it? This is the power Christ, and there is nothing impossible with the Lord our God. Christ possesses the power to save all that genuine place their commitment and trust in Him. As Hebrews says,

> But this *man*, because he [*Christ the Lord*] *continues* ever, *has* an unchangeable [*inviolable*] priesthood. 25Wherefore he is **able also to save them to the uttermost** that come unto God by him, seeing he ever *lives* [*lives forever*] to make intercession for them. 26For such *a* high priest became us, *who is* holy, harmless, undefiled, separate from sinners, and made higher than the heavens; 27Who *need* not daily, as those high priests, to offer up sacrifice, first for his own sins, and then for the people's: for this he did once, when he offered up himself.   (Heb. 7:24-27 KJV)

B. To keep you from stumbling

Here Jude demonstrates the use of grace, and grace that is completely unmerited by anyone. This is unmerited *sustaining grace of God*. Like the mighty universe, the Lord sustains it by His infinite power and grace. As Job said to his fault-finding friends, "He hangs the earth upon nothing."Job 26:7 MSB

Friend, the Lord not only saves you by His grace; it is grace and grace alone that sustains you.

The human nature is so fickle. We blow with the wind. As we note previously, this is like what Jacob said concerning firstborn son Reuben, but also characteristic of the human natural,

> "Reuben, you are my firstborn; My might, the beginning of my strength *and* vigor, Preeminent in dignity and preeminent in power [that should have been your birthright]. But unstable *and* reckless *and* boiling over like water [in sinful lust] —" (Gen. 49:3, 4a AMP)

After feeding the five thousand men, which did not include the counting the feeding the women and all the children, Jesus tells the apostles to get into the boat and go across the Sea of Galilee and He would meet them on the other-side.[Mark 6:45] The disciples did as they were told, but we don't read anywhere that they asked the Lord, *How are going get to the other-side* of the Sea of Galilee? (Jesus spends the night on the mountain in prayer.[v 46])

Jesus is on the mountain, but **He see the disciples** struggling with the oars mid-way across Galilee.[v 47, 48] The disciples at once seems to notice something coming towards them on the sea; it is Jesus walking on the sea.[v 49, 50]

Then, we read this account, which is incredible,

> But immediately Jesus spoke to them, saying, "Take courage, it is I; do not be afraid."
>
> Peter said to Him, "Lord, if it is You, **command me to come** to You on the water." And He said, "**Come!**" And Peter got out of the boat, and walked on the water and came toward Jesus. But seeing the wind,[waves of the sea] he became frightened, and **beginning to sink**, he cried out, "**Lord, save me!**" Immediately Jesus **stretched out His hand and took hold of him**, and said to him, "You of little faith, why did you doubt?"
>
> (Matt. 14:27-31)

Some today are oblivious to the mighty sustaining grace of the Lord Jesus. Some today ignorantly suppose that Peter by his inherent or intrinsic faith mustered up faith to walk on water. Perish the thought my brother! Those with such assertion are indeed blind! Peter said, "Lord, if it is really You, then **COMMAND ME TO COME**." Jesus said, "**COME!**" Friend, Peter walked on water by the **power** and the **grace** of the Lord Jesus. You might laugh at Peter and his lack of faith. However, let us remember that eleven others remained in the little boat. Friend, only Peter excised faith by stepping out of boat on to the turbulent sea at Jesus' command. Would you step out of the boat? Friend, be careful how you answer. The Lord truly knows what we would do in the same situation. So, again, exercise care since the Lord knows our every *thought* and every *probable action.*

Do you now get it my friend? Peter defied and overcame the natural law of gravity. Peter broke the Law Gravity at Jesus' command and by His sustaining grace, mercy, and power of Christ. Christ as Creator established and sustains all the natural laws in the universe. Only Christ can supersede the natural laws and laws of man since He is the Creator and Sustainer of all things.[Col. 1:16, 17] Yea, "For in Christ all the fullness of the Deity [*Godhead*] lives in bodily form."[Col. 2:9 NIV]

Can you now see my brother, it's all by the grace and wonderful mercy of the Lord Jesus that sustains you and me? As Jude says, "Now unto him that is **able** to keep you from falling."[Jude 1:24 KJV]

Now, you might understand what is meant when our Lord asked Peter who was in "the hot-seat" being drilled concerning which Peter loved more, fishing or Christ.[John 21:15-22]

> Jesus replied, "If **I WANT HIM** [*John*] **TO LIVE UNTIL I COME BACK**, what concern is that of yours? You follow me!"
>
> (John 21:22 NET)

We do not realize how precious we are in the eyes of the Lord Jesus who knows that we are frail and flesh, but said,

> "Look at the birds of the air, for they neither sow nor reap nor gather into barns; yet your heavenly Father feeds them. Are you not of more value than they?" (Matt. 6:26 NKJ)

It is all by the sustaining grace and mercy of the Lord Jesus that He sustains us. Let us realize as the centurion said to Jesus that we now may understand a little more fully who Jesus Christ really is,

> The centurion answered and said, "Lord, I am not worthy that You should come under my roof. **But only speak a word, and my servant will be healed.** [9]"For I also am a man under authority, having soldiers under me. And I say to this *one*, 'Go,' and he goes; and to another, 'Come,' and he comes; and to my servant, 'Do this,' and he does *it*." [10]When Jesus heard *it*, He marveled, and said to those who followed, "Assuredly, I say to you, I have not found such great faith, not even in Israel! [11]"And I say to you that many will come from east and west, and sit down with Abraham, Isaac, and Jacob in the kingdom of heaven. [12]"But the sons of the kingdom will be cast out into outer darkness.

There will be weeping and gnashing of teeth." [13]Then Jesus said to the centurion, "Go your way; and as you have believed, *so* let it be done for you." And his servant was healed that same hour.   (Matt. 8:8-13 NKJ)

C. To make you stand in the presence of His glory

Here we see again how mighty and wonderful is grace that extended to sinful mankind that truly embrace and receive the Lord Jesus as the only Sovereign and Redeemer. Jude says,

> Now unto him that is able to keep you from falling, and **to present** *you* **faultless before the presence of his glory**   (Jude 1:24 KJV)

This is a mind blower and totally incomprehensible to those with some sense of awareness of the infinite holiness and righteousness of the Lord our God. And why, you might ask is Jude's statement such a mind blower? The Lord told Moses who wanted to see God in His face of glory:

> [18]Then *Moses* said, "Please, show me Your glory!" [19]And He said, "I Myself will make all My goodness pass before you, and will proclaim the name of the LORD before you; and I will be gracious to whom I will be gracious, and will show compassion to whom I will show compassion." [20]He further said, **"You cannot see My face**, for **mankind shall not see Me and live!"** [21]Then the LORD said, "Behold, there is a place by Me, and you shall stand *there* on the rock; [22]and it will come about, while My glory is passing by, that I will put you in the cleft of the rock and cover you with My hand until I have passed by. [23]Then I will take My hand away and you shall see My back, but My face shall not be seen."   (Exodus 33:18-23)

Sinful mankind cannot look upon the Lord. He is infinite in holiness and righteousness. No man shall look upon the Lord who is alone in His holiness. Even at the calling of Isaiah the prophet, after a very great king dies, King Uzziah, the people were wondering what will happen now that our great king has died. Isaiah is called at this time as a prophet,

> In the year of King Uzziah's death, I saw the sovereign master [HEB *Adonay, Lord*] seated on a high, elevated throne. The hem of his robe filled the temple. [2]Seraphs [*Seraphim, plural angels*] stood over him; each one had six wings. With two wings **they** covered **their faces**, with two **they** covered their feet, and they used the remaining two to fly. [3]**They** called out to one another, "Holy, holy, holy is the Lord [HEB *YHWH*, LORD, Ex. 3:13-15]

who commands armies! His majestic splendor fills the entire earth!" [4]The sound of **their voices** shook the door frames, and the temple was filled with smoke. [5]I said, "Too bad for me! I am destroyed, for my lips are contaminated by sin, and I live among people whose lips are contaminated by sin. **My eyes have seen the king** [e.g. I am a dead man now c], **the LORD** [HEB *YHWH*] who commands armies." [6]But then one of the seraphs flew toward me. In his hand was a hot coal he had taken from the altar with tongs. [7]He touched my mouth with it and said, "Look, this coal has touched your lips. Your evil is removed; your sin is forgiven." [8]I heard the voice of the sovereign master say, "Whom will I send? Who will go on our behalf?" I answered, "Here I am, send me!"

(Isa. 6:1-8 NET)

cNote: Isaiah assumes that "*I am a dead man now*" since he said, '**My eyes have seen the king   the LORD** who commands armies.' This is Christ the Lord whom Isaiah sees as a theophany. God is invisible. [John 1:18; Col. 1:15; 1 Tim. 1:17; 1 John 4:12] The Lord is so holy that with four wings seraphs **covered their faces** and **feet** in God's presence, and the angels did not look upon the Lord.

The apostle John is transported to Heaven into the presence of the risen Lord Jesus Christ and the Bible says,

When **I saw Him** [*the Lord Jesus Christ*], **I FELL AT HIS FEET LIKE A DEAD MAN**. He laid his right hand on me, saying, "Don't be afraid. I am the first and the last.d"   (Rev. 1:17 WEB)

dNote: "first and last" the emphasis is that Jesus Christ is indeed "the Eternal One, from all eternity and the Everlasting God."

Moses, Isaiah, and even the apostle John came into the presence of Christ, the Lord our God. Awesome and petrifying must have been their experience. Nevertheless, we have these assuring words by Jude,

Now unto him that is able to keep you from falling, and **to present *you* faultless** before the **presence** of **his glory**.   (Jude 1:24 KJV)

Friend, we are going into the **presence of glory** of our God. This my friend ought to tell us just how valuable and preciseness is the shed blood and death Christ the cross.

Forasmuch as ye know that ye were not redeemed with corruptible things, *as* silver and gold, from your vain conversation *received* by tradition from your fathers; But with **THE PRECIOUS BLOOD OF CHRIST**, as of a lamb without blemish and without spot:

(1 Peter 1:18, 19 KJV)

Therefore remember that once you, the Gentiles in the flesh, who are called "uncircumcision" by that which is called "circumcision" (in the flesh, made by hands), that you were at that time separate from Christ, alienated from the commonwealth [citizenship] of Israel, and strangers from the covenants of the promise, having no hope and without God [GK atheos, actual word for atheist] in the world. But **now in Christ Jesus** you who once were far off **ARE MADE NEAR IN THE BLOOD OF CHRIST**. For he is our peace, who made both one [Jews and Gentiles], and broke down the middle wall of separation. (Eph. 2:11-14 WEB)

Friend, this is all possible because, hallelujah, Jude says,

— and to present *you* faultless before the presence of his glory -

(Jude 1:24 KJV)

D. In His Presence blameless with great joy

Jude is giving one crescendo[2] after another mighty crescendo throughout his great doxology. This is like a mighty and great orchestra and every musical instrument playing loud and louder.

Jude continues with another mighty crescendo by saying,

— before the presence of his glory **with exceeding joy-**

(Jude 1:24 KJV)

There is no hanging our heads down in Heaven. Praise the Lord! This is the greeting of the Lord our God in His presence. Sadly, we just do not fully grasp the significance here. This is the Lord our God (infinitely holy and righteous) rejoicing as He greets us. The Lord Himself is overtly rejoicing in seeing you and me in Heaven whom He redeemed by grace and mercy. Heaven is the holiest place in all creation, bar-none. Yet, Jude says,

— before the **PRESENCE** of his glory **with exceeding joy-**

(Jude 1:24 KJV)

Hallelujah! We ought to prostrate or even fall as dead men before Him and in the presence of the **KING** of kings, the **LORD** of lords, and the **ALMIGHTY SOVEREIGN ONE** overall and in all His redeemed. This is all possible because of the Savior who shed His blood and died in our place for sin, praise God, He has imputed to us the very righteousness of Christ the Lord.[2 Cor. 5:21; Phi. 3:9] Lord Jesus paid for all our sins in His mighty redemption on the cross. We atoned for nothing; our sins have been propitiated by the redemption in Christ.[Rom. 3:25; Heb. 2:17; 1 John 2:2; 4:10] Our salvation is not by human works or supposed suffering in so-called purgatory, which is a preposterous lie of tradition and ecclesiastical leaders. Jesus paid for all our sins in full measure. Glory to God, He has imputed to us the righteousness of Christ Lord, which made us fit for Heaven today. As the apostle Paul says,

> And be found in him [*Christ*], not having a righteousness of my own that comes from [*works of*] the law, but that [*righteousness*] which is through faith in Christ— the **RIGHTEOUSNESS THAT COMES FROM GOD** on the basis of faith [*in Christ*].   (Phil. 3:9 NIV)

Now hear me: we are not righteous because of our generated faith. Get it right: we are righteous due to **the object of our faith, our commitment and complete trust in the Lord Christ and His work on Calvary**. It is not our faith that makes us righteous before God; it is the object of our faith which is Christ the Lord. Again, the apostle says,

> He [*Triune God*] made Him [*Christ*] who knew no sin *to be* sin on our behalf,[e] so that we might *become the righteousness of God* in Him[*Christ*].

> (2 Cor. 5:21)

> [e]Note: the meaning of the preposition "*for*" (GK *huper*): Christ Jesus took our place on the cross, and He died in the believer's place. Yet, the offer of propitiation is available to the whole world.[1 John 2:2]

Friend, this is more than joy of seeing someone. When we see a loved-one or a longtime friend we have not seen for many years, we are somewhat overwhelmed with joy. We are very glad to see them once again. God is rejoicing as we come into **His presence**.

Jude says,

> — before the **PRESENCE** of his glory **with exceeding joy**-

> (Jude 1:24 KJV)

My brother, this is "**exceeding joy**." The GK word is *agalliasis*. This is an **exuberant joy**. This is a joy that is bubbling over with joy. This is a joy of *excitement* and *enthusiasm*. Yea, this is more than excitement; this is joy that can be seen and noticed by everyone without hesitation or doubt.

When there is **exuberant joy**, this is more than holy angels rising to their feet. This is even more than the holy angels standing up. This is the holy angels standing, clapping their hands, stomping their feet as they yell, "**Amen, amen, amen, and glory to God**."

Have you ever read the lesson on "the prodigal son?"[Luke 15:11-32] The prodigal son is a portrait of you and me. Like prodigal son, we are bankrupt and in bondage and destitute and in utter hopelessness before the Lord our God. We deserve the Lake of Fire.

Ah, but we have embraced Jesus Christ, the Son of God, as our personal Lord and only Savior who bore our sins on cross and imputed His righteous to His redeemed. We are coming into the Father's presence and remembering the reproach and shame we brought on His blessed name.

While we are still some distance away and before we reach the Father's presence, He comes to greet us with *exceeding joy*, and He put a ring on our hand signifying we are indeed His sons or daughters, and He has now clothed us with royalty of holiness and righteousness. We are His heirs forever and ever in Christ, hallelujah, glory to God.

Now before I close this chapter, I want to say a word concerning the last phrase in Jude 1:24 as given by the Latin Vulgate. Which reads,

"- in the coming of our Lord Jesus Christ-"   (Jude 1:24 LVE)

The Latin Vulgate is indeed a monumental and very great work by Jerome. The Latin Vulgate dominated the world for over a millennium, and that alone, this makes it unequal to any other translation of the Bible during those times. The Latin Vulgate continues to be used by thousands and thousands around the world.

Moreover, the above phrase ("- in the coming of our Lord Jesus Christ-") is certainly worthy of our Lord, but the phrase unfortunately is an insertion. The phrase is **not** an authentic statement by Jude. The manuscripts show conclusively the phrase does not belong in Jude. Regrettably, the phrase has been unwarrantedly added to the text of Scripture.

The same can be said of the name "*Jesus*" instead the word "*Lord*" in Jude 1:5. The word in GK is definitely "Lord." Note the comparison:

Now I desire to put you in remembrance, though ye know all things once for all, that **the Lord**, having saved a people out of the land of Egypt, afterward destroyed them that believed not. (ASV)	I want to remind you, though you once knew this, that **the Lord**, having saved the people out of the land of Egypt, afterward destroyed those who did not believe. (Coptic)	Therefore I want to remind you, although you once knew this, that **the Lord**, having saved the people out of the land of Egypt, afterward destroyed those who did not believe. (TRE)	I will therefore admonish you, though ye once knew all things, that **Jesus**, having saved the people out of the land of Egypt, did afterwards destroy them that believed not: (LVE)

Whether Jerome replaced the phrase "the Lord" for "Jesus" I do not know, but as I have said, the context supports the translation "the Lord." In the same way in Jude 1:24, the phrase in Latin "- in the coming of our Lord Jesus Christ-" is an insertion. The clause is not part of the original GK text in Jude. Here is the parallel again in v 24.

Now unto him that is able to guard you from stumbling, and to set you before the presence of his glory without blemish in exceeding joy. ASV	"Now to Him who is able to keep you from stumbling, and to present you faultless before the presence of His glory with exceeding joy-" Coptic	"Now all glory to God, who is able to keep you from falling away and will bring you with great joy into his glorious presence without a single fault" TRE	Now to him who is able to preserve you without sin, and to present you spotless before the presence of his glory with exceeding joy, **in the coming of our Lord Jesus Christ** LVE

I do not like point out flaws or defects especially with such monumental works like the Latin Vulgate. I have no pleasure in speaking against Jerome's mighty translation. Jerome's insertion is evident to those who have eyes to see. Unfortunately, he is the one that made the insertions. He bears the responsibility on his own work. Even as we shall each bear responsibility for our works whether they be good or bad. Therefore, I must affirm again that the last phrase in the Latin Vulgate of Jude 1:24 is unfortunately an insertion and **not authentic**.

Conclusion

In this first section of this mighty doxology, Jude 1:24, focuses on the mighty blessings of being in Christ. Jude accentuates the excitement and joy God has in greeting us in Heaven. Friend, this is not a greeting after the rapture. Listen, this is a greeting and blessings at death as our souls enter the Portals of

Heaven. There is no *drooping* of our heads or a *solemn* looking down. There is joy when we see Jesus. Friend, don't you get it? There is joy on Jesus' face as we meet Him face to face. As the hymn writer wrote,

Face to Face with Christ my Savior[3]

1. Face to face with Christ, my Savior,
Face to face- what will it be
When with rapture I behold him,
Jesus Christ who died for me?

Refrain:
Face to face I shall behold him,
Far beyond the starry sky;
Face to face in all his glory,
I shall see him by and by.

4. Face to face- oh, blissful moment!
Face to face- see and know;
Face to face with my Redeemer,
Jesus Christ who loves me so. [Refrain]

Everyone will indeed meet the Lord Jesus face to face. For those who have placed their trust in Christ Jesus as Lord and Redeemer, it will be a blissful moment. For those who only knew Him through history but never placed their trusting faith in Him, friend, it will be the beginning of the most terrify and dreadful event for them in all eternity.

Jesus is beckoning for all who desire to come to Him while there is still time.

> Come unto me, all *ye* that *labor* and are heavy laden, and I will give you rest. Take my yoke upon you, and learn of me; for I am meek and lowly in heart: and ye shall find rest unto your souls. For my yoke *is* easy, and my burden is light. (Matt. 11:28-30 KJV)

Footnotes:

1. "Able," Jude 1:24: Friberg's Analytical GK Lexicon from Bible Works 10.

2. "Crescendo," in reference to an orchestra: "A gradual increase in loudness in a piece of music. It can also refer to the musical passage itself, or the direction to indicate increasing loudness." From Google Website

3. "Face to Face with Christ my Savior," written by Carrie Ellis Breck
    https://hymnary.org/text/face_to_face_with_christ_my_savior

CHAPTER 20

The Doxology that is beyond Time and Immortal

(Section two, "To whom are all the blessing belong?")

Memory verse

Let everything that has breath praise the LORD. Praise the LORD!

(Psa. 150:6)

Introduction

In the first part of this mighty doxology, Jude emphasizes the awesome blessing of God and particularly the tremendous welcoming by the LORD our God of His redeemed into Heaven. Jude now shifts to whom are blessings belong. That is, the blessings flow from the Lord our God. (This is no generic "God." This is praise to the Lord our God. Hallelujah!) And to whom are blessings and praise due? All the praise, glory, and worship belong to Christ the Lord who is worthy and blessed forever and ever.

Let us note the complete doxology. There is an extremely important phrase here in the GK text, but unfortunately, the phrase is omitted in BYZ and Coptic texts. Still, the key phrase is found in most GK texts, including the Latin text. The phrase is found in older GK texts.

KJV	Coptic	LV/ENG	ASV
[24]Now unto him that is able to keep you from falling, and to present *you* faultless before the presence of his glory with exceeding joy, [25] To the only wise God our *Savior,*[a] be glory and majesty, dominion and power, both now and ever. Amen.	[24]Now to Him who is able to keep you from stumbling, and to present you faultless before the presence of His glory with exceeding joy, [25] To God our *Savior,*[a] who alone is wise, Be glory and majesty, dominion, and power, both now and forever, Amen	[24]Now to him who is able to preserve you without sin, and to present you spotless before the presence of his glory with exceeding joy, in the coming of our Lord Jesus Christ, [25]To the only God our *Savior*[a] **through Jesus Christ our Lord,** be glory and magnificence, empire and power, before all ages, and now, and for all ages of ages. Amen.	[24]Now unto him that is able to guard you from stumbling, and to set you before the presence of his glory without blemish in exceeding joy, [25]to the only God our *Savior,*[a] **through Jesus Christ our Lord,** be glory, majesty, dominion and power, before all time, and now, and for evermore. Amen.

Note: in italics, "*Savior,*" change from ENG to USA spelling.

In the KJV and the Coptic, the text reads, "**wise** [GK *sophos*] God our *Savior.*" The word **wise** does not appears in in the many GK texts. The phrase appears in the Byzantine and Coptic texts. So, the initial phrase reads this way by most newer versions, "to the only God our Savior."

The Latin reads in the end of verse 24, "**in the coming of our Lord Jesus Christ**." Then in verse 25, the verse begins saying, "To the only God our *Savior.*" Notice the additional phrase, "in the coming of our Lord Jesus Christ," verse 24. The phrase is indeed in some GK MSS and even in the Latin version. Unfortunately, as noted above, the phrase is rightly omitted in the BYZ and Coptic texts, and does not belong in the original text. Regrettably, it is an insertion, and it is not part of the original text.

The phrase in majority of GK texts reads, as noted below, but the phrase is not in the Byzantine or the Coptic texts,

> To the only God our Savior, **THROUGH JESUS CHRIST OUR LORD** — (Jude 1:25)

The phrase is omitted in the KJV, the Coptic, and earlier ENG versions like Geneva Bible does not appear in those texts [Jude 1:25]. Still, there are some newer translations that follow the BYZ text. For example, those following BYZ texts are: the World ENG Bible (2013), the Literal Standard Version (2022), and the Majority Standard Bible (2024). Such newer versions appear to be following the BYZ text; meaning the phrase "through Jesus Christ our Lord" is also omitted.

I am going to side with the more contemporary scholarship on this issue that reads, ("through Jesus Christ our Lord"). The omission of the phrase is indeed unfortunate by BYZ and Coptic texts. However, due the immense importance of the phrase, I **do not** think it prudent to omit the phrase "through Jesus Christ our Lord." The phrase appears authentic, and hence, it was written by Jude.

> To the only God our Savior, **through Jesus Christ our Lord,** *be* glory, majesty, dominion, and authority before all time and now and forever. Amen. (Jude 1:25 NAS)

Interestingly, in verse 25, the phrase **does** definitely appear in the Latin Vulgate, and here is the translation again the Vulgate in ENG,

> To the only God our *Savior* **through Jesus Christ our Lord,** be glory and magnificence, empire and power, before all ages, and now, and for all ages of ages. Amen.[1]   (Jude 1:25 Latin Vulgate in ENG)

The Lord Jesus Christ is the center of all that God is. The omission of the phrase ("through Jesus Christ our Lord") is significant because the phrase gives Jesus His complete title, **"through Jesus Christ our Lord-"** [NAS]. Thus, such omission gives raise to question those texts that omit the phrase. The omission is a very serious red flag me. The phrase is a very important NT doctrine in the study Christology.

However, if you lean more to tradition of the Byzantine or Coptic text, then, you might favor the KJV or GNV. For me, **Christ as Lord** is indeed the center of all sound Biblical Theology, Scripture, and genuine faith in the Lord our God. The omission of the phrase that **JESUS** is **THE CHRIST** and He is **LORD OF ALL** by the BYZ and Coptic is too serious of an omission to ignore, [Jude 1:25]. Yet, the phrase is found in many older GK texts including the Latin Vulgate. These other GK texts date much earlier than the oldest known BYZ text. In addition, the Latin Vulgate goes back to the 5th century. This is too strong of evidence to ignore!

A. To the only [*wise*] God our Savior

While the word "wise" does not appear in many older GK texts, we know that the Lord our God is the only wise God. First, the phrase is **not** a comparative to other so-called gods. That is, Jude is not comparing the Lord to any other so-called *gods* or *goddesses*. There is no other God besides the Lord. The Lord alone is eternal and blessed forever and ever.

Again, as given in the Byzantine text by GNV Bible,

> That is, to God only wise, our *Savior*, be *glory*, and *majesty*, and dominion, and power, both *now* and *forever*, Amen.   (Jude 1:25 GNV)

Interestingly, the exact phrase is used by Paul,

> So that, as sin reigned in death, even so grace would reign through righteousness to eternal life **through Jesus Christ our Lord**.
>
> (Rom. 5:21 NAS)

> Thanks be to God **through Jesus Christ our Lord**! So then, on the one hand I myself with my mind am serving the law of God, but on the other, with my flesh the law of sin.   (Rom. 7:25 NAS)

The apostle Paul uses a similar phraseology in his doxology in closing of the great Epistle to the Romans.

> Now to Him who is able to establish you according to my gospel and the preaching of Jesus Christ, according to the revelation of the mystery which has been kept secret for long ages past, but now has been disclosed, and through the Scriptures of the prophets, in accordance with the commandment of the eternal God, has been made known to all the nations, *leading* to obedience of faith; **to the only wise God**, **through Jesus Christ**, be the glory forever. Amen.   (Rom. 16:25-27)

So, this phrase is used elsewhere in the NT. This helps to cement some bases for the phrase in Jude. The phrase in BYZ text is given more validity in Jude when the phrase is used in other NT documents. Whether one agrees or disagrees that the phrases are authentic rests with you, the reader. The phrase "to the only wise God, through Jesus Christ"[(Rom. 16:27 ASV)] is support by the apostle Paul. In the same way, the phrase is found with Paul, e.g. "through Jesus Christ our Lord-" [(Rom. 7:25 ASV)]

There is no one else in the universe and creation other than God who has infinite wisdom. Scripture says,

> For that preaching of the cross is to them that perish, *foolishness*[b]: but *unto us*, which are *saved*, it is the power of God. [19]For it is written, I will destroy the *wisdom* of the wise, and will cast away the *understanding* of the prudent. [20]Where is the wise? where is the Scribe? where is the disputer of this *world*? *has* not God made the *wisdom* of this *world* *foolishness*? [21]For seeing the *world* by *wisdom* *knew* not God in the

wisdom of GOD, it pleased God by the *foolishness* of preaching to *save* them that *believe*: [22]Seeing also that the *Jews* require a *sign*, and the Grecians [*Greeks*] *seek* after *wisdom*. [23]But *we* preach Christ crucified: *unto* the *Jews*, *even* a stumbling *block*, and unto the Grecians [*Greeks*], *foolishness*: [24]But *unto* them which are called, both of the Jews and Grecians [*Greeks*], we preach Christ, the power of God, and the *wisdom* of God. (1 Cor. 1:18-24 GNV)

[*b*]Note: no words have been changed except for the update in the spelling in modern ENG, and what is in brackets [].

Again, the apostle Paul declares in Christ **there is wisdom** and **knowledge**.

In whom are **hid ALL THE TREASURES of WISDOM and KNOWLEDGE**. (Col. 2:3 KJV)

In Paul's doxology of praise in Romans 11, draws upon the book of Isaiah and he summarizes the mystery of the church and Israel by saying,

For God hath shut up all [*Jews* and Gentiles] unto disobedience,[*c*] that he might have mercy upon all. [*Jews* and Gentiles] [33]O the depth of the riches both of the wisdom and the knowledge of God! how unsearchable are his judgments, and his ways past tracing out! [34]For who hath known the mind of the Lord? or who hath been his counsellor? [35]or who hath first given to him, and it shall be recompensed unto him again? [36]For of him, and through him, and unto him, are all things. To him *be* the glory *forever*. Amen. (Rom. 11:32-36 ASV)

[*c*]Note: the word *"disobedience"* is the GK *apeitheia*. Though the word *apeitheia* literally means *"disobedience,"* the KJV uses the word "unbelief."[Rom. 11:32] In verse 30, he says, "For as ye in times past have not believed God, yet have no obtained mercy through their unbelief [GK apeitheia, disobedient]·Rom. 16:26.

Oh, my friend, please listen to me. There is no redemption for evil angels that sinned. The fallen angels have no recourse or appeal for their sin of rebellion. Hell was prepared for the devil and his angels.[Matt. 25:41; 2 Peter 2:4; Jude 1:6; Rev. 20:10] Judas Iscariot saw the mighty miracles and wonders of Jesus, and he was given the power to heal through the authority of Christ the Lord though he did not genuinely believe in Jesus. Judas Iscariot's healing was not based on his own intrinsic will or faith. Judas Iscariot's healing was based on the sole authority of Christ the Lord who gave him the power to heal.[Matt. 10:1ff] Yet, Judas Iscariot did not believe in Christ the Lord despite seeing all the mighty power and deeds of our Lord. Judas Iscariot only had historical faith within himself, but he reflected no evidence of genuine personal commitment and genuine trust in Christ. Jesus said of Judas Iscariot,

> The Son of Man goes as it is written of him, but woe to that man by whom the Son of Man is betrayed! It would have been better for that man if he had not been born." (Matt. 26:24 ESV)

While salvation is unquestionably available and extended to everyone who wants to come to Jesus, our Lord warns:

> Enter in at the *straight*[d] gate: for it is the wide gate, and *broad* way that *leads* to destruction: and many there be which *goes* in thereat, Because the gate is *straight*, and the way *narrow* that *leads into* life, and *few* **there be that** *find* **it**. [15] Beware of false prophets, which come to you, in *sheep's* clothing, but inwardly they are *ravening wolves*.
>
> (Matt. 7:13-15 GNV)
>
> [d]Note: old ENG spelling has been updated and noted in *italics*, but there are no words in the GNV Bible that have been changed.

Why are there few saved? People are blinded due to the world, flesh, and the devil. Some only have intellectual acknowledgement of the historical fact of the Gospel of Christ Jesus on Calvary, but they are **without commitment and complete trust** in Jesus as Lord and His redemption on Calvary. They may be relying on their religious acts, religious rites, or religious institution. Yet, still others see Jesus as little mere man, a religious guru. Others see our Lord as deceiver and false prophet. Others, though they believe the historical facts of the Gospel, they have not genuinely and personally trusted and received Jesus Christ and His finished work on Calvary.

Salvation is not Jesus plus [+] works. It is Jesus alone: *sola fide*, **by faith alone** is the hallmark call of the saved in Christ since the apostles. Let us keep in mind that it is not faith that saves. Hear me now: **we are saved by faith in the object of our faith, the Lord Jesus Christ**. Hence, salvation is completely and only by faith in Christ and His redemption on the cross alone. It is not faith that saves us. It is our faith in Christ, which saves us alone. As I have already said: it is not faith that saves anyone. Get it right: *we are saved **through the object of our faith that saves, the Lord Jesus***. We are saved through trusting in Jesus as Lord and Him alone.[Acts 4:12] Jesus saves through our faith in Him alone.

Amen! The Lord our God is the only wise God.

B. "- through Jesus Christ our Lord"

The next phrase "through Jesus Christ our Lord" [Jude 1:25], as noted above that the phrase does not appear in the BYZ and Coptic texts. This is very unfortunate, but the phrase is definitely genuine and belongs in Scripture. Why the omission by the BYZ and Coptic texts is one of mystery to me. Some are so zealous for only the BYZ text that they cry out, *"Well, it is not in the text."* Friend, you better be careful what you think or say concerning God's Word least you get bite by your zealous for ecclesiastical tradition.

I think speculation as to the phrase being omitted by BYZ and Coptic texts it is better to make no comment. Nevertheless, the phrase, *"through Jesus Christ our Lord,"* is extremely important in the doctrine of Christology. The text is too important to ignore or overlook. This is why I believe the phrase is part of original GK text by Jude. Still, let everyone be persuaded in their own mind.

Jude is not using the phrase (*through Jesus Christ our Lord*) as simply a supplement. The phrase is included to clarify that redemption of mankind is only **"through Jesus Christ our Lord."** In others words, if a person desires to be righteous before God and enter Heaven, everyone can only be righteous **through Jesus Christ as Lord** and the only Savior. There is no other way to God.[Acts 4:12]

The doctrine that salvation is only through Jesus is disturbing and very upsetting to many people. Some hate the idea being told that "Jesus is the only way," [John 14:6]. Humankind wants to set the condition or standard in coming to God. However, God sets the standard for humanity to come to Him. Rejecting the Gospel is in essentially declaring God and His Word a lie.[1 John 5:10-13] Friend, anyone declaring God a liar is a fool of all fools.

Humankind is expecting the God of Heaven to honor *humanity's reasoning, his carnal works* as righteousness, and *rebellious humanity's standard* for Heaven. Man does not like to be told he is a wicked sinner, and he needs to repent and receive Jesus Christ as his personal Lord and only Redeemer. Nevertheless, everyone that is without Christ Jesus as Lord and Savior shall most certainly perish in their sin.[John 3:16-18, 36; 8:24; 14:6] The bottom line here is that humankind rejects God's Word. The rejection of God's Word is declaring God a liar[1 John 5:10-13] is indeed the greatest fool of all. Friend, only a fool would dare call God a liar.

Here in lies the lightyears difference between religion and genuine faith in Jesus. This is the difference between reality which Jesus Christ is Lord and only Redeemer and *manmade religion* which is only fantasy and illusion.

Religion in my mind is humanity attempting to reach *a god of his own manufacturing through his corrupt and depraved mind.* Man's standard of faith is *plastic* and *manufactured* through his corrupt mind. So, it is easy to understand man's displeasure with the Gospel of God.

Nevertheless, if the Lord had not first communicated to all of humanity by His grace and mercy, we could not know God. Fact! Furthermore, how would depraved man ever know God's will apart from Divine Revelation given to us by God Himself? Friend, we could never know God or know His will in approaching Him unless He initiated and established communication to humankind. Therefore, it seems to me that the Lord must establish communication if we are going know God's will. The Lord has established communication to all humankind. The Lord alone sets the standard through His Word, the Bible!

So, the Lord our God initiated the first step towards communicating to all of mankind. The Lord is a just God. He initiated and established communication with the first man, Adam. He also communicated Himself through Jesus Christ our Lord. Let us also keep in mind that humankind is totally **alienated** and **completely separated** from God **due his sin** and **rebellion**.

> And you *He made alive*, who were **dead in trespasses and sins**, in which you once walked according to the course of this world, **according to the prince of the power of the air** [Satan], the spirit who now works in the sons of disobedience, among whom also we all once conducted ourselves **in the lusts of our flesh**, fulfilling the desires of the flesh and of the mind, and **WERE BY NATURE CHILDREN OF WRATH**, just as the others. (Eph. 2:1-3 NKJ)

The unregenerate imagines that he can come to God based upon his own merit and religious works and religious rites. Here again, man is attempting to establish the standard, though it is an ecclesiastical standard and not God's standard by His Word. The reason man sets the standard is because humankind has created *a god* that he manufactured in his own carnal and depraved mind.

In addition, humankind has rejected the revelations of God, the Bible. There are many ways humankind has reject the revelations of God. Below are some the various ways the Lord has definitely established communication with all mankind. (Humankind may deny the various ways God has establish Himself before all mankind, but man's denial cannot change the fact that God has indeed established the various means below.) Hence, this leaves man without excuse in coming *through Jesus Christ our Lord.*

Man has rejected: *the natural revelation of God*

Natural revelation is seeing all the wonders of the universe, which include the most intricate and meticulous interworking of life. Then man ought to rightly conclude that these wonderous things in the universe are from God and including even to the microscopic detail how life exists and is maintained. Life is too complex to arrive by chance such as evolution. Hence, there is indeed a Creator since none these wonderful things came into existence by chance. Christ the Lord is that Creator. Even Dr. Albert Einstein concluded near the end of his life the universe was created by God, and he openly renounced atheism.

The power to bring all these things into being, who or what power is capable of bringing all these things into existence? God is the only logical answer. Even more amazing is that all things are **sustained** and **maintained** by Christ the Lord ^{Col. 1:16f}. Only God possesses such infinite and immeasurable power and authority. To allege the universe possesses the power to create itself is beyond absolute madness. The **atheist knows** the power that unleashed the universe was immeasurable and unimaginable and beyond comprehension. The **atheist knows** the universe cannot harness or mustered such power on its own. Yet, many depraved among humanity are unwilling to entertain what is totally the rational conclusion: God created the universe. The Lord our God created it. As David said,

> The heavens are telling the glory of God; and the firmament proclaims his handiwork. (Psa. 19:1 NRS)

Paul said,

> For the wrath of God is revealed from heaven against all ungodliness and unrighteousness of people who **SUPPRESS THE TRUTH** by their unrighteousness, because **what can be known about God is plain to them**, because **GOD HAS MADE IT PLAIN** to them. For since **the creation** of the world **his invisible attributes**—his **eternal power** and **divine nature**—have been clearly seen, because they are **understood through what has been made**. So people are without excuse. For although they knew God, they did not glorify him as God or give him thanks, but they became futile in their thoughts and their **senseless hearts were darkened**. (Rom. 1:18-21 NET)

Man has rejected: *the supernatural revelations of God*
Supernatural revelations are many, but we will only note three:
<u>One</u>: there is the **written Word of God**. The written Word of God was all patterned after Moses ^{Deut. 18:15ff}. These were all godly men of the Lord chosen

303

to write down His revelation and as He revealed it to them. There were over forty authorities, sixty-six books empowered and guided by the blessed Holy Spirit of God.

Two: there is also the **spoken of Word of God** declared by holy men of God. There were prophets raised up by the Lord who were chosen spokesmen for God. (Also, patterned after the standard of Moses.) These were men of God like Elijah who fearlessly spoke the Word of God, but these men were not writers of any revelation from God, but their words were *just as authoritative* as the written Word of God and *binding*. They only spoke the Word of God as it was revealed to them.

Three: there are the **holy angelic beings that spoke** or **announced the Word of God** to mankind. This was the awesome and fearful Word announced through holy angelic beings. As Stephen himself says in his message to Israel,

> "You stiff-necked people, uncircumcised in heart and ears, you always **RESIST THE HOLY SPIRIT**. As your fathers did, so do you. Which of the prophets did your fathers not persecute? And they killed those who announced beforehand the coming of the Righteous One, whom you have now betrayed and murdered, you who **received the law as delivered by angels** and did not keep it."   (Acts 7:51-53 ESV)

> Why **the Law** then? It was added on account of the violations, **having been ordered through angels** at the hand of a mediator, until the Seed [which is Christ the Lord] would come to whom the promise had been made.
>
> (Gal. 3:19)

Man has rejected: *the innate revelations of God*.

Solomon tell us that humankind ought to realize there is indeed a clock ticking eternally within the human consciousness inside every human being that gives them the sense of God and His presence. The Amplified Bible makes this very clear in Ecclesiastes,

> He has made everything beautiful *and* appropriate in its time. He has also **PLANTED ETERNITY** [a sense of divine purpose] **IN THE HUMAN HEART** [a mysterious longing which nothing under the sun can satisfy, except God]—yet man cannot find out (comprehend, grasp) what God has done (His overall plan) from the beginning to the end.
>
> (Ecc. 3:11 AMP)

Death does not end all. Death is the commencement into eternity. Death will unveil reality of the universe and all creation. Life of every person is too precious in the infinite love of God. He desires that mankind would choose eternal life with Him.[1Tim.2:3, 4; Titus 2:11; 2 Peter 3:9] However, keep in mind that God is first and foremost infinitely holiness and righteousness. So, even His infinite love and benevolence are subject to His infinite holiness and righteousness. Therefore, God will judge sin!

Man has rejected: *the Incarnation revelations of God.*

The doctrine of the incarnation is so very imperative and monumental. The incarnation alone is the most significant event in the revelation of God and history of mankind, bar none! There are no words sufficient to adequately explain the immense importance of God tabernacling Himself in flesh. Watch out if you dare say that God has not tabernacled as a human being. God has indeed manifested Himself in the past through Theophanies. Theophanies were appearances or manifestations of God in the history of humankind. (Hence, theophanies literally meaning: God manifesting or God appearing in human history during the OT.)

Therefore, the appearance of God is indeed very rational. Please listen, theophanies reveal how **intimate** and **compassionate** God is to all sinful humanity. Theophanies are sometimes unknown or overlooked by some students of the Scripture. Theophanies or appearances of God are clearly revealed in Scripture. Theophanies are definitely very important declarations in the doctrine and revelations of God. But as I have said, theophanies are less known or overlooked by some Christians. For shame!

So then, when we consider the incarnation of the Lord Jesus, this is indeed the very greatest beacon of Light to all humankind![John 1:4, 5, 9; 9:5; 12:46] There is nothing greater in the revelation of God. The apostle John says that during the Lord's earthly ministry to the nation Israel,

> This is the disciple who is testifying to these things and wrote these things, and we know that his testimony is true. And there are also many other things which Jesus did, which if they were written in detail, I suppose that even the world itself would not contain the books that would be written. (John 21:24, 25)

> Therefore many other signs Jesus also performed in the presence of the disciples, which are not written in this book; but these have been written so that you may believe that Jesus is the Christ, the Son of God; and that believing you may have [*eternal*] life in His name. (John 20:30, 31)

305

It is very evident that God manifested Himself in the Garden of Eden with Adam and Eve. What many probably do not realize is that this was Christ the Lord appearing as a theophany to our first parents. Hence, God initiates the first communication to man before sin entered the world.[John 1:14] When man sinned and rebelled against God, the Lord sought out man and even provided the first sacrifice and covered man with animal sacrifice for forgiveness. Hallelujah!

Another theophany occurred at the Tower of Babel. This is where we have very unique appearance. This is where there may have been the manifestation of the blessed Trinity. This is a *mystery of all mysteries* since God is invisible. Not only is the Holy Spirit His spirit and invisible; is Father also spirit and invisible? please **read Deut. 4:12-20** *slowly* and *methodically*. The apostle says, "By common confession, the mystery of godliness is great: God appeared in the flesh."[1 Tim. 3:16 MSB] Is the Christ the only One that became manifest? We know that while angels are spirit beings,[Heb. 1:14] angels are capable of appearing in human form.

As to the theophany in Genesis 11, we read as given by Amplified Bible,

> Now the whole earth spoke one language and used the same words (vocabulary). And as people journeyed eastward, they found a plain in the land of Shinar and they settled there. They said one to another, "Come, let us make bricks and fire them thoroughly [in a kiln, to harden and strengthen them]." So they used brick for stone [as building material], and they used tar (bitumen, asphalt) for mortar. They said, "Come, let us build a city for ourselves, and a tower whose top *will reach* into the heavens, and let us make a [famous] name for ourselves, so that we will not be scattered [into separate groups] *and* be dispersed [scattered] over the surface of the entire earth [as the LORD instructed]."
>
> Now the LORD came down to see the city and the tower which the sons of men had built. And the LORD said, "Behold, they are one [unified] people, and they all have the same language. This is only the beginning of what they will do [in rebellion against Me], and now no evil thing they imagine they can do will be impossible for them.
>
> Come, **LET US** (Father, Son, Holy Spirit) go down and there confuse *and* mix up their language, so that they will not understand one another's speech." So the LORD scattered them [all of mankind] abroad from there over the surface of the entire earth; and they stopped building the city. Therefore the name of the city was Babel--because there the LORD

confused the language of the entire earth; and from that place the LORD scattered *and* dispersed them over the surface of all the earth.

(Gen. 11:1-9 AMP)

The Angel [*Messenger*] of the Lord:

(This is inwoven with the theophanies of God.) There are over fifty references to theophanies in the HEB Bible concerning the appearances "*Angel of the Lord.*" It is also likely the phrases, "the *Angel of God*" and "*His Angel*" may equally apply to Christ's preincarnate appearances. The HEB word for angel is *malak*. *Malak* is used of humans and angels. *Malak*, like the GK word *aggelos* (angel), literally means "*messenger.*" Hence, the Angel of the Lord is **the Messenger of the Lord**. The study of this topic of the Theophanes of God in OT could not be contained properly in just one volume. This topic alone ought to alert everyone to the extreme importance of the study of the Theophanies in the OT.

As to the incarnation (the Christ *tabernacling* in flesh), Jesus told the leaders in Jerusalem, 'It is written in the prophets, and they shall be all taught of God.'[(John 6:45 KJV & cf. Isa. 54:13)] As we have already noted, Psalm 2:7 declares that the Son would begotten. That is, the Messiah would be sent into the world to redeem mankind.

Once again, the apostle Paul declared as given by the World ENG Bible,

Without controversy, the mystery of godliness is great: **God[e] was revealed in the flesh**, justified in the spirit, seen by angels, preached among the nations, believed on in the world, and received up in glory.

(1 Tim. 3:16 WEB)

[e]Note: some GK MSS use the pronoun "*He*" rather than the noun "*God.*"

Man has rejected *the wooing and convicting of the Holy Spirit*.

Though the illuminating and convicting power of the Holy Spirit is also often overlooked, Jesus declares the necessity of the Holy Spirit's coming,

Nevertheless, I am telling you the truth. It is for your benefit that I go away, because if I don't go away the Counselor [*the Holy Spirit*] will not come to you. If I go, I will send Him to you. [8] When He comes, **He WILL CONVICT the world ABOUT SIN, RIGHTEOUSNESS**, and **JUDGMENT**: [9]About sin, because they do not believe in Me; [10]about righteousness, because I am going to the Father and you will no longer

see Me; [11]and about judgment, because the ruler of this world has been
judged.   (John 16:7-11 CSB)

The Holy Spirit *convicts* people of their sin. In addition, the Spirit also
illuminates the unregenerate. Furthermore, the Holy Spirit *illuminates* the
saints as well. The unregenerate man may deny the Spirit's *convicting* and
illuminating him, but his denial does not cancel out the truth of God's working
in him. The Holy Spirit even *draws* people to hear the Word of God. The Holy
Spirit even *witnesses* to the things of God. Hence, the Holy Spirit's working
upon humankind leaves all of humankind **totally inexcusable** before God.
The Holy Spirit *woos* and *beckons* us to come to Christ while there is time.
"You don't believe the Spirit is witnessing to people?" Then, sir what does the
apostle John mean when he says,

> The Spirit and the bride [*believers in Heaven*] say[*f*] [plural, *saying*], "Come." And let the
> one [*also*] who hears say, "Come." And let the one who is thirsty come;
> let the one who wishes take the water of life without cost. (Rev. 22:17)

> [f]Note: the word "*say*" in GK is *lego*; it is plural *legousin*, "saying."
> There are two asking people come to Christ: the Holy Spirit and the
> bride (believers in Heaven.) The Lord is the God of living who are alive
> even after death [Luke 20:38].

Therefore, the Lord has made Himself plainly known. If some refuse to
believe God's Word, then they have called God a liar [1 John 5:10-13]. To call God a
liar, my friend is the final "coup de grace" (or coup de grâce). Their rejection
of Jesus Christ as Lord and Savior brings the final death blow down on their
own heads.

C. To Whom *be* glory, majesty, dominion and authority, before all time and now and forever. Amen.

Now, we come to last mighty "crescendo" in this awesome doxology as
we look at the complete doxology once more by Jude,

> Now to Him who is able to keep you from stumbling, and to make you
> stand in the presence of His glory blameless with great [*exuberant*] joy,
> to the only God our Savior, through Jesus Christ our Lord, *be* glory,
> majesty, dominion and authority, before all time and now and forever.
> Amen.   (Jude 1:24, 25)

First, we must understand and know without any doubt that the whole and
complete doxology point to and centers upon Jesus Christ as Lord of all. This

is why the phrase (*through Jesus Christ our Lord*) omission in the BYZ and the Coptic texts raises serious doubts about the omission. The phrase is definitely authentic and belongs in the GK text. Christ the Lord is the Creator, Sustainer, and Sovereign One overall creation, [Col. 1:16, 17]. In Christ,

> In whom are hid all the treasures of wisdom and knowledge.
>
> (Col. 2:3 KJV)

Again,

> For in him dwelleth all the fulness of the Godhead bodily.
>
> (Col. 2:9 ASV)

The doctrine of Jesus Christ as Lord and Sovereign One is a serious omission by the BYZ and the Coptic texts. In addition, many stumble at the phrase, "Son of God." *As noted earlier*, today there are people simply reading into the Bible their own depraved meaning. These are people, many are indeed that are no doubt very sincere, but such people sadly are completely deficient of illumination from on High. We must allow the Bible to interpret itself. The Bible will declare its own inherent meaning. This is indeed the point that liberalism, cults, and many unbelievers do not fully realize or even grasp.

Many people because they lack the biblical meaning of "Son of God" misread the biblical authors' intended declaration. As result, a lot of people have followed the cults without knowing it. That is, people are reading into the Scripture very serious error, and in their deadly error, they miss the wonderful grace of God. This is especially true as we noted the meaning for the word "son."

So, Jude devotes the whole doxology to Jesus Christ as Lord of all. This in itself is a very important observation. This truth must not be overlooked nor minimized!

> Now to Him who is able to keep you from stumbling, and to make you stand in the presence of His glory blameless with great [*exuberant*] joy, to the only God our Savior, through Jesus Christ our Lord, *be* glory, majesty, dominion and authority, before all time and now and forever. Amen.   (Jude 1:24, 25)

Now to the last phase in Jude's epistle. The last phrase is equally pungent and fully packed. The phrase is indeed significant and needs to be meticulously emphasized. Let us take each aspect of the doxology *phrase* by *phrase*:

> "- [*to whom*] be glory, majesty, dominion and authority, before all time and now and forever. Amen."

309

"[*to whom*] be [*the*] glory"

Listen and pay close attention to God's Word here. Isaiah tell us,

> I am the LORD! That is my name! I will not share my glory with anyone [*or anything*] else, or the praise due me with idols.   (Isa. 42:8 NET)

Woe unto those who only place Christ as some sidebar, and then, in so doing, they unfortunately defame His glory and honor that truly belongs to Him. The word "*worship*" means "He is <u>worthy</u>."[Rev. 5] Amen, as the apostle says,

> Wherefore God also hath highly exalted him, and given him a name which is above every name: That **at the name of JESUS**[g] every knee should bow, of *things* in heaven, and *things* in earth, and *things* under the earth; And *that* every tongue should confess that Jesus Christ *is* **LORD**, to the glory of God the Father.   (Phil. 2:9-11 KJV)

> [g]Note: the name Jesus in HEB is *__YEHOSHUA__* (earlier spelling was thought to be *Joshua*). Jesus in GK is *__Iesous__*, and the root meaning is to *__save__*. In HEB, *YEHOSHUA* meaning is *the **LORD** saves* or *the **LORD** will save you*.

Jesus said,

> Furthermore, the Father judges no one, but has assigned [GK *didomi*, *given*, *handed over*] all judgment to the Son, so **that all may honor the SON just as they honor the FATHER**. Whoever does not honor the Son does not honor the Father who sent Him. Truly, truly, I tell you, **whoever hears My word and believes Him who sent Me has eternal life and will not come under judgment**. Indeed, he has crossed over from death to life.
>
> (John 5:22-24 MSB)

Therefore, all glory, honor, and praise belong to Christ the Lord. He who honors Jesus honors God the Father. He that does not honor Jesus does not honor God the Father.

"[*to whom be the*] majesty"

The GK lexicon by VGNT (Vocabulary of the GK NT, Bible Works 10) says of the word *majesty*, "God does not smite them according to their sins nor according to the greatness of His might, but uses forbearance" (Thackeray). In other words, the Lord is longsuffering or very patient in order reach the unsaved.

God is greater than all our sin and wickedness by His *majesty* or *infinite greatness*. Peter says,

But do not ignore this one fact, beloved, that with the Lord one day is like a thousand years, and a thousand years are like one day. The Lord is not slow about his promise, as some think of slowness, but is patient with you, **not wanting any to perish, but all to come to repentance**.

(2 Peter 3:8, 9 NRS)

The meaning of majesty here refers to the infinite greatness of the Lord. Jude is not thinking of Royality (though God is the Lord and King and such attributes belong to Him), but here the phrase by Jude is referring to the very greatness of God, GK *megalosune*. In the mighty greatness of God, He is *long-suffering* or *patient* in order that He might save or redeem all that genuinely call upon the Lord Jesus as their personal Lord and Savior.[John 1:12f, Acts 16:31; Rom. 10:13] Friend, if you do not call upon Jesus to save you, you cannot be saved.

Therefore, out of infinite majesty God is very patient and longsuffering towards the sinner in order that mankind might believe and receive eternal life through Jesus Christ our Lord. As noted earlier, the apostle Paul says,

Or do you disregard the riches of His kindness, tolerance, and patience, not realizing that God's kindness leads you to repentance?

(Rom. 2:4 MSB)

"[to whom be the] dominion"

The word is *dominion* (GK *kratos*) denoting the possession of force or strength that affords supremacy or control; (1) of God *sovereignty, power, might, dominion* (1 Tim. 6.16); (2) of the devil *power, control* (Heb. 2.14); (3) concretely *mighty deed, miracle* (Luke 1.51) Friberg, Analytical Greek Lexicon

As the apostle Peter says,

Whoever speaks, *let him speak*, as it were, the utterances of God; whoever serves, *let him do so* as by the strength which God supplies; so that in all things God may be glorified through Jesus Christ, to whom belongs the glory and dominion [kratos] forever and ever. Amen.

(1 Peter 4:11)

The power or strength of the Lord is one of total and complete power and sovereignty over all creation and all things. Christ the Lord by His will and word alone, He spoke the universe into being.

The psalmist says as given by the GK OT in ENG,

[6]By the word of the Lord the heavens were established; and all the host of them by the breath of his *mouth*. [7]Who gathers the waters of the sea as

in a bottle; who lays up the deeps in treasuries. ⁸Let all the earth fear the Lord; and let all that dwell in the world be moved because of him. ⁹For he spoke, and they were made; he commanded, and they were created. ¹⁰The Lord frustrates the counsels of the nations; he brings to nought also the reasonings of the peoples, and brings to nought the counsels of princes. ¹¹But the counsel of the Lord endures forever, the thoughts of his heart from generation to generation [*his plans abide throughout the ages* NET]. ¹²Blessed is the nation whose God is the Lord; the people whom he has chosen for his own inheritance.   (Psa. 33:6-12 LXE)

Therefore, all dominion and rule reside in Christ the Lord. There is no dominion or rule higher that Christ the Lord. All things belong to Him, and He is the One that rules all the universe and creation accord to His will.Eph. 1:11

"[*to whom be the*] authority"

The GK word here is "*exousia*." Jesus said just before His ascension,

All authority [*exousia*] has been given to Me in heaven and on earth

(Matt. 28:18)

Here is an example of the word "*exousia*,"

When He entered the temple, the chief priests and the elders of the people came to Him while He was teaching, and said, "By what authority [*exousia*] are You doing these things, and who gave You this authority [*exousia*]?" Jesus said to them, "I will also ask you one thing, which if you tell Me, I will also tell you by what authority I do these things. "The baptism of John was from what *source*, from heaven or from men?" And they *began* reasoning among themselves, saying, "If we say, 'From heaven,' He will say to us, 'Then why did you not believe him?' "But if we say, 'From men,' we fear the people; for they all regard John as a prophet." And answering Jesus, they said, "We do not know." He also said to them, "Neither will I tell you by what authority [*exousia*] I do these things.

(Matt. 21:23-27)

Christ the Lord **possesses all authority over all things**. As I have said, there is no authority higher Christ Lord. All power and authority reside in the blessed Lord Jesus Christ. As the apostle wonderfully declares,

He is the image of the invisible God, the firstborn [*the Preeminent* One] over all creation, ¹⁶ for all things in heaven and on earth were created by him– all things, whether visible or invisible, whether thrones or dominions, whether principalities or powers– all things were created through him

312

and for him. [17] He himself is before all things [the Eternal One] and all things are held together [and sustained and maintained] in [by] him. [18] He is the head [Supreme Ruler] of the body, the church, as well as the beginning,[h] the firstborn [the Preeminent One] from among the dead, so that he himself may become first firstborn [the Preeminent One] in all things. [19] For [*Triune*] God was pleased to have all his fullness dwell in the Son [20] and through him to reconcile all things to himself by making peace through the blood of his cross– through him, whether things on earth or things in heaven.

(Col. 1:15-20 NET)

[h]Note: "*beginning*" is a noun (GK *arche*). *Arche* probably better translated "*originator*:" That is, Christ the Lord, the **Originator** or **Source** from which all things came into the beginning. "*Beginning*" is not the intended meaning here given the context in Col. 1:15ff.

ESV also likely gives a closer meaning to v 19, "For in him all the fullness of God was pleased to dwell."[Col. 1:15 ESV] The words "the Father" is not in the GK, though many translators followed the KJV here.

Consequently and unequivocally, all authority resides in Christ the Lord. Christ is Lord Supreme over all things. Everything in creation will submit to His Sovereign Lordship! Some submit to Christ's Lordship in this life and shall be saved. Others wait until the judgment when they must submit to Christ's Lordship. Then, unregenerate having condemned themselves, they shall regrettably shall be sent to an eternal Hell, the Lake of Fire.

"- before all time and now and forever. Amen."

All praise and worship is due Christ the Lord for He is indeed worthy. First, all of those headed for hell will first bow their knee to Jesus[Phil. 2:9-11] that "yes, Yehoshua (Jesus) is Lord and He is worthy of all "*glory, majesty, dominion and authority.*"

The angels and all of Heaven will join in the praise and worship to Christ the Lord:

And they sung a new song, saying, Thou art worthy to take the book, and to open the seals thereof: for thou was slain, and hast redeemed us to God by thy blood out of every kindred, and tongue, and people, and nation; [10]And hast made us unto our God kings and priests: and we shall reign on the earth. [11]And I beheld, and I heard the voice of many angels round about the throne and the beasts[i] and the elders: and the number of them was ten thousand times ten thousand, and thousands of thousands; [12]Saying with a loud voice, Worthy is the Lamb that was slain to receive power, and riches, and wisdom, and strength, and *honor*, and glory, and blessing. [13]And every creature which is in heaven, and on the earth, and under the earth, and such as are in the sea, and all that are in them, heard I saying, Blessing, and *honor*, and glory, and power, *be* unto him that *sits* upon the throne, and unto the Lamb for ever and ever. [14]And the four beasts said, Amen. And the four *and* twenty elders fell down and worshipped him that *lives forever* and ever.   (Rev. 5:9-14 KJV)

Note: the word in the KJV is <u>not</u> <u>beast</u>, but the GK is "<u>*zoon*</u>," *living creatures.*

Friend, this is what Heaven is all about. Heaven is all about praise and worship of the Son of God. We shall be singing about and to Christ the Lord for He is worthy. We shall sing praises because the Lord Jesus is worthy of worship; yes, the Lord Jesus Christ is worthy; He worthy in this life and worthy forever ever, amen.

The unregenerate will **not** be allowed to sing the endless praises and worship of the Lamb of God. The unregenerate can only blasphemy and profane His blessed Name since their nature is unchanged. The unregenerate continue in their unredeemed state forever and ever. Thus, unsaved have no right to speak our Lord's blessed name. Therefore, they are without the redemption of Christ Jesus, and they do not possess the new natural given by the Spirit of God.

Like the wicked angels, the unsaved people are filled with bitterness and contempt. The unsaved are filled and overcome with rage. The unsaved in their old Adamic nature *have no room for repentance*. Yeah, the unregenerate cannot repent! The unsaved will be cast into the Lake of Fire where evil angels shall reside. The Lake of Fire is not only endless suffering, it is utter darkness and totally solitary and isolated. The unregenerate had chosen rather to follow the world, flesh, and the devil. Friend, "It is a terrifying thing to fall into the hands of the living God."[Heb. 10:31] Repent while there is still time and believe the Good News that Jesus died for your sin and arose the third day. And friend, He is indeed coming back soon. Hallelujah!

The unregenerate have rejected Jesus Christ. Like the rich man in Luke 16:19ff in Hades, who did not ask why he was in Hades. He did not wonder why his judgment was so severity and his condemnation. He **already knew** why such severe judgment. He entered the door into eternity. He did not choose eternal life with Christ. He had rejected the witness of God. The very own words of the unregenerate will condemn himself. For those who reject the Son of God, their judgment is sealed, and there is no appeal. Their judgment is final, forever and ever. Friend, I must tell you once again: *it is a terrifying thing to fall into hands of the living in judgment*!

The apostle John says that if we are willing to hear and accept the testimony of most any human being, how much greater then when God Himself gives His testimony concerning the Son of God?

> Even if we accept human testimony [*witness*], the testimony [*witness*] of God is greater. For this is the testimony [*witness*] that God has given about His Son. Whoever believes in the Son of God has this testimony [*witness*] within him; whoever does not believe God has made Him out to be a liar, because he has not believed in the testimony [*witness*] that God has given about His Son. And this is that testimony [*witness*]: God has given us eternal life, and this [*eternal*] life is in His Son. Whoever has the Son has [*eternal*] life; whoever does not have the Son of God does not have [*eternal*] life. I have written these things to you who believe in the name of the Son of God, so that you may know that you have eternal life and that you may believe in the name of the Son of God. (1 John 5:9-13 MSB)

Friend throughout eternity the redeemed shall indeed give praises and sing hymns to the Lord our God. The unregenerate will be in total darkness in the Lake of Fire. This is what it will be for those who rejected or did not trust in Christ the Lord. All shall perish in their sin who have trusted religion, trusted religious rites, relied on religious works, or who relied on tradition. They had failed to put their complete trust in the Word of God. They failed to commit their life and trust in Christ Jesus as their redemption. But remember: trust Jesus Christ and Him alone, for He died on the cross in His love for you.John 3:16; Rom. 5:8 Yes, they refused Him who died for our sins on Calvary and rose again on the third day, and hallelujah, He is coming again.

Friend, this is most serious and dreadful question. To whom will you worship and praise forever and ever? Do not put your trust in manmade religion. Do not even put trust in your gut feeling which is your natural man. If you put your trust in manmade religion, you will surely **perish in your sin without mercy**. Believe and trust only in Christ Jesus' redemption and in God's Word. "Faith comes through hearing the Word of God."Rom. 10:17 Once again, the Hebrews warns everyone,

> He that despised Moses' law died without mercy under two or three witnesses: [29]Of how much sorer [*severer*] punishment, suppose ye, shall he be thought worthy, who hath trodden underfoot the Son of God, and hath counted the blood of the covenant, wherewith he was sanctified, an unholy thing, and hath done despite [*insulted*] unto the Spirit of grace?

315

> ³⁰For we know him that hath said, Vengeance *belongs* unto me, I will recompense, saith the Lord. And again, The Lord shall judge his people. ³¹*It is* **a fearful** [*terrifying*] **thing to fall into the hands of the living God**.
>
> (Heb. 10:28-31 KJV)

Jesus said very plainly,

> I said therefore to you, that ye shall die in your sins: for if ye believe not that I AM, ye shall die in your sins."
>
> (John 8:24 SLT)

Conclusion

Jude's epistle is certainly fully packed. He is exhorting the saints that since we now have the complete deposit of God's Word, let us **"earnestly contend for the faith which was once delivered unto the saints**."^{Jude 1:3 KJV}

Jude does not mean just hold on to the faith, but he means let us watch out for deceivers and those who corrupt the Word of God. There are people out there turning the grace of God in wickedness.

> Beloved, when I gave all diligence to write unto you of the common salvation, it was needful for me to write unto you, and exhort *you* that ye should earnestly contend for the faith which was once delivered unto the saints. For there are certain men crept in unawares, who were before of old ordained to this condemnation, ungodly men, turning the grace of our God into lasciviousness, and denying the only Lord God, and our Lord Jesus Christ.   (Jude 1:3, 4 KJV)

Let us fervently and faithfully declare His Word. Listen my friend, God is calling upon people everywhere to repent and receive Jesus as the Lord and Savior.^{Acts 17:30; Rom. 10:13}

Our Lord warns us concerning false prophets, false teachers, and false Messiahs leading people astray even as it is taking place this very day. There is a war going on everywhere. Open your eyes friend and look around you. This is a spiritual warfare that is unparalleled in all of human wars of history combined. There is an urgent need for godly men to rise to the challenge. The Lord is looking for men to stand in the gap and join in the battle. Will you say **"yes**," I shall stand in the gap? Then, make your commitment right today, and says to the Lord, "Here I am; Lord, send me!"

God is longsuffering and very patient in order that many people might still be redeemed by faith in Christ through His infinite mercy and grace. Yes, even the most wicked person can be saved and cleaned up from the inside out. The Lord is merciful. The Lord in the same way wants His people to be merciful on those doubting. "And others saved with fear, pulling *them* out of the fire; hating even the garment spotted by the flesh."[Jude 1:23]

Above all, Jude gives an extraordinary doxology that is centered in and through Jesus Christ who is Lord overall and He is indeed worthy of all our worship and praises.

> Now to Him who is able to keep you from stumbling, and to make you stand in the presence of His glory blameless with great joy, to the only God our Savior, through Jesus Christ our Lord, *be* glory, majesty, dominion and authority, before all time and now and forever. Amen.
>
> (Jude 1:24, 25)

Footnotes:

1. Jude 1:25, Latin Vulgate in ENG: Biblia Sacra Vulgata, https://vulgata.net/judas?chapter=1&en=true

ABBREVIATIONS AND ACRONYMS

ABPE = Aramaic Bible in Plain English
AFV = A Faithful Version
AKJV = American King James Version 1999, by Michael Peter (Stone) Engelbrite
AMP = Amplified Bible
ARA or ARC = Aramaic
ASV = American Standard Version
BSB = Berean Study Bible and BLB = Berean Literal Bible
BYZ = Byzantine manuscripts
CEB = Common English Bible
CEV = Contemporary English Version
cf. = clarified
Coptic = referring Egyptian text; Egyptian Christians
Coverdale Bible = Miles Coverdale Bible 1535
CSB or HCSB = Holman Christian Standard Bible
1 Chro. = 1 Chronicles, OT
2 Chro. = 2 Chronicles, OT
1 Cor. = 1 Corinthians, NT epistle
2 Cor. = 2 Corinthians, NT epistle
CJB = Complete Jewish Bible
DBT = Darby Bible Translation,
Deut. = Deuteronomy, OT
Ecc. or Eccl. = Ecclesiastes, OT
ENG = English
Eph. = Ephesians, NT epistle
ERV = English Revised Version, 1885
ESV = English Standard Version
Ezek. = Ezekiel, OT
f = the following verse
ff = the following verses
Gal. = Galatians, NT epistle
Gen. = Genesis, OT
GK = Greek NT
GNV = Geneva Bible (1599 edition) Bible Gateway
GNT = Good News Translation
GWT = God's Word Translation
HEB = Hebrew language of the OT

Heb. =Hebrews, NT epistle
Isa. = Isaiah, OT
ISV = International Standard Version
James = NT epistle
Job = book of the OT
John = the Gospel of John, NT
1 John = the First Epistle of John, NT epistle
2 John = the Second Epistle of John, NT epistle
3 John = the Third Epistle of John, NT epistle
Josh. = Joshua, OT
Jude = NT epistle
Judges = book of the OT
1 Kings = book of the OT
2 Kings = book of the OT
KJV = King James Version; NKJV = New King James Version
lit. = literally
Latin = LAT.
Latin/English = LAT/ENG
LSV = Literal Standard Version 2020
Luke = the Gospel of Luke, NT
LVE = Latin Vulgate in ENG
LXE (& LXA) = GK OT (Septuagint) in ENG
LXX = Septuagint, GK OT
Mark = Gospel of Mark, NT
MSS = manuscript(s)
Matt. or Mat = Gospel of Matthew
MSG = The Message
NAS = New American Standard2020 and Update 1995
NCV = New Century Version
NEB = New English Bible
NEH = Nehemiah, OT
NHEB = New Heart English Bible, update 201 e
NIV = New International Version
NKJV = New King James Version, Thomas Nelson, 1982
NLT = New Living Translation
NRS = New Revised Standard 1989
NT = New Testament
OT = Old Testament

p = page

pp = pages

OJB = Orthodox Jewish Bible

1 Peter = NT epistle

2 Peter = NT epistle

Psa. = Psalm, OT

Phi. Or Phil. = Philippines, NT epistle

PTL = Praise the Lord

PNT or Philips NT = J B Philip's NT

Prov. = Proverbs, OT

Rev. = Revelation, NT epistle

Rom. = Romans, NT epistle

1 Tim. = 1 Timothy, NT epistle

2 Tim. = 2 Timothy, NT epistle

1 Sam. = 1 Samuel, OT

SLT = Smith's Literal Translation

1 Thess. = 1 Thessalonians, NT epistle

2 Thess. = 2 Thessalonians, NT epistle

TNT = Tyndale New Testament, 1534

Titus = NT epistle

TRE = Textus Receptus in ENG (GK text of the KJV)

VUL = Latin Vulgate

WBT = Webster's Bible Translation

WEB = World English Bible

WNT = Weymouth NT

WYC = Wycliffe Bible

YLT = Young's Literal Translation

BOOKS, TRACTS, AND SONGS BY THE AUTHOR

Books by the author
Understanding Salvation by Faith in Christ
Understanding the Biblical Principles of Bible Study
Understanding the Biblical Principles of Witnessing
Understanding Prayer
Understanding Christian Doctrine, vol. 1: The Doctrine of God
Understanding Christian Doctrine, vol. 2: The Doctrine of Creation
Understanding Christian Doctrine, vol. 3: The Doctrine of Redemption
A Short Outline on Christian Doctrine
Christ's Supreme Sovereignty Over All (Commentary on Hebrews)
The Seven Mandates of Christ
Two of the Greatest Truths in Universe and their Significances
The Greatest Contemplation of Thought Ever!
Christ the Lord, the absolute center of Theology
Meeting the Greatest Friend You'll Ever Have
The Way of the Lord more Accurately
The Lord is Faithful who calls you into His Kingdom (A Study in 1
    Thessalonians)
Earnestly Contend for the Faith, (Study of the Epistle of Jude)

Gospel Tracts
Eternal Life, Yours for the Asking
Have You Received the Gift of God?

Songs
Thou Art Worthy, O Lamb of God (Chair song set to music)
Tis All to Him I Owe (not set to music)
Jesus' Precious Blood Avails for You (not set to music)
Mangrove Song (Filipino children's song in English, to the tune: I'm in
    the Lord's Army)

Index